HISTORY OF PHILOSOPHY IN THE MAKING

*A Symposium of Essays
to Honor
Professor James D. Collins
on his 65th Birthday*

By his Colleagues and Friends

Edited by
Linus J. Thro, S.J.
St. Louis University

University Press of America
1982

Copyright © 1982 by

University Press of America, Inc.

P.O. Box 19101, Washington, D.C. 20036

All rights reserved

Printed in the United States of America

ISBN (Perfect): 0-8191-2659-4
ISBN   (Cloth): 0-8191-2658-6

B
29
H495
1982

Library of Congress Catalog Card Number: **81-43840**

ACKNOWLEDGMENTS

Grateful acknowledgment is hereby given to the following for the use of quotations from their copyrighted works:

DOVER PUBLICATIONS, INC.
The Philosophical Works of Descartes, translated by E. S. Haldane and G. R. T. Ross. Volume I. Copyright 1955. Quoted with permission of the publisher.

HARPER AND ROW, PUBLISHERS, INC.
Søren Kierkegaard, *Works of Love*. Translated and edited by Howard V. Hong and Edna H. Hong. Copyright 1962.

HARVARD UNIVERSITY PRESS
Collected Papers of Charles Sanders Peirce. Edited by Charles Hartshorne, Paul Weiss and Arthur Burks. Eight volumes, 1931-1958. Copyright 1931, 1934, 1938, 1939, 1962.

INDIANA UNIVERSITY PRESS
Søren Kierkegaard's Journals and Papers. Translated and edited by Howard V. Hong and Edna H. Hong. Seven volumes, 1967-1968. Copyright 1967. Quoted with permission of the publisher.

PRINCETON UNIVERSITY PRESS
James D. Collins, *Interpreting Modern Philosophy*. Copyright 1972.
Søren Kierkegaard, *For Self-Examination*. Translated by Walter Lowrie. Copyright 1968.
John Duns Scotus, *God and Creatures: The Quodlibetal Questions*, translated and edited by Allan B. Wolter and F. Alluntis. Copyright 1975. Quoted with permission of the publisher.

CHARLES SCRIBNER'S SONS
Jacques Maritain, *The Range of Reason*. Copyright 1952 by Jacques Maritain; copyright renewed 1980 by Eveline Garnier (Scribner's). Quoted with the permission of Charles Scribner's Sons.

THE REVEREND GEORGE EARLE, S.J., AND THE SOCIETY OF JESUS (LONDON)
"God's Grandeur" from *The Poems of Gerard Manley Hopkins* (Oxford University Press). Copyright 1967, 1970.

CONTENTS

PREFACE   vii

1 INTRODUCTORY: "James Collins — the Man,
the Scholar, the Teacher"
John Patrick Murray and *Daniel O. Dahlstrom*   1

PART I   SOURCE THINKERS UNDER HISTORICAL QUESTIONING

2 "Plato's Dialectic of the Sun"
Leonard J. Eslick   19

3 "Eternity and Time in Boethius: his *Complicatio-Explicatio* Method"
Thomas P. McTighe   35

4 "Act, the Self-Revelation of Being in St. Thomas"
W. Norris Clarke, S. J.   63

5 "Duns Scotus on Intuition, Memory and Knowledge of Individuals"
Allan B. Wolter, O.F.M.   81

6 "The Suarezian Proof of God's Existence"
John P. Doyle   105

7 "Reflections on Descartes' Methods of Analysis and Synthesis"
Richard J. Blackwell   119

8 "Hobbes and Skepticism"
Richard H. Popkin   133

9 "The *Deutsche Metaphysik* of Christian Wolff: Text and Transitions"
Charles A. Corr   149

10 "Kierkegaard, Abraham and the Modern State"
John W. Elrod   165

11 "Peirce and the Conditions of Possibility of Science"
C. F. Delaney   177

PART II PROBLEMATIC OPENINGS TO QUESTIONS OF TODAY

12 "The Question of Recurrent Problems
   in Philosophy"   *Frederick C. Copleston, S.J.* 197

13 "Metaphysics and the History of Philosophy:
   The Case of Whitehead"   *Albert William Levi* 213

14 "Collins and Gadamer on Interpretation"
                                     James L. Marsh 231

15 "Religion within the Scope of Philosophy"
                                     John E. Smith 247

16 "Wittgenstein and Philosophy of Religion: an Application
   of *Emergence* Themes"   *John W. Carlson* 255

17 "Jacques Maritain on the Future: in Search of
   a Concrete Historical Ideal"   *Vincent C. Punzo* 275

18 "History, Futurology and the Future of
   Philosophy"   *Vernon J. Bourke* 299

   BIBLIOGRAPHY
                     Lee C. Rice and *Joseph W. Koterski* 313

   RESPONSE: "Conspectus"
                                     James D. Collins 321

   NOTES ON THE CONTRIBUTORS   327

PREFACE

It is nearly forty years since James Collins began his intensive academic career at St. Louis University. His sixty-fifth birthday this year affords an occasion for his colleagues and friends to render him grateful appreciation of the rich endowment his years thus far have brought to philosophical scholarship as well as to the lives of innumerable students.

As a specialist in the history of modern philosophy, he has said often enough in his writings precisely what he conceived his professional task to be. It is, first of all, to gain an accurate and sympathetic understanding of the methods, general standpoints, and special doctrines of the great thinkers; nothing can replace a careful, enlightened study of the sources, with the purpose of sharing in the outlook of these men through an act of historical insight *(A History of Modern European Philosophy,* p. 3). But mere fact-gathering is not enough: the data in question are the efforts of human minds to reach some permanent truths, so that fidelity to them places upon us the responsibility of evaluating the various historical solutions and of measuring them by the evidence as we ourselves can view it. "The historical study of philosophy integrates itself with philosophy proper and serves the ends of the search for wisdom" *(ibid.,* p. 4).

Philosophy is not something completely achieved in which the mind rests. Rather, this effort of human reason is a historical process ever growing as it engages in self-criticism. There is critical assimilation, there are creative advances, but truth is not easily come by. It beckons as an ideal, yet its promise cannot be fulfilled without strenuous, disciplined devotion to its pursuit. So very many participants in this high human endeavor make for an overwhelming diversity of stances on every problem and unreconcilable conclusions. Serious history of philosophy is a stern workshop.

But the work of history of philosophy cannot be achieved with sights trained only on the source thinkers themselves. Valid generalizations about the course of modern philosophy can hardly be made without fastening upon standard problems traced through several centuries and many minds. This and other sorts of comparative investigation help to uncover the "potential meaning which remains latent in the individual philosopher because of the limiting influence of his own age and his personal inner weather. Philosophy secures its continuity and progress by mining this hidden deposit, assaying its actual worth, and then searching elsewhere for fresh sources..." *(God in Modern Philosophy,* p. x).

This sort of problem approach is well exemplified, although in rather different ways, in his later works, *God in Modern Philosophy* and *The*

Emergence of Philosophy of Religion. Even more significantly, perhaps, a problem-centered re-assessment of the primary sources in the light of the later literature has characterized the cyclical treatment of modern philosophy in Dr. Collins' seminars of the last twenty years, as the first essay in our volume elaborates.

In the last couple of decades he has turned his attention more directly toward the formal nature and practice of his own discipline. Through reflection upon the whole range of recent historical-philosophical literature he strives to achieve a unified understanding of the methodology and purposeful intent of the historian of philosophy. This is plainly in his mind as he writes for a 1968 collection of studies on the human implications of the present-day knowledge explosion. A simple dualism of philosophical theory and historical study of philosophy is quite untenable. The low regard for historical studies in philosophy entertained by analysts and some phenomenologists of thirty to fifty years ago has duly given way to a considerable engagement in such work on the part of the philosophical community. The treasure is there awaiting further exploration. "What assures our interest in a philosophical source is the proven presence there of pools of meaning, which remain unsuspected or unemphasized until they are found to respond to some current problem in philosophy or some line of research developing in other fields" ("Developing Patterns in Philosophy," in *Knowledge and the Future of Man*, p. 221).

Finally, less than ten years ago he published *Interpreting Modern Philosophy*, his professional statement of what he sees his work to be. Curiously, instead of the empirical study it actually is, this book has been misread by the unwary as a historicist philosophy of history and, ultimately, a relativistic judgment on the philosophical enterprise itself. By contrast, its announced purpose is "to illuminate the methodology and epistemology of history of modern philosophy by reflecting upon the concrete ways of historians in this field" (p.viii).

Pointing toward the ideal of a general theory of historical knowledge in philosophy, the investigation focuses in turn upon three co-essential ingredients of the complex activity of doing historical work in philosophy: the pressure of the basic modern source texts seen against their own rich backgrounds; the art and the techniques of historical questioning; and the urgent present philosophical concerns of the investigator. The great philosophers and their work are found to come alive again and speak to us anew under the persistent, imaginative search for the present significance of past philosophizing (p. 204). And, since the successful historian of philosophy must himself be a philosopher, his work is marked by an overarching pursuit of philosophical wisdom. With the overriding "intent to do historical justice, all the methods and acts of inquiry are teleologically directed toward developing a faithful and pertinent image of modern philosophy, one that will somehow illuminate our humanity in its historical and contemporary reality" (p. 405).

*****

The vision of a dedicated historian of philosophy enshrined in James Collins' works and in his life will continue to exert its influence upon students and professional philosophers alike, as it has long inspired his colleagues and friends. It seems peculiarly appropriate that the essays prepared by some of them for the present volume should fall neatly into two classifications which he will recognize. The first set are studies of source texts of major philosophers submitted to the techniques of historical questioning. The second set fasten more prominently upon contemporary problems whose urgency opens the source documents to fresh light and new insights for the human present and future.

Hence, following upon the introductory biobibliographical study, Part I comprises ten essays with the title "Source Thinkers Under Historical Questioning." The seven essays of Part II, "Problematic Openings to Questions of Today," range through various issues of methodology and interpretation raised by the jubilarian's own works and probe into the ultimate significance of philosophy and its future prospects.

It is most gratifying to be able to complete the volume with a generous response from Dr. Collins himself. Special thanks are due him, as well as to Dr. Marianne Childress and Dr. Richard Blackwell for their generous and indispensable editorial help.

Linus J. Thro, S.J.
St. Louis University

1.

JAMES COLLINS:
A PERSONAL PORTRAIT OF THE MAN,
THE TEACHER, AND THE SCHOLAR

J. Patrick Murray & Daniel O. Dahlstrom

There is a fine wholeness to James Collins' life. In his teaching as in his philosophizing he remembers to be human, to relish his life. Continuity persists in his life history. A deep-rootedness in family, faith, and cultural tradition marks the man. One sees in his maturing the formation of the philosophic temper of his later work as a teacher and scholar. Love of the human is Collins' taproot. His, however, is not a humanism that stacks itself up against the presence of God. Rather, one gets the sense that Collins experiences a gentle providence co-operating in the continuity of his life.[1]

I.

James Daniel Collins was born during the first world war on July 12, 1917 in Holyoke, Massachusetts. Recalling his early days, he speaks of the friendship, warmth, and immediate faith of his first generation Irish Catholic parents, Michael Joseph and Mary Magdalen (Rooney) Collins, and his sister, Elinor. Religion was a natural part of life in the Collins' household and politics a standing topic of lively family discussions. Though in an area once known as "Ireland Parish," Holyoke's citizens included French Canadians who came down to work its paper and silk mills and English people, who held most of the power. Yet there were no terrible tensions, and young James was bred into pluralism, making friends among Protestants, Jews, and blacks.

In August of 1931, at age fourteen, Collins fell ill with polio. He speaks of it without hesitation, not slighting its effect on his childhood and the course of his life, yet without a sense of tragedy. It was the course his life took; it brought hardships, but also new experiences, new friends. With typical toughness, Collins would remark that you make your opportunities where you are. After that summer of 1931 Collins found himself in beds, hot springs, and wheelchairs; there he created his opportunities. In the face of the frightening, little-known foe polio, the Collins family united in support of their stricken teenager. Seeking the best help possible led to the Yale University hospital; in turn the Yale doctors recommended an extended stay at Warm Springs, Georgia. Franklin Delano Roosevelt had been to the ramshackle springs in 1924, and after his stay the place became an important polio treatment center, attracting victims of all ages to its warm water baths and regimen of exercises. Arriving at Warm Springs in September, 1932, Collins joined a band of FDR enthusiasts in celebrating the victory of the New Dealer. Young James lived with fourteen to seventeen year olds in cabins near the baths, starting up what would become several lifelong friendships. Already a voracious reader, Collins worked through the library's fare with a special relish for literature and science.

Upon Collins' return home, efforts were made to insure his continued schooling. An aunt had some influence with the school board director, who saw to it that Collins received a private tutor, Helen Griffin, for three years. Together they worked on English, history, French, and Latin, while Collins received supplementary tutoring in math. Collins had always attended public schools, getting his catechesis elsewhere, and this experience of personal and humane treatment long before the days of any special consciousness for handicapped persons gave Collins an abiding respect for the public education system. During these years Collins' reading, especially in English literature, history, and the life sciences, went on unabated. Once the Holyoke public library collection had been exhausted, the same friendly school board director (Nathan P. Avery) retrieved books from the library of his alma mater, Amherst College.

Nothing seems forced or discontinuous in Collins' life, and this is true of his decision to pursue philosophy. The call to philosophy was present amid the many sounds Collins heard in the literature he loved. With time it simply stood out and became more insistent. From literary classics like Dante's *Divine Comedy*, though, it was a short journey to the concerns of philosophy. By seventeen or eighteen, Collins had settled into philosophy. During the Catholic literary and philosophical renaissance of the mid-thirties, Collins became an avid reader of *America, Commonweal*, and *Saturday Review*. He read the works of Christopher Dawson, Paul Claudel, Etienne Gilson, and Jacques Maritain as soon as they came out. Indeed, another friend (Mollie Greeley), with connections at the local Catholic book store, would get the new books to Collins before they reached the shelf. Signs of things to come — how many a book manuscript has passed the scrutiny of James Collins before the type is set?

When it came time for college, the natural choice of Amherst was passed up in favor of Catholic University and the warmer climes of the nation's capital. So in September, 1937, in the midst of the Depression, James Collins was one of approximately 75 incoming freshmen at Catholic University. Here FDR made himself felt in Collins' life once again, for it was from National Youth Administration funds that Collins' classmates were paid to wheel him around the campus and to bring him meals.

Two undergraduate teachers stand out in Collins' memory. John Tracy Ellis, who was soon to be ordained a priest, taught Collins the history of Europe and provided him with a standard for well-organized lecturing combined with fine scholarship. From Reverend Mr. Ellis too, Collins apparently came to appreciate a heavy workload, a lesson he ably passed on in his own teaching career. Though Collins had entered college as a declared philosophy major and had been reading philosophy books for some time, not before enrolling at Catholic University did he see a philosopher in the flesh. Fr. Charles Aloysius Hart was a first and lasting personal model of a philosopher. Hart's philosophizing came from the heart stamped with humanness and punctuated with humor.

By successfully competing for a Knights of Columbus fellowship Collins was able to be on his own financially in graduate school and ease the burden on his parents. This was 1941 and a war year. The School of Philosophy at Catholic University was small and populated largely by clerical students such as Allan Wolter, now professor of philosophy at Catholic University. At the end of his first year, Collins wrote his master's thesis on St. Thomas Aquinas' theory of the essence and existence of angels and followed two years later with a comprehensive study of St. Thomas' theory of the angels for his doctoral dissertation.

One event in particular stands out in Collins' reminiscences about his years as a graduate student. Rudolf Allers and his Jewish wife came to Washington after fleeing Vienna. One evening his wife came to her husband's seminar and whispered to him while Collins was presenting a paper. Rudolf Allers interrupted the presentation with news from the Dutch Underground. Edith Stein had been put to death at Auschwitz. Collins' paper had been on the philosophy of Edith Stein.

Collins began writing articles for publication during these graduate years, but the summer of 1944 was no time to be fresh out of graduate school and looking for a job. Fortunately, Collins won the Catholic University Penfield Traveling Fellowship in Philosophy and chose to do his research at Harvard University's Widener Library. During this year as a research fellow at Harvard, Collins lived in Lowell House, a student hall. The noted philologist and Boethius scholar, E. K. Rand, was in the Widener Library much of the time, and Collins struck up friendly working relations with him. This experience firmed up Collins' convictions on the need for interdisciplinary work.

From December till June of 1945 Collins turned his attention to Immanuel Kant. Though this was perhaps Collins' most intensive encounter with modern philosophy to date, his graduate studies had not been narrowly Scholastic or Thomistic. Collins recalls that the Catholic University faculty was itself not a bed of Thomists; it had its own pluralism. Moreover, his own decision to write on St. Thomas was, as he puts it, a basal act of returning to a major source — not pamphleteering for some Thomistic school.[2]

Collins' move to Harvard University was not the end of his ties to Catholic University. There was a certain librarian there, Yvonne Marie Stafford, whom Collins returned to wed on June 6, 1945. This gentle lady's quiet kindness and courteous support through the years are well known to all of us who have had the pleasure of being received in the comfortable Collins home in Normandy, Missouri. Her cheerful concern for Dr. Collins and their son, Michael Leo, ought not go unmentioned in paying tribute to Dr. Collins.

During his second semester at Harvard, Collins had sent out a number of letters inquiring about teaching positions. He received but one positive response. Fr. William Wade, S.J., was building up the department of philosophy at St. Louis University and he wanted Collins. When Wade learned that Collins was working on Kant, Wade figured he had hired a modern philosophy professor. He had indeed. In September of 1945 Collins taught the undergraduate history of modern philosophy course and a graduate offering on Descartes. The tradition at St. Louis University of sifting the incoming graduate students by putting them through the undergraduate history of modern philosophy course started already in Collins' second year, once Wade had seen the winnowing capacities of Collins in the classroom.

Collins' subsequent career at St. Louis University is the history of a scholar and teacher, winning recognition first for the subtlety and breadth of articles ranging over contemporary and historical themes, and then for his extraordinary, synoptic studies *The Existentialists* (1952), *The Mind of Kierkegaard* (1953), *A History of Modern European Philosophy* (1954), and *God in Modern Philosophy* (1959). When, in 1953, he delivered the Suarez lecture at Fordham University on the problems of a perennial philosophy, Collins was vice president of the American Catholic Philosophical Association and would become president in the following year. Other awards were to follow such as the Award for Scholarship from the National Council of Catholic Men in 1961. In 1962, while president of the Metaphysical Society of America, Dr. Collins received the Catholic University of America Alumni Award and the Cardinal Newman medal and gave the Aquinas lectures at Marquette University, later published as *The Lure of Wisdom* (1962). While delivering the second series of the Thomas More lectures at Yale in 1963 and doing research as a Guggenheim fellow during 1963-1964, Collins worked out the basis of *The Emergence of the Philosophy of Religion*, published in 1967. The American Catholic Philosophical Association bestowed its highest honor, the Aquinas Medal, on Dr. Collins in 1965.

Throughout Collins' career his output in the form of articles and reviews has been prolific. Perhaps the most notable example of these prodigious efforts is his Annual Review of Philosophy, appearing in *Thought* every year from 1951 through 1955, then in *Cross Currents* from 1956 to the present. The sweep of these reviews is matched only by Collins' uncanny knack for getting to the heart of the matter time after time. In these review Collins shares his own feel for the intellectual pulse of current philosophical scholarship. Several early articles form the basis of *Three Paths in Philosophy* (1960), reissued in 1969 as *Crossroads in Philosophy*. Collins dedicated this book, which outlines the main directions of existentialism, naturalism, and theistic realism, to his colleagues at St. Louis University. A monograph entitled *Descartes' Philosophy of Nature* followed in 1971, and Collins' most mature work, *Interpreting Modern Philosophy*, appeared in 1972.

II.

James Collins is a philosopher living in what Albert William Levi calls "the age of the professional." This phrase has several significances, but we will draw on its pointing to a confluence of university teaching and philosophical research. This university milieu and more particularly the graduate philosophy seminar setting for most philosophical work in our day has been thoughtfully taken up by Collins both in his practice as a teacher and in his writings, most thoroughly in *Interpreting Modern Philosophy*. Indeed, the book is in no small measure a theoretical reflection, or *Nachdenken*, on a lifetime of the practice of educating in graduate seminars. As we now consider in turn Collins' teaching and research, we hope to keep in mind their mutual reinforcement.

When James Collins' name crops up in a group of former students, faces loosen, eyes brighten, and reminiscences flow. There is much to recall. Collins never lets the mountain of his knowledge come down on his students; his personal charm, demeanor, and convictions overcome the potential for self-elevation and distancing.[3] Likewise, Collins somehow conveys that humane sense of the equal importance of the philosopher's thought expressed in the text and the student, alive with his or her own moral dilemmas and desire for wisdom. Perhaps the palpable respect and care he shows each student is the key to the remarkable motivation he induces. Students always seem to take up the heavy load of papers, reports, and research with a great deal of eagerness, not to win Collins' approval or to be able to climb some academic ladder with his recommendations, but because of the contagion of his own love of philosophy.

What is it that you learn from this man? You come to grips with a terrific amount of material, though for the most part you do this on your own, learning autonomy the hard way. You develop habits of control, discipline, and hard work. He stimulates your appreciation of language and impresses on you the need to study philosophers in their native tongues. He teaches you to experiment, to try different approaches, to examine different problems, to consult different teachers, and to sensitize yourself to many human values. You acquire a respect for the philosopher of the past as a human being groping with his own unique mix of typically human confusions and insights.[4] By example, you learn that the religious mind in philosophy can mean open-mindedness and a celebration of our humanness.

Collins puts a lot of stock in university seminars, describing them as "the creative source for most major advances now being made in history of modern philosophy."[5] His own graduate seminars are a kind of philosophical bootcamp and yet a privileged time of apprenticeship with a master. Twenty-four hours of every day for four months, or so it seems, you do practically nothing but work into shape the basic skills of reading, analyzing, and writing under Collins' watchful and demanding eye. The seminars are generally conducted on a two-year cycle of four semesters, passing from a figure in continental rationalism to one in British empiricism the first year and from Kant to Hegel the second. The cycles center on some theme of contemporary significance such as "cognitive models" or "theory and practice," aimed at preventing you from construing the historian's task as that of a mere chronicler of ideas or caretaker of some philosophic graveyard. "The historian's proper concern is neither with an archaicized past nor with a detemporalized present but with seeking the significance of past philosophizing, as being brought in relation to the present existence and problems of men. Such a relationship supposes that we are not in possession of complete lucidity about either pole: whether ourselves or the great philosophers of the modern centuries."[6]

At the first meeting of the seminar Collins tantalizes and intrigues, hinting at how the theme of the seminar emerges in the main text of the course.[7] The main text is some major work or collection of works, e.g., the *Critique of Pure Reason* for "Cognitive Models in Kant" or Wiener's edited collection of Leibniz's works for "Cognitive Models in Leibniz." Collins then divides the text into three sections (approximately 250-300 pages each) on the basis of which students are required to write three successive, ten-page expository papers on each section at three-week intervals. These papers are always returned one week after their submission, accompanied by a slip of paper filled with handwritten comments upon which Collins elaborates privately in his office. These little slips of paper, as every Collins student can attest, are treasures of insight, revealing implications far beyond what the author of the paper could have ever dreamed. How many dissertations, articles, and books are born of these humble suggestions and admonitions!

Early meetings of the seminar include discussion of topics for term papers and seminar reports. Usually Collins suggests from thirty to forty topics in all, two-thirds of which deal with major works of the philosopher on whom the course is centered (e.g., Leibniz's *Monadology* or Hegel's *Philosophy of Right*). The remaining third concern other important figures more or less contemporary to the philosopher. For initiates in the history of philosophy these suggestions can be a learning experience in itself. For example, in a seminar on Hegel, Collins mentions not only Fichte, Schelling, Bolzano, and Bentham but also such wayside figures as Charles Lyell, author of *The Principles of Geology*. By calling attention to these "middle-range and paraphilosophers," Collins communicates his concern for avoiding any rigid segregation or isolation of philosophical genius from its time and cohorts.[8]

Term papers are to be written on the topics that form the subject matter of seminar reports. These seminar reports are to be reproduced and placed in the hands of other members of the seminar one week before an oral presentation of the report. Although it is intended to reflect only the extent of one's research at the time of its presentation, the report must conform to very specific guidelines spelled out by Dr. Collins. A fifteen to twenty page, single-spaced affair, these reports begin with a title and outline or table of contents on the first page or two, followed by a bibliography of texts which had in fact proved relevant to the researcher. The body of the report contains the headings of the outline with short paragraphs of explanation, intended to place a particular part within the study as a whole or to project some yet to be completed research. Joined to these section headings and paragraphs of explanation were to be the most significant and relevant passages, cited in full, from the text(s) of the philosopher under investigation. The usefulness of these reports, both for their authors and for the seminar's participants, is enormous. Through these reports Collins teaches the nuts and bolts of the synthetic side of historical understanding, viz., how to put together a creative and responsible study of a philosopher's thinking. Moreover these reports realize the ideal of a seminar experience, so rarely achieved, in which members of the seminar genuinely instruct and help one another, forming a *concordia discors*.[9]

The presentations of the seminar reports comprise the greater part of the seminar meetings but before they begin Collins devotes at least the third and sometimes part of the fourth meeting of the seminar to a bibliography. The bibliography normally numbers about seventy-five to one hundred carefully selected books. The first twenty or so selections consist of the "creative fundament," i.e., the original, the latest, and the most adequate editions (and, where relevant, translations) of a philosopher's works. Next come general studies of the philosopher's thought as a whole, followed by one or two biographies of the philosopher, and finally groups of more particular studies, genetic and systematic accounts devoted entirely to, for example, a philosopher's epistemology, ethics, or aesthetics. Collins goes through these lists, book by book, frankly and respectfully appraising the strengths and weaknesses of each work. These concise estimates of major research, recent and past, set high standards of erudition and fairness, trademarks of Collins' work.

After the bibliographic sessions, Collins begins to lecture in earnest. For the members of the seminar these lectures are the event of the week, but it is not easy to characterize such understated masterpieces. Occasionally they touch down on the seminar's text, but they are largely creative "meta-reflections" inspired by Collins' re-reading of the text and his study of the most current philological and historical work. These artfully crafted lectures are concentrated with philosophical life and human sensibilities.[10] Some Collins peppers with his dry wit. Their meaning is not immediately assimilated; you have to keep sounding and resounding them as you trudge through the seminar's primary reading.

During the oral presentations of the seminar reports Collins imparts invaluable lessons in reading, analyzing, and writing a philosophical text. His attention first focuses on the report's table of contents. "Why did you decide to organize the material in this way? Does the symmetry (or asymmetry) in your ordering have any special significance? Does it perhaps match the philosopher's own account or reflect general methodological considerations?" With such questions Collins attracts attention to the philosopher's own decisions regarding method and structure. These questions lead to others concerning "the communicational spectrum," the when, why, and for whom the work was composed. In this regard, Collins alerts seminar members to the strategic importance of introductions and prefaces.[11]

Collins never leaves the seminar report itself for long. Often he links up quotations printed on the pages of the report and asks a rather anxious student what he or she made of them. The quotations inevitably illustrate some neglected perspective or correct a standard misconception of the philosopher's views. Through this strategy, Collins teaches you to be suspicious of facile and over-worked interpretations. In the same vein, Collins insists on avoiding monistic references to a philosopher (e.g., *the* philosophy of x or *his* position). Any talk of completely mastering the philosophical sources Collins greets with a withering reply. Constantly he urges "historical re-education," a conscious endeavor to understand a text differently in several subsequent readings.[12]

Frequently members of Collins' seminar will make the decision to write their dissertation under his direction. It may be that a dissertation topic emerges naturally from a final paper done in the seminar. In any case, writing a dissertation with Dr. Collins promises the opportunity to deepen the education begun in the seminar, to work with him more personally and at a higher, even more demanding level of scholarship. It is not surprising that more than forty doctoral dissertations have been completed under his direction. The topics they take up vary greatly and include: freedom, religion, community, essence and subjectivity, mathematics, physics, proofs of God's existence, nature, relations between nature and man, method, self and identity, Deism, Personalism, language, moral anthropology, and cognitive models. Each of the major modern philosophers are represented in this group of dissertations, as are the major American pragmatists and naturalists, Vico, John Toland, Marx, Bradley, Scheler, and Buber.

In terms of contact hours, working with Collins on a dissertation is a lean experience, but you remember the intensity of the working relationship. You struggle on your own to achieve a basic understanding of the relevant problems and texts. There are no loose-talking, free-floating sessions. From the outset, when you begin to pull a proposal together, Collins wants you to have something written, in as final a form as possible, before each meeting. Once your proposal is accepted you are on your own until a chapter or chapters are ready. To say that you are on your own is a bit misleading, for you are sure to find Collins ubiquitous. The lessons he teaches are so deeply ingrained that he seems to be at your side as you thumb through the card catalog, consider some research short-cut, or grapple with a difficult German text.

For the dissertation writer, the hours spent in Collins' home discussing your chapter or chapters can be a peak experience. If you have done your work well, these sessions run on that distinctive "meta-level" at which Collins lectures. You join him in dialogue, you think together, new connections are knit. At these times, Collins is aglow with love of the material and personal attentiveness to you and your work. His energy for these meetings is tremendous. Ron Talmadge recalls discussing his first chapter, "I remember going out to Dr. Collins' house hoping not to take too much of his time, knowing his health was 'precarious' and all. As it turned out, we spent five hours going over that one chapter detail by detail, and he wore me out after the third hour or so. I left with the impression he could've gone on much longer, whereas I, in the bloom of youth, had completely lost focus."

At the beginning of this look at Collins' teaching career, we emphasized the mutuality of his teaching and scholarship. This bond between teaching and research can be pinned down in terms of his graduate seminar and dissertation direction work. Their closest relationship lies in Collins' practice of uniting the four semester cycle of the seminar under a common theme. Organizing topics such as "Interpretation Theory," "God," and "Philosophy of Religion" bear directly on Collins' research. A more tenuous relationship holds between Collins' direction of dissertations and his own research. He stresses the person to person character of the relationship between director and writer. The choice of topic should come, at least in its rough form, from the student. On the basis of current research trends, his judgment of the opportunities which might be opened up, and his own research interests, Collins will make certain finer specifications of the topic. Though he regards the whole dissertation experience as a learning process, he calls special attention to those hours devoted to going over dissertation chapters. These times he calls "gracious interchanges."

III.

One way of getting in touch with a philosopher's fundament[13] is to watch the project of the youthful philosopher take shape against the grid of the intellectual milieu of his or her maturing years. From the mid-nineteen-thirties up into the fifties in the USA, the history of philosophy stood in danger of being severed from institutional connections with current philosophy, and the renaissance of Catholic intellectual life was threatened by its insularity. James Collins has powerfully influenced our intellectual climate by setting himself against these two currents. Through a wealth of studies, Collins has helped keep the history of philosophy and current philosophy on working terms within the same academic department, and he has pressed Catholic philosophers outward to probe all philosophical traditions.

Throughout his writings Collins employs a wide range of strategies for undermining what he terms the "purist split"[14] between the history of philosophy and philosophy. Here just a few of the important ways Collins contributes to the reunion of philosophy and its history can be touched upon: his clearing the way to the modern sources through meticulous scholarship, his ability to actually bring contemporary and modern philosophies into conversation, and his decision to center his studies of modern philosophy on those matters which are very much with us in the "interpreting present."

In her essay on school studies Simone Weil urges us to study our mistakes, for there we catch outselves in an inattentive rush to impose our own preconceived notions on a problem.[15] To guard against this way of obstructing our path to the modern philosophers, Collins sets a stringent standard of scholarship. To write his study of Kierkegaard, Collins learned Danish. He digests the biographies and autobiographies of philosophers, he picks over their letters and journals, their library shelves and their marginal notes. He scrupulously follows and fosters developments in translations, text editing, and philological methods. He is a virtuoso in the history of philosophy.

Collins brings to life the reciprocity of philosophy and its history by studying the great twentieth century philosophers: Wittgenstein, Dewey, Carnap, Husserl, Heidegger, Merleau-Ponty, Sartre, Ricoeur, Sellars, and more. Besides methodically reviewing their books, Collins constantly brings their various philosophical initiatives to bear on his seminars and studies of modern philosophy.

Look over the topics which have guided Collins' studies in the history of modern philosophy: God, religion, nature, wisdom, and history or tradition. These display Collins' pursuit of themes of the classical modern philosophers which continue to open up to us. Perhaps this is too mild, for these are a bundle of issues which the modern philosophers have rudely dumped on us to shun or puzzle over as we choose. Collins' lesson is that if we risk the puzzling, the modern philosophers will prove their pluck. They can help us find our way.

For Collins' views on a proper Christian approach to the study of philosophy in this post-modern period, we turn to his three essays "The Problem of a Perennial Philosophy," "Toward a Philosophically Ordered Thomism," and "Leo XIII and the Philosophical Approach to Modernity," in *Crossroads in Philosophy*, and the address he gave to the ACPA in 1965, "Christian Philosophers and the Modern Turn." Collins insists that the name "Christian" or "Catholic" or more specifically, "Thomist," does not lift a philosopher out of history and the human condition. He criticizes an understanding of "perennial philosophy" which fixates on a particular doctrinal system, rather he takes the term in a methodological sense which allows for enduring truths but establishes no doctrinal norm. He disagrees with Gilson that reconstructed Thomism must follow the theological order going from God to finite things, and that to do otherwise necessarily leads one into either Aristotelian essentialism or Cartesian post-Christian naturalism. Pope Leo he praises as "pre-eminently *the Pope of the open tradition in philosophy*," a tradition which recognizes that in God's providence the seeds of truth are scattered widely. His address to the ACPA underlines both the hope and the risk his position involves. "The Christian philosopher who assimilates the temper of modern philosophizing can better appreciate the kind of human world in which he lives and which he should want to enrich. He realizes that his own religious faith cannot and should not be made an exception to the vocation of radical and persistent questioning to which the philosopher is called."[16]

Enlivened by the tradition of Christian revelation and philosophy, Collins has hewn to the hard path of the philosophical order, sympathetically yet critically immersing himself in existentialism, phenomenology, naturalism, and modern philosophy. Keeping to his aspiration has not left Collins' thought unaffected — it was not intended to. One discerns in Collins' writings a shift away from interpolating Thomistic criticism into his treatments of various philosophers. This trend points up the unsettling implications of his open-ended concept of "perennial philosophy" and his conviction that modern and contemporary philosophies really do gleam with truth. It is a shift which signifies a maturation of Collins' vocation as a Christian philosopher, not its fading away.

Collins' lifelong strainings against the "purist split" and against insularity in Catholic philosophy may be pressure points of his intellectual project; they certainly are not the sum total of his contributions. Only brief mention can be made of some others. As a professional, Collins takes responsibility for the state of his art. His involvement in matters of translation, text editing, and philological method have already been noted. Collins has taken on a good share of formal editorial work.[17] Less formally, Collins makes himself available to other scholars to help evaluate their work or place it with a publisher, or simply for on-going intellectual interchange. For example, Collins corresponded with novelist Walker Percy on existentialist themes before Percy wrote his novel, *The Moviegoer*.

Through various articles and his books *The Existentialists* and *The Mind of Kierkegaard*, Collins helped put existentialism and phenomenology on the agenda at a time when they were widely disdained by English-speaking philosophers. This was but one of the ways in which he resisted the near stranglehold of analytic philosophy on American philosophy. With studies of "paraphilosophers"[18] such as Kierkegaard, Newman, and the evolutionary naturalists, Collins has kept philosophy aware of its own permeable limits. While books such as *The Existentialists* and *The mind of Kierkegaard* have helped philosophy stay open to a non-technical public, Collins has written superb technical studies of modern philosophers.

Though such studies as *The Emergence of the Philosophy of Religion* and *Descartes' Philosophy of Nature* confirm Collins as a world renowned historian, his most distinguishing philosophical accomplishment to date is *Interpreting Modern Philosophy*. This book harvests the learning achieved over years and years of studying, teaching, and researching. By his own reckoning, *Interpreting Modern Philosophy* holds a special place among Collins' writings. Though Collins' name does not appear in the index, it is very much a personal act of self-reflection. In it he addresses methodological issues at the center of his work. It also brings into sharp relief the importance of Collins' years of teaching for his development as an interpreter of modern philosophy. It serves as a case study in the meaning of history and the ways of historical interpretation. He fashions a synthetic theory of interpreting modern philosophy by sticking close to the practices of interpretation employed by historians of modern philosophy, while he keeps in mind the human purposes served by their historical investigations. *Interpreting Modern Philosophy* is a major contribution to philosophical hermeneutics,[19] and it distills in a single volume Collins' persistent values.

* * *

Wonder is a special gift of children and a constant spur to philosophers. A child's eyes grow big at the sight of yellow chicks bursting their white confines or at the unfamiliar pictures in a new storybook; Kant kept wondering at those starry skies above and that inner moral law inscribed on the human heart. James Collins was a child-wonderer, and he is a philosopher-wonderer. Through a lifetime he has husbanded and communicated this sparkle. It leavens the life of this master teacher and scholar.

Thirty-five years of dredging dead men's papers might snuff out one's spark, but Collins' mind is always re-ignited. Instead of trailing off into a monotonous roll call, the names Descartes, Hume, Kant, Hegel, and the others, ever more signal to Collins a society of friendly minds. In discussing Heidegger's reflections on his own lifelong reading of Kant, Collins highlights the term "*Wiederholung*," meaning a retrieval and a creative repeating. Collins has conducted this wonder-infused *Wiederholung* through all the classical modern writings. Perhaps the final stanzas of Gerard Manley Hopkins' poem provide the best image for Collins' relation to the much traveled texts.

> Generation have trod, have trod, have trod;
> And all is seared with trade; bleared, smeared with toil;
> And wears man's smudge and shares man's smell:
>   the soil
> Is bare now, nor can foot feel, being shod.
>
> And for all this, nature is never spent;
> There lives the dearest freshness deep down things;
> And though the last lights off the black West went
> Oh, Morning at the brown brink eastward, springs —
> Because the Holy Ghost over the bent
> World broods with warm breast and with ah!
>   bright wings.[20]

Collins has no less a sense for the "pied beauty" of the modern sources. Although in his essay on perennial philosophy Collins rejected a "pluralism-in-principle" as a dogmatic claim ill justified by the actuality of pluralism, he cultivates a respect for it as an indispensable human virtue. Collins keeps a tolerant mind; he experiments and he encourages others to do so. He digs in against the spirit of imperialism in philosophy, constantly reminding us that philosophy is but one of many modes of human experiencing. He uses and fosters a multiplicity of approaches within the history of philosophy. Like the great modern philosophers themselves, he rubs up against that whetstone of tolerance — skepticism. In this age of specialization Collins takes his stand with Kant against "Cyclopism"[21] and other brands of reductionism. He has a keen eye for reciprocities among the modes of human knowing and experiencing — to counter the "purist split" Collins cites the actual reciprocities between philosophy and its history. His attentiveness to story, model, and metaphor, likewise enable us to appreciate reciprocities within plurality.

"*Nihil humani a me alienum puto* are words that spring to mind when I think of my teacher and Ph.D. mentor James Collins," writes Edward Stevens. This captures not just Collins' pluralism but its humanistic setting. For Kant, the fourth and overarching critical question is, what is man? In concluding *Interpreting Modern Philosophy* Collins writes, "Our inquiry into the modern source philosophers aims at *such* an interpretation of their thought as will illumine and improve the meaning of humanity among us. This more comprehensive purpose .... dictates nothing determinate and exclusive about *how* the reality of man is to be explored, . . . These matters have to be determined in accord with the internal procedures and interpretive modes of history of modern philosophy. But the teleological dynamism of these procedures and interpretive acts points toward the meaning of humanity as the unifying center of reference for all specific investigations. And it is the pivot whereby historical inquiries can be given practical significance for human action today."[22]

The task of building the human is not the work of a single person; it is a community task. The theme of human community — the community of philosophers, of scientists and artists, the university community, the community of seminar members, church as community, language communities — is ever-present in Collins' teaching and writing.

In building human community wisdom has a special place. It stretches us, bonds us together, brings us joy, and gives us hope. The philosopher is a lover of wisdom. When modern philosophers search for harmony, try to reconcile human reason and passion, or strive to mend the torn fabric of our social, intellectual and religious worlds, they prove themselves no exception to this rule. Kant worked hard to draw together the vast spray of human experience and knowledge. His was a religiously sensitive "mundane wisdom." In James Collins' life and work wisdom's glint is bright too.

Notes

[1] We would like to thank Dr. Collins, who helped us in the preparation of this essay by sharing some of his personal history with us in an interview. We would also like to acknowledge the letters and other help offered by some of Dr. Collins' former students: Edward Stevens, Ron Talmadge, Rev. Harry Burns, S.J., Sr. Rosemary Flanigan, Rev. W. Henry Kenney, S.J., Sr. Marie G. Hungerman, IHM, James H. Hamby, Sr. Mary Alice Haley, and Jeanne Schuler.

[2] For Collins' account of the basal act of philosophizing, see James Collins, *Interpreting Modern Philosophy* (Princeton: Princeton University Press, 1972), pp. 44-53.

[3] Edward Stevens writes, "A brilliant man — but you don't feel like you have to be brilliant to talk with him. His respect for people and their views is boundless."

[4] This sense, which many of us consider one of Collins' greatest gifts to us as students, emerged as the "rule of historical comportment" in *Interpreting Modern Philosophy*. "We must learn to comport ourselves toward the source men and their works *as we would toward a company of critical inquirers*, with whom we are in personal relationship" (*Interpreting*, p. 43).

[5] *Interpreting*, p. 204.

[6] *Interpreting*, p. 267.

[7] "Without always reflecting upon it, the seminar members have a lived comprehension of many fundamental aspects of historical understanding. Their very convening together in an atmosphere of expectation — of engaging in work that is to be exploratory rather than repetitive, a testing of new interpretations rather than a recall of old ones — tells something about the source under study. . . . the seminar's sense of expectation about new findings, yet to be made, in a much surveyed land, is the proper historical correlate of the original source's own classical nature and futural intent." *Interpreting*, pp. 268-269.

[8] "We do not truly know the historical landscape in modern philosophy until we come to discern the values found upon the middle plateau and in the fertile lowlands, as well as those found on the highest mountains." *Interpreting*, pp. 232-233.

[9] "Thus the seminar experience reinforces the conclusion that historical interpretation of modern philosophy is a community operation, and at the same time specifies that this inquiring community consists of the teachers and students bound together in a common work and not solely of the lone research writer." *Interpreting*, p. 271.

[10] We remember in particular the timely second lecture of the Hegel seminar offered in Spring of 1974. Collins' take-off point was Leibniz's maxim, "scholars and students ought to be engaged as much as possible in conversation, and be as much as possible with people and in the world." He went on to consider philosophers' decisions on whether to work within or outside the university and how the press of modern barbarism shapes these decisions.

[11] "*The strategic introduction.* It is a safe rule of thumb that we should never ignore or glide over a philosopher's 'front matter': the dedicatory letter, preface, or introduction to which he devotes so much care." *Interpreting*, p. 80.

[12] "This constant renewal of historical questioning does not depend primarily upon the historian's modesty as a private trait of temperament, but rather upon his very realistic appraisal of the non-conquering nature of his relationship with the written achievements of the great modern philosophers." *Interpreting*, pp. 42-43.

[13] On the difference between "fundament" and fundamentals" see *Interpreting*, pp. 102-103.

[14] See *Interpreting*, p. 14.

[15] See "Reflections on the Right Use of School Studies with a View to the Love of God" in Simone Weil, *Waiting for God*, translated by Emma Craufurd (New York: Harper ¿ Row, 1951).

[16] James Collins, "Christian Philosophers and the Modern Turn" in *Proceedings of the American Catholic Philosophical Association*, Volume XXXIX, edited by George F. McLean (Washington, D.C.: Catholic University of America Press, 1965), p. 23.

[17] He serves as a member of the boards of *International Archives of the History of Ideas, American Philosophical Quarterly, The Modern Schoolman, Journal of the History of Philosophy, The Philosopher's Index*, and *Southern Journal of Philosophy*.

[18] See *Interpreting*, pp. 242-252.

[19] See James L. Marsh's essay in this volume.

[20] Gerard Manley Hopkins, "God's Grandeur," in *Gerard Manley Hopkins: Poems and Prose*, edited by W.H. Gardner (Baltimore: Penguin Books, 1953), p. 27.

[21] "Cyclopism is a disease of civilized men, who find that they can make notable advances in knowledge and the control of nature only by concentrating all of their energy and skill upon particular fields of research . . . . They are apt to dry up the vision in 'the other eye,' the one which should keep them aware of, and sympathetic toward, the viewpoint of others and the common concerns of humanity." James Collins, *The Emergence of the Philosophy of Religion* (New Haven: Yale University Press, 1967), p. 92.

[22] *Interpreting*, pp. 407-408.

PART I

SOURCE THINKERS UNDER HISTORICAL QUESTIONING

*...Plato...Boethius...
Aquinas...Scotus...
...Suarez...Descartes
...Hobbes...Wolff...
Kierkegaard...Peirce...*

2.

PLATO'S DIALECTIC OF THE SUN

Leonard J. Eslick

My choice of this topic for the Collins Festschrift is, I think, especially appropriate. For much of Collins' work has been in the area of what might be called the philosophy of philosophy, particularly as manifested in the history of modern and contemporary philosophy. This is an inquiry which begins with Socrates and Plato. According to one tradition, the *Charmides* was the earliest of Plato's dialogues, and was even read by Plato in the presence of Socrates. Central to the *Charmides*, seeking a definition of *sophrosyne*, temperance, is the Socratic "dream of wisdom," as a science of science and of its absence. Socrates is unsure at this early date whether such a dream comes from the gate of horn from which true dreams issue, or the gate of ivory, the source of lying dreams. It is quickly made clear that such a science is useless unless it is of the good, and if it is not of the good it is not even science in the sense of wisdom. But it is clear that the only wisdom which Socrates at his trial professed to have was this self-reflective type, a knowing that he did not know, and that this is the therapeutic "charm" he offers to the young Charmides for the cure of his "headache", that is to say, for the cure of his soul. In the *Republic* the cure both for the ills of the soul and the state is to be effected by the dialectical wisdom of philosophy. The central books of that dialogue are accordingly concerned with the nature of dialectic, and its distinctions from other, inferior modes of cognition.

There is no philosopher who has been more written about than Plato, and no passages in all philosophical literature better known than the Divided Line at the end of *Republic VI* and the illustrating Allegory of the Cave at the beginning of book VII. One might suppose that such almost universal familiarity has long since exhausted the possibility of fresh insights or discoveries about Platonic doctrine, at least in these areas. But Platonic thought is inexhaustible, and there are still mysteries to be further penetrated. One of the major mysteries which still awaits a definitive resolution is the apparent fact that there is not just one Platonic dialectic, but two — the so-called "earlier" dialectic and the "later" dialectic of Collection and Division, which makes what is perhaps its earliest appearance in the *Phaedrus*.[1] Is there doctrinal continuity or real divergence between them? The question is too vast to be answered in this essay, though I will try to point in the direction in which I think the answer is to be found.[2] But preliminary to any attempt at a resolution, the exact nature of the "early" dialect, which I am calling, for obvious reasons, that of the Sun, must be determined. In spite of the quantity of modern and contemporary scholarship in this area, including the well-known work of Richard Robinson[3] and the recent study of Kenneth Sayers,[4] much more needs to be said. In particular Plato's indebtedness to developments in ancient Greek mathematics needs to be clearly pointed out.[5]

Knowledge and Opinion; Being and Becoming

The central texts in the *Republic* concerning scientific and dialectical methods arise in the context of the third and greatest "wave" which the Socratic theory of Justice must surmount. This is the proposal for the union of royal power and philosophic wisdom. Socrates is constrained to identify the nature of the latter. The philosopher has infallible knowledge of eternal, immutable, and necessary Being. The cause of such Being, and the knowledge of it, is the Good, which, in a passage which had the authority of revealed scripture for the later neo-Platonists, is said to be beyond both Being and knowledge. The Good is not directly defined, though the hedonistic identification of it with pleasure, and even the theory of "the finer sorts of wits," who identify it with knowledge are quickly and summarily dismissed. The refutation of hedonism is the briefest to be found in the *Dialogues* — if one admits that some pleasures are evil and should not be enjoyed[6]; hedonism falls into contradiction. The identification of the Good with knowledge is not the same as the Socratic-Platonic equation of virtue with knowledge. It falls into circularity. One must ask, knowledge of what? The only answer is knowledge of the Good.

Instead of a direct reply as to the nature of the Good we are given a causal analogy. In the physical world of Becoming, the Sun causes generation, light, and vision, without being identical with these effects. The Good is the Sun of the intelligible world, the cause of Being, Essence, and knowledge, without being identical with its effects.

Clearly all of this is functioning in the pattern of a sharp and definitive *chorismos*, a separation of Being (the Forms) and Becoming, of the objects of knowledge from the objects of opinion (*doxa*). What Aristotle calls "the argument from the sciences" was perhaps the most popular Academic argument for the separation of the Forms. Fallible opinion deals with objects which become, which are mutable and contingent, temporal and non-eternal. They are like the moving images of Daedalus, probably children's wind-up toys which if placed upon a flat surface never stay in the same place. Such objects are not utterly unreal, as the Eleatics had supposed. They participate in Being, but such participation makes them like "punning riddles" — they both are and are not. They are blends of Being and of Non-Being.[7] As such they cannot be objects of knowledge, but only of opinion. Plato is as confident as Kant will later be that sciences actually do exist, the mathematical sciences in particular. For neither Plato nor Kant could they have exclusively empirical origin. For Kant the certitude and necessity of such sciences comes from the subject; for Plato they come from the *objects* known, which are, therefore, completely trans-empirical and altogether separated from the ever-changing, Heraclitean world of Becoming. Such mathematical sciences *do* exist, and hence also the objects known by them. But Plato, as we will see, is well aware that science on this level — *dianoia*, thinking or understanding — cannot be self-founding. It cannot justify whatever ultimate truth values it may attain, either empirically or within its own systematic framework. The final appeal must be to a higher — the highest — court of arbitration, and this is Dialectic, the Dialectic of the Good, the Sun of the intelligible world.

Dialectic and the Good.

In the *Phaedo*,[8] in the interlude between the preliminary and the final arguments for immortality of the soul, Socrates recalls his discovery in his youth of the book of Anaxagoras, and his excitement on reading therein that the cause of nature was *nous* or mind. He supposed that this could only mean that mind causes by ordering all things to the best or the Good. In reading further he was disappointed to find Anaxagoras making no such use of *nous*, but employing it solely as a mechanical agent, a catalyst to initiate the endless process of differentiation in the original mixture. But the real, the primary cause, is indeed the ordering by mind to the Good. To scientifically explain exclusively in terms of material conditions, as for example, to account for life solely by chemical arrangements of non-living materials, is to leave out this real cause. Whatever may be the case in the special sciences, on the level of *dianoia* or understanding, Dialectic must be essentially teleological, and its possibility rests upon a noetic grasp of the Good, the reason of all reasons, the Form of all Forms. It is, therefore, astounding to find a recent commentator on Plato's analytic method, Kenneth Sayers,[9] minimizing and even ignoring the role in that method of the Good. Indeed, as we will shortly see, Burnet's characterization of Plato's earlier dialectic as a "teleological algebra" is well founded.

The Divided Line: The Levels of Cognition.

The status of dialectic as the highest level of cognition is most extensively presented in the *Republic VI — VII*. The Divided Line is an epistemological-metaphysical hierarchy whose supreme rule is that verification is always from above, never from below. Plato does indeed possess an *analytic* method in the strictest and most precise sense. But the rule of his analysis is diametrically opposed to the "analysis" of the Anglo-American logical empiricists of the 20th century. The latter, exemplified by the "logical constructionism" of Russell and Carnap, is a reductive analysis of the compound sentences of the sciences into so-called 'protocol sentences' denoting the sensory atoms of Hume. Verification, and even meaning, is supposed (at least in the younger, more innocent period of the movement) to be a function of such reductive analysis. It is impossible to understand Plato apart from his fundamental opposition to empiricism, an opposition which is as evident in the *Republic* as it is in the much later *Theaetetus*, the most sustained and powerful critique of empiricism in Western philosophy.

The lowest level in the Divided Line is *eikasia*, a word difficult to translate into English. "Conjecture', which is sometimes used, is certainly incorrect. 'Imaging' or even 'imagining' are better, but still not satisfying. The objects of such operations are clearly images, but Plato's example is misleading and much too narrow. He compares them to reflections on shiny surfaces or pools of water.[10] Narcissus, to be sure, according to legend was deceived by seeing his own reflected image in such a pool, fell in love with it, and was drowned in the attempt to embrace it. More light on the actual objects of *eikasia* is shed by the Cave Allegory, in which *eikasia* is symbolized by the chained cave-dwellers, who see only the moving shadows and hear only the sounds reflected on the wall in front of them. These are the reflected images in firelight of artifacts carried above the heads of walkers moving behind the prisoners' backs. Shadows of the walkers themselves are not cast, since they are hidden by a curtain screen. How are we to interpret this strange allegory? It seems evident to me that *eikasia* is sense perception. We know what Plato's own theory of sense perception was, in the later dialogues *Theaetetus* and *Timaeus*.[11] It is reasonable to suppose that he was in full possession of it when writing the *Republic*. It is a crucial part of the background evidence for the separation of Forms and the theory of Reminiscence. Perception is accounted for as the result of the confluence of two motions, the external and the internal movement of the sense organs. A third motion, different from the first two, is thereby produced, the sense image. Such a theory is attributed in the *Theaetetus* to Protagoras, as the interpretation of the great sophist's dictum, "Man is the measure of all things." If such images are indeed the only measures of the truth of opinion, then *all* opinions are true, since their objects exist only subjectively and relatively. Empiricism, which seeks to verify from below, for Plato leads ineluctably to a universal skepticism with respect to *objective* standards for truth and falsity.

The next highest level is *pistis* or belief, which together with *eikasia* exhaust the world of *doxa* — opinion concerning Becoming. Such beliefs are already acts of intellectual *inference*, judgments beyond the data of sense perception to their supposed causes, which cannot themselves be directly sensed. They imply, therefore, a certain turning or conversion of the soul, away from visible images to invisible, though physical, causes. A certain confusion at this point is difficult to avoid, and Plato's own language abets it. He talks as if the objects of *pistis* were things perceived, sensible things themselves. This would imply a perceptual realism which is foreign to Plato, however at home it might be in an Aristotelian empiricism. Beliefs are *intellectual* judgments, not immediately about the data of the senses — except for hardened logical positivists we seldom utter protocol sentences such as 'red here.' They are opinions about the physical causes of such sensible effects, causes which are not themselves immediately perceptible at all. In the Cave Allegory such believers are released prisoners, who have turned around to face a higher level of reality, so that they face the fire and the objects moving in its light. They are 'looking' at objects which the senses as such cannot perceive. Indeed, to remain always on the level of *eikasia* would be to experience "sound and fury signifying nothing." For a newborn infant, William James once speculated, the world would be "one big buzzing blooming confusion." The beliefs we form even about the physical world are trans-empirical, and, as Plato was later to say in the *Theaetetus*,[12] are expressed in judgments which employ objects of intellect, and not of sense — Forms of Being, Same, Different. The problem is how such beliefs are to be verified. If only from below, and if such data are private and relative, none of them is falsifiable. If one can only talk about what he perceives, he perceives what he does perceive, and that is the end of it. But even if one believes more than he can perceive, beliefs are not self-validating. Their truth or falsity must be determined on a higher level still.

In any case, the physical things ('events' would be more accurate, since for Plato, with his Heraclitean heritage from Cratylus, the physical world is in process) are themselves only images, moving images of eternal spiritual realities. Their very motions, as the Cave Allegory intimates, are not spontaneous and self-derived. The motions are communicated to them by the invisible walkers holding them, hidden by the curtain screen. Who are these walkers? Plato does not tell us in the *Republic*, but it is clear to readers of the *Phaedrus, Timaeus*, and *Laws X* that they are *souls*, self-moving movers, who are the sources of all physical (moved) movers. The description of the moved bodies as *artifacts* is also significant. For *nature* itself is, for Plato, artificial, the work of soul, which the *Laws* declares to be the 'eldest of all things'.[13]

To verify (or falsify) beliefs from above is to cross the great divide which separates the world of Becoming and the opinions about it from the intelligible world of Being and Knowledge. It is to move, at first, into the domain of *dianoia*.

Dianoia, hypothetical understanding, thinking under a hypothesis, is exemplified for Plato by the mathematical sciences. Plato knows five, arithmetic, plane geometry, solid geometry (whose pioneering development was largely the work of Academicians in Plato's lifetime), harmonics, and astronomy. The proliferation of such sciences in later centuries would hardly have surprised Plato. It is important to understand that sciences, for Plato, are *purely* mathematical, and do not deal with physical objects or motions, even in the cases of harmonics and astronomy. Harmonics deals with *intelligible* ratios and proportions, the *inaudible* 'music' exemplified in the great diatonic scale. Astronomy deals not directly with the physical motions of celestial bodies, but with purely intelligible motions. The latter science does seek, to be sure, to "save the appearances" (a phrase perhaps invented in the Academy) by formulating hypothetical systems of "real regular motions" to explain or account for the anomalies, the apparent irregularities, of observed planetary motions. The lawfulness of the realm of physical becoming is imaged, participated, and is the product of a 'persuasion' of material 'necessity' by Reason[14] which can never be total and complete. Reason's persuasion in the domain of physical becoming can never eliminate contingency.[15] The most that physics, the so-called natural 'sciences', can achieve is the *probable* account or 'likely story' of the *Timaeus*, far superior to ordinary belief (because it involves the application of mathematical models to phenomena), but inferior to the necessity of pure science. The problem, however, even with these pure mathematical sciences is that the necessities so discerned and demonstrated remain, on the level of these sciences, hypothetical only, in an if-then connection in which the *If* cannot be eliminated.

There are two methods of scientific demonstration on the level of *dianoia*, synthesis and analysis. Their use is most clearly evident in geometry. It is worthwhile to recall the tradition, mentioned by Tzetzes in his *Book of Histories* viii, 972-973,[16] "over his front door Plato wrote: 'Let no one unversed in geometry come under my roof.' " Geometrical synthesis is best, and almost uniquely, illustrated by Euclid's *Elements*. The theorems in Euclid were largely the discoveries of earlier Pythagorean and Academic mathematicians. (For example, those in Book X on the irrationals come from Plato's colleague in the Academy, Theaetetus, and the great Definition V., Book V, of *proportion*, which restored geometry after the supreme trauma of the Pythagorean discovery of incommensurability, was due to Eudoxus.) But the synthetic ordering of the *Elements* is the work of Euclid, beginning with the first principles of the science (definitions, common notions, postulates) and moving downwards deductively to theorems. *If* those first principles are assumed, *then* their assumed truth causes necessarily the truth of the theorems as effects. (One is presupposing, of course, the coherence of the original categorial set, and the logical correctness of the reasoning from them.) The movement of thought in synthesis is from (assumed) causes to effects. In the later Aristotelian tradition proof of this kind will be called demonstration *propter quid* — of the reasoned fact.

Traditionally, in this kind of reasoning, an appeal will be made to the supposedly intuitive, self-evidential character of the starting points. There must, to be sure (unless one is operating in a purely nominalistic formalism) be some such founding moment of intellectual intuition. But Plato's point is that as long as one remains on the level of *dianoia*, the hypothetical character of the starting points, the presumed causes, cannot be exorcised. Verification, once again, is from above, and involves an intellectual intuition into an *unhypothetical* principle, an ultimate reason which is unconditioned, the Good.

The other kind of geometrical method is *analysis*. Instead of moving from hypothetical cause to effect, its movement is the reverse, from effects to hypothetical causes. Actually, most attempts at scientific demonstration in the history of science, even in geometry, develop in this pattern. We have already mentioned that Euclid's example of a synthetic ordering of the elements of his sciences is almost unparalleled. It is rather curious, therefore to find an ancient mathematical philosopher, Theon of Smyrna,[1] crediting Plato with the *invention* of geometrical analysis. It must have always been the normal method of discovery. But I think what Theon meant was that Plato was the first to become fully and explicitly conscious of its implications in the *positive* mode of analysis.

Certainly this indirect method of proof had long been familiar in its negative form, the *reductio ad absurdum*, and had been generalized from mathematical argument into philosophy by the Eleatics. The principle is logically simple, familiar to anyone who has learned to ring the changes of the Aristotelian square of opposition. If propositions are related as contradictories, the truth of one entails the falsity of the other, *and* vice versa. For Parmenides and Zeno, the absurdity of the hypothesis of pluralism led to the necessary truth of absolute monism. Many, if not most, of the Socratic arguments in the *Dialogues* employ this negative kind of analysis, usually on the level of *dianoia* rather than of dialectic.

It is, however, the positive mode of geometrical analysis which is most philosophically interesting, and which Plato will transmute, by the alchemy of his genius, into *dialectical* analysis. If a proposition which one desires to prove can be shown to imply the truth of an already granted proposition, then the truth of the original is proved. The logical form is, if A then B. But B's truth is already (or can be) established — and therefore A. There is, however, to the logically tutored, a bare-faced logical fallacy in this, even though it is what many people, including many scientists, talk about as scientific verification. Hypothesis A upon analysis yields consequences x,y,z. We then, if it is an empirical science, resort to the appropriate laboratory or observatory and happily discover x,y,z, and triumphantly announce that hypothesis A has been confirmed. To use more Platonic language, the appearances have been saved. The fallacy is to suppose that affirming the consequences allows us to affirm the antecedent.

Plato was well aware of this problem, even at the heart of what he regarded as a pure mathematical science, astronomy. According to tradition, while presiding over the Academy, he set for his faculty the project of working out as many different hypotheses of planetary motions as they could devise, all of them 'saving' the same apparent motions. In the process, besides variants of geocentric theories (including a particularly ingenious one of Eudoxus, which Aristotle was later to greatly admire) there may be been an anticipation of heliocentric theory.[18] Each would successfully account, by different hypothetical systems of real regular motions, for the apparent irregularities or anomalies of the observed motions (e.g. station and retrogradation in the planetary motions.) The same effects may be predicted by different hypothetical causes.

How does one, in these circumstances, choose between alternative hypotheses? On the level of *dianoia,* of the mathematical sciences, decision would seem impossible. First of all, it can be proved that mathematically speaking, they are *equivalent,* whether it be a Ptolemaic epicycle theory, an eccentric circle theory, or a Copernican heliocentric theory. Even if new observations provide apparent motions which seem not to be 'saved' by a particular hypothesis, say Ptolemy's epicycles, it may be possible to so adjust the hypothesis, perhaps by the incorporation of additional epicycles, to accommodate the new evidence. The criterion of relative simplicity, while attractive, is difficult to apply. Anyone, for example, who has labored over both Ptolemy's and Copernicus' theories of the moon would judge the latter to be more complex.

Another episode in the history of mathematical science which occurred many centuries after Plato was the advent of non-Euclidian geometries. It would have surprised Plato not at all, although it is embarrassing to neo-Kantians. In Euclid it is simply *postulated* that straight lines will intersect when the angles between them are less than 180°. It is not laid down as a primitive meaning assumption (definition) or as axiomatic, in the sense of a commonly accepted notion. This long occasioned uneasiness, and in the 18th century the Jesuit mathematician Saccheri wrote a book "in vindication of Euclid," in which he attempted to *geometrically* prove the parallel postulate.[19] The failure of the attempt opened the Pandora's box of non-Euclidean geometries in the 19th century. There is an instructive difference as compared with our astronomical problems. There *is* convertibility between the proposition that the internal angles of triangles equal 180° and the parallel postulate of Euclid, each implies the other, and hence there is no violation in this case of the logical law against affirming the consequent and then affirming the antecedent. It is this property of convertibility of geometrical propositions *within* a particular geometry that makes geometrical analysis work. But in non-Euclidean geometries, dependent upon the parallel postulates chosen, the interior angles of triangles may be either greater than 180° or less. How does one *mathematically* choose between Euclidian and non-Euclidian geometries?

There is a further point of importance to Plato and to many others in the history of science, including recent logical positivists and empiricists. This is the age-old dream of the Unity of Science. Can thinking, remaining on the level of *dianoia,* unify all science, so that ultimately, instead of many different sets of first principles, each for a different science, all would follow from a single set. From Plato's point of view the synoptic unity of all science is impossible to attain in principle on this level. The usual way of trying to do this is reductionism, a reduction to some one privileged science, usually physics. The *physicalism* of Carnap is a typical example and its organon is the positivistic method of analysis, logical constructionism, which is the inversion of Platonic analysis. The obvious failure of the *Aufbau* led to a retreat to linguistic syntax, without abandoning physicalist dreams.

The Platonic Dialectic of the Sun: Synthesis and Analysis

The base metals of synthesis and analysis on the level of *dianoia* are transmuted into the gold of dialectic by an intellectual intuition *(noesis)* into the cause of the essence of all Being, the Good. The *Republic* (Bk. VII) will distinguish an ascending (analytic) and a descending (synthetic) dialectic, ascending to the Good and descending downward from it, like the angels on Jacob's ladder. In the descent the hypotheses of the special sciences are "destroyed"[20], which means that they lose their hypothetical character and are seen as necessary consequences of the unhypothetical first principle. The ideal method of proving anything, whether virtue is teachable or the soul is immortal, would be synthetic, starting with the beatific vision of the Good seen face to face, and in it seeing the necessary reasons for all things.

It is significant that Socrates nowhere in the *Dialogues,* including the *Phaedo* whose setting is the prison cell on the last day of his life, claims such ultimate wisdom. (I can think of only two major writings in Western philosophical literature which are ordered synthetically: Proclus' *Elements of Theology* and Spinoza's *Ethics.*) The Socratic philosopher, lover of wisdom, is like Eros in the *Symposium,* a child of poverty and plenty[21], a *daimon* intermediate between the heaven of perfect knowledge and the darkness of total ignorance. Learning, which is remembering, can take place only in the light of the Good, and without inheritance from Plenty the soul would lack intellectual intuition and could not ascend to the universal source. Consequently, Socrates in the *Phaedo,* in the great final argument for immortality, employs an ascending dialectic, the "second-best mode of inquiry," dialectical analysis. He will use only hypotheses consonant with the unhypothetical first principle of the whole, the Good. Such dialectical analysis,[22] unlike thinking in the mathematical sciences, makes no use of physical models, of images taken from the level of *pistis.* Unlike astronomy, there are no 'appearances' to be 'saved.' For Plato, like Charles Hartshorne in our own day,[23] metaphysics (for this is what dialectic is about) is not subject to empirical falsification. Rather, it "begins with forms, moves through them, and ends with them."[24]

Fortunately, Plato has provided us with a kind of "Rosetta Stone", by which we can identify the logical structure of all such dialectical analyses, whenever they appear in the *Dialogues.* This is an argument appearing late in the *Meno*,[25] in the context of the so-called second (and less famous) mathematical example. It is valuable for us precisely because of its relative simplicity and even because of its apparent failure.

The *Meno* begins, as do most of the early and middle dialogues, with a "what is x" question, in this case, "what is virtue?" Such questions, in these dialogues, have a way of turning, almost before the reader is sensible of it, into a different type of question, does x, as yet undefined, have the quality y? It would seem in principle impossible to answer the second without first having answered the first, to answer the question of *quality* without knowing *essence*. Towards the end of *Republic I,* Socrates and Thrasymachus are debating whether Justice (not defined) has the quality of being superior to Injustice in intelligence, power, and happiness. Socrates' arguments in that place that justice has this quality are based upon implied assumed definitions of justice and injustice. Since they remain (in Book I) unproved hypotheses, the arguments are not dialectical, but remain on the level of *dianoia*. In the *Euthyphro* Euthyphro tells Socrates that piety is that which is pleasing to the gods, an answer in terms of *quality* without even an implied hypothesis about the essence of justice.

Is there any way of scientifically answering *quality* questions before answering *essence* questions? The *Meno's* second mathematical example is the "diorismos", or limiting condition for the solution of a problem, in this case whether it is possible or not to inscribe in a circle an isosceles triangle equal to a given area x. The *diorismos* is a hypothetical definition. Is virtue teachable? It is, *if* and only if virtue is knowledge, but such reasoning remains on the level of *dianoia,* and does not establish the hypothetical condition for virtue's teachability. Can *dialectical* analysis turn back upon the hypothesis and prove it as following from an unhypothetical principle?

It is at this point that Plato provides us with his 'Rosetta stone' example: Virtue is teachable (v is t) if and only if virtue is knowledge (v is k). To dialectically establish the hypothesis both v and k must be subsumed under the highest formality of the Good (G). The premises, v is G and k is G, seem unexceptionable, but to immediately conclude to the identity of v and k would commit what Aristotle would call the fallacy of undistributed middle. This brings us to the noetic moment of the argument, an intellectual intuition into the argument's middle term, the Good. The insight here in the *Meno* is minimal, and will turn out to be insufficient to dialectically establish the hypothesis of the equation of v and k. Good is identified with the Beneficial. So-called goods of soul, body, and fortune are not really good unless they benefit their possessor. G is B. But benefit (B) is declared to be the function of knowledge, k. The conclusion is then drawn, v is k, which is the limiting condition for v is t.

The argument, as it stands, is flawed, since it turns out that true opinion, which is not knowledge, is as beneficial as knowledge. Furthermore, if virtue is knowledge, it would be teachable, and would have been taught by men of eminent virtue to their own children. But such a man of undoubted virtue as Pericles had a son who turned out badly. So v is not k. The resolution of these difficulties will await the *Republic,* but it is hinted at in the *Meno* in the distinction between real virtue (based on knowledge) and images of virtue, based upon habitual true opinion. The guarantee of the truth of opinion is knowledge, the wisdom of the philosopher-kings. But the *Meno* example has the great merit of showing the basic logical structure of dialectical analysis, minor and flawed as it may be.

Another minor example, from the *Protagoras,* raises a difficulty which is not pointed out in that dialogue. The hypothesis to be proved is once again the same, the equation of virtue and knowledge which is the *diorismos* of virtue's teachability. For Plato, as for Aristotle,[26] only those who possess art or science based upon universal principles can teach; men of experience only cannot. The Sophist's rhetorical "art" of persuasion is not a true art at all, but a species of flattery.[27] The Protagorean sophist, like Zeus in the myth told by Protagoras in the dialogue named after him,[28] gives the gift of the civic virtues to men not by teaching them knowledge (there is none), but only by persuading them through rhetoric to adopt those opinions which are socially useful (the laws). It seems highly likely that Protagoras was a social utilitarian, like Bentham, whose aim is to maximize pleasure for the greatest number. The first two premises of the *Protagoras* analysis are the same as the *Meno's,* v is G and k is G. The intuition into the Good, however, identifies it with social utility as the greatest *pleasure* and the least pain for the greatest number. It is then easy to show that this is the function of a hedonistic *calculus,* which is knowledge, and the Socratic hypothesis of the equation of v and k, and its corollary, v is t, are dialectically established. For readers of other Platonic dialogues, warning signals should flash at this point. The evidence is overwhelming that Plato rejects hedonism. If a false intuition into the Good still leads to the verification of the same hypothesis, surely something is wrong with the method, but reflection upon Plato's treatment of pleasure in other dialogues, notably *Republic IX* and the *Philebus,* should relieve the reader's shock. For Plato, although no hedonist, never denied that pleasures and a rational calculus of them (not merely quantitative but respecting their real differences of quality) were an element of the good life, though far from being of first rank.

We have now seen two minor examples of dialectical analysis. In the *Phaedo* and *Republic* the examples are major, and the art has reached its maturity. Because of their incomparably greater complexity and sophistication, they are also harder to discern.

The *diorismos* or limiting condition for the soul's immortality in the *Phaedo* is the hypothesis which makes the soul the first principle of life. The problem which made analysis so risky, in moving from the analysis of effects to cause, was the logical possibility of other hypothetical causes for the same effects. In the dialectical maturity of the *Phaedo* and the *Republic* two, and only two, possible contenders exhaust the field. (In the great cosmological arguments for the existence of God, which are analytic — demonstrations *quia* — moving from effects to cause, theism is resting its case upon the supposed impossibility of an infinite causal regress, which atheism must espouse.)[29] Life is *either* the product of a first principle of life, essentially living with a life not received from another, for which the name is *soul, or* it is an epiphenomenal by-product, the result of the chance arrangement of non-living materials. The first hypothesis is Plato's; the second mechanistic theory is represented in the dialogue by the Pythagorean definition of the soul as the harmony of the body. The dialectical choice between the two is obvious. A materialistic, mechanistic account of life cannot in principle be subsumed under the Good.

Soul as the first principle of life must participate in the Form Life essentially, in such a way that it could not participate in the opposite of life, death, just as the number three, which is essentially odd, could not participate in even. Bodies, which can alternate between life and death, must have their life caused. Implicitly, there cannot be an infinite regress of such causes. There must be a first cause of life, soul, whose life is not caused by another. Already the *Phaedo* is pointing toward the later Platonic definition of soul as self-moving mover, cause of all moved movers *(Phaedrus, Timaeus, Laws X)*, and dialectical analysis in the *Phaedo* has engendered the prototype of all subsequent cosmological theistic arguments.

In the *Republic* dialectical analysis does not begin until Book II, when Glaucon makes the three-fold division of kinds of goods. There are things which are both good in themselves and in their consequences. This class is called in later philosophy *bonum honestum.* There are goods desirable for themselves but not for their consequences *(bonum delectabile)*. Finally there are things not good in themselves, but *only* in their consequences *(bonum utile)*. This articulation of the kinds of goods enables Plato to set up the decisive dialectical contrast between two theories of Justice which exhaust the field. The first, which is developed in Book I by Thrasymachus and with more subtlety in Book Two by Glaucon and Adeimantus, I will call the T-G-A hypothesis. What is good for man depends upon the nature of man. For the T-G-A hypothesis, man is by nature a predatory, egoistic animal. In a state of nature, therefore, 'justice' would be, as Thrasymachus claimed in Book I, the 'interest of the stronger,' might makes right. The paragon of true virtue (human excellence) according to nature is the successful despot or tyrant, a life desirable both in itself and in the consequences. But if unlimited aggressiveness is naturally right and desirable for oneself, it is so also for our neighbors, which means that a state of nature is a state of war, in which, as Hobbes was to put it many centuries later, life is "nasty, brutish, and short," lived in constant fear of violent death and aggression at the hands of our fellow men. The naturally best, most truly good (*bonum honestum*) of all lives would be that of Gyges whose aggressions are protected from retribution by a magic ring. But the worst of all evils is to suffer such aggression from others without retribution. The T-G-A hypothesis finds the origin of the state, of political justice, like Hobbes in a 'social contract.' The state and its laws are fabrics of convention (*nomos*), not founded, except negatively, in human nature (*physis*). Justice in the political sense, supported by legal sanctions of punishments and rewards, is not something naturally good and desirable in itself, but only in its consequences (*bonum utile*). It is a compromise between the best of lives and the worst of lives, adopted out of fear, and essentially negative, for the sake of police protection of lives and property.

The Socratic hypothesis, which is under development from the end of Book II through Book IV, maintains that Justice, seen first 'writ large' in the State, and then in smaller letters in the soul, is indeed *bonum honestum*. It is no part of the task of this essay to traverse such familiar ground again. Obviously, for it, man is by nature a political animal, whose natural welfare requires social co-operation and vocational differentiation according to natural talents. The state has a natural origin, and a positive, rather than merely negative, purpose. The principle of Justice is to secure the order of nature, in which each does his own job and not another, and in which the natural hierarchy in society and in the soul is preserved. I, and countless others, have discussed the details and problems of the Socratic hypothesis of justice.[30]

Again, the dialectical decision between the two hypotheses is, from Plato's point of view, easy. It is a choice between natural unity and harmony and their opposites. The decline from the ideal republic (Books VIII, IX) through the successive stages of timocracy, oligarchy, democracy, and tyranny is a descent from organic unity into increasing alienation and the disorder of lawless appetites. The real meaning of the Good, the Sun of the intelligible world, for Plato is Unity.

Final Problems

We have mentioned before that one of the great mysteries in Platonic scholarship is that we find in the later dialogues what is seemingly a new kind of dialectic, that of Collection and Division. I do not propose to expound this so-called later dialectic here. This would be an enormous undertaking in its own right. I will only mention certain problems which *may* have led Plato in the direction of a dialectical method which is not simply an extension of the dialectic of the Sun.

The earlier dialectic hinges upon the possibility of *intellectual* intuition into the Good, as the cause of Being, essence, and knowledge. That the Good is Unity we have already seen, and there is massive evidence, including the testimony of Aristotle, for such Platonic identification. The One which is the essential principle is the one which is the principle (*arche*) of number, simple and indivisible. Anything which is a true Being (a Form) must be what Aristotle calls *ousia*, substance, possessed of *inseity* or self-existence. The contrast is between *essence* and *quality*, what something is in itself and by itself, and what something is only in a context of relational dependence upon others. The *diorismos* of the earlier dialectic supposes that *quality* is ontologically founded in essence, which is in turn what it is good for it to be or express. This provides the energy for the effect-to-cause implication, which is the heart of dialectical analysis.

But it is precisely at this point that crisis develops, and appears in the dialogues written in Plato's early sixties (*Parmenides, Theaetetus, Sophist*). The supreme point of crisis is found in the so-called first hypothesis of the latter part of the *Parmenides*. What can really be said or predicated about a unity which is just one, simple and without parts, without reference to anything else? The answer is stunning. *Nothing whatsoever* can be predicated of such a one, including Being. The neo-Platonists supposed (I think incorrectly) that Plato was talking about the ultimate Godhead, thus founding the long tradition of negative theology. Whether this theological interpretation was correct or incorrect, they saw clearly that any kind of intellectual grasp of such a one, intuitive or discursive, was out of the question.

Plato in the later *Sophist*, tells us that nothing can either exist or be known just by itself, in isolation from all dependent relations upon others. The hallmark of Being is *dynamis* (power), the power of making a difference to others, and of having differences made by others.[31] *To be* is to exist both in *itself* and *in relation*, and the latter is relative non-being as compared to essential unity.[32] It follows that every predicate said of any subject is *quality*, rather than *essence*, what the subject is not in itself but in its relative non-being, relative to others than itself. The 'new' dialectic of collection and division thus becomes a calculus of relations, a "dialectic of non-being", a dialectic which is two-principled rather than single-principled.

The reader must judge for himself. Let me end by quoting a strange, remarkable, and little noted text from the *Seventh Epistle*.[33] Plato begins by distinguishing three things, name, definition, and image, which are the means by which knowledge, the fourth thing, seeks to know the fifth, the object itself. He goes on to say that "with each of the Four, their inaccuracy is an endless topic, but...the main point is this, that while there are two separate things, the real essence and the quality, and the soul seeks to know not the quality, but the essence, each of the Four proffers to the soul either in word or in concrete form that which is not sought..."[34] He speaks of himself as one who is "capable of analysing and convicting the Four... But in all cases where we compel a man to give the Fifth as his answer and to explain it, anyone who is able and willing to upset the argument gains the day, and makes the person who is expounding his view by speech or writing or answers appear to most of his hearers to be wholly ignorant of the subjects about which he is attempting to write or speak; for they are ignorant sometimes of the fact that it is not the soul of the writer or speaker that is being convicted but the nature of each of the Four, which is essentially defective."

Notes

[1] Now generally agreed to be chronologically closer to the 'later' dialogues of the period 368-7 B.C. to 348-7 (Plato's death) than to the 'middle' dialogues (*Republic, Phaedo, Symposium*). One 19th century theory made the *Phaedrus* the earliest of all dialogues, on the grounds that its florid rhetorical style could only have been that of a young man. This position no longer has adherents.

[2] See my "The Platonic Dialectic of Non-Being", *New Scholasticism* 29 (1955), pp. 33-49.

[3] Richard Robinson, *Plato's Earlier Dialectic*. Oxford: Clarendon, 1953.

[4] K. Sayers, *Plato's Analytic Method*. Chicago: University of Chicago Press, 1969.

[5] Here the pioneering studies of Sir Thomas Heath in the history of Ancient Greek mathematics are especially relevant. In particular, see Heath's excellent discussion of Greek geometrical synthesis and analysis, *The Thirteen Books of Euclid's Elements* (Cambridge: University Press, 1926), vol. I, pp. 137-142.

[6] The canny and wily Jeremy Bentham will avoid such an admission: "Push-pin is as good as poetry."

[7] Plato has not, at this stage of his life, directly, addressed the problem of the metaphysical and epistemological status of Non-Being: how or whether Non-being can exist and be thought. It will not be until perhaps 20 years after the *Republic*, in the *Sophist*, that the final resolution will occur.

[8] Phaedo, 97c-99d.

[9] Kenneth Sayers, *op. cit.*, pp. 46-47.

[10] *Rep.* VI, 509a-510a.

[11] *Theaet.* 151e-160d.; *Tim.* 45b-46d.

[12] *Theaet.* 184b-186a.

[13] *Laws X*, 892a-d.

[14] *Timaeus*, 47e-48b.

[15] Lest it be objected that my reference to the *Timaeus* is to a much later dialogue, whose teachings cannot without danger be read back into Plato of the middle dialogues, recall Plato's insistence, in the beginning of *Rep. IX*, that even if a close approximation to the ideal Republic should ever come into existence (by the 'persuasion' of philosophic rulers) it could not last forever. Anything in the sphere of Becoming is corruptible and will pass away. Whatever is meant by the playful reference to the 'nuptial Number', of which even philosopher-kings will be ignorant, thay are ruling in the darkness and shadows of the Cave.

[16] Ivor Thomas, *Selections Illustrating the History of Greek Mathematics*, vol. I (London and Cambridge, Mass., 1939), p. 387.

[17] Theon of Smyrna, *An Exposition of Things Mathematical Useful for the Understanding of Plato*.

[18] In any event, Aristarchus of Samos was soon enough to devise one.

[19]G. Saccheri, *Euclides Vindicatus*, ed., trans. G.B. Halstead. Chicago, London: Open Court, 1920.

[20]*Republic* VII 533c-d.

[21]*Symposium*, 203a-204e.

[22]*Republic* VI, 511 b-d.

[23]Charles Hartshorne, *Creative Synthesis and Philosophic Method.* LaSalle, Ill.: Open Court, 1970.

[24]*Rep.* IV, *ibid.*

[25]*Meno*, 86-87.

[26]Aristotle, *Metaphysics* A.

[27]Plato, *Gorgias*, 463a-d.

[28]Plato, *Protagoras*, 320c-322d.

[29]The first appearance of the cosmological theistic argument is in Book X of Plato's *Laws*. The principles of that argument are already present in the *Phaedo*.

[30]L. J. Eslick, "The Republic Revisited," in *Human Dignity*, ed. by R. Gotesky and E. Lazlo. New York: Gordon and Beach, 1971.

[31]Plato, *Sophist*, 247d-e.

[32]L. J. Eslick, "The Dyadic Character of Being in Plato," *The Modern Schoolman*, 21 (1953), pp. 11-18.

[33]Epistle VII, 342 A-344 C.

[34]*Ibid*, 343 B-D.

3.

ETERNITY AND TIME IN BOETHIUS

Thomas P. McTighe

I

A*eternitas igitur est interminabilis vitae tota simul ac perfecta possessio.*[1] What does Boethius mean by his famous definition? And, also how does he conceive time? For in the clause which directly follows the statement of the definition he asserts that eternity can be understood by comparison *(collatione)* with temporal change.[2] But surely, it may be asked, what possible reason can there be for raising these questions once again? Is there any need to add to the already abundant literature on these and other dimensions of Boethius' thought?

The fact of the matter is that the literature is not all that abundant. To be sure commentators by the score have pored over Boethius' definition. But by and large their efforts have been limited to establishing the sources of the Boethian doctrine of eternity. There have been few efforts to determine its philosophical meaning. Even in the case of such a respected Boethian scholar as Pierre Courcelle[3] there is little effort to analyze closely the language Boethius uses to express the nature of time and eternity and their relationship. Courcelle, like so many others, concentrates on the distinction between the eternity of divine being and the perpetuity which characterizes the world. Courcelle even claims, wrongly, as I hope to show, that the problem posed by this issue is one of the central problems of the last portion of the *Consolation*. What leads him to this view is, of course, the vexing question of the Christianity of the author of the *Consolation*. Quite apart from the curious absence of Christian themes in the last testament of a man under sentence of death, how could Boethius be Christian and at the same time maintain the perpetuity of the world? Some of his Christian contemporaries, not to speak of his predecessor, St. Augustine, were quite clear in denying both the eternity and the perpetuity of the world. Courcelle's account of this problem is indeed magistral. But the question still remains: apart from whether or not the world's time is perpetual, just what is the nature of time and of eternity for Boethius and how does he conceive their

[35]

relationship?

Nonetheless, if most of Boethian scholarship has been mired in *Quellenforschungen* and in the endlessly debated issue of Boethius' Christianity, there have been some recent attempts to offer a response to these questions. The most interesting and challenging one is that of Lewis Ford.[4] His account of Boethius' theory of time and eternity is, I believe, ultimately untenable. But the way in which it goes wrong is most instructive; it can serve as a useful entree to a reconsideration of the Boethian texts themselves.

Ford's approach to these texts is that of the process philosophy of Whitehead. Eventually his Whiteheadian a prioris lead him astray. But in the beginning they serve him well. The big issue in an interpretation of Boethius' famous definition is, Ford rightly notes, the meaning of *possessio*. Eternity, he claims, may be said to possess the temporal in the way in which an "inclusive simplicity" possesses a multiplicity. Eternity is an "inclusive" rather than an "exclusive" simplicity. As the terms suggest, the former contains and preserves subordinate multiplicity while the latter stands above its multiplicity in lonely isolation. In an inclusive multiplicity the underlying diversity is retained and indeed functions as "the necessary basis for the higher unity." Moreover, since this underlying diversity retains its "extensiveness" in the inclusive simplicity, it is as such "available for analysis and becomes our best means for indirectly understanding the simplicity itself."[5]

Ford claims that Boethius first develops this notion of simplicity with respect to divine knowledge and then goes on to use it to describe eternity. According to Boethius, as Ford reads him, divine and human knowledge differ on the basis of exclusion or inclusion of multiplicity. Human knowledge is partially abstractive since in forming its universals it leaves behind the diversity of particulars. Divine knowledge on the other hand does not shed its subordinate multiplicity. God knows all things, which means that the multiplicity He knows is retained as present within the unicity of His knowledge. And what is most important in Ford's eyes is "that the divine powers of unification are not threatened by the continued presence of the diverse elements so unified."[6]

Boethius' eternity is according to Ford just such a simplicity— a whole in which the diversity unified is possessed in simplicity, yet present in that simplicity in such a way as to be accessible to analysis.[7] The *totum simul* of the definition designates the simplicity of eternity and the *possessio* signifies its inclusivity, the retention of the diverse moments of time within it.[8]

In short, Boethius is a Whiteheadian *avant la lettre*. Eternity is not for Boethius as it also is not for Whitehead a *stasis* posed in absolute majesty above the temporal flow. The latter conception of eternity is that of St. Thomas, who, by disregarding the inclusive nature of Boethian simplicity, is led to the "disastrous consequence" of a God utterly divorced from the pulse and flow of the temporal.[9] Process thinkers need not turn up their noses at all of classical theology. The Boethian eternity like that of Whitehead himself "includes time because it is based upon an inclusive simplicity. Such a simplicity invites us to analyze the subordinate multiplicity."[10]

What are we to make of this interpretation? The Boethius of Ford fits comfortably within a Whiteheadian framework, but does it square with the texts? I think not. Certainly the expression, inclusive simplicity, is a felicitous one and eminently applicable to Boethius' thought. For, as I shall try to show, eternity is for Boethius a simplicity, and, moreover, a simplicity which includes time. But *how* does it include or contain time? That is the nub of the issue. Ford claims that as a simplicity, eternity's perfect possession is "non-extensive and unanalyzable", but that as an inclusive simplicity, however, "it contains the subordinate multiplicity."[11] But how can eternity be both a simplicity and an inclusive simplicity? How can eternity embrace all moments of time all at once and yet leave the diversity of these moments "available for analysis"? Surely analysis entails distinction, discrimination and differentation. How, then, can the many of time be in the unicity of the eternal all the while retaining its manyness? Furthermore, can it be true for Boethius, as it apparently is for process philosophers, that "the underlying diversity is preserved as the necessary basis for the higher unity"? Are we to understand that the multiple moments of time are the *ground* of eternity? L. Obertello, in his recently published two-volume study, quite properly, it seems to me, arches an eyebrow at the suggestion that for Boethius the temporal is the foundation of the eternal.[12]

First things first, however. Ford claims that the principle Boethius enunciates in his account of knowledge in Bk V, pr. 4 is the basis for his discussion of eternity and time. In a sense he is correct. The principle that the higher includes the lower, which is central to the theory of knowledge, is also operative in the theory of eternity and time.[13] But what Ford failed to appreciate was that both accounts are grounded in a still more ultimate theoretical structure. Ford limited his textual analysis to prose 5 and prose 6 of Bk V. What he and, indeed, most other commentators overlook is a universal theory of inclusion and emergence from inclusion which is set forth in prose 6 of Bk IV.

The following passage summarizes that general theory:

> Igitur uti est ad intellectum ratiocinatio, ad id quod est id quod gignitur, ad aeternitatem tempus, ad punctum medium circulus, ita est fati series mobilis ad providentiae stabilem simplicitatem.[14]

In these very revealing lines Boethius is setting up a series of multiplicity-unity relationships. Indeed, they are among the most fundamental in in metaphysics and theory of knowledge. Being, eternity, intellectual intuition and the center of the circle stand to becoming, time, discursive thinking and the circle, as Providence stands to fate. The obvious, but it should be added, rarely asked question is: how are Providence and fate related?

Once we have established an answer to that question we will be able to determine just what Boethius' own notion of inclusive simplicity is. From there it will then be possible to appreciate more fully the highly suggestive language that Boethius uses in Book V to expand his doctrine of eternity and time.

II

As so many commentators have noted, Bk IV, pr. 6 marks a decisive turn in the progression of the *Consolation*. The *quaestio vexata*— why do the good suffer and the evil prosper?— takes on a new dimension with the establishment of God as cause and governor of all that happens in the world. For, as Boethius complains to Lady Philosophy, it is one thing to be astonished by the disproportion of awards to the good and to the evil, if everything happens by chance. But that God is the ruler of the universe and still the disproporton obtains, serves only to increase his astonishment.[15] To this plaint Lady Philosophy responds by invoking the hidden order of things. And, pressed by Boethius to "disclose the causes of hidden things and to unfold the reasons veiled in darkness," she identifies five relevant issues: the simplicity of providence, the course of fate, chance, divine foreknowledge and freedom of choice.[16] All these issues are connected in such a way as to lead up to the final problem of the *Consolation*: how can contingent events and free acts of the will retain their contingency and freedom given God's omniscience?

Lady Philosophy at this point in Bk IV begins the long process of resolving this issue with an account of the *simplicitas providentiae* and the *series fati*. The importance of the text warrants its citation in full:

> Tunc uelut ab alio orsa principio ita disseruit: Omnium generatio rerum cunctusque mutabilium naturarum progressus et quidquid aliquo mouetur modo causas, ordinem, formas ex diuinae mentis stabilitate sortitur. Haec in sua simplicitatis arce composita multiplicem rebus gerendis modum statuit. Qui modus cum in ipsa diuinae intellegentiae puritate conspicitur, prouidentia nominatur; cum uero ad ea quae mouet atque disponit refertur, fatum a ueteribus appellatum est. Quae diuersa esse facile liquebit si quis utriusque uim mente conspexerit; nam prouidentia est ipsa illa diuina ratio in summo omnium principe constituta quae cuncta disponit, fatum uero inhaerens rebus mobilibus dispositio per quam prouidentia suis quaeque nectit ordinibus. Prouidentia namque cuncta pariter quamuis diuersa quamuis infinita complectitur, fatum uero singula digerit in motum locis, formis ac temporibus distributa, ut haec temporalis ordinis explicatio in diuinae mentis adunata prospectum prouidentia sit,

eadem uero adunatio digesta atque explicata temporibus fatum uocetur. Quae licet diuersa sint, alterum tamen pendet ex altero; ordo namque fatalis ex prouidentiae simplicitate procedit.[17]

As Courcelle points out, the full doctrine of providence and fate includes both a theoretical and a moral dimension.[18] To put the point even more strongly, the theoretical part, in effect, constitutes the outline of a fundamental metaphysical schema, in terms of which the emergence of the finite order from God is explained. It is, therefore, somewhat surprising that amidst the luxuriant Boethian bibliography so little attention has been paid to its doctrinal import.[19]

Even Courcelle, having made his felicitous distinction, summarizes in a line the theoretical part of the doctrine and then passes on to an investigation of its antecedents. Providence and fate, he says, are two dimensions of the same divine "action." The one, providence, is the act by which God embraces outside space and time, the infinity of beings; the other, fate, is the "agent of the execution of providence..."[20]

If only he had paused to reflect upon the significance of his own word, "embrace"! Instead, as the language of action, agent and execution, suggests, he interprets the relationship of providence to fate as one of efficient cause to its effects. And this, as we shall see, is to obscure the actual contours of that relationship. To be sure, fate is the terminus of a procession from providence, as Boethius' use of *progressio* and *procedit* shows.[21] But not every procession is one of efficient causality. Indeed in the Neo-Platonic tradition to which most commentators assign Boethius, procession never means efficient causality. Still it may be objected that the image of an artisan producing an artifact, which Boethius invokes some lines later on, confirms or seems to confirm Courcelle's interpretation.[22] A more careful reading of our text, however, will prove otherwise.

The very language of *modus* belies an interpretation of the fate's procession from providence in terms of efficient causality. The divine mind fixed in the citadel of its simplicity established a *multiplex modus* for things. This *modus*, one in itself, can be considered as it is in the purity, the simplicity of the divine mind; or it can be considered with respect to its finite manifestations. The former, providence, is pure undifferentiated unity. The latter, fate, is multiplicity, the other side of the coin *(modus),* so to speak. We are, therefore, before a version of Neo-Platonic metaphysics in which the many emerge from the One because they are already present in the One. This is precisely what Boethius' subsequent formulas convey. Providence is said to enfold *(complectitur)* all things equally, however diverse, however endless they are.

Here is the crux of Boethius' theory of exclusive simplicity. The language he uses to express it needs careful elaboration. Providence is, first of all, an enfolding *simplicitas*. But what does it enfold and how does it enfold its content? *Quamvis diversa, quamvis infinita*— the radical diversity of things. However different things are one from the other, however endless their multiplicity they are all within the enfolding unity of God. But how are they present in that unity? As a collection each item of which retains its diversity from the others? No. They are all there *pariter*— equally. In the absolute simplicity of God-providence all differentiation is overcome. Opposites sink out of sight in this enfolding unity.[23] Providence is an *adunatio* in which everything is everything else. In a word, providence is a *complicatio*[24], the envelopment of all things in the pure identity of God. Note that Boethius rejects the notion of providence as a lesser unity mediating the things ordered by fate and a transcendent One. Providence is the divine mind which is identical with the *summus omnium princeps*. Its unity, therefore, is absolutely transcendent.

From this transcendent unity proceeds the ordered multiplicity of finite things, the *series fati*. Fate is an *ordo*, a *series*, a nexus. It is the *dispositio* inherent in spatio-temporal things. Thus, the term fate is not a collective term designating the added-up totality of all things. It designates, rather, the principle which binds together all the members of the finite multiplicity. Consider the language Boethius uses to describe fate: *nexus, connectit, texitur*.[25] Again, fate is said to constrain within the structure of its own sort of immutability that which would otherwise be *temere fluituras*.[26] All this suggests, therefore, that fate is a relational system. Finite things are not atomic isolates nor are they substantial entities to which relations accrue *ab extra*. Rather, they are in their very finitude, relational.[27] This thesis is confirmed by the account Boethius gives of the type of procession involved in the emergence of fate from providence.

Fate is described as *haec temporalis ordinis explicatio*. It is the unfolding into multiplicity of what is one *(adunata)* in the divine mind. The procession, thus, is the emergence of multiplicity from unity by a kind of relaxing of the One into manyness. Fate, the ordered structure of spatiotemporal things, is the unity of providence made other *(digesta)* than itself.

In sum, then, providence and fate, God and creatures are related as *complicatio* to *explicatio*, as pure unity to the "outering" of that unity into multiplicity. It was this couple which was to become so influential in sectors of later medieval philosophy. Thierry of Chartres will make extensive use of it.[28] Much later Nicholas of Cusa will appropriate (one is tempted to say, plagiarize) Thierry's development of the Boethian schema.[29].

But already for Boethius it is clear that the *complicatio-explicatio* couple is intended to serve as a universal schema for all unity-multiplicity relationship and not merely as an *ad hoc* device to explain providence and fate. As the sentence, already cited, which terminates the theoretical exposition, indicates, the fundamental oppositions in metaphysics and theory of knowledge display the same structure as the providence-fate opposition does. Intellectual intuition, being, eternity and providence are to discursive thinking, becoming, time and fate as *complicatio* to *explicatio*. Each of the former is a unity enfolding within its pure simplicity the multiplicities of each of the latter. And each of the latter is a multiplicity that unfolds its appropriate unity.[30]

There is, however, one feature of Boethius' account to which we have not yet attended, the all-important geometrical image of the circle and its center. The use of this image is itself decisive evidence that Boethius' theory of reality is an *Einheitsmetaphysik* of a clearly Neo-Platonic cast. Once we have investigated the meaning of this image in the earlier Hellenistic Neo-Platonisms we will be able to appreciate its role in the account of the *Consolation*. The image will be of immense significance in determining what sort of an "inclusive simplicity" a Boethian *complicatio* is. At this point, however, let us search out further evidence that Boethius is a unity-metaphysician.

In Bk III, pr. 11 he states the fundamental thesis of such a metaphysics: "...each thing subsists so long as it is one; when it ceases to be one, it perishes."[32] Later in the same section it is said that "if unity be taken away, being *(esse)* will not endure."[31] Perhaps, however, Boethius is simply equating unity and being as transcendentals and not asserting a priority of unity over being.

Such is not the case. The whole thrust of his discussion of partial, imperfect goods versus the complete perfect good makes this point clear. To be good is to be one. The highest good is God who is *one by nature*.[33] Nothing else is one by nature. All else is one in the way in which a whole of parts is one. Finite wholes are not, as in an Aristotelian metaphysics, grounded in their wholeness by virtue of their positive natures. Rather, for Boethius, finite wholes are each an unfolding of the pure whole in which all goods are identical.[34] For these ideas Boethius is clearly relying upon a well-known text of Plato's *Protagoras* (329c-d), though almost certainly he knows of the text through an intermediary. Further evidence of the identification of God with absolute unity is to be seen in Boethius' citation of a text from the poem of Parmenides: "In body like a sphere well-rounded on all sides." This description of the Parmenidean One serves to characterize the *divinae forma substantiae*.[35]

Passages in the last sections of Bk III express the relationship between God and the world in terms akin to the language of Bk IV, pr.6. Thus prose 10 of Bk III specifies the procession of finite things from God as a falling away *(dilabitur)* from the integral and perfect into that which is weak and outermost.[36] The verb has the same sense of a descent into multiplicity that *explicare* has. In prose 12 of the same book the theme of the world as "unfolded" multiplicity is explicitly asserted?

> Mundus hic ex tam diversis contrariisque partibus in unam formam minime convenisset, nisi unus esset qui tam diversa coniungeret. Coniuncta vero naturarum ipsa diversitas invicem discors dissociaret atque divelleret, nisi unus esset qui quod nexuit contineret.[37]

The force of the verbs *coniungeret* and *contineret* is to emphasize the role of the One in containing all things. The multiplicity would sunder into a chaos of incommensurable items, lacking even the minimal unity sufficient to be a multiplicity, were it not for God, the one who unites the diversity of things. This is the order of fate. Again, the *mundus* would sunder unless there were a unity which contains its diversity. *Contineret* seems to be the equivalent of the *complectitur* of Bk IV, pr. 6.

Finally, the "fixed order of nature would not proceed forth *(procederet)*, nor would it unfold *(explicarent)* its motions which are so well disposed...unless there were One who, by remaining Himself *(manens ipse)* disposes the variety of these changes..."[38] We see in this text the same formula as the one at work in the account of fate and providence. *Procedere* is equated with the *explicare*. The procession of things is not via efficient causality, but by a kind of *detente* or declension into otherness, change and multiplicity.

There is another interesting feature to the text just cited. God is described as *manens ipse*. This formula, describing God as abiding or remaining in Himself occurs in a number of other places in the *Consolation*.[40] The term *manens* may simply be a synonym for immutable. It is significant, however, that in at least some of its usages it is linked with the idea of God as enfolding all things. Now if it is true that God enfolds all things in His simplicity, it is also true that all things are unfolded from Him. Indeed, the finite order *is* God unfolded into plurality. But such an unfolding cannot, of course, mean the disappearance of the divine into multiplicity. All the while that the divine is unfolded, it "remains" itself. It remains itself and that which is unfolded from it remains within it. In this sense, the unity of the *complicatio* is not unfolded.

My hypothesis, therefore, is that *manens* is not simply a synonym for *stabilis*, or the like, but has a certain technical meaning. And it is further hypothesized that this technical sense is derived either directly or through an intermediary from Proclus, in whose metaphysics the idea of something engendering a lower order, all the while remaining itself, and that which is to be engendered, plays an important role.

Proclus distinguishes three stages in the derivation of *Nous* from the One: *mone, proodos* and *epistrophe*. *Mone* from the verb *menein* (to remain) expresses the condition of the original coincidence of the lower in the higher.[41] As Trouillard, who has studied this Proclean notion very carefully, points out, the prior state of *mone* cannot be taken as simply equivalent to rest *(stasis)*.[42] One of its derived senses, expressed by our word "monastery" conveys more accurately the sense of the original: a remaining, but with the added sense of a kind of retreat or sheltering in silence, a hidden life more powerful than any public manifestation. *Mone*, then, denotes the non-processive moment of procession, the stage of unity prior to and sustaining all multiplicity. In the stage of *mone* is to be found the point of indissoluble coincidence between the enfolding prior reality and the to-be-unfolded subsequent realities.[43]

One of the clearest statements of the idea of *mone* occurs in Proclus' *Commentary on the Timaeus*. In this passage he makes the same connection that we observed in the *Consolation* between "abiding" and "enfolding." Moreover, he makes use of the very same geometrical analogy, circle to center, that is so crucial to Boethius' theory of enfolding-unfolding:

> ...the Intellect *(nous)* has precedence over the Soul. For it envelops the Soul without itself being divided...Thus it is from the Intellect, as from a sort of interior sanctuary, that the essence of the Soul arises disclosing the indivisibility of the Intellect...As to the Intellect it is firmly established in itself; it understands all things in a tranquil way since, compared to the Soul it is...center. For if the Soul is circle, the Intellect is itself the center, the potentiality of the circle...And it [Intellect] contains the extended in an unextended way, the divisible in an indivisible way, the circular in a central way.[44]

Thus the similarity of Boethius' *manens* and Proclus' *mone* allow us to claim, at least as an hypothesis, that the *Consolation* may be echoing Proclean themes.[45] Like *mone, manens* cannot be translated by terms that signify the mere absence of motion. The term seems to suggest that for Boethius as for Proclus the higher unity abides with itself and that the generated multiplicity abides with the enveloping unity of the higher. For Proclus this notion is applied all along the various levels of emanation. In Boethius' case the doctrine of *manens ipse* is applied exclusively to God, in whose enveloping unity creatures abide. Moreover, as both thinkers make clear, the lower abides in the higher according to the mode of the higher. The divisibility, the plurality of soul and souls is, for Proclus, present in Intellect in an indivisible and non-plural way. So for Boethius all things, however diverse, however endless, are present *pariter* in God's *complicatio*. This point will have considerable significance for the relationship of time's successive moments to eternity. If, as we shall see, eternity is the *complicatio* of all the successive moments of time, it is impossible for it to contain "the underlying diversity [of temporal moments]...preserved as the necessary basis for the higher unity."[46]

One final remark is necessary concerning Boethius' possible indebtedness to Proclus for his notion of *Deus manens ipse*. If he is, in fact, reflecting the Proclean doctrine, he does not appropriate all its features. For one thing Proclus' conception of *mone* is designed to account for the doctrine that the lower, derived orders, notably Soul and Intellect, are processes of self-constitution. Each is an *authupostaton*. It is precisely because the derived reality is first coincident with its principle, that it can separate itself from that principle and so constitute itself. In Trouillard's words, *"'pour un autoconstituant, procéder de ses principes et procéder de soi-même sont une seule et même chose.'"*[47] No such doctrine of self-constitution appears in the *Consolation*. Boethius, if our hypothesis is correct, is picking and choosing, disengaging from his sources whatever fits his needs.

Moreover, his principle of appropriation and rejection seems to be governed by a central option possibly arising from his Christianity, viz., the rejection of the more (Proclus) or less (Plotinus) complex hierarchies that intervene between God and the world in Neo-Platonism.[48] As we have already seen, Providence and fate are related, respectively, as the unity side and the multiplicity side of the same *modus*. Fate, therefore, proceeds immediately from providence. It is true that Boethius mentions some possible candidates for mediators between fate and providence: certain divine spirits, a world soul, nature, the motion of the stars, angelic power, demonic ingenuity or any or all of these. But it seems clear that this list is a kind of summary round-up having no real significance and mentioned only in passing. For he immediately adds that providence and fate are directly related as *simplex forma* and its manifestation in the order of finite multiplicity, *mobilem nexum et ordinem temporalem*.[49] Thus, Boethius has no need for a doctrine of *authupostata* whereby intervening hypostases are at once engendered from above and self-constituted within. Nonetheless, it is not true, as Obertello claims, that "the elimination of the Neo-Platonic hierarchy is equivalent to a refutation of the fundamental characteristics of that speculative system."[50] On the contrary, the "fundamental characteristics" of the Neo-Platonic schema of enfolding-unfolding are very much present in Boethius' philosophy together with their metaphysical and epistemological consequences.

Let us turn now to a more extended treatment of Boethius' Neo-Platonic sources.[51] Is the schema of enfolding-unfolding operative in a significant way in their metaphysics and if so, how? How also do they utilize the image of the circle and its center? Our concern is less with the details of *Quellenforschungen* than with a determination of the philosophical meanings involved. Hence the controversy raised by Courcelle's critique of Patch's thesis concerning the circle (or sphere) image in Boethius need not concern us.[52] Patch had claimed that Boethius' use of the image involved a correction of Proclus by Plotinus, i.e., that from Proclus he borrowed the image of the circular movement of fate and from Plotinus the notion of providence as the center of the universe.[53] Courcelle, it seems to me, contra de Vogel and Obertello[54] is right in rejecting Patch's conclusions. In point of fact, as I hope to show, the use of the image is fundamentally the same in both thinkers. Courcelle is also correct, I believe, in claiming Proclus or a Proclean intermediary as the main source of Boethius' doctrine of providence and fate.[55] It is highly doubtful that Boethius had any direct knowledge of the *Enneads* of Plotinus. In any case, the controversy aside, none of these commentators note the similarities between Boethius' *complicatio-explicatio* couple and the corresponding language in Plotinus and Proclus. And none of them attempts to probe the significance of the circle-center image.

In point of fact the Neo-Platonic tradition is rich in texts which turn upon the enfolding-unfolding correlation and the metaphor of the circle and its center. The *Enneads*, if they do not originate these ideas, certainly seal their approval in the writings of the later Neo-Platonist. Plotinus' words for *complecti* and *complicatio* are *perilambanein* and *perilepsis* along with *periechein*. His equivalent for *explicare* is *exelittein*. In all cases these correlatives are used to express the original presence of a multiplicity in a higher unity and the evolution or, rather, devolution of the multiplicity from that unity.[56]

The passage which most explicitly links the enfolding-unfolding schema to that of the circle-center image is VI, 8, 18 1-25. The problem Plotinus is dealing with here is the familiar one of the procession of *nous* and being from the One. This procession is likened to that of the radii of a circle from its center such that a circle results. Thus the center is as unity and the radii are as multiplicity. What, then, does this image tell us of the status of the unity, the status of the multiplicity and the relationship between the two?

The circle, Plotinus says, receives in some way its form from the center because it "touches" the center. It does so by virtue of its radii, whose tips are, as it were, anchored in the center. But the unity of the center is not merely an additive totality, the sum of all the tips. The center is "more than" the tips. The center is all the tips, indeed all the radii, in indistinction. The center, as Plotinus puts it, contains them in potency. But the state of being "in potency" does not have for him the same sense as it does for Aristotle. For Plotinus the expression signifies a state of possession in which the things possessed are present by a kind of latent actuality in which everything is everything else. In this instance every radius is every other radius in the pure identity of the center's unity. They are all in the center "as a state of involution."[57] The radii in their plurality are the center outered, as it were, relaxed into multiplicity— in a word, unfolded from the center. Yet at the same time the center maintains its integrity as an undifferentiated whole. In the words of Plotinus the center "is unfolded, but it does not unfold itself."

Thus, to use a now familiar term, the center is an inclusive unity. But its mode of inclusion is neither that of a collection nor that of some paradoxical simplicity in which a multiplicity somehow retains its diversity. Yet for all that the Plotinian unity is genuinely inclusive. If there is enfolding, there must be the enfolded.

The radii are by contrast the center as unfolded into plurality. How, then, is one radius distinct from another? Though Plotinus does not respond explicitly to this question, it is clear from the thrust of his metaphor that it cannot be by virtue of some positive content. In the metaphysics imaged in the circle-center metaphor, no term of a plurality is what it is by virtue of its own positive content. There is, of course, something positive in the radius, viz., the center, its unity. But that positivity is the positivity of all the radii. The members of a multiplicity must therefore be distinct from each other, simply because they are other than their unity and other than each other. Otherness or negation is the ground of plurality. This, then, is the basic import of the circle-center image in Plotinus.

Proclus, whose Neo-Platonism often departs significantly from that of Plotinus, nonetheless makes liberal use of the same enfolding-unfolding schema. As S. Gersh notes, "The verb 'to unfold' *(anelittein)* is very common in Proclus and is usually employed in passages where the evolution of a multiplicity from a unity is described."[58] His comment is very much to the point. The emergence of a multiplicity from a higher unity is explained in Proclus as the unfolding of that multiplicity from the antecedent inclusive unity wherein the multiplicity dwells in pure simplicity. And, just as in Plotinus, the enfolding-unfolding couple is analogized to the center and the circle.

In the *Elements of Theology* Proclus describes the lower as unfolding *(exelitte)*[59] the powers contained in the higher. Despite this process of unfolding, however, what remains in the higher is "secret and ungraspable." The unity of the higher is "an unexpanded life which escapes unfolding *(anelixeas)*." The notion of the secrecy of the recesses of unity by relationship to the multiplicity which "outers" that unity is described in the *Platonic Theology*.[60] The multiplicity engendered by a monad pluralizes the powers which pre-existed in a hidden way in the monad. Thus "what is in the monad in a unitary way *(enoeides)* and in an enfolded way (literally, "wrapped up") is a manifestation in a divided way in the offspring of that monad." One of the examples he gives of this thesis is the monadic unit which, as the source and ground of all numbers, enfolds them within itself. Hence, that which preexists as a multiplicity contains that multiplicity in simplicity. Correlatively the multiplicity manifests the fecundity of the prior unitary whole, though it never receives what is engendered. The lower multiplicity is, therefore, not so much an imitation as it is an expression of the antecedent unity. For the procession of multiplicity from unity is a kind of slackening *(hyphesis)* or relaxation into plurality.[61] Earlier in the *Platonic Theology* Proclus applies these notions to nous and the soul. "Thus the soul unfolds *(anelittei) nous*, whereas *nous* unfolds itself as Plotinus rightly says when he deals with the declension of the intelligible."[62] The same theme of soul unfolding into plurality what *nous* enfolds in its unity is applied to the problem of the unity of mathematics in the *Commentary on Euclid*.[63]

Like Plotinus, Proclus uses the circle-center image to express the relationship of the enfolding to the unfolded. He also employs the companion arithmetical metaphor of the derivation of the numbers from the monadic unit. In the *Commentary on the Timaeus* the soul is compared to the Intellect *(nous)* as circle to center. "For if the Soul is circle, it [Intellect] is itself the center, the power of the circle... And it contains the extended in an unextended way, the divided in an undivided way, the circle in a central way..."[64] In the *Commentary on the Parmenides*, in a passage which echoes remarkably *Enneads* VI, 8, 18, Proclus shows us what the image truly means.[65] His problem is to explain how *nous* is "the place of ideas." It is so not as substance is a substratum for accidents or matter for form. Rather, it is their place in the way in which the center has within itself the multiple tips of the radii which are drawn from it and as a science contains its theorems. How, then, does each unity possess its multiplicity? "Not as a composite of the many, but as prior to the many and present in its totality in each."

Here in a lapidary formula is the crux of the Neo-Platonic metaphysics of containment. An enfolding unity is not a synthesis built up from its components. It is not a whole subsequent to its parts. Enfolding unities such as center, science or *nous* itself are prior to their multiplicities. They envelop their multiplicities in indistinction. And each member of the unfolded multiplicity contains the unity wholly and entirely. Once again it is made clear to us that Neo-Platonic inclusive simplicities are a far cry from those in whom "the underlying diversity is preserved as a necessary basis for the higher unity."

In his old age, Proclus applies this metaphysics of enfolding unity and unfolded multiplicity and its attendant metaphor of the circle and its center to the problem of the relationship of providence to fate. He does this in three short works[66] which Courcelle claims— rightly, I believe— "la théorie de Boèce semble reproduire exactement."[67] In one of the opuscula, the *De Decem Dubitationibus*, the One of Providence is said to be one "insofar as it envelops *(periechon, continens)* all other things, is present to all things of whom it is a cause, and preserves them." Later in this same passage Proclus stresses that it is not possible for the things that subsist by Providence "to unfold *(anelixai)* the power which pre-exists in it, nor is it possible for those to grasp themselves in it or to rest in its bosom."[68] In this dense text which comes to us via the barbarous Latin of William of Moerbeke, Proclus is contrasting the envelopment characteristic of Providence to that of lesser unities, some of which also enfold plurality within themselves. Thus by his enigmatic remark that Providence cannot be unfolded, Proclus is not denying to it unfolding as such. Rather he means to deny of it precisely the kind of unfolding in which the unfolded somehow retain their diversity within the antecedent unity.

Elsewhere in the same opusculum in a text much cited by Boethian scholars, Proclus expresses his doctrine of providence in terms of the usual circle-center image plus an arithmetical image.

> It has been said, and rightly so, that the whole circle exists centrally in the center...and for the same reason every number exists monadically in the monad. In the One of Providence, then, all things exist in an even greater way, if it is the case that Providence is one in a way greater than that of the center and the monad. If, therefore, the center had knowledge of the circle, it would have knowledge that is as absolutely central as is its own reality and it would not be divided into the parts of the circle. In like fashion the unitary knowledge of Providence is, within the same indivision, knowledge of all divided things...The knowledge, since it is one enfolds *(periechei)* the infinity of knowable things...[69]

Providence possesses the multiplicity of things in its enfolding unity and these things are in that unity after the manner of unity and not according to their diversity. Here the geometrical image is complemented by an arithmetical image, also quite common in Neo-Platonism. For the ancients the number series begins with two, since number is defined as a collection of units. The unit, or the monad as Proclus calls it, is regarded as the essence of all the numbers. Hence in the monad (the number one by our standards) all numbers are present in identity. The monad enfolds them in its simplicity just as the center enfolds in its simplicity all the radii that make up a circle. And just as the radii are a devolution of the center into otherness, so numbers are the unfolding of the monad into otherness or diversity. For Proclus, therefore, no number in its distinctiveness as a member of the plurality of numbers possesses a positive nature of its own, as it does according to Aristotle. For the latter, a number, let us say, three, has a positive essence of its own and, thereby, enjoys its own irreducible unity. Its unity is a function of its positive essential content. Not so for Proclus. The number three is either a collection of ones (its unfolded condition) or it is in and is identical to the monad itself. And there it is every other number in indistinction. The same is true for the circle. An Aristotelian circle is a per se whole, not the center relaxed into a multiplicity of radii. A metaphysics of *complicatio-explicatio* cannot co-exist with a metaphysics of positive essences. The long detour through Boethius' Neo-Platonic antecedents shows us that this, too, is the thrust of the metaphysics of the *Consolation*.[70] His *complicatio-explicatio* schema also precludes any ontology of essences dense with positivity as it also must exclude a noetics in which universals are the result of an abstraction of positive natures.[71]

One final point before we turn to an analysis of the texts dealing with time and eternity. It should now be clear that the enfolding One of Boethius and his predecessors cannot be taken as a unity in which the multiple remain multiple and serve as the foundation of the unity. The *perilepsis* of Plotinus and Proclus, the *complicatio* of Boethius, all can be quite properly called inclusive simplicities. But their inclusion is neither the preservation of a multiplicity nor a whole subsequent to its parts. It is an identity in which diversity sinks out of sight. Hegel's famous thrust at Schelling's Absolute is not an inaccurate description of Boethius' *complicatio*: "like a night in which all cows are black."

III

Boethius raises the question of eternity and time in the context of his central problem, the reconciliation of divine foreknowledge and human freedom. The key to its solution is the nature of divine knowledge, which like all modes of knowing is a function of the nature of the knower, not the known. A prior condition for establishing the character of God's knowledge is a consideration of the *status divinae substantiae*. This status[72] is without further ado identified as eternity. Since eternity can be understood by comparison to time, Boethius proceeds to a discussion of each and of their relationship in an abbreviated account occupying only some fifty-one lines in the critical edition. This passage together with a brief discussion in the *De Trinitate* is all that we have available to determine his theory of time and eternity.

Before considering the text of the *Consolation* some preliminary remarks are in order. In the first place, Boethius like all Neo-Platonists is concerned with time and eternity, not separately but in relationship to each other.[73] But by virtue of the main problem he has set for himself, his emphasis will obviously be put on the question of eternity. Hence he gives us a definition of eternity, but nowhere in the *Consolation* account or, for that matter, in the *De Trinitate*, does he give us a definition of time. We shall have to infer one, if that is possible.

There is another matter that ought to be attended to before we come to a close analysis of the text. Besides the definition of eternity Boethius' remarks on the perpetuity of the world have attracted a good deal of attention. Thereby hangs a problem. The tendency among commentators has been to isolate the issue of perpetuity from its full context and to elevate it to the status of a major problem in its own right. The result of this move, is, I believe, to obscure the distinctive features of Boethius' theory of eternity and time. Courcelle is one who errs in this regard. Having reduced Lady Philosophy's five problems to three (providence and fate, foreknowledge and freedom, and perpetuity and the world), he is then perplexed at finding the bond linking the problem of perpetuity to foreknowledge to be *tres tenu*[74]. The truth is that the bond is not so much tenuous as non-existent. The introduction of the issue of perpetuity seems to violate logical order only if one wrongly assumes, as Courcelle does, that it is a separate problem in its own right. It is not. Whether the world is eternal or perpetual or created in time is irrelevant to the problem of divine foreknowledge and human freedom, since the question of how God knows the future without it being necessitated remains whether that future grows out of an eternal or created past. Why, then, does Boethius raise the question of the world's duration? His primary purpose is to institute a contrast between perpetuity and eternity so as to highlight the distinctive character of the latter. As he notes, it is one thing to be led through an endless succession of temporal moments. It is quite another to *envelop* all moments all at once in a total presence. The former is perpetuity, the latter eternity.[75] Thus the question of perpetuity is neither a major issue in its own right, nor a mere excursus designed to put Boethius on record concerning a controversial issue of the day. The doctrine, if the brief remarks devoted to it can be so called, is logically required by the exigencies of the theory of eternity. In fact we have here a clear indication that the theory of eternity and time is an application of the metaphysics laid out in Books III and IV. As prose 6 of Bk IV puts it, eternity is to time as providence is to fate, which later are in turn to each other respectively as *complicatio* to *explicatio*. Thus, whatever perpetuity is, it is not a *complicatio*.

With these preliminary remarks in mind, let us proceed to a careful analysis of Boethius' definition of eternity and an all too brief elaboration of the definition which he supplies. What does *possessio* mean? Its sense begins to emerge through a comparison with temporal things. The latter are subject to what Boethius calls the *condicio temporis*, succession from the past through the present to the future. Consequently, "nothing subject to time can enfold *(amplecti)* the entire extent of its existence all at once *(pariter)*."[76] Time is, therefore, the opposite of a condition of enfolding in which what is enfolded is present in simultaneity, not succession. The text goes on then to distinguish carefully between what is and what is not rightly characterized as eternal *(ut aeternum esse jure credatur)*. It is at this point that Boethius introduces the possibility that the world exists through an endless extent of time, never beginning to be and never ceasing to be. The implication is that, according to this view— identified as that of Aristotle— the duration of the world transcends the transitory character of ordinary time and may, perhaps, be rightly called eternal. The thesis is, however, immediately rejected. For even granting Aristotle's claim that the world never began and will never cease, such a duration cannot properly be qualified as eternal. The reason is that it does not "embrace and enfold *(comprehendit atque complectitur)* in simultaneity"[77] its duration in a successionless whole. For endless though the duration of the world may be, at any given moment "it does not possess the still to be accomplished future."[78]

Thus Boethius, following his method of *collatio*, has identified two cases where the kind of *possessio* appropriate to eternity is absent. Neither any individual thing *(quidquid vivit in tempore)* whose present is transitory and fleeting nor the *mundus* whose duration may be, as Aristotle thought, infinite, qualify as eternal. For the *possessio* of each lacks the condition of simultaneity. In short the *possessio* of neither is a *complicatio*. Now at last it is possible to identify the authentic sense of eternity:

> That which embraces *(comprehendit)* and possesses in simultaneity the whole plenitude of an endless existence from which neither anything future is absent nor from which anything past has vanished...Necessarily [such a being] must in possessing itself be both always present to itself and have present the infinity of moving time.[79]

In this text Boethius is evidently taking pains to specify carefully the meaning of *possessio*. In the first place it signifies a *complicatio*, an enfolding within itself of the plenitude of endless existence. Secondly, the enfolding involves the total self-presence of the eternal being, God, to itself. Thirdly, *possessio* signifies the presence within eternity of all time, past, present and future. In other words if there is enfolding, there must be that which is enfolded. In this case the enfolding which is eternity includes within itself all the moments in the succession of time. But these successive moments are not present in God's simplicity *qua* successive, but *qua* simultaneous. Nonetheless it remains true to say that these successive moments are genuinely present within eternity. And to emphasize the distinctive feature of eternity, Boethius once again brings in the question of perpetuity, i.e., a time that has no beginning or end. It is quite wrong, he says, to claim that Plato made the world co-eternal with God simply because he held that the world's time is without beginning or end. This is to misconceive the nature of eternity which is "to enfold all at once *(pariter complexum esse)* the total presence of an endless life."[80] Only the eternal qualifies as a *complicatio*, an enfolding both of itself and the infinite succession of time. For it and that infinite succession are one in the pure identity of the divine *simplicitas*.

Boethius' description of God's *aeternus ac praesentarius status* provides further confirmation of the "double" possession. His *praesentia* is pure simplicity transcending all temporal succession *(omnem temporis supergressa motionem)*. At the same time this status is, to use Ford's term, an inclusive simplicity enfolding within itself all moments of temporal progression *(infinitaque praeteriti ac futuri spatia complectens omnia)*.[81]

It should now be clear what Boethius himself means by an "inclusive simplicity." Over and over again he insists that it is an enfolding whole.[82] The verb forms of *complecti* are used six times throughout Bk V, prose 6, not to mention its synonyms: *amplecti, comprehendere* and *possidere*. What one commentator remarked of the classical theories of time (those of Plato, Aristotle, Plotinus and St. Augustine) is true of Boethius. His theory of time and eternity is "in accordance with his theory of reality as a whole."[83] The metaphysics of the third and fourth books of the *Consolation* provide the groundwork of the theory.

This last point provides us with a basis for a final estimate of Professor Ford's interpretation of Boethius' theory. Limiting his efforts to determine Boethius' notion of simplicity to the account in Bk V of divine knowledge, he fails to appreciate the metaphysics of *complicatio-explicatio*. To be sure, he is partially right since both the nature of divine knowledge and the issue of eternity and time are explained in terms of this schema. In any case, on a rather skimpy textual basis he concludes that the unity of divine knowledge is the sort of simplicity which embraces its subordinate multiplicity in such a way that it "is not threatened by the continual presence of the diverse elements so unified."[84] So far, so good. A Boethian *complicatio* is an inclusive simplicity, an enfolding of the many in the one. The important question, however, is: how are the many in the one? In response to this question Ford cites not Boethius, but a contemporary writer, Martin Foss, who describes the simple as that which "not only transcends all division but in its transcending keeps the divisibility as overcome..." Such a simple, according to Foss, entails "the manifold, not as excluded but included, and we, therefore, consider the simple together with its *unfolding*. A simple is never only a whole; we can consider it as a mere whole of the *unfolded*. But if we do this, we distract from the beyond which makes it simple."[85] Ford's claim is that Foss' account of the simple is an accurate reflection of Boethian doctrine.

As is evident, Foss uses language that is vaguely reminiscent of Boethius. But by contrast to the latter, his account is quite confused. In the Boethian simplicity, the many are not present as *unfolded*. And to speak of "the simple together with its unfolding" makes no sense in terms of the Boethian schema, since it implies that the manifold is *qua* manifold present in the simple. That is simply not true. Ford, misled by this conception, then concludes that Boethius' eternity is the kind of simplicity which includes its manifold as unfolded: "As a simplicity this perfect possession [of eternity] is nonextensive and unanalyzable; as an *inclusive* simplicity, however, it contains a subordinate multiplicity, everlastingness, which can be examined and by means of which we can indirectly approach the mystery of divine eternity."[86]

This passage contains some puzzling, if not outrightly contradictory, statements. For one thing, how can eternity be both simplicity unqualified, in which what is possessed is non-multiple and unanalyzable, and also an inclusive simplicity in which the manifold of temporal succession retains its multiple character and so is in some sense analyzable? What is at work here are the pressures of process philosophy and not fidelity to the text. Ford does cite one text to support his position. It is one we have already seen, in which Boethius describes God's eternal status. Unaccountably, he misses another which superficially at least might seem to justify his view: *infinitatem mobilis temporis habere praesentem*.[87] But in fact, neither text does. The trouble is that he uses an outdated translation and only rarely, but not in these instances, does he cite the Latin. Hence he misses the sense of the key term, *complectens*, or, rather, he imposes upon it a meaning alien to Boethius' own usage.

Then there is Ford's curious interpretation of *interminabilis vitae*.[88] To explain this expression he first formulates a distinction between abstract and concrete time. The former has no ontological significance since it is simply a succession of empty "befores" and "afters", a series of empty dates. Concrete time signifies the events that occupy these, hitherto, empty loci. Now it is this concrete time, "everlastingness," as he calls it, which he identifies with the Boethian *interminabilis vitae*. This is the "subordinate multiplicity" which is retained in the inclusive simplicity of eternity and which is available for analysis. But Ford's account leads only to a dilemma from which there is no exit.

Either this subordinate multiplicity is present in eternity in all its diversity—but then, the divine simplicity is shattered, for how can the simple remain simple all the while including a multiplicity that retains its diversity? or the subordinate multiplicity is not present *qua* multiple, in which case (Boethius' own) it is neither multiple nor subordinate, nor still less available for analysis. What is Ford's way out? The thesis that "what is experienced is successive, but not the experience itself."[90] God's experience is non-successive, a pure simplicity, but what He experiences is successive and therefore plural.

But again this will not do, at any rate, for Boethius. Nowhere does Boethius state or imply that *intelligentia*, God's mode of knowing, is somehow the unity and simplicity of an experience whose objects are other than itself. How, indeed, could Boethius maintain with consistency the simplicity of divine knowledge if there is within it a distinction between knower and known. In point of fact the object of divine knowledge is the *simplex forma*,[90] i.e., the *complicatio*, which is God Himself. There can be no distinction between the divine experience and what it experiences. Both are non-successive. Hence, the *interminabilis vitae* of the definition refers not to the simultaneity of God's enfolding unity. This is precisely the point of Boethius' carefully formulated contrast between perpetuity and eternity.

In short, the inclusive simplicity of Boethius is not the God of process philosophy. For him the temporal is, indeed, truly present in the eternal. All temporal moments are present there, not divided off from each other, but each identical to the other in the encompassing *(complectens)* identity of eternity. Indeed, each temporal moment is most truly itself insofar as it is identical with all other moments in the pure simplicity of eternity in *complicatio*. This was the lesson of the geometrical image so dear to all Neo-Platonists: the different radii of the circle and the circle itself are most truly themselves in the identity, the simplicity of the center. Each *is* the center in the center.

So much for Boethius' theory of eternity. How does he conceive time? The answer, already explicitly in Bk IV, pr. 6, is that time is an unfolding: *haec temporalis ordinis explicatio*. It is the divine unity unfolded into plurality: *adunatio digesta atque explicata temporibus*.[91] But, alas, Boethius in Bk V, pr. 6 gives us no extended development of the implication of this thesis. In an already foreshortened treatment of eternity and time only some fourteen lines are devoted to the relation. Nothing resembling a definition or succinct characterization after the manner of Plato, Aristotle, Plotinus or St. Augustine is offered.

One point is immediately clear. Boethius' reflections on time show no trace of the psychological approach to time of Plotinus and St. Augustine. Countless commentators claim without the slightest evidence to see in Boethius the influence of Augustine not only in respect to time and eternity but also many other issues. The truth is that Boethius' account owes nothing to Augustine. Courcelle is, however, quite right in rejecting Silk's and Carton's elaborate but unfounded claims of Augustinian influence.[92] Nothing like the *complicatio-explicatio* couple is operative in Augustine's conception of the relationship between time and eternity. And by the same token nothing like the psychological view of time as a *distensio animae* is present in Boethius.

That said, let us consider the few lines that Boethius devotes to time. His main concern is not so much the nature of time considered by itself, but rather its relationship to eternity. That relationship is characterized as one of imitation: *quoniam manentis illius praesentiae quandam gestat imaginem*.[93] What, then, does he mean when he says time is an image of eternity? Is imitation to be taken here as part of a doctrine of exemplarism according to which the copy is an imitation of the model? I think not. Recall that Boethius began his elaboration of the definition of eternity by invoking a comparison with time. What is most striking about this comparison is the form it takes— negation. "Nothing established in time can enfold in a simultaneity the complete extent of its existence."[94] Time "cannot possess the plenitude of its existence all at once."[95] "It cannot remain."[96] It must, therefore, "accomplish successively by going *(continuaret eundo)* the existence whose plenitude it cannot envelop *(complecti)* by remaining."[97] All this suggests that time is a negation of eternity and not so much a weakened but positive version of it. Thus time as an image is not a reproduction at a lower level of the perfection of the higher, but a kind of declension or deterioration of simplicity into the plurality of the successive. "Since the infinite motion of temporal things cannot reproduce or equal the present state of immutable being, it falls away *(deficit)* from immobility into motion and declines *(decrescit)* from the simplicity of the present into the infinite extent of past and future..."[98]

The result is that the present moment of the temporal succession, as short and fleeting as it is, because it bears within itself a kind of image of the *praesentia* of eternity, can at best "make things only seem to be."[99] True, the language of imitation is explicit enough. But note the qualification— a sort of *(quandam)* image. Not the image entailed in a doctrine of exemplarism, but rather image in the qualified sense in which an *explicatio* can be said to be an image. Clearly the language of *deficit* and *decrescit* expresses the same meaning as the term *explicatio* does. Thus, the temporal is an *explicatio* of the eternal as the eternal is the *complicatio* of the temporal. But an *explicatio* is not an image of a *complicatio* in the way in which in Platonic exemplarism a particular is a likeness or copy of an eternal model. *Explicatio* stands to *complicatio* as multiplicity to unity. But multiplicity is not a likeness, a copy of unity. It is, in fact, its very opposite. It is unity relaxed into otherness. Trouillard's remark said originally of the relationship of the sensible to the intelligible in Plotinus is applicable to the relationship of time to eternity in Boethius. *"Le sensible n'est pas imitation, mais expression."*[100] So, too, for Boethius time is an expression, not an imitation of eternity. Time unfolds into succession *(continuaret eundo)* that life or existence whose plenitude it cannot enfold in permanence *(cuius plenitudinem complecti non valuit permanendo.)*[101]

IV

As we noted earlier, Boethius deals with the problem of time and eternity in only one other work, the *De Trinitate*. Is its treatment of the problem at variance with the account in the *Consolation*? The theological tractate does not make use of the *complicatio-explicatio* couple. And the focus of its brief treatment of time and eternity is quite different from that of the *Consolation*. The concern of the latter is to establish the ontological status of time and eternity. In the *De Trinitate* the focus is logical: the applicability of the Aristotelian categories to God and to creatures. What does it mean, it asks, to predicate *quando* of creatures and what does it mean to assert of God that He always exists *(semper est)*? Nonetheless the *De Trinitate* account is fundamentally in harmony with that of the *Consolation*.

According to the tractate when *semper est* is predicated of God, it signifies a unity in which He is present, as it were, to all of the past, present and future: *unam quidem significat, quasi omni praeterito fuerit, omni quoquo modo sit praesenti est, omni futuro erit.*[102] The *quasi* is significant. Clearly it is a qualifier indicating that God's duration is not spread out from a past through a present to a future. Rather, the *unum* which is God's duration contains all these moments of time concentrated (enfolded) in the indistinction of the *nunc divinum*. E. K. Rand's translation of this passage is, to say the least, very free, as is to a fault much of his rendition of the *Tractates*. But in this case it conveys well the sense of the original: "The expression 'God is ever' denotes a single Present, summing up His continual presence in all the past, in all the present... and in all the future."[103] Thus the *unum* of the *De Trinitate* seems to be the equivalent of the *simplicitas* of the divine *praesentia* in the *Consolation*. Each is a simplicity including within itself in indistinction all moments of time. The *unum* of the *De Trinitate* is, in short, a *complicatio*.

Thierry of Chartres makes the same identification in his commentaries on the *De Trinitate*. In the *Glosa* he remarks that some manuscripts have a *non* preceding the *quasi omni praeterito*. Hence in the reading which omits the negative we might be led to interpret the text as meaning that God is involved in temporal succession. This, of course, is not true. Hence we should interpret these lines as signifying "the three-fold state *simpliciter et complicite sine discretione statuum trium*."[104] Elsewhere in the same commentary he clearly identifies eternity with *complicatio successionis temporum*.[105] And in the *Commentum* Thierry unites in one lapidary formula the doctrines of the *Consolation* and the *De Trinitate*: *...ibi quidem vocabulum illud quod semper est* [Deus] *eternitatem designat, que omnia tempora in presentis simplicitatem conplicat.*[106]

In summary, then, Boethius appears to us once again in the role traditionally assigned to him, that of a transmitter of Greek philosophical culture to the Christian West. It is not only the logic of the Greeks and a few important definitions that he hands on to his successors. He is also the source for an overarching metaphysical schema. Not St. Thomas but Thierry of Chartres and after him, Nicholas of Cusa, are the authentic heirs of Boethius' philosophy of eternity and time.

Notes

[1]Boethius. *Corpus Christianorum. Series latina* Vol. 94. Ed. L. Bieler. Brepols, Turnhout, 1957. Bk V, pr. 6 p. 101. All references to the *Consolation* will be to this edition.

[2]*Ibid.*

[3] Courcelle, P. *La consolation de philosophie dans la tradition littéraire*. Etudes Augustiniennes. Paris, 1967, pp. 208-231.

[4] Ford, Lewis S. "Boethius and Whitehead on Time and Eternity," *International Philosophical Quarterly* 8 (1968), 38-67

[5] *Ibid.*, p. 42.

[6] *Ibid.*, p. 41.

[7] *Ibid.*, p. 42.

[8] *Ibid.*, p. 43.

[9] *Loc. cit.*

[10] *Ibid.*, pp. 49-50.

[11] *Loc. cit.*

[12] Obertello, L., *Severino Boezio*. Genoa: Ligurian Academy, 1974.

[13] V. pr. 4. "In quo illud maxime considerandum est: nam superior comprehendendi vis amplectitur inferiorem, inferior vero ad superiorem nullo modo consurgit."

[14] IV, pr. 6, p. 80.

[15] IV, pr. 5, pp. 77-78.

[16] IV, pr. 6, p. 79.

[17] *Ibid.*, pp. 79-80.

[18] Courcelle, p. 203.

[19] See, for example, besides Courcelle and Obertello: Klinger, F., *De Boethii Consolatione Philosophiae* (Reprint. Zurich/Dublin, 1966); Patch, H., "Fate in Boethius and the Neo-Platonists," *Speculum* 10 (1935) 62-72; Carton, R., "Le christianisme et l'augustinisme de Boèce" in *Mélanges augustiniens* (Paris, 1931), pp. 243-329; DeVogel, C., "Boethiana I", *Vivarium* 9 (1971), pp. 49-66.

[20] Courcelle, p. 203.

[21] IV, pr. 6, p. 79. "...Ordo namque fatalis ex providentiae simplicitate procedit."

[22] *Ibid.*, pp. 79-80. "Sicut enim artifex faciendae rei formam mente praecipiens movet operis effectum..." The next lines, however, clearly establish the Neo-Platonic opposition between *singulariter stabiliterque* (providence) and *multipliciter ac temporaliter* (fate).

[23] Here, perhaps, is the distant origin of Nicholas of Cusa's *coincidentia oppositorum*.

[24] The use of the noun form is taking some liberties with the text. In most cases Boethius uses the verbal forms: *complecti, amplecti, comprehendere*. Only once does he use the verbal form, *complicare*, and never the noun, *complicatio*. The former occurs in III, pr. 12 (p. 62): "...an mirabilem quedam divinae simplicitatis orbem complicas." It is difficult to determine whether or not this is a technical usage of the word. English translations usually fudge the issue, rendering

it as "make," "create" or "frame," but it may mean: "Do you [Lady Philosophy] envelop a sort of wondrous circle of divine simplicity?" In any case, given the nature of the work and the conditions under which it was written, Boethius' terminology was bound to be somewhat fluid. In the tradition which developed out of Boethius, notably in Thierry of Chartres, Clarembald of Arras and Nicholas of Cusa, the couple, *complicatio-explicatio* settled into technical form. For the sake of convenience, then, its use throughout this paper seems not unwarranted.

[25] IV, pr. 6, p. 80. "...fatalis series texitur" and "fatum...mobilem nexum atque ordinem temporalem." See also III, pr. 12, p. 60: "...nisi unus esset quod nexuit contineret."

[26] IV, pr. 6, p. 81.

[27] Obertello (p. 679) comes to the same conclusion though without any solid textual evidence. "La realtà mondana e eminente relazionale: ogni cosa ha legame con altre, l'universo e una rete di riferimenti reciproci ...Tutto e in relazione a tutto, per esprimere con una formula, sintetica il nesso di interdipendenza che regge dal suo interno la realtà." Fortescue (p. 167) is right, it seems to me, in rejecting F. Nitzsch's interpretation of *fatum* as a kind of substance which functions as a medium between God and finite things. See Nitzsch, F., *Das System des Boethius und die ihm zugeschriebenen theologischen Schriften* (Berlin, 1860), p. 62. Fortesque also appreciates the relational character of the order of fate: "Non est igitur substantia fatum sed relatio quaedem inter ipsas res" (p. 167).

[28] Thierry's Commentaries have been brilliantly edited by N. M. Häring. *Commentaries on Boethius by Thierry of Chartres and his School* (Toronto, 1971). See, for example, the *Lectiones* (p. 156): "Fatum vero est explicatio divine providentie quod Boetius in libro de Consolatione testatur. Unde patet divinam providentiam precedere fatum. Conplicatio enim semper precedit explicationem sicut unitas pluralitatem."

[29] As Pierre Duhem claims in "Thierry de Chartres et Nicolas de Cusa", *Revue des sciences philosophiques et théologiques* 3 (1909), 525-30.

[30] Only two commentators have, as far as I know, alluded to Boethius' use of the *complicatio-explicatio* couple, and that only in passing. They are M. de Gandillac and P. Hadot. The former in his excellent study of Nicholas of Cusa, *Nikolaus de Cues, Studien zu seiner Philosophie und philosophischen Weltanschauung* (Dusseldorf, 1953) p. 120, n. 72, claims that "Boethius betont wiederholt die Korrelation *explicatio-complicatio* besonders in De Trin. (IV, 5) wo von Gott gesagt wird, dass er alles Sein 'conjuncte et copulative' enthalte..." There is a slight error in his reference to the *De Trinitate*, the text in question reading not *copulative* but *copulate*. This text may, indeed, be parallel to Book IV, pr. 6 of the *Consolation*. What it asserts is that the Aristotelian categories signify "divise quidem in ceteris, in deo vero conjuncte et copulate." But in any case it is surely the *Consolation* and not the *De Trinitate* that "repeatedly emphasizes" the *complicatio-explicatio* couple. Hadot's reference occurs in his magnificent work: *Porphyre et Victorinus*. 2 vols. Etudes augustiniennes (Paris, 1968). His problem at a certain point was to determine the meaning of an enigmatic expression of Victorinus: *explicavit imaginationem*. He established that *explicare* here means dérouler, i.e., that for Victorinus the soul in producing an image unfolds "ce qui est avant elle dans un état d'involution". In the course of identifying earlier Greek equivalents of *explicare* (*exelittein* in Plotinus and *anelittein* in Proclus) he alludes (p. 334, n.2) to the link Boethius makes between time and *explicatio* in IV, prose 6.

[31] Bieler, p. 57.

[32] *Ibid.*, p. 59.

[33] III, pr. 10, p. 54.

[34] See III, pr. 10 and pr. 11, pp. 52-59. See also Courcelle, pp. 168-189.

[35] III, pr. 12, p. 62.

[36] *Ibid.*, p. 53.

[37] *Ibid.*, p. 60.

[38] *Ibid.*, p. 60.

[39] The grammar of this sentence is puzzling. Its subject *certus naturae ordo* takes, of course, the singular verb form, *procederet*. But why, then, is *explicarent*, which is clearly in parallel with *procederet*, in the plural form? The critical editions of Weinberger (CSEL. V. 27, Vienna 1935) and Bieler both list *explicaret* as the reading of several manuscripts. The text of the *Patrologia Latina* edition has *explicaret* and one is tempted, against all canons of scholarship, to accept the Migne reading. But, alas, one cannot. Professor Bieler has communicated to me by letter that there can be no mistake in the reading. The textual evidence is solidly on the side of the plural, though Bieler also concedes that the puzzle remains as to its subject.

[40] Bk III, m. 9. *(stabilisque manens)*; IV, pr. 6 *(manens in divina mente simplicitas)*; V, pr. 6 *(uno ictu mutationes tuas manens...complectitur)*; V, pr. 6, *(in sua simplicitate manet...complectens)*.

[41] Dodds, E.R. (tr.), *The Elements of Theology* (2nd ed. Oxford, 1963), Prop. 35, p. 38.

[42] Trouillard, J., *L'Un et l'âme selon Proclus* (Paris, 1972), Ch. III, pp. 91-109. He has even coined a French word to translate it, *manence*.

[43] Trouillard. p. 98. Trouillard says simply that "procession et conversion sont fondées toutes les deux sur un point de coincidence indissoluble entre générateur et engendré."

[44] Diehl, E. (ed.) *Proclus in Timaeum* (Leipzig, 1903-06), II, 243. See the excellent French translation of A. Festugière, *Proclus: Commentaire sur le Timée* (Paris, 1967), III, p. 287.

[45] W. Theiler in a brief reference relates the *stabilisque manens* of III, m. 9 to Proclus' *mone* in his essay: "Antike und christliche Rückkehr zu Gott" in *Forschungen zum Neuplatonismus* (Berlin, 1966), p. 322. Klinger (pp. 44-45) had earlier emphasized the importance of Proclus' *Commentary on the Timaeus* as a source for III, m. 9. See also C. deVogel, "Boethiana II," *Vivarium* 10 (1972) p. 7.

[46] Ford, p. 42.

[47] Trouillard, J., "L'Antithèse fondamentale de la procession selon Proclos," *Archives de Philosophie* 34 (1971), 437.

[48] The absence of such a hierarchy has been noted by many commentators. See e.g. Courcelle, p. 205; Fortescue, pp. 165-168; Obertello, p. 704; and Carton, pp 276-77: "...Boèce ne reprend pas la cascade néo-platonicienne des intermédiaires..." Carton is also right in rejecting E.K. Rand's thesis that Boethius' treatment of providence and fate is not an appreciation of but rather a systematic critique of Neo-Platonism. See E.K. Rand "On the Composition of Boethius' *Consolatio Philosophiae*," *Harvard Studies in Classical Philology* 15 (1904), pp. 16-24.

[49] IV, pr. 6, p. 80.

[50] Obertello, p. 704.

[51] Boethius seems to have been influenced almost exclusively by Greek sources and only very little by Latin authors. Still there are echoes in the *Consolation* of some of Cicero's language and it may be that Boethius found in Cicero's *De Divinatione* (I, 127) a clue to his own use of the term *explicatio*. "Non enim illa quae futura sunt subito exsistunt, sed est quasi rudentis explicatio sic traductio temporis nihil novi efficientis et primum quidque replicantis". See also W. Theiler, *Die Vorbereitung des Neuplatonismus* (Berlin, 1930), p. 96. Theiler notes that the notion of unfolding may originate with Posidonius.

[52] Courcelle, P., *La Consolation...*, pp. 206-7.

[53] Patch, H.R., "Fate in Boethius...," pp. 62-72.

[54] deVogel, C., "Boethiana I," p. 56, and Obertello, L., pp. 517-18.

[55] The intermediary is Ammonius Hermias according to Courcelle. But is Courcelle right in claiming that the fifth book of the *Consolation* in inspired *tout entier* by the commentaries of Ammonius?

[56] The texts which employ the language of enfolding and unfolding are too numerous to list here. See e.g. V, 3, 10, lines 46-51; V, 8, 6, lines 9-11; VI, 6, 9, lines 27-31; V, 9, 6, lines 7-13; III, 7, 6, lines 15-16, and 11, lines 23-27. The line references are to the Henry-Schwyzer edition, *Plotini Opera*, 3 vols., Paris, 1951-1973.

[57] I borrow this expression from Hadot who uses it to explain Victorinus' meaning for "in potency" and who also notes its appearance in Plotinus. See his *Porphyre et Victorinus* I, p. 228, and especially n. 2. Cf. also J. Trouillard, *La purification plotinienne* (Paris, 1955), pp. 56-75; C. Rutten, *Les catégories du monde sensible dans les Ennéades de Plotin* (Paris, 1961), p. 21; Lloyd, A.C. "Neo-Platonic Logic and Aristotelian Logic II", *Phronesis* 2 (1956), pp. 146-150.

[58] Gersh, S.E., *KINESIS AKINETOS. A Study of Spiritual Motion in the Philosophy of Proclus* (Leiden, 1973), p. 105 and notes 3 and 4.

[59] Dodds, E.R. *The Elements of Theology. A Revised Text with Translation, Introduction and Commentary* (Oxford, 1963), Prop. 93, p. 84. See also props. 65 (p. 62) and 176 (p. 154). The translation is my own.

[60] Saffrey, H.D., and Westerink, L.G., (ed.), *Proclus. Théologie Platonicienne* (Paris, 1978), Bk. III, 2, p. 8. This excellent critical edition is accompanied by a facing French translation.

[61] Saffrey-Westerink, p. 7. "Cette dimunition d'unité...explique seule l'apparition de la multiplicité des êtres secondaires. Tout devrait rester 'caché'...dans l'unité originelle, c'est un relâchement de cette unité...qui produit le multiple..."

[62] Saffrey-Westerink (1968), Bk I, 19. p. 93. See also *Notes complémentaires*, p. 155, n. 2, in which the editors identify Proclus' reference to Plotinus. It is to *Ennead* III, 8, 8.

[63] Friedlein, G. (ed.), *Procli Diadochi in Primum Euclidis Elementorum Librum Commentarii* (Leipzig, 1983), 44, 1-22. The word which "enfolds" translates is *symptussein* (literally "wrap up"). It is similar to an expression used in the *Platonic Theology*.

[64] Diehl, E. (ed.), *In Platonis Timaeum Commentaria* (Leipzig, 1903-06), II, 243. See A.J. Festugière, *Proclus Commentaire sur le Timée* (Paris, 1967), Vol. III, p. 287.

[65] *In Platonis Parmenidem IV*, 930, lines 11-20. The reference is to the edition of V. Cousin: *Procli...opera inedita*. Reprint Georg Olms, Hildesheim, 1961.

[66] The three opuscula, *De Decem Dubitationibus, De Providentia et Fato* and *De Malorum Subsistentia* survive only in an execrable Latin version made by William of Moerbeke. In some passages the original Greek has been reconstructed from the works of a Byzantine author, Isaac Sebastocrater, first by H. Boese, *Procli Diadochi Tria Opuscula*, Berlin, 1960. A more recent edition with text newly established and with a facing French translation is being made by D. Isaac, *Proclus. Trois Études sur la Providence*: Vol. I *(De Decem Dubitationibus)*, Paris, 1977, and Vol. II *(De Providentia et Fato)*, Paris, 1979. My citations are from this edition.

[67] Courcelle, *La consolation*, p. 206. Obertello agrees with Courcelle's estimate of influence of these works on Boethius. One cannot, however, agree with Obertello's claim that "l'immagine del cerchio non ha inoltre, in Boezio come in Proclo, che un valore limatato" (p. 518, n. 54).

[68] *De Decem Dub*. III, 10-12; Isaac, pp. 66-68 (Latin and French); pp. 165-67 (Greek).

[69] *De Decem Dub*. II, 5; Isaac, p. 60 and p. 158.

[70] If this account of the metaphysics of the *Consolation* is correct, how is one to account for the ontology of being as form which Boethius, according to many commentators, outlines in the *Tractates*? Limitations of space do not allow for a full treatment of this problem. This much, however, can be said. The interpretation of the famous axiom: *diversum est esse et id quod est* as equating *esse* with form has recently been vigorously challenged by Pierre Hadot. (See his "*Forma essendi*. Interprétation...d'une formule de Boèce," *Les études classiques* 38 [1970], 143-56.) If his Neo-Platonic exegesis of the axiom is, as I believe, correct, the metaphysics of the *De Hebdomadibus* and that of the *Consolation* can be shown to display a fundamental harmony. There would, however, still remain the problem of accounting for the texts in the *De Trinitate* where the identification of *esse* with *forma* seems even more decisive. The striking contrast between the metaphysics of the two great Chartrian commentators of the *De Trinitate*, Thierry of Chartres and Gilbert of Poitiers may provide a clue to the resolution of this problem. In his commentaries Thierry unites in a coherent way the *complicatio-explicatio* structure of the *Consolation* with the texts which equate *esse* with *forma*. Gilbert, on the other hand, completely ignores the doctrine of the *Consolation* and arrives at an ontology of being as essence.

[71] For an appraisal of the role of the *complicatio-explicatio* couple in Boethius' theory of universals, see my "Boethius on Universals: a Reconsideration," in *Proceedings of the Patristic-Mediaeval-Renaissance Conference* II (1977), pp. 113-121.

[72] *Consolation*, Bk V, pr. 6, pp. 100-101.

[73] See the remarks of Bréhier in the *Notice* to *Ennead* III, 7, "Les Ennéades de Plotin;" Vol. III, p. 123.

[74] Courcelle, *La Consolation...*, pp. 221-22.

[75] Bk V, pr. 6, p. 101.

[76] *Loc. cit.*

[77] *Loc. cit.*

[78] *Loc. cit.*

[79] *Loc. cit.*

⁸⁰*Loc. cit.*

⁸¹*Ibid.*, p. 102.

⁸²Philip Wicksteed in his work, *The Religion of Time and the Religion of Eternity*, has a remarkably accurate summary of Boethius' conception of eternity: "...Eternity is not an endless time, but a state in which perfection is found in coexistence, not in the succession of the parts that make up the whole." This passage is cited in H. Barrett, *Boethius. Some Aspects of His Times and Work* (New York, 1965), p. 136.

⁸³Callahan, J., *Four Views of Time in Ancient Philosophy* (Cambridge, Mass., 1948), p. 189.

⁸⁴Ford, p. 41.

⁸⁵Foss, M., *The Idea of Perfection in the Western World* (Princeton, 1946), as cited by Ford, p. 41.

⁸⁶Ford, p. 49.

⁸⁷*Consolation*, Bk V, pr. 6, p. 101.

⁸⁸Ford, pp. 43-49.

⁸⁹Ford, p. 50.

⁹⁰*Consolation*, Bk V, pr. 4, p. 97: "...simplicem formam pura mentis acie contuetur [intelligentia]." Prose 5 (p. 99) makes it clear that "intelligentia sola divini."

⁹¹*Ibid*, p. 79.

⁹²*La Consolation* p. 340, n. 1, and p. 221.

⁹³Bieler, p. 102.

⁹⁴*Ibid.*, p. 101.

⁹⁵*Ibid.*, p. 102.

⁹⁶*Loc. cit.*

⁹⁷*Loc. cit.*

⁹⁸*Loc. cit.*

⁹⁹*Loc. cit.*

¹⁰⁰See n. 42.

¹⁰¹*Ibid.*, p. 102.

¹⁰²*De Trinitate* IV (Stewart-Rand), p. 20.

¹⁰³*Ibid.*, p. 21.

¹⁰⁴*Glosa* IV, 29 (Häring), p. 291.

[105] *Glosa* II, 15 (Häring), p. 272.

[106] *Commentum*, IV, 42 (Häring), p. 107.

4.

ACTION AS THE SELF-REVELATION OF BEING: A CENTRAL THEME IN THE THOUGHT OF ST. THOMAS

W. Norris Clarke, S.J.

It is a strange fact, well enough known to Thomistic scholars familiar with the whole of St. Thomas' thought, that the great underlying themes, the central structural principles organizing his philosophical world-view, are not ordinarily highlighted explicitly in their own right, as a modern philosopher would tend to do. The explicit focus of his writing, following the medieval scholastic custom in university teaching, is directed toward the solving of an integrated series of key problems in a given area—for example, "Whether the soul is the Form of the Body," etc. The central governing principles are *used* constantly, and indeed quite explicitly, to solve these problems, but St. Thomas does not ordinarily thematize them directly in a full-fledged exposition of them in their own right as universal principles. Thus one does not find articles entitled: "Whether Act and Potency (or the Theory of Participation) Are Universal Principles for Understanding All Things." Yet one has not really understood the Thomistic system in its holistic unity and depth until one has thematized explicitly for himself these great underlying principles precisely as universal explanatory principles.

One of these great central organizing themes in St. Thomas' thought, too often left in the shadow, yet running through not only his whole philosophy but also his theology, is the principle that *action is the self-revelation of being*.[1] By this is meant that action, activity, not only follows naturally from being, but is also a natural self-communication and self-revelation of the being that acts, "pointing out," as St. Thomas graphically puts it, both its existence and its essence, both *that* it is and *what* it is.[2] The centrality of such a principle is particularly evident throughout the whole of metaphysics and epistemology. For without it no universe, properly speaking, could exist, that is, the multiplicity of beings would not be "turned toward each other to form a unity" *(universum)*, i.e. a real order or system unified by existential bonds between the members: without action there can be no existential bond between beings. Nor would knowledge be possible of anything real beyond the knower. For unless a being manifested or reveal-

[63]

ed its presence and nature by some action, it would be impossible to know that it was present at all, let alone its nature (unless, of course, the knower had directly caused its whole being, which would involve action at least on the part of the knower). A being that did not manifest its existence and essence to others by some form of self-revealing action would make no difference at all to the other beings in the universe, and hence might just as well not be at all. A totally unmanifest existence, unreachable even potentially by any kind of action, would be to all intents and purposes equivalent to non-existence, if it could indeed be conceptualized at all.

As a result, I am willing to venture the following risky, but I think well defensible, statement, that the whole of Thomistic epistemology, in its large lines, can be summed up as follows: all human knowledge of the real is an interpretation of action. Yet it is hard to find this basic principle thematized explicitly for itself, in St. Thomas, abstracted from its particular applications. This is what I would like to do in large lines in this essay. The fruit of such an exploration will be, I hope, to highlight not only the unity but the profoundly dynamic character of the entire world-view of St. Thomas, together with its ability to shed light on certain troublesome "bridge" problems that have plagued modern Western epistemology since its new start with Descartes.

I. Action as the Natural Overflow of Being

It is impossible to read St. Thomas at any length and not come across the oft-repeated refrain: *agere sequitur esse* (to act follows upon to be). Here are some characteristic texts:

> Every agent acts according as it is in actuality.[3] From the very fact that something exists in act, it is active.[4] Active power follows upon being in act; for anything acts in consequence of its being in act.[5]

Thus it is proper to every being, insofar as it is in act, to overflow into action, to act according to its nature, whether such action be free or necessitated in its modality. The act of existence of any being (its "to be" or *esse*) is its "first act," its abiding inner act, which tends naturally, by the very innate dynamism of the act of existence itself, to overflow into a "second act," which is called action or activity. Every second act of a being points back toward its first act as to its ground and source, and every first act, in turn, points forward to its natural self-expression in a second act. This action may be an *immanent action*, which terminates within the agent itself, as in the case of knowledge or love, or a *transient action*, which terminates outside the agent by exercising some influence on another, as cause on effect, thus manifesting itself to another than itself.[6] In what follows we are thinking more particularly, though not exclusively, of this second kind of action, without which no non-creative being could know any other being in the universe distinct from it.

It might be asked how St. Thomas establishes the natural connection between being and its overflow into action. There is no logical or other way of *deducing* this property of being from anything else more fundamental. It can only be reached by a reflective insight arising from an inductive examination which observes it constantly at work in all the cases and at all the levels of being we know, until we are finally brought to the level of a "metaphysical insight" that this property somehow belongs to the very nature of existential being as such, and could not be intelligibly otherwise, in that any being without it would remain beyond the pale of intelligibility, inaccessible to the rest of the real universe in the darkness of its total isolation from all others. To be, in the strong sense of to be real or actually existing, is seen to be ambiguous, incomplete, empty of evidential grounding, unless it includes, as natural corollary, *active presence*, that which *presents* itself positively to others through some mode of action. To be is to be actively co-present to the community of existents, of other active presences. Presence that is not presence in some way *to* the community or other existents slips into the unreachable darkness of the totally unmanifest, the totally concealed (unrevealed), indistinguishable from nothingness to all other beings (one might perhaps argue, even to itself, though we will not venture into these particularly deep waters right now).

II. Action as the Self-Communication of Being

Let us now unpack further the implications of action as the natural overflow of existential being. This is where the full significance of the link between being and action begins to emerge, as St. Thomas sees it. Every being, he says, insofar as it *is* in act, tends naturally to overflow into action, and this action is a *self-communication*, a self-giving in some way. This theme recurs over and over again, in many contexts. Here are a few characteristic texts:

> It is in the nature of every actuality to communicate itself insofar as it is possible. Hence every agent acts according as it exists in actuality.[7]

> To bring forth an actuality is, of itself, proper to a being in act: for every agent acts according as it is in act. Therefore every being in act is by its nature apt to bring forth something in act. But God is a being in act...Therefore it is proper to Him to bring forth some being in act, to which He is the cause of being.[8]

> It follows upon the superabundance proper to perfection as such that the perfection which something has it can communicate to

another.[9]

Communication follows upon the very intelligibility *(ratio)* of actuality. Hence every form is of itself communicable.[10]

For natural things have a natural inclination not only toward their own proper good, to acquire it, if not possessed, and, if possessed, to rest therein; but also to diffuse their own goodness among others as far as possible. Hence we see that every agent, insofar as it exists in act and possesses some perfection, produces something similar to itself. It pertains, therefore, to the nature of the will to communicate to others as far as possible the good possessed; and especially does this pertain to the divine will, from which all perfection is derived in some kind of likeness. Hence if natural things, insofar as they are perfect, communicate their goodness to others, much more does it pertain to the divine will to communicate by likeness its own goodness to others as far as possible.[11]

Here we touch on the most fundamental dynamism of being itself for St. Thomas. Not only does every being tend, by the inner dynamism of its act of existence, to overflow into action, but this action is both a self-manifestation and a self-communication, a self-sharing, of the being's own inner ontological perfection, with others. This natural tendency to self-giving is a revelation of the natural fecundity or "generosity" rooted in the very nature of being itself. We are immediately reminded of the ancient Platonic tradition—well known to St. Thomas—of the "self-diffusiveness of the Good" *(bonum est diffusivum sui*, as the Latins put it). What St. Thomas has done is to incorporate this whole rich tradition of the fecundity of the Good into his own philosophy of being, turning this self-diffusiveness, which the Platonic tradition identified as proper to what they considered the ultimate ground of reality, the Good, into a *property of being* itself, of which the good now becomes one inseparable aspect (or transcendental property).[12] Whereas in Platonism, and especially Neoplatonism, being itself is only a lesser dimension, on the finite level, of the primal self-diffusiveness or self-communication of the Good, for St. Thomas the good is a derivative property of existential being itself, expressing more explicitly the primal dynamism of self-expansiveness and self-giving inherent in the very nature of being as act of existence. The primacy always lies with existence for St. Thomas. Nothing can be good unless it first actually is; and from the very fact that it is, it naturally follows that it is good, since the act of existence is the root of all perfection in any domain, "the actuality of all acts, and the perfection of all perfections."[13]

We have here penetrated to the very roots of being itself, to the primal spring of its activity without which there would be no universe. There is something mysterious, ultimate, and undeducible about this inherent self-diffusive dynamism of all being, as about all primary things. It cannot be deduced from anything more ultimate, but is reached by insight through induction, when we finally see that not only is it a fact about all the beings we know, but that it must be so if there is to be a universe, an intercommunicating community of co-existents, at all. It is the dynamo that makes the whole world go round. In its highest form as self-communicative altruistic love, it is the ultimate reason why the Many emerges from the One at all, without which sheerly gratuitous emanation there would be no Many, hence no universe at all.

It is true, of course, that in St. Thomas' participation universe, as in the Neoplatonic one, the self-diffusiveness of all finite participated beings can be traced back to its primal source, the infinite essential goodness of God himself, who, as pure Subsistent Act of Existence *(ipsum esse Subsistens)*, is also Love itself. And Revelation here gives us a marvelous further insight, inaccessible to strictly philosophical penetration, into the interior depths of the divine self-communicativeness within His own being, manifesting to us that it is of the very nature of the divine being to pour over into two supreme eternal acts of self-communication of the perfection of His nature, first from the Father to the Son, then from the Father and Son together to the Holy Spirit, the procession of the Son or Logos according to self-knowledge, and the procession of the Holy Spirit according to self-love. The rest of the universe dimly imitates, each thing in its own way, this infinite fullness of self-giving. But it still remains that this mysterious inner process of thoughtful, loving self-communication is not a free decision but belongs to the very nature of the Supreme Being as pure Subsistent Act of Existence. If we try to pursue this trail further, and ask why this should be so, why Being itself should *be* self-expansive Love, all trails end in the silence of *the* Mystery. The Ultimate Fact that Being is identically Love precludes all further explanatory moves, and serves itself as the ultimate explanatory reason for the entire dynamic nature of the universe.

The principal difference, of course, between St. Thomas and the Neoplatonic tradition of the self-diffusiveness of the Good, to which he clearly owes so much, is that for the latter the self-communication of the supreme source, the One or the Good, is presented as a *necessary* process of emanation, at all levels, including the highest. St. Thomas, both as a Christian *and* as a philosopher, holds firmly to the divine freedom in creation, that God is free to create or not to create finite beings. Because he fears that the "self-diffusiveness of the good" doctrine, if taken too strictly in the order of efficient casuality, might compromise this freedom of creation, he tones down the meaning of the adage, *bonum est diffusivum sui*, to mean the self-diffusiveness of the good in the order of final casuality, the order of the good as attractive goal, not as causal source. In the order of efficient causality, he is willing to concede only that every being is *capable* of active self-communication, has a natural aptitude for it, but does not necessarily have to actualize this aptitude. This is clearly not the original Neoplatonic meaning of the principle, which insists on the active overflow of a kind of natural law, an exigency of the very nature of the good. St. Thomas is also being considerably more cautious here than St. Bonaventure and other Christian Neoplatonists, who remain closer to the stronger Neoplatonic doctrine while not denying the freedom of creation, by appealing to a kind of spiritual exigency of love, by which it would be somehow "out of character" for a loving person, above all God, not to share freely his goodness with others.

It seems to me that St. Thomas is indeed somewhat overcautious here. His own strong statements, quoted above, that it is proper to every being in act to be self-communicative through action, do not easily fit together with his restriction of the law of the self-diffusiveness of the good to the order of final causality. It seems to me he could have kept the stronger meaning of the principle and taken care of the freedom of creation by several other qualifications: (1) He could have appealed to the revealed doctrine of the Three Persons in the Trinity, to show that the necessary law of the self-communication of the good has already been fulfilled in an infinitely perfect way in the inner procession of the Son and the Holy Spirit, which is not free, but of the very nature of divine being; then the further pouring over into finite creation no longer becomes necessary but is free; (2) he could have held, as some Christian philosophers have, that while on the one hand it is impossible to deduce from the existence of an infinite Source the necessity of any *one* finite universe flowing from it—since an infinite number of other finite universes is always possible, and the choice must pass through the filters of intelligence and freedom—still one might say that there is a kind of moral exigency of perfect love that it share itself in *some* way, that it would be "out of character," hence not fully intelligible for it not to. But his caution may have been the better part of prudence, especially in his own day, when the Christian world was facing the strong intellectual threat of the great Arabic necessary-emanation theories of the universe, which clearly left too little place for the divine freedom in creation.

At any rate, once the universe is launched into existence by the loving self-communication of God as First Cause, all finite beings, which are imperfect images of the Source, bear within their very natures this same divinely originated dynamism of active self-communication to others. Thus the many existential bonds of the finite universe come into being. But because *finite* beings are both rich and poor, these bonds go both ways: every finite being insofar as it is in act, is rich, pours over to share its perfection with others; but insofar as it is poor, deficient in the full plenitude of being, it reaches out to receive enrichments of being from others sharing their riches.[14] Thus the universe becomes a vast interconnected web of interacting beings, reciprocally acting on and being acted on by others, giving and receiving. *To be finite* is *to share*, in all the active and passive meanings of that term.

To sum up this whole section, action, as the natural overflow and selfcommunicative dynamism of existential being, is the indispensable shuttle on which is woven the web of this, and any other, universe.

III. Action as the Self-Revelation of Being

The implications of the above doctrine of action as the self-communication of being are profound and rich, lending themselves to the deepest metaphysical, artistic, and religious meditation, opening out easily into mysticism. We shall now turn our attention to one of the richest philosophical implications or corollaries of the doctrine, namely, that this self-communication of being is also necessarily a *self-revelation* or *self-manifestation* of being. This is where the role of action as the ground of a realistic epistemology emerges more explicitly.

But first let us take a quick look at one of the interesting ontological implications of being as self-communicative. For St. Thomas, as for Aristotle and Neoplatonism, every being, by the very fact that it communicates itself through action, also produces in the recipients of this communication an ontological *self-expression*, a likeness or image of itself. The reason for this flows from the nature of the cause-effect relationship: every effect must in some way resemble its cause, and vice versa. Since the effect proceeds from the cause, receives its being or mode of being, insofar as it is an effect, from its cause, and since a cause cannot give what it does not possess, at least in some equivalent higher way, there must be a relation of at least analogous similitude between effect and cause. Hence every self-communication of one being to another through action of one on the other necessarily brings forth a self-imaging, a self-expression, one might say a self-symbolization, of the cause in the effect. If every being, then, turns out to include a natural dynamism toward self-communication through action, we can say truly, in more than a metaphorical sense, that every being is naturally a *self-symbolizer*, an icon or image-maker, in some analogous way like an artist, expressing itself symbolically, whether consciously or unconsciously.[15] No wonder that man has an innate drive toward image-making, if *all* beings do, from the very fact that they are beings in act. The difference between man and lower beings, why we call one an artist and not the others, is that those below man are limited to an endlessly repetitive self-imaging according to their already determined nature, whereas man has the freedom to make images not only of himself but of the whole universe in relation to himself in endlessly creative new perspectives and angles of insight.

We might add that this notion of every being as innately ordered toward self-symbolization opens up a profoundly illuminating harmony between philosophy and theology, reason and faith, in St. Thomas' worldview: the self-symbolizing tendency in all the finite beings we know turns out to be an imperfect participation or imitation of the inner being of God himself, revealed to be supremely and perfectly self-symbolizing in its eternal interior procession of the Son from the Father and the Holy Spirit from both. But again why the divine being should be this way, why it is the "nature" of Being itself to be this way, leads our minds to the end of explanation in the unsoundable depths of the Ultimate Mystery, expressed impersonally as the fecundity of being as the good, personally as the identity of Being and Love.

IV. Action as the Key to a Realistic Epistemology

The key problem in any realistic epistemology is how a finite non-creative knower like man can know a world of real beings "outside of" or distinct from his own consciousness, so that his immanent knowledge or conscious representation of these beings *corresponds* authentically with the reality of this world as it is in itself, in a word, so that his knowledge of it is *true*. The basic type of Platonic solution to the problem, echoed creatively but always recognizably through the Augustinian and other later derivatives of the Platonic tradition, is that the knower is illuminated from within himself and from above, by a direct intuitive insight, however dimmed it may be for various historical contingent reasons, into the ideal forms or pure intelligible patterns that are constitutive of the intelligible core of these things; but the locus of these intelligible forms, from which they are received by the knower, is not the imperfect individually existing instances of these forms found around us in our horizontal world of change and action, but the separate, pre-existent ideal world of these forms in their pure intelligible state, either as found in the apparently self-subsisting Platonic World of Ideas, or in the Divine Ideas of Neoplatonism and St. Augustine, eternally existing in the Divine Mind itself (i.e. the secondary level of the Divine *Nous* for Plotinus; the Divine Logos, co-equal with the Father, for Augustine and all orthodox Christian Platonists). We must turn within and be illumined from above, not directly from individually existing things themselves, if we are to know their true being.

The fundamental criticism of this theory of direct intuitive knowing of the essence of other beings advanced by the whole Aristotelian-Thomistic tradition is that it does not do justice to, or cannot be squared with, our actual experience of human knowing: its dependence on sense knowledge, its slowly growing character through trial and error and interactive feedback with the real through experiential contact with it, its always incomplete perspectival character, its non-intuitive character, for which the intentionality of judgment is a substitute, etc. We need not elaborate on this here, well known as it is to most of our readers. For St. Thomas, then, although we do have a general divine illumination in the form of a created participation in the divine light by our own individual agent intellect, all knowledge of particular real beings or kinds of being must come through the illumination or selfrevelation of things themselves in direct contact with us. Since we have no direct intuition into the substantial forms of things immanent within them—not only of beings distinct from us but even of our own being—there must be some mediating bridge by which real beings distinct from us enter into the interiority of our consciousness in some way and manifest themselves trustworthily to us.

The only such bridge is the mediation of action, if understood in its full ontological depth as the self-revelation of the being of the agent that is its source. Since all beings are constantly in some way (though perhaps intermittently) flowing over from their inner act of being into self-communicative, self-revealing action on the beings within their range of action, any being capable of receiving these influences immediately becomes a receiving center for the surrounding world, a kind of crossroads information-receiving center for the universe as it impinges on that particular location. All that a being has to do is to become conscious, to become aware of itself *as* a receiving set, as the recipient of self-revealing action from the surrounding world, and it is now enabled to interpret the messages, the *information*, contained within this incoming action, *as* messages from these surrounding beings, *as* the self-revelation of these beings to it through the mediation of their structured action upon it. Man is precisely such a self-conscious receiving set, a *Dasein*, as Heidegger beautifully puts it, a *There*-Being, placed in the midst of the material cosmos with the ability to receive the self-imaging messages of all the material beings around him, insofar as they can act upon his body with a high enough energy input to be able to be brought up, first beyond the minimum threshold of sense perception, and then interpreted by intelligence. It is man's destiny, written into him by the very structure of his nature, to be the one to *listen* to being, as it reveals itself to him through the mute message of its action, interpret its significance, gather into unity its multifarious voices, speak out the *logos* of Being (as mediated by the many beings which are its bearers), and respond accordingly by his own action.

Action as the self-revelation of being is thus the key for St. Thomas to all knowledge of all beings other than itself by a knower that must be receptive and not creative of its objects. Since the action that flows out from a being is not simply an indeterminate surge of raw energy, but pours out from, and is self-expressive of, the whole unified inner being of the thing, both its act of existence and its essence, its action cannot help but be *essence-structured action* revealing or manifesting to any potential receiver both the actual existence and the essence of the being from which the action originates. As St. Thomas puts it, with his typical condensed brevity:

> The operation of a thing manifests both its substance [essence] and its existence.[16]

> The operation of a thing shows forth its power, which in turn points to [or points out: *indicat*] its essence.[17]

The action of a being upon us as a conscious receiving set reveals to us first, therefore, the actual existence of the being in question, *that* it is, is really present, in the world of actual existents. Action, by the very fact that we do not originate or control it, but receive it to some degree passively, "suffer" its influence, and are controlled or determined by it willynilly, is the natural sign of the real presence of another-than-self. It then at the same time, because it is structured action, reveals to us the essence or nature of the agent precisely as *this kind of actor on me* (and subsequently on others, as our observation widens). This is precisely what our knowledge of the essences of real beings comes down to: we know them as such and such *kinds of actors*, distinguished from others by such and such a set of *characteristic actions*. Such knowledge is genuinely revelatory of the essence, for it enables us to know that the being truly has within itself such a nature, possessing such a degree of perfection and power, that it can originate such a self-communicating, self-expressing, self-imaging action.

But notice immediately the built-in limitations of such a mode of knowing through the interpretation of action. We cannot "zap in" by direct unmediated intuition to "see" intellectually the inner act of existence and especially the nature of the agent as it abides in itself behind the actions, *apart from and independently of these actions*. Man has no such intuitive knowledge of essences—including his own—for St. Thomas. We can know real beings—including ourselves in fact—only to the extent that they actually reveal their natures by their actions. But no single action of a finite being can ever reveal totally, in a single exhaustive flash, the entire essence of that being. Every action of a finite being (or even the action of an Infinite Being as received in a finite being) is always at once revealing and concealing, to use Heidegger's marvelously apt language. It does reveal something of the inner nature; otherwise it would not be action at all. But it also leaves unrevealed further depths or aspects of the reservoir of active potency within it; and though finite in itself, the latter is still inexhaustible by our knowledge because of its hidden ontological connections with every other being in the universe and especially with its Infinite Source, God himself. To know even the least finite thing fully as it is, with all its relations, we would have to know it precisely as an image of God, and how it proceeds from and expresses its original, which is hidden from us in the depths of the Infinite.[18]

It is not generally recognized how modest St. Thomas is in his claims for our knowledge of the essences of real things.[19] Yet he says with all the explicitness desirable that we human knowers cannot know the inner essential forms of things directly as they are in themselves:

> The substantial forms of things, which, according as they are in themselves, are unknown to us, shine forth to us *(innotescunt)* through their accidental properties.[20]

Sometimes a created intellect does not arrive at the essence of what it knows directly through itself (as do the angels), but only through the mediation of what surrounds the essence, as though through doors placed around it; and this is the mode of apprehending in man, who proceeds to the knowledge of the essence of a thing from its effects and properties. Hence in this knowledge there must be a certain discursive character.[21]

As a result St. Thomas does not hesitate to maintain that no human knower can ever come to know perfectly the essence of anything, even a fly:

Our knowledge is so weak that no philosopher was ever able to investigate perfectly the nature of a single fly. Hence we read that one philosopher passed thirty years in solitude in order that he might know the nature of the bee.[22]

Thus the abstraction of form from matter in St. Thomas' theory of knowledge cannot be equated with the popular misapprehension that the whole essential form of material beings somehow pops out automatically whole and entire under the X-rays of the agent intellect, somewhat as a sausage pops out of a sausage machine. The abstraction of form does indeed give us an authentic *sighting* on the form, but always incompletely, according to the perspective of our horizon of inquiry and the aspects of the form which are revealed by the particular action received.[23]

In the light of this doctrine of knowledge through action as the partial self-revelation of a being to a given knower, the necessary incompleteness of all human knowledge of essences turns out to be derived from two complementary sources. On the other hand, there is the limitation on the side of the self-revealing action, which, as we have seen above, can never totally reveal in a single act or series of them the full essence of a finite being in all its natural depths of potentiality and act. The second source of limitation comes from the side of the knower himself. As St. Thomas never tires of repeating in its application to knowledge, "Whatever is received is received according to the mode of the receiver."[24] Hence, whatever the knower receives from the self-communication of the known to it through action will always be measured by the receptive capacities of the knower, especially evident in the thresholds and channels of receptivity at the primary level of data input, our sense receiving sets. Thus we can perceive light rays only within a limited section of its total spectrum of wavelengths; we can only see a body from one visual perspective at a time, etc. Here the whole contemporary insistence on the perspectival character of all human knowing can be assimilated easily enough into Thomistic epistemology, even including the partially active a priori contributions and transformations brought to the knowledge relation by the knower, though St. Thomas himself has only laid down the basic principles of receptivity through action and has not worked out all the far-reaching philosophical and theological consequences.

We could also express the above doctrine of action as the bridge between knower and known in the language of *intentionality*, as St. Thomas himself regularly does. Intentionality in general is that property of something by which it tends dynamically and relationally toward something else *(intendere)*. This can either be in the ontological order by active tendency, or in the cognitive order in the form of a natural sign or image which points back to the source which it manifests and represents. Intentionality understood in its full richness as including both of the above is indeed the key to knowledge for St. Thomas. It includes a double movement of intentionality, only one aspect of which has been recovered by Brentano, Husserl, and contemporary phenomenology. There is first the incoming *ontological intentionality of action* itself into the knower, which tends naturally to produce a self-expression, a similitude, of itself in an apt receiver. This similitude, which is a selfexpression of the agent projected through its form, leaving the being's matter and actual existence behind, is not the physical or natural being *(esse naturale)* of the agent, which remains within itself, but a projected similitude, (an *esse intentionale*) received in the knower according to the mode of the knower, and, when recognized as a *natural similitude, image, or sign* of its source, points back by the whole dynamism of its relational being to the source from which it came and of which it is the projected self-image. The second, complementary movement of *cognitive intentionality* now occurs when the consciousness of the knower, fecundated or informed by the image brought into it by the incoming intentionality of action, recognizes it explicitly *as a sign* or message from another and reaches out dynamically in the cognitive order, through the mediation of the sign, to *refer it by an intending relation* back to the thing itself from which it came. Thus, it retraces the incoming path of ontological intentionality by its own cognitive movement within consciousness, pointing back to the thing through the referential act of judgment. St. Thomas even sums up the whole activity of the universe in a dazzling synthetic vision under the image of the great circle of intentionality, proceeding from God to the universe, through the universe's action into man as knower, and from man back again to God its source. God by his creative action first projects his own divine ideas by ontological intentionality into created things, where they become the substantial forms of active natures; then the latter project themselves by self-communicative, self-imaging action into apt conscious receivers such as man, again by ontological intentionality; man, then, recognizing the projected intentional similitudes within his consciousness *as* signs and intentional similitudes, retraces by cognitive intentionality the incoming ontological intentionality of things back to their original sources in the active natures of the beings themselves, and then further traces these by causal inference back to their own original Creative Source, recognizing and paying homage to Him as such. Thus, the great circle of intentionality begins from God, passes through the created universe to man, then through man as knower and lover back to its Source again. Such is the dynamism of action, as it originates in the order of consciousness, passes into the ontological order, then transforms itself again into the order of consciousness, thus synthesizing being and consciousness into a single unified cosmic process of self-manifestation. To be, once again, is to be self-communicative.[25]

V. *Application to Kantian Agnosticism*

It seems to me that here lies the only satisfactory response to the challenge of Immanuel Kant that the human mind is incapable of transcending its own consciousness to know things-in-themselves, that it is not informed by the real world from without but projects its own a priori forms to inform the raw material of sensation from within. We notice first that Kant himself admits the necessary role of action in our knowledge. He insists that the human knower is not creative of its objects, as in idealism, but must wait for the world to act upon it. On the other hand, he insists that we cannot reach outside the immanent circle of our own consciousness to know the thing-in-itself, as it is in itself, but only as we structure the incoming raw material of sense by our own innate a priori forms. What this comes down to is that Kant on the one hand admits the necessity of the action of the thing-in-itself on us, but on the other hand denies that such action is in any way *revelatory* of the being from which it proceeds. Action is not in any way a self-communication, an information-bearing message from its source, but merely the delivery of amorphous material with no intelligible structure of its own, waiting to be intelligibly structured by us. The intelligible message is ours, not the thing's itself.

But Kant cannot have it both ways. He cannot hold *both* that the things in themselves truly act upon us, penetrate our consciousness, and at the same time that this action is non-informative, non-communicative of anything in the nature of these agents, in a word, that action is completely non-revelatory of nature. For such a notion of non-communicative action cannot be thought through coherently; it is an emasculated mental construct or abstraction, leaving out an integral part of what it abstracts, as though the conceptual abstraction of action from form and structure allowed an actual separation in reality. Real action of its very nature proceeds from the total being of the agent that is its source, according to its nature, and thus cannot help but be essence-structured action that is a self-manifestation precisely of that nature as actually existing. To be consistent Kant should either deny the role of action entirely, and thus move over to idealism—which he vehemently rejects—or accept the role of action and then admit that it is *to some degree* revelatory of its source.[26]

We might speculate that one consideration that blocks Kant's acceptance of action as an information-bearing medium, revelatory of the thing-in-itself, is an impossibly high ideal, inspired by the rationalists before him, of what such objective knowledge would have to be. He seems to be convinced that if we do not know the thing-in-itself directly and intuitively, without mediation of any kind, precisely as it is in itself apart from, prior to, and independently of any action emerging from it, then we do not know it all. There is no middle ground, i.e. the knowledge of a thing through the mediation of a self-manifesting action received in another, which action as a natural sign or icon of the agent *points back* to what the agent *must be* in itself in order to originate such an action. Knowledge of a nature as *this kind of actor* is for Kant no knowledge of the nature at all, which presumably would have to be in purely formal static terms, like the objects of geometry. Action is not a *natural sign* of anything. But it is precisely this middle ground of moderate "relational realism" that St. Thomas occupies—the only kind of epistemological realism, it seems to me, that fits our human condition. And after all, what is it that is most significant and crucial for us to know about the real world around us: the static inner essences of things as they abide in themselves alone in splendid isolation, or as they actually relate to us existentially and *make a difference* to us by their self-communicative action? The notion of a real being totally prescinding from all self-communication is probably not intelligible at all. If to be self-communicative belongs to the very inner nature of being in act, as St. Thomas invites us to recognize, then to form a notion of real being that abstracts from this is to leave behind the living core and abstract only an empty formal shell.

Thus Kant, demanding a utopian ideal of objectivity for realistic knowledge, which he rightly saw was unattainable, abandons realism entirely, throwing the baby out with the bath. On the other hand, the more modest action-mediated realism of St. Thomas we have outlined above does indeed provide adequate support for a carefully qualified *correspondence theory* of truth. Such a correspondence, however, can only be a dynamic correspondence or correlation between knowledge and known, not at all a naive picture theory representation purporting to mirror the object statically exactly as it "looks" if seen in itself apart from all action. What action as a natural sign reveals of its agent-source is not a mirror image or picture copy, but the presence in the thing of a set of *dispositional properties* (active potencies, in Thomistic terms) *for action* that characterize this being as distinct from others. It is quite possible for us through the mediation of action to recognize, classify, and draw out the implications of such active potentialities. But it is impossible in principle to draw exact pictures or copies of them. No active potentiality as such can be seen, touched, heard, felt, etc. (which is one reason empiricists must banish them like poison from their universe). Yet the knowledge of the dispositional properties of things is the most important and consequence-laden thing we need to know about them. It is just what Kant rejects as not up to his standards for objective knowing that is what we most want and need to know about things in order to live with them safely and fruitfully.

One of the surprising results of taking over this action-mediated realism as the basis for one's epistemology is to discover how aptly it fits the needs of contemporary physicists as they advance into the increasingly strange world of subatomic quantum physics. Physicists have now, they tell me, had to give up any attempt to describe subatomic matter in the old mechanistic terms of fully determinate measurable states of particles as they are in themselves independently of any interaction with the physical observer and his instruments. They have had to settle for a description of the subatomic world in terms of dispositional properties to react within such and such a limited range of ways to the active intervention of an observer using such and such instruments as intermediaries. Subatomic particles are known as *potential actors* on the stage with so and so, as potential "dance partners" with so and so. Surprising as it may seem to some, I am convinced that St. Thomas himself would be (or should be, if he understood the data and remained consistent with his own principles) quite at home with such a knowledge of the real world as true (humanly accessible) knowledge of the real world *the way it really is*, as the kind of world it really is.

We are now in a position to sum up our whole analysis of Thomistic epistemological realism as follows: action as the self-communication and self-revelation of being is the key to the whole of Thomistic epistemology: all knowledge of the real, for St. Thomas, is an interpretation of action. But accepting action as the medium of knowledge of the real also commits us to accepting the limitations built into its revelatory power both on the part of the finite communicator and the finite receiver: all action is both revealing *and* concealing. The self-revelation of being to the human observer is necessarily a *chiaroscuro* of light and darkness.

VI. Action as the Self-Fulfilment of Being

We have seen above how for St. Thomas all being naturally tends to overflow into action, and how such action is the natural self-communication and self-revelation of being, thus becoming the key to a realistic knowledge of being. Let us return now very briefly to a last crowning piece in St. Thomas' metaphysics of action. It is that action is not only the natural self-communication and self-manifestation of being, but also the final perfection of its *self-realization* or *self-fulfilment*. He is quite explicit on this point, as a few texts will suffice to show:

> The proper operation of each thing is...its end [or goal].[27]

> Every substance exists for the sake of its operation.[28]

> Each and every thing shows forth that it exists for the sake of its operation; indeed operation [activity] is the ultimate perfection of each thing.[29]

All things exist for the sake of their operations.[30]

The reason is that operation or activity is the passing into actuality of the active potencies of a being, and actuality is always better than potency, as the natural self-realization or self-fulfilment of its corresponding potency. Action is thus the final natural fruition or self-expression of any real nature, which *is* a unified center of natural potencies or dispositional properties for action. It follows that the final fruition of any being, its peak of self-realization, is reached only in its *self-communication to others*, its self-sharing with others. The final perfection of the whole of being, therefore, is to form a community of reciprocally self-communicating actors, which, on the level of self-conscious beings, is but another name for love. We leave the reader to meditate on his own on the mind-(and heart-) expanding implications of such a metaphysics of being and action.

Let us pause, before concluding, only to note how radically different is this notion of substance, as abiding center of activity, naturally oriented towards self-fulfillment through activity, from the so-called "classical" notion of substance attacked and rejected by so many, if not most, modern philosophers after Descartes and Locke. For Descartes, substance is defined as a self-enclosed essence which needs nothing, save God, to exist. For Locke, substance seems to be an inert, static, unknowable, underlying something whose sole role is to support accidents, somewhat like a pincushion in which pins are stuck. Bergson, process philosophers like Whitehead, and many others have justifiably criticized this static, self-enclosed notion of substance; but thinking this is *the* or the only classical notion of substance, they have gone on to reject the notion of substance entirely. How far removed both from this notion of substance and its criticisms is the authentic Thomistic conception! With its roots sunk deep in the metaphysics of action, it defines substance as an abiding center of activity, subsisting in itself as an autonomous center, but totally oriented toward self-communication through action as the supreme fulfilment of its being, a fulfilment which necessarily draws it into the vast web of interacting co-existents which make up the community of real beings. It would be a shame if contemporary philosophy, with its sensitivity to process and dynamism, were to let slip away from it unrecognized the rich resources of this highly dynamic notion of substance, just because modern philosophy has lost the secret of it from Descartes on, just because its Heideggerian "forgetfulness of being" has included the forgetfulness of being as active.

Conclusion

To sum up in a nutshell all that I have tried to unfold in the above paper: (1) Action, for St Thomas, is the *natural overflow of being in act*. (2) This overflow of action becomes the self-communication of being, thus drawing together the multiplicity of real beings into a true *universe*, a community of interacting members turned toward each other to form a dynamic unity of order among themselves through the bonds of action. (3) As the *self-revelation* of being, action lights up beings for each other, making mutual knowledge of each other possible, thus drawing the universe together in an *intentional* unity through knowledge and love, where the whole is recreated consciously in every personal member. To be is to self-communicate; to know is to pick up within oneself the self-communication of being. For "the actuality of each thing," St. Thomas tells us, in an extraordinarily pregnant phrase that integrates into his own system the whole Neoplatonic metaphysics of light—and also quite a bit of Heidegger—"is like an inner light, proper to that being,"[31] which shines forth through action to light up other beings. To know is to be "lit up" within oneself by the self-illumination of active being. And finally, (4) this process of self-communication and self-revelation manifests itself as the *supreme perfection* and *self-realization* of every being, the final *raison d'etre*, of being itself.

Notes

[1] Perhaps the finest study developing this whole theme on action and being is the still unsurpassed work of Joseph de Finance, *Être et agir dans la philosophie de S. Thomas* (2nd. ed.; Rome: Università Gregoriana, 1960).

[2] *Summa contra Gentes*, Bk. II, ch. 79. All translations will be my own.

[3] *De Potentia*, q. 2, art. 1.

[4] *Sum. c. Gentes*, I, 43.

[5] *Ibid.*, II, 7.

[6] Cf. De Finance, *Être et agir*, Ch. VII, sect. 3: "L'acte second", pp. 241-53.

[7] *De Potentia*, q. 2, art. 1.

[8] *Sum. c. Gentes*, II, 6.

[9] *Ibid.*, III, 69.

[10] *Comment. in Libros Sententiarum*, Bk. I, dist. 4, q. 1, art. 1.

[11] *Summa Theologiae*, Part I, q. 19, art. 2.

[12] On this whole question, cf. J. Péghaire, "L'axiôme *bonum est diffusivum sui* dans le néoplatonisme et le thomisme," *Revue de l'Université d'Ottawa*, 2 (1932), 5*-32*; M. J. Nicolas, "Bonum est diffusivum sui," *Revue Thomiste*, 55 (1955) 363-76; De Finance, *Être et agir*, Ch. II: Le dynamisme de l'acte.

[13] *De Potentia*, q. 7, art. 2. ad 9.

[14] Cf. text in note 11.

[15] Cf. *Sum. Theol.* I, q. 19. art. 2; *Sum. c. Gent.* I. 19; II. 16, 23, 43, etc. and De Finance, *Être et agir*, p. 71. This is also a favorite theme of the philosopher-theologian, Karl Rahner. See his "The Theology of the Symbol," in *Theological Investigations*, Vol. IV (London: Darton-Longmans-Todd, 1966), esp. Section 1: "The Ontology of Symbolic Reality in General," p. 224: "Our first statement, which we put forward as the basic principle of an ontology of symbolism, is as follows: all beings are by their very nature symbolic, because they necessarily 'express' themselves in order to attain their own nature." And again, p. 228: "Being *as such*, and hence as one, for the fulfilment of its being and its unity, emerges into a plurality—of which the supreme mode is the Trinity." Even within a finite being, this self-expression takes first place within the being itself, in that the finite substance expresses itself in emanating first its faculties, then its accidental operations, from within itself, which then return, so to speak, through their fruition in operation, to fulfill the substance itself, completing the cycle of self-realization through self-expression.

[16] *Sum. c. Gent.* II, 79.

[17] *Ibid.*, II. 94.

[18] See the profound treatment of this in Josef Pieper, *The Silence of St. Thomas* (New York: Pantheon, 1957).

[19] Two fine treatments of this much-neglected point can be found in: G. B. Arbuckle, "St. Thomas Aquinas and the Doctrine of Essence," in J. K. Ryan, ed., *Studies in Philosophy and the History of Philosophy* (Washington: Cath. Univ. of America Press, 1963), II, 104-36; Ralph Gehring, S.J., "The Knowledge of Material Essences according to St. Thomas Aquinas," *Modern Schoolman*, 33 (1955-56), 153-81.

[20] *Sum. Theol.*, I, q. 77, art. 1 ad 7.

[21] *Comment. in III Sent.*, d. 35, q. 2, art. 2, sol. 1.

[22] *In Symbolum Apostolorum Expositio*.

[23] Cf. especially the article of Arbuckle cited in note 19.

[24] *Sum. c. Gent.*, II, 74, etc.

[25] On the great circle of intentionality, see *Sum. Theol.*, I, q. 105, art. 3; I, 56, 2; *De Anima*, art. 20; *Comment. in II Sent.*, d. 12, q. 1, art. 3 ad 5; and the fine article of André Hayen, "L'intentionnalité de l'être et métaphysique de la participation," *Revue néoscolastique*, 42 (1939), 385-410, clearer on this point than his book *L'intentionnel selon s. Thomas* (Paris: Desclée de Brouwer, 1954; 2nd ed.).

[26] See the critique of Kant in my article, "Interpersonal Dialogue as the Key to Realism," in Robert Roth, ed., *Person and Community* (New York: Fordham Univ. Press, 1975), 141-75.

[27] *Sum. c. Gent.*, III, 26.

[28] *Ibid.*, I, 45.

[29] *Ibid.*, III, 113.

[30] *Sum. Theol.*, I, 105, 5.

[31] *Expositio in Librum de Causis*, cap. 1, lectio 6.

5.

DUNS SCOTUS ON INTUITION, MEMORY AND OUR KNOWLEDGE OF INDIVIDUALS

Allan B. Wolter, O.F.M.

Perhaps Scotus' most important contribution to medieval epistemology was his theory of intellectual intuition. He clearly regarded it as a departure from Aristotle, who "frequently talks about an intellection of the quiddity, but seems to say nothing about intellectual vision".[1] The terms, *intuition, intuitive* or *intuere*, of course, are of earlier origin, having been applied both to the introspective insight into the soul or its functions as well as to the 'face-to-face' vision of God in the after-life.[2] But Scotus gave the term a new existential twist, distinguished it sharply from its sense perceptual counterpart, and combined it with a non-intuitive theory of how substances and singulars are known.[3] The cautious and tentative way in which his conception of intuition matured would suggest he believed himself to be playing a pioneering role, — an hypothesis confirmed to some extent by the attitudes of William of Ockham and Peter Aureoli. The first cites Scotus to prove his own theory of an intellectual intuition of both sensible and intelligible objects was not an Ockhamistic innovation.[4] The second questions whether we actually have in this life any truly intellectual intuition such as Scotus or Ockham claim.[5] From the time of Scotus onward, however, the subject is never ignored by the late scholastics and continues to surface in various controversial contexts until given a new twist by John Major, Calvin's teacher, where it becomes a turning point in the history of theology.[6]

In this paper I would like to sketch briefly the main steps I see in the evolution of Scotus' thought until it reaches full bloom in the key text quoted at length by Ockham, where the implications of intuition for memory are explored. But first a word as to what he means by intuitive cognition.

The Nature and Types of Intuitive Cognition

From the many places where he describes it, intuitive cognition in general is a form of existential awareness.[7] At the intellectual level, it is an act of simple awareness or intelligence in which some object is grasped holistically [*simul totum*] as present and existing here and now. Hence it is not to be confused with the subsequent contingent or existential judgments that explicate its conceptual content. Rather it is contrasted primarily with abstractive cognition, which is simple awareness or understanding of the meaning of a term or proposition, and prescinds from whether the object or situation conceived of either exists in actuality or is here and now present.[8] At the level of sense cognition, Scotus attributes abstraction to the phantasy or sense imagination, and intuition to the external sense of sight. The former can conjure up a sensible *species* or representative likeness of an object no longer present or perceived as existing by some external sense.[9] In similar fashion at the intellective level, abstractive cognition depends causally upon some naturally prior intelligible species which goes proxy for the object it represents. By contrast, intuitive intellection has the thing itself, rather than a substitute species, interacting with the mind or soul to cause actual knowledge of itself.[10] Unlike Ockham, who critically developed and extended Scotus' conception to include the supernatural possibility of an intuition of nonexistence, Scotus sees the creature's awareness of existence as essential to any intuition it may have.

But because the memory of an initial intellectual intuition can linger on, Scotus found it necessary to expand his notion to include a distinction between perfect and imperfect intuition.[11] The need for such may have become apparent to him when he considered the implications of his argument for intellective intuition in the present life, based on our assurance of the truth of certain primitive contingent propositions. Perfect intuition is the awareness of a present existential situation; imperfect intuition, an opinion about a past or future existential situation. One might speculate as to how intuition of the future should be understood. It seems to refer to the veridical prophecies theologians attributed to Christ and the prophets, but it could also be an allusion to the reputedly high incidence of 'second sight' among the Scots. Be that as it may, it is only the memory of the past that Scotus explains in any detail, and here an antecedent perfect intellectual intuition is a necessary, but not sufficient, condition for our subsequent imperfect intuition. Though perfect intuition dispenses with a naturally prior intelligible species, the same is not true of imperfect intuition. Some form of intelligible species produced by the original perfect intuition must be impressed upon the memorative faculty.[12] And so imperfect intuition, inasmuch as it functions at a time when the object is not intuited as here and now present, introduces features common either to abstractive knowledge and/or Ockham's famed intuition of nonexistence.

A still further expansion of the notion of intuition seems warranted in view of the role Scotus assigns to intellective memory, in terms of its proximate and remote object of recall, a subject I will discuss later vis-a-vis the final stage of development. Before we can trace any growth in his thought, however, some relative dating of the works we shall be using is needed.

Chronological Note on Scotus' Works

Any attempt at a definitive chronology of Scotus' major works, perhaps, is at present premature. Yet enough data is available to suggest a working hypothesis for the four we wish to compare. There seems general agreement that the *Lectura* came at the beginning, and the *Quodlibetal Questions* near the end of his academic career. It seems fair then to take these as our boundary conditions. As for the *Ordinatio*, or revised commentary on the *Sentences* of Peter Lombard, work on the Prologue was under way at Oxford in 1300, a date mentioned in the second question,[13] and was still in progress at Paris in 1304, for Scotus refers in Bk. IV, distinction 25, to a papal bull he had seen with his own eyes that was issued by Benedict XI in the early months of that year.[14] A note in Scotus' own hand indicating the number of questions yet to be dictated in the last two distinctions of Bk. IV, reported by the scribe of the important Codex A,[15] would imply the revision was never completed, like that of the last question of the *Quodlibet*, which exists only in a partially emended form.[16] We seem justified in assuming that while Scotus may have by-passed certain particular questions en route, he had pushed on to drafting all but the final portions of Bk. IV before leaving Paris for his final teaching assignment in Cologne, where he died. Hence the questions in distinction 45 of this book we rank with questions six and thirteen of the *Quodlibet* as the most mature expressions of his thought on intuitive cognition. As for the two questions on intuition in his *Questions on the Metaphysics*, for internal reasons as well as Lottin's observations on the subject,[17] we date them after the *Lectura*, but prior to the question in *Ordinatio*, Bk III, on Christ's intuitive knowledge. This would permit us to demark four or five very broad steps in the evolution of his ideas on the intellect's powers of intuition.

Lectura I, the Incipient State of Development

In these lectures given before the turn of the century, the technical distinction between abstractive and intuitive cognition appears only in the second book, when Scotus speaks of angelic knowledge. In the first book, the doctrine of intellective intuition seems only implicit, and even the term "intuitive", as opposed to "vision", seems to have been *obiter dictum*.[18] Whereas Ockham introduced his theory of intellectual intuition already in the Prologue to his *Ordinatio* and made it central to his whole epistemology, Scotus sets forth his ideas as to how our intellect functions only in distinction 3, and with no explicit mention of its capacity for intuition. His main concern was what a theologically tenable account of its adequate object might be. His first ideas on the subject appear in simplified form in the *Lectura* as part of the larger question: Is God the first object of knowledge as Henry of Ghent claimed?[19] And the expanded version of the *Ordinatio* devotes an entire question to the topic.[20]

Like most of his contemporaries, Scotus held a basically Aristotelian theory of knowledge, which he modified only slightly in the interests of an earlier Franciscan-Augustinian tradition.[21] Roughly what is relevant about this common theory is that man's intellect lies midway between the cognitive powers of the brute beast on the one hand and the Judeo-Christian "angel" or the philosophers' "Intelligence" on the other. Where the brute knew only material and sensible things and the angel the spiritual and immaterial, man's proper intellectual object is the essence or quiddity of what is sensible or material. Working with the aid of an agent intellect, man's mind is able to grasp the universal or immaterial aspects, whereas his senses by contrast are concerned with the particular material or accidental features. Hence the cognitive maxim: *Intellectus est universalium, sensus particularium.*

While Scotus as a philosopher was willing to accept this tripartite division of cognitive faculties as a fair description of what normally moved brute, man and angel to know, he could not, as a theologian, regard it as an adequate account of the nature of the human intellect as such.[22] For if the face-to-face beatific vision of God that Paul spoke of was to be explained in terms of some sort of Aristotelian intellectual habit given in heaven, then by its nature, our intellect must at least be able both to know and be moved by something other than sensible quiddities. Hence Scotus' complex counter proposal as to what constitutes the adequate object of our intellect, based on what we can know under optimum conditions and not just what we know at present through the medium of the senses.

Implicit in this enlarged conception of our intellect's nature as a cognitive potency is its natural capacity to know intuitively as well as abstractly, once the soul is freed from the body. Since we have treated elsewhere of the manifold distinctions Scotus makes in this connection,[23] we only note briefly here that he distinguishes between the intuitive cognition we can receive naturally and what can be obtained through the interaction of natural causes. Since no form of intuitive cognition does violence to the intellect, but perfects it as a receptive potency, we can even be said to be "naturally inclined" to receive knowledge impressed directly by anything as existing and present to it, be it the divine nature or the essence of a creature. Nevertheless, even in its separated state, our intellect — which is but little less than the angel's in this respect — can only be moved naturally to such intuitive knowledge by created beings.[24] And in such a case, the intellect is not purely passive, but it cooperates as a partial, essentially ordered efficient cause, with the created object itself (for natural intuitive cognition), just as it cooperates with an intelligible species that represents the object (for natural abstractive cognition).[25] In the supernatural face-to-face vision promised in heaven, however, God's essence is not a naturally moving object, nor does the created intellect act or coact with it, but God moves the passive intellect of the blessed through his will, and thus properly speaking he is a voluntary or supernaturally gratuitous object. But because God's will and essence are really identical, the intuition that results is not primarily a knowledge of

God's voluntary action as such but rather a vision of the divine essence itself. Here, at least, Scotus seems to have introduced a distinction between the direct causal action of the object known intuitively and what terminates the intentional act of knowing. We shall have occasion to return to this distinction in discussing the dual object that seems to be involved in imperfect intuition of past experiences.

Second Stage: Lectura II on Angelic Intuition

In the first distinction, question six, of Bk. II Scotus discusses the precise formal reason why the human soul and an angel are specifically different, and why the latter is more perfect in nature than the former. But he makes it quite clear that the reason is not to be found in any intrinsic specific difference in their respective intellectual powers. Once our soul is freed from its embodied state, our mind might even equal an angel's.[26] Consequently, when he raises the question of angelic knowledge later in the second part of distinction three, he can appeal to his theory of what we can know in the afterlife to indicate how his account of angelic cognition differs from that of Henry of Ghent, Aquinas and others. Speaking of the created intellect's power he writes:

> Know that an intellect is capable of two sorts of knowledge and intellection, for it can have one that abstracts from all existence, and another of a thing present in its own existence... The first sort of knowledge, according to which the intellect abstracts from all existence, is called "abstractive", whereas the other, according to which the intellect sees the thing in its existence, is called "intuitive". It is not called "intuitive" because it is not "discursive", however, but rather because it is distinguished from that abstractive knowledge, which knows a thing in itself through a species.[27]

The *Ordinatio* version is essentially the same except that Scotus suggests this technical usage is peculiarly his own. "I may speak briefly, I call knowledge of the quiddity itself 'abstractive'...[and] that of a thing according to its actual existence or of a thing present in its existence I call 'intuitive intellection' ".[28] Henry of Ghent had used the term "intuitive" as opposed to "discursive" reasoning, and earlier Scotus himself had employed it in this sense when he wrote of the univocal concept of being or *ens*, predicable of substance but abstracted from accidents: "This is all that we know intuitively of substance, and no more".[29] But here he is using it in the sense of an intellectual vision of existence or the existent. And since many of his colleagues, unlike Henry of Ghent, were asserting that the beatific vision of the divine involved a created species infused by God,[30] Scotus insists that even an infused species yields nothing but abstract knowledge, a point he will bring up again in discussing Christ's knowledge.

Though he illustrates the difference between these two types of knowledge with our intellect in mind, and by analogy with our external and internal sense knowledge,[31] in neither the *Lectura* nor the Ordinatio versions does he hint that we possess intellective intuition already in this life, but only that we look forward to having it in the next. Once he had introduced the intuitive-abstractive distinction in the second book of the *Lectura*, he had occasion to refer to it several times in revising the first book as an *Ordinatio*, for instance, in his famous "coloratio" of Anselm's *Proslogion* argument for God, absent in the *Lectura*, where he is referring ahead to distinction three that deals with the object of the intellect and the knowledge it possesses.[32] But even in stressing the certitude we have of our own cognitive acts, he apparently failed to recognize that this reflective knowledge is itself a clear-cut case of intellectual intuition, as he later did, for instance, in the *Quodlibet*.[33] Indeed, the admission that we already may enjoy some measure of intellective intuition at present marks the advent of the next step in his thinking.

Third Stage: Scotus' Questions on the Metaphysics

The first of the two questions relevant to intuition is question three of Bk. II.[34] It asks whether the essence of God or any other immaterial substance can be known by us in this life. To solve it Scotus turns once more to the parallel between the sense and intellective functions. There are four degrees of sense knowledge, he informs us. The first is the intuition of a thing as present in its own nature and not known either through a species or a process of reasoning. Seeing color is the sense perceptual example given. The second degree is knowledge through a species or likeness produced by the thing itself, e.g. our phantasy imagines some color we have seen. The third degree is through a species fabricated by the cognitive power itself from several proper species initially impressed upon it, for instance, when we picture a gold mountain to ourselves, or imagine something seen as gray or pale black to be pitch black. Beyond these three forms of *per se* knowledge are *per accidens* "perceptions" which involve opposites or a subject consisting of an aggregate of accidents. Each type of sense knowledge has its analogue at the intellectual level. The first two correspond to intuitive and abstractive cognition as explained at the previous stage. That of creative imagination has its intellectual counterpart in the essential definitions we form by putting together the differential notions arrived at by the classical "via divisionis" or investigative technique of Plato. Beyond these three degrees of *per se* knowledge is the way in which we construct descriptions of what is transempirical, using negative and accidental features which we add to the core notion of "thing" or being". In analyzing the nature of our God-notions in question 1, distinction 3, Bk. I of both the *Ordinatio* and *Lectura*, Scotus had made use of this constructive technique. But what is interesting about the present question, so far as intuition is concerned, is his admission: "As for the first degree, namely intuitive cognition, it is doubtful whether it is in the intellect in our present life. It seems however that it is".[36] Here for the first time, if our dating is correct, Scotus recognizes the fact that we may have intuitive cognition in this life. The argument he gives is the familiar one used to prove we shall have it in the afterlife, namely our intellect is not by its nature an inferior power to that of vision in the eye. This is not an apodictic proof and leaves the question open to doubt, however. The reason for the doubt becomes more apparent when he cites an instance of what he had in mind as a possible candidate. "If one could hold that to know intuitively can pertain to the intellect, then one could say that some act of the intellect accompanies every distinct act of the sense, and this intellection is vision".[37] The reason this is open to doubt, I suspect, is that it seems to belong to the indistinct, or semiconscious peripheral intellections he speaks of in another context,[38] and that we can say of it, as he says of a similar intellection later on in the *Metaphysics*:[39] "Here is another act which is reflex, but is not perceived because it occurs simultaneously" with some act of direct knowledge. Even in as late a work as the *Quodlibet*, he admitted "we do not experience it as certainly" as we do abstractive cognition, "but it is possible" to do so.[40] This I think became apparent in the subsequent two stages of development, when he discussed the knowledge of Christ in this life and our own ability to recall past existential situations.

But there is still another interesting point about the present text we are considering. Whatever is to be said about whether or not we have such intuition at present, it is quite clear to him that "here at least, no separate substance is known by us according to this first degree of knowledge, or even in the second way, for the species would have to originate immediately from that object — which never happens. For the only species we receive is through the sense, or is fashioned by the intellect from what it receives".[41] And he goes on to show that this limitation imposed on our intellect through its linkage with the senses, excludes it from knowing intuitively not only separate or purely spiritual substances, but any substance whatsoever. And he explains precisely how we construct descriptions of corporeal substances, or a spiritual but not "separate" substance like our soul, in terms of what is accidental to it (acts of intellection and volition). In short, we have no intuitive intellection of material substances as such, and the same holds good for the *haecceity* or individuating difference, as Bk. VII of the *Metaphysics* makes clear. In all such cases our intellection of substance and the individual *qua* individual is not knowledge by acquaintance, but by description, to use Russell's distinction.

Though Scotus deals extensively with the metaphysical question of what makes creatures individual in both the *Sentence* commentaries and the *Questions on Metaphysics*,[42] it is only in the latter that he devotes a special question to whether the singular is *per se* knowable by us. And in his reply he distinguishes between two aspects. "The question is metaphysical insofar as it asks about the intelligibility in an unqualified sense; it pertains to a treatise on the soul insofar as one inquires about our intellection of the singular".[43] In reply to the metaphysical question, he shows first of all that the singular is intelligible *per se*, something certain "Aristotelians" had called into question; secondly, how it is a primitive intelligible, because the individuating difference or *haecceity* is something positive in addition to a thing's specific nature; and thirdly, how as a primitive intelligible it relates to the two types of intellection, intuitive and abstractive cognition.

> There are two sorts of intellection, one quidditative, which abstracts from existence; the other, called vision, which is of the existent *qua* existing. Though the first usually concerns the universal, it can also be primarily of the singular. And whenever it is, it has to do primarily with the singular [rather than the specific] nature. For the singular as such is further determined by existence, for *qua* singular it abstracts from existence, just as the universal [nature] does. The second sort of intellection is of the simultaneous whole, that is of the singular *qua* existing. And in this way Aristotle's *simul totum* is glossed. It includes no accident, but only existence which is not of the essence of anything, neither as a *quid* nor as an individual that participates in a *quid*. Now the singular is not primarily an object of this second type of intellection, nor vice versa.[44]

Having shown at the metaphysical level that intellection of singularity and intuitive intellection are essentially independent of one another, Scotus takes up the psychological problem. How is the singular known if our intellect only grasps what is common and is intricately linked with on-going sense functions in its initial intellections? Since Scotus has often been misrepresented as holding we intuit the singular intellectually, it is interesting to find him insisting we have no *per se* knowledge of the singular at all, be it intuitive or abstractive, sense perceptual or intellectual. His task, as he sees it, is twofold. "First we must see just why our intellect in its present state does not grasp the singular *per se*, nor does the sense sense it; secondly, how in some way we do understand and sense the singular, while in another way we do not".[45] If twin objects of the same species were to appear at the same time and place, our intellect would judge them to be one individual, not two; nor would our senses discern them as two. Yet each has its own *haecceity*, he argues, and does not lose it because it happens to be in the same place simultaneously with another. How then do we know the singular? By reflecting upon the phantasm, it is said, for according to Aristotle in *De anima* III,[46] we know it be a process that is not straightforward, but like a line that bends back upon itself. Though Scotus does not seem particularly interested *per se* in exploring the precise feedback mechanism involved, he does express dissatisfaction with Averroes' account and suggests an alternative.

Another explanation is that in the sense imagination there is a confused something either of substance with accidents or an aggregate of many accidents modifying one another. Now the intellect in grasping the universal abstracts each of these until finally it understands the universal, namely its nature, which is in fact a 'this', but is not grasped intellectually as such, but rather with those accidents that are proper to it. And to this the intellect joins the notion of a subject with accidents... The resulting concept is neither irreducibly simple like "being", nor is it a quidditative concept like "man", but is only a quasi-*per accidens* notion, like "a white man" — although it is not really *per accidens* in that way. But this is the more determinate conception we come to in this life. For we never arrive at anything such that, as we conceive of it, to be in another would be contradictory for it, and without such a concept we shall never conceive the singular distinctly.[47]

The same construction process seems operative here as in the case of forming a concept of substance, be it immaterial or material, described in the earlier text from the *Metaphysics*. We are not only not intuitively in contact with the *haecceity* associated with any singular object but we have no proper abstract knowledge of it *per se*. In the first case, that of the substantive aspects of the object holistically presented in the perceptual field, we eventually come up with a description that zeroes in on one particular species. Here, in the case of the individual our description specifies the accidents peculiar to it. I have suggested that here Scotus is using a technique resembling, if not identical with, that of Russell's "principle of abstraction that dispenses with abstraction", but yields concepts that are not second intentions but first intentions directly predicable of the object described.[48] There is no reason for thinking Scotus ever abandoned the position that the first indistinct concept we have is of the "species specialissima" of that sense object that most forcibly impresses our senses.[49] "Only an intellect that could receive the action of the object immediately could be moved by its singularity; not one which is only receptive through some intermediary action. Only the angelic intellect is of the first sort; it sees immediately the singular material object. Our intellect is of the second sort where the nature only acts by means of something produced in the sense".[50] Since we are object orientated in our initial awareness of the world, our first intellectual cognition will not be intuitive, as it is for Ockham, but abstractive. Not until Scotus recognizes that the conscious reflection upon our own cognitive acts is a form of intuition, and that these acts as real accidents in the mind or soul are the "things" that interact directly with the intellect without benefit of species, are there grounds for ascribing to him, at least implicitly, the doctrine that we have an intuitive intellection of singular mental events. But this recognition of reflection as a form of intuition, though hinted at here, is asserted categorically only at the next stage in the evolution of his thought.

Fourth Stage: Christ's Intuitive Cognition

As Peirce was quick to perceive, it was their meticulous philosophical analysis of what they believed that made the theological speculations of Scotus and Ockham of more than passing historical interest to a philosopher-scientist like himself. In his Christology, which is the subject of the first half of his commentaries on Bk. III of the *Sentences*, Scotus is content to explore the possibilities open to a human nature in which the Word, a divine person, became incarnate. For here too he has a methodological principle that allows him to move from possibility to probable actuality. "In extolling Christ, I prefer to praise him too much than fail by defect, if through ignorance I must fall into either excess".[51] In distinction 14 he applies this technique to a discussion of what Christ's soul could have known. The Gospel's description of the Word, "through him all things came into being" (Jn. 1, 3) suggested the Son, as the Wisdom of the Father, was in a special way the locus of the archetypal creatural ideas described by Augustine. Medieval theologians generally agreed Christ's soul must have possessed from the outset the most perfect vision of the Word granted to any creature. But how reconcile this with that other Gospel statement, "Jesus, for his part, progressed in wisdom and age and grace before God and man" (Lk. 2, 52). Many intriguing solutions were suggested by contemporaries and their pros and cons weighed carefully by Scotus. One was that of Aquinas.[52] In addition to its vision of the Word with its creatural archetypes and scenario of creation, Christ's soul, like the angels on the morn they were created, was also impressed with the intelligible species or forms of each creature in its own nature. This infused knowledge in Christ's possible intellect permitted no growth. But he also had an agent intellect, whose function it was to make the intelligible species actual by abstracting them from the sense images or phantasms and impressing them in the possible intellect. It was in this way that Luke's Gospel is to be understood.

Scotus' main difficulty with this theory stemmed from its use of "intelligible species". Since they abstracted from both singularity and existence, according to Aristotle, it was difficult to see how they would do the job Aquinas assigned to them. It would take us too far afield to detail his counter proposal. What is of interest is the new light it sheds on his notions of intuition and abstraction. We can bypass the first two questions which concern Christ's intuitive human knowledge or vision of the Word, and turn to the third, which treats of what his soul could know of things in themselves.[53]

Cognition of this sort is twofold, abstractive and intuitive, as was pointed out in the case of the angels. Both the nature which precedes singularity and the singular itself can be known in either way. Furthermore, it seems probable to attribute to the soul of Christ the perfection the angels had as regards intelligibles, since according to Augustine cognition of things in the Word *(cognitio matutina)* is compatible with a cognition of things in themselves *(cognitio vespertina)*. If one looks simply to the different kinds of things, one could say Christ's soul knew all universals or quiddities through infused species, since the kinds of things are not infinite, as opposed to the possible individual instantiations thereof. And this would yield what is technically confused knowledge of singulars. And the knowledge would be abstractive and habitual. But since singulars are knowable in themselves, i.e. any possible *haecceity* could be known by acquaintance, if it existed, and remembered afterwards as something unique and distinct from any other singular, it would also be possible to infuse a distinct form or species proper to the individual, and then one would have to face the problem: could any finite intellect have an infinity of such individualized forms, even habitually? If one did not wish to make this move, one could admit at least that Christ's soul knew habitually and abstractively some singulars, those of the more noble natures, by infused species. And one would not have to assume either that his soul knew all these quiddities and singulars actually at one and the same time, since once habitual knowledge is in the mind, one can recall it in thought by a natural process.

But even proper species will not account for Christ's human existential knowledge. Here we need to turn to intuition. This can be of the nature or of the singular, but *qua* existing. It can also be perfect or imperfect, according to the time factor. Perfect intuition concerns an object existing here and now. Imperfect intuition is an opinion about the future or a memory about the past. Now it is obvious that Christ's soul did not have intuitively acquired knowledge of everything that existed. For Peter's sitting would not be suited to be known in this fashion unless it were present either in itself or in something in which it has existence in a more perfect way than in itself. But since we are not speaking here of what Christ envisioned in the Word, ths second alternative is excluded. And since many things never were present nor will be present to that human intellect in this fashion, Christ's soul could not have known all existents irrespective of the time of their occurrence in this fashion. Hence he concludes:

> If one claims [this soul] could have knowledge of all existents for all the different times when they existed by means of infused species, this is false. First because infused species represent the object as it prescinds from actual existence, since it represents things in the same way whether the object exists or does not exist and hence cannot be the ground for knowing the existent qua existent. Second, because truths knowable by intuitive cognition about existing things qua existing, viz. contingent truths, could not be known through any sort of innate species, since from a knowledge of its terms the truth of a combination of contingents could not be known, for the truth of their com-

bination is not included in the terms as the necessary truth of a scientific combination is included in the species and their terms. Therefore, both because of contingent truths knowable by intuitive cognition (which are contingent truths about existents insofar as they are existing) and in order to know existents actually in themselves, it is necessary to have the objects themselves present that they could be intuitively known and intuitively seen in themselves. This could never happen in regard to things themselves on their own unless these things in themselves according to their own proper existence were present. Only in this way could this intuitive cognition, be it actual or habitual, of everything whatsoever in itself be given to this soul [of Christ]...

But so far as imperfect intuition is concerned, which is an opinion about the future and memory of the past, which remains after perfect intuition — because from many such things known intuitively in a perfect way, many experiences and memories are left behind in the intellect, whereby those objects could be known according to their existential conditions, not as past but as present — I still say that this soul does not know all things in themselves.[54]

Here for the first time we find Scotus introducing a new argument for intuition. We need it to know in a non-inferential manner that anything exists, and we need it to account for the truth of contingent existential statements. And as if realizing this statement is not something applicable to what is special about Christ's intellect, but assumes something about the normal mechanism of how we know, he goes on to explain:

And if it be objected that all that remains behind from the presence of a thing is an intelligible species impressed upon the intellect and in the sensitive portion [of the soul], such as the imaginative power, an imaginable species, this is false, for what is left behind from a thing's presence is not only an intelligible species in the intellect whereby it is known with no time specification added, but another in the memorative potency. And these several potencies know the object under different aspects. One knows it as it exists presentially, the other knows it as something apprehended in the past, so that the apprehension of the past is the immediate object of the memory, and the immediate object of this past apprehension is the mediate object of recall. Also if some sensible is presented to a sense in this way, a twofold cognition can be caused in the intellect in virtue of this: one abstractive, whereby the agent intellect abstracts from a species in the phantasm a species of the quiddity qua quiddity, which represents the object absolutely and not as existing now or then. The other can be an intuitive cognition in the intellect whereby the object as existing cooperates with the intellect, and this can leave behind in the intellective memory an habitual intuitive cognition, which is not of the quiddity absolutely, as was the other abstractive cognition, but of the known object as existing, namely the way it was apprehended in the past. And by this experience Christ could be said to have learned many things, i.e. by intuitive cognitions, of those things known existentially and through the memories they left behind.

It is arbitrary whether we wish to consider this a separate stage or part of the following or final stage, for Scotus has capsulated the essentials of his mature position in what he says of Christ's experiential knowledge. In distinction 45 of *Ordinatio* IV he spells out in greater detail the intuitive powers he ascribes to a human intellect not united to the Word in speaking of what the departed souls could know.

Fifth Stage: Intuition Here and Hereafter

The first question is whether the intellect could use the habitual knowledge of quiddities acquired in this life when no longer linked to the phantasy or senses. The second asks: Could the soul acquire new knowledge in this state? Or must it be content to work with species or forms infused by God or the angels, as many of his colleagues maintained? He argues this theory denigrates the intellective nature of the human soul by implying it is functionally less perfect than a stone which seeks the center of the earth and rests there on its own. He argues that the soul could acquire both intuitive and abstractive knowledge, intuitive, because the intellect, working with the object itself rather than a substitute object or the phantasm, should be even more effective. "Such cognition, which is called intuitive, can be intellective, otherwise the intellect would not be certain about the existence of any object".[55] Abstractive knowledge would also be possible, since the agent intellect could produce intelligible species working directly on material objects just as it now does working with the sense image. This theory is recapitulated in question four to answer the question: Do the blessed know of the prayers we offer? But it is question three that throws light on what intuitive cognition Scotus thought we had in this life. It reads: "Could the separated soul remember past events that occurred when it was joined to the body?" To answer it, he sets forth his most complete analysis of sense and intellective memory.

> Assuming as certain there could be in us an act whereby the past *qua* object is known, I add that this act, which we call

"remembering", is not immediately about any past event, but only about some act of the remembering subject, and to exclude vegetative acts, chance actions or imperceptible acts generally, we limit ourselves to human acts. For I only remember that you sat here because I recall I saw or knew you sat here. On the other hand, though I know I was born, or that the world was created, I don't remember either, for I recall no act of mine that had this or that as its object. "Remembering is cognition of some past act of the person remembering where the act is recognized as being past". Given this definition of the term, certain things follow from the fact it is known as past and others from the sort of past object involved. From the fact that this knowledge is of the past four conclusions follow: First, we must understand that the potency or capacity to remember has an act after a lapse of time, otherwise it would not be the past *qua* past that is remembered. ...Second, memory perceives the flow of time between that instant or time in which the object remembered existed and the present instant of perception. Third, the remembered object confronting the person remembering is not present in itself, otherwise it would not be remembered as past. Fourth, since the object must in some sense be present to the act and it cannot be present in itself, it must be present in a likeness or species and then the memory will be conserving the species... Because of the special character of the object remembered, however, namely that it is a past act of the individual who remembers, three more certain conclusions follow: First, remembering will involve a double object: one ultimate or remote (viz. the something about which the person remembering had at one time a conscious or human act); the other, the proximate (viz. the past human act whereby he reached out to that other object). Second, since the potency for remembering requires a species, speaking of what is required for remembering *in toto*, this could not be impressed by the object when the latter no longer exists or is actually present. But this proximate object is a human act of the past. Therefore, while it did exist, the necessary species was impressed. And since the species of a past human act could not be impressed in any potency other than that which had this act as object, it follows then that the past act of knowing has to be the object of the potency for remembering. Third, only what concerns one's own act — where this is human — is subject to remembrance, for it is only through knowing one's own act as proximate object that we know its object qua remote object. Hence a person cannot remember the same sort of act in another as he can in himself. [56]

Scotus then goes on to discuss to what extent memory is a sense function and whether animals possess it; and then the question of whether Aristotle admitted intellective memory, and eventually continues with the passage Ockham thought embodied much of what he considered original and important, and quoted at length.

> As for this article, then, I say that in the intellective part there is memory and remembering, properly so called. For I presuppose that the intellect not only knows universals (which is true indeed of its abstractive ability that the Philosopher speaks of, for it alone is scientific), but also that it can know intuitively what the sense knows (for the more perfect and higher cognitive power in the same subject knows what the inferior power knows) and that it can also know of sensations. Both assumptions are proved from the fact that the intellect knows contingently true propositions and draws inferences from them. For to form propositions and to syllogize is proper to the intellect. But the truth of these concerns objects known intuitively, that is to say, under their existential aspect, which is something known by sense. Hence, all the aforesaid conditions for remembering can be found in the intellect. For it can perceive time, and has an act after a lapse of time, and so on. To put it briefly, it is possible to remember any object whose sense memory can be recalled. For the act which is the proximate object can be intuitively known when it exists and thus can be remembered later. Also many proximate objects that were never matters for sense remembrance, such as any past intellection or volition, can be recollected. Proof that man can remember such: Otherwise he could not repent of his bad will, make use of intellectual experience in the future, or from the fact that he had thought about such matters, set out to explore other consequences thereof. In short, we could do none of this were we unable to recollect past intellections and volitions... Clearly then some remembrance of both objects of its act, proximate and remote, is proper to the intellect. Some remembrance is so proper by reason of the proximate object, too, that it could not pertain to the sense, whereas some which pertains to the intellect in virtue of its proximate object, could also pertain to the sense, for instance, if the intellect intuitively recognized that I see something white and afterwards retains this knowledge and remembers that I saw something white. And here is a case where both proximate and remote objects are matter of intellective remembrance; it occurs whenever on the basis of such a past remembrance we draw a syllogistic inference to something else. In such a case, the proximate object cannot be the sensation of even the highest

sense... It can only be a remembrance of something intellective.[57]

Scotus' sharp distinction between remote and proximate objects of imperfect intuition suggests something similar is required for the original intuition. This was recognized by Ockham, and more recently by Bérubé.[58] The latter argues that Scotus professes an immediate realism in enumerating sensible objects before sensation as instances of intellectual intuition, and that this implies a direct and immediate grasp of the exterior object and of the singular by the intellect. Ockham, it seems, drew much the same conclusion, in appealing to Scotus as a precursor of his own position. All this overlooks, however, (1) the difference between Scotus' and Ockham's theories of cognition,[59] (2) the different mechanism Scotus ascribed to intellectual and sense perceptual intuition,[60] and (3) the difference between the existential status of the proximate and remote objects of memory (and presumably of the initial cognitive experience) that is recalled,[61] as well as (4) the different epistemic values Scotus attached to immediate introspective awareness of internal acts and that of "de cognitis a nobis ut nunc per sensus",[62] and perhaps most of all (5) Scotus' recognition, as indicated by his frequent references to the opening chapter of Aristotle's and Avicenna's *Physics*,[63] that perception is a process that moves from the indistinct to the distinct, and involves features that are both — upon later analysis — singular and universal, sensible and intelligible, intuitive and abstractive. "Indistinct" is the Anglo-Latin translation of συγκεχυμενον, which suggests the initial, unanalyzed, sense perceptual ὅλον, is not like a piece of granite in which the distinct minerals can be pointed out, but is rather like an amalgam or liquid mixture requiring distinct analytic techniques to isolate the components. To show why the second model fits better Scotus' account of how the intellect extracts the intelligible content, or analyzes the initial sense perceptual whole, would require another paper. Let me close, however, on this note. Earlier I suggested why Scotus was slow to recognize intellectual intuition as a distinct, yet integral, component of the perceptual process.[64] It is because the focal point of our intial interest and attention centers on what stands out most impressively in the perceptual field, whereas the awareness of its existence and presence, like that of being awake, lies in the penumbra of indistinct, peripheral intellections and visions. A special act of the will is required to bring to center stage, as it were, what is lurking in the wings. And this is precisely what happens when after the fact, we deliberately try to recall distinctly the bits of information that entered into our initial on-going experience. It is not surprising then that Scotus' most lucid account of intellectual intuition occurs in his description of intellectual memory, or that he feels the need to prove we had some intellectual awareness of the existential situation that serves as evidence for the two types of primitive contingent statements one needs to explicate its cognitive content. As for Bérubé's contention that Scotus deserves to be called an immediate, rather than a mediate realist, if this means nothing more than that *qua* intentional or tendential the cognitive act terminates directly with what is known, one can admit this. But this does not imply Scotus believed our intellect was ever in direct causal, as opposed to intentional, "contact" with the extramental object in the physical world. And it also leaves us with many of the epistemic problems associated with mediate realism. But then Scotus, unlike Ockham, had no desire to make intuition the keystone of his epistemology.

Notes

[1] *Quaestiones subtilissimae super libros Metaphysicorum Aristotelis*, VII, q.15, n. 9 (Vivès ed. VII, 404). Hereafter this work is referred to in the text as *Questions on the Metaphysics* and in the footnotes as *Meta*.

[2] M.-D. Roland-Gosselin, "Peut-on parler d'intuition intellectuelle dans la philosophie thomiste?", *Philosophia perennis*, hrsg. von F.J von Rintelen (Regensburg: J. Habbel, 1930) Bd.II, p. 711, suggests the term "intuitive knowledge" was introduced by the Franciscan school after the death of St. Thomas and entered Thomistic terminology through discussions with the Franciscans. He distinguishes four senses in which it was used: first as "vision" in opposition to faith (pp. 712-14); "direct insight" as opposed to discourse (pp. 714-715); "immediate knowledge" as opposed to mediate knowledge (pp. 716-720) and "vision of the individual" as opposed to that of the universal (pp. 721-730). On the history of the last sense, see Camille Bérubé, *La connaissance de l'individuel au moyen age* (Montréal: Presses de l'Université de Montréal/ Paris: Presses Universitaires de France, 1964). Henry of Ghent's distinction between the two ways in which we can know *(scire)* the existence of a thing, one "per seipsam ex evidentia existentiae suae apud scientem: ad modum quo scit ignem esse ille qui videt ignem praesentem oculis"; the other by inference (cf. Henricus Gandavensis, *Summa quaestionum ordinariarum*, art. 22, qq. 1 & 5 [Paris, 1520, photoreprint St. Bonaventure, N.Y: Franciscan Institute, 1953], I, 130L & 134C), and his critique of the "species" theory of the vision of God (Quodl.3, q.1[Paris, 1518, photoreprint Louvain: Bibliothèque S.J., 1961], f.47-48) undoubtedly influenced Scotus. Cf. Lectura I, prol.n.108 (XVI, 40).

[3] C. Bérubé, *op. cit.*, p. 179ff.

[4] Guillelmi de Ockham, *Scriptum in librum I Sententiarum Ordinatio*, prol. *Opera theologica* I (St. Bonaventure, N.Y.: Franciscan Institute, 1967), p. 44: "Ne autem ista opinio quantum ad notitiam intuitivam sensibilium et aliquorum mere intelligibilum tamquam nova contemnatur, adduco verba Doctoris Subtilis libro IV, distinctione 45, quaestione 3, duas praedictas conclusiones expresse ponentis, videlicet quod intellectus noster intuitive cognoscit sensibilia et quod intuitive cognoscit aliqua mere intelligibilia".

[5] Philotheus Boehner, *"Notitia Intuitiva* of Non-Existents According to Peter Aureoli, O.F.M. (1332)," *Franciscan Studies* 8 (1948), 399-410. "The importance of Scotus in regard to the theory of intuitive and abstractive cognition is shown by the fact that Aureoli, like Ockham, starts the explanation of his own theory with a critical discussion of that of Duns Scotus" (p. 391).

[6] Thomas F. Torrence, "Intuitive and Abstractive Knowledge from Duns Scotus to John Calvin", *De doctrina Ioannis Duns Scoti* (Romae: Commissio Scotistica, 1968), v. 4, pp. 291-305.

[7] Sebastian J. Day has given a virtually complete listing of the passages in the Wadding-Vivès

edition where Scotus treats the subject, together with a helpful analysis of the implications of each. See *Intuitive Cognition: A Key to the Significance of the Later Scholastics* (St. Bonaventure, N.Y.: The Franciscan Institute, 1947), pp. 48-139. To these should be added the texts from the *Lectura* and some references in Scotus' notes available in the *Ordinatio* or revised commentary on the *Sentences*, parts of which are available in the critical edition edited by the Scotistic Commission, *Ioannis Duns Scoti Opera* omnia (Civitas Vaticana: Typis Polyglottis Vaticanis, 1950-). Unless otherwise noted, quotations from the *Lectura* and *Ordinatio* I & II are from the Vatican edition, whereas those from *Ordinatio* III & IV are from Codex A, described at length in C. Balić's "De Ordinatione I. Duns Scoti disquisitio historico-critica", pp. 12*-28* in the first volume of this edition.

[8] To quote from a translation of his most mature work: "It is helpful to distinguish two acts of the intellect at the level of simple apprehension or intellection of a simple object. One is indifferent as to whether the object is existing or not, and also whether it is present in reality or not. We often experience this act in ourselves, for universals and the essences of things we grasp equally well whether they exist extramentally in some subject or not, or whether we have an instance of them actually present or not. We also have an empirical or *a posteriori* proof of this, for scientific knowledge of a conclusion or understanding of a principle can be equally present to the intellect whether what they are about is existing or not, or is present or absent. In either case, then, one can have an equal understanding of that term on which an understanding of the principle or conclusion depends. This act of understanding, which can be called 'scientific', because it is a prerequisite condition for knowing the conclusion and understanding the principle, can very appropriately be called 'abstractive' because it 'abstracts' the object from existence or non-existence, from presence or absence. But there is another act of understanding, though we do not experience it in ourselves as certainly, but it is possible. It is knowledge precisely of a present object as present and of an existing object as existing... This is so when it is attained in itself and not just in some diminished or derivative likeness of itself [i.e. an intelligible species]" *John Duns Scotus, God and Creatures: The Quodlibetal Questions*, trs. with an introduction, F. Alluntis and A.B. Wolter (Princeton and London: Princeton University Press, 1975; reprinted Washington, D.C.: The Catholic University of America Press, 1981), par. 6.18-6.19, pp.135-136; hereafter cited as *God and Creatures*.

[9] *Ibid*. par. 13.27 (p. 290): "There is some knowledge of the existent as such, such as that which grasps the object in its actual existence, e.g., the sight of color and in general of any sense perception involving the external senses. There is also knowledge of the object, but not as existing as such, either because the object does not exist or at least the knowledge is not of the object as actually existing. One can imagine color, for example, both when it exists and when it does not".

[10] Day sees the question of whether or not a species is involved in intuitive cognition "a problem that has exercised the ingenuity of Scotistic commentators for centuries" (*op. cit.* p. 105). In what follows, I hope to make clear to what extent a "species", in any capacity, functions in intuitive cognition.

[11] *Ordinatio* III, dist. 14, qu.3; Codex A, f. 155vb: "Loquendo autem de alia cognitione, scilicet intuitiva, quae est de natura vel singulari, ut concernit actualem exsistentiam, dico quod illa est vel perfecta, qualis est de obiecto ut exsistens praesentialiter, vel imperfecta, qualis est opinio de futuro vel memoria de praeterito". Cf. Vivès ed. XIV, 527.

[12] *Ibid.*, ff. 155vd-156ra: "Obiectum isto modo [scil. intuitive] non est cognoscibile nisi ut actualiter praesens in se vel in aliquo in quo habet esse perfectius quam in se [scil. in essentia divina]... Non esset igitur nata cognosci sessio Petri, nisi praesens esset sessio Petri in se; et ita cum multa obiecta nec fuerint nec esse potuerint praesentia illi intellectui [Christi] secundum exsistentiam actualem illorum, non potuit habere cognitionem intuitivam illorum. Et si dicatur quod [Christus] potuit habere cognitionem omnium exsistentium pro quacumque differentia

temporis per species infusas, hoc falsum est; tum quia species infusae repraesentant obiectum ut abstrahit ab exsistentia actuali, quia eodem modo repraesentat sive obiectum exsistat sive non exsistat, et per consequens non sunt ratio cognoscendi exsistens ut exsistens; tum quia veritates quae sunt cognoscibiles cognitione intuitiva de exsistentibus ut sunt exsistentia, videlicet veritates contingentes, non possunt cognosci per species qualescumque innatas, quia ex cognitione terminorm contingentium non potest cognosci veritas complexionis contingentium de illis terminis, quia illarum complexionum veritas non includitur in terminis, sicut in speciebus et terminis eorum includitur veritas necessaria complexionis scientialis. Oportet ergo — etiam propter veritates cognoscibiles cognitione intuitiva, quae sunt veritates contingentes quae sunt de exsistentibus ut exsistentia sunt, et propter exsistentia ipsa in se actualiter cognoscenda — habere ipsa obiecta in se praesentia, ut intuitive possint cognosci et intuitive in se videri. Et hoc non potest fieri in ipsis rebus in genere proprio, nisi ipsis rebus in se secundum suam propriam exsistentiam praesentibus et ita potest ista cognitio in genere proprio intuitiva actualis vel habitualis illi animae dari de omnibus. Et quoad hoc necesse est dicere quod profecit sicut alia anima, et obiecta alia aliquo modo cognoscit. Sed quantum ad intuitivam imperfectam, qualis est opinio de futuro et memoria de praeterito, quae relinquitur ex ista perfecta, quia de talibus pluribus perfecte intuitive cognitis derelicta sunt plura experimenta et plures memoriae in intellectu, quibus cognosci possint illa obiecta quantum ad conditiones exsistentiae, non ut praeterita, sed ut praesentia, adhuc dico quod etiam [non] novit omnia in genere proprio. Et si obiicitur quod ex re praesente non derelinquitur nisi species intelligibilis impressa in intellectu et in parte sensitiva, ut in virtute phantastica, species imaginabiles, hoc falsum est, quia de re praesente non tantum derelinquitur species intelligibilis in intellectu qua cognoscitur sub nulla differentia temporis, sed alia in potentia memorativa. Et istae potentiae cognoscunt obiectum sub alia et alia ratione. Una cognoscit obiectum ut exsistit praesentialiter, alia cognoscit ipsum ut in praeterito apprehensum ita quod apprehensio praeteriti est immediatum obiectum memoriae et immediatum obiectum illius apprehensionis praeteritae est obiectum mediatum recordationis. Ita etiam praesente aliquo sensibili sensui, potest virtute illius causari in intellectu duplex cognitio, una abstractiva, qua intellectus agens abstrahit speciem quidditatis, ut quidditas est, a specie in phantasmate, quae reprasentat obiectum absolute, non ut exsistit nunc et tunc; alia potest esse cognitio in intellectu intuitiva, qua obiectum cooperatur intellectui ut exsistens, et ab hac potest derelinqui habitualis cognitio intuitiva importata in memoria intellectiva, quae non sit quidditatis absolute, sicut fuit alia prima abstractiva, sed cogniti ut exsistens, scil. quomodo in praeterito apprehendebatur. Hoc modo per experientiam dicitur Christus multa didicisse, i.e. per cognitiones intuitivas, hoc est, illorum cognitorum quantum ad existentiam et per memorias derelictas ab eis''. Codex S (f. 191va/b) has virtually the same wording.

[13] *Ordinatio*, prol., n. 112 (I, 77). See A. G. Little, "Chronological Notes on the Life of Duns Scotus", *English Historical Review* 47 (1932), 573 and C. K. Brampton, "Duns Scotus at Oxford, 1288-1301", *Franciscan Studies* 24 (1964), 9-10, for an interpretation of this passage. If it refers to the short-lived euphoria the news of the defeat of the Egyptians by the Turks in alliance with the Christians in the battle of Medjamâa el-Morûdj on Dec. 23, 1299 brought to Oxford in June of 1300, one would have expected Scotus to qualify, or eliminate the remark, had he lived to complete the final revision of the *Ordinatio*. The internal structure of this question (absent from the earlier *Lectura*) suggests it may have been a university sermon.

[14] Little, *art. cit.*, p. 577; C. K. Brampton, *art. cit.*, pp. 9-10.

[15] See C. Balić, "De ordinatione...disquisitio historico-critica", p. 28*.

[16] *God and Creatures*, p. xxxiii.

[17] Odon Lottin, "L' *Ordination* de Jean Duns Scot sur le livre III des Sentences", *Recherches de théologie ancienne et médiévale* 20 (1953), 102-119.

[18] Of the six explicit uses in *Lectura* I a cursory reading revealed (viz. prol. n. 108; dist.3, n. 59, n. 112; dist. 8, n. 174; dist. 10, n. 3; dist. 13, n. 17), the first three seem to refer to "intuition" as opposed to "discursus" or reasoning; the last three refer to God's intuitive cognition. Only the first of these seems to contrast intuition with abstractive knowledge, and the second is of interest because it suggests that God, at least, has an intuitive cognition of nonexistence: "...in essentia cognoscitur creatura intuitive antequam sit" (dist. 10, n. 3; XVII, 115).

[19] *Lectura* I, dist. 3, nn. 88-123 (XVI, 258-273).

[20] *Ordinatio* I, dist. 3, nn. 108-201 (III, 68-123).

[21] On this tradition and Scotus' reaction to it, see the editorial notes re *Lectura* I, dist. 3, n. 313 (XVI, 350-351).

[22] *Lectura* I, dist. 3, n. 92 (XVI, 259): "Opinio, quae ponit quod quiditas rei materialis sit primum obiectum adaequatum ipsius intellectus, non est vera... Nullus catholicus potest hoc dicere, quia tunc esset alia potentia quando videret essentiam divinam in patria et alia immaterialia"; *Ordinatio* I, dist. 3, n. 113 (III, 70): "Istud non potest sustineri a theologo, quia intellectus exsistens eadem potentia naturaliter, cognoscet per se quiditatem substantiae immaterialis, sicut patet secundum fidem de anima beata".

[23] A.B. Wolter, "Duns Scotus on the Natural Desire for the Supernatural", *The New Scholasticism* 23 (1949), 281-317.

[24] *Ibid.*, pp. 294-300. Especially illuminating are Scotus' remarks on how the blessed in heaven can acquire new knowledge of the creatural world. See *Ordinatio* IV, dist. 45, q.2; Codex A, f. 267vb: "Ad quaestionem ergo dico quod anima separata potest acquirere cognitionem prius ignoti, et hoc tam cognitionem abstractivam quam intuitivam... Patet secundum, scilicet de cognitione intuitiva, nam causae illius sufficientes sunt obiectum in actuali exsistentia praesens, et intellectus agens et possibilis... Sed nec ista intellectio intuitiva haberi potest per speciem praesentem, quia illa repraesentat rem indifferenter exsistentem et non exsistentem, praesentem et non praesentem".

[25] Scotus' concession to the older Franciscan position (ascribed to Augustine) that the intellect is the sole efficient or active cause in intellection, was to admit that Augustine only attributed a partial activity to the soul or intellect; hence his frequent citation of that text from the *De Trinitate*, Bk. 9, ch. 12: "Obviously we must hold fast to the principle that everything which we know begets the knowledge of itself within us. For knowledge is born from both the one who knows and the object known". See e.g., *Lect.* I, dist. 3, n. 320 (XVI, 352); also n. 365 (p. 367) where he asks: "What then is the sufficient and precise cause of the knowledge produced? I say that the precise cause of intellection and of the knowledge produced is the intellective soul...and the object in itself, if it is present to the intellect according to itself, or the object in some representation, as in a species representing the object. Neither the object *per se* nor the intellect *per se*, but both together, form one sufficient cause". And he goes on to show how these two essentially ordered efficient causes coact to produce either intuitive or abstractive cognition. To the objection that when an intelligible species goes proxy for the existing object in abstractive cognition, it does so as a form in the possible intellect, he insists: "It is only coincidental so far as the basis for causing [*ratio causandi*] is concerned that one [the species] perfects the other [*qua* form]... Indeed, if the object itself were present, or if through some [divine] assistance, the species was present in a way other than as an [accidental] form of the intellect, still the intellect would understand in no less degree" (*ibid.* n.370, p. 369).

[26] *Lectura* II, dist. 1, q. 6, n. 291 (XVIII, 58): "Dico quod [anima et angelus] distinguuntur specie, et tamen non in ratione intellectivi et volitivi, nec ut comparantur ad actus; nec intellectiones

eorum et volitiones distinguuntur specie, licet limpidius unus intelligat alio". We are grateful to Father Luke Modrić, O.F.M., Praeses of the Scotistic Commission, for supplying page proofs of this forthcoming volume. See also *Ordinatio* II, dist. 1, q. 6, n. 319 (VII, 155).

[27]*Lectura* II, dist. 3, nn. 285, 287-288: "Sciendum est quod in intellectu potest esse duplex cognitio et intellectio, nam una intellectio potest esse in intellectu prout abstrahit ab omni exsistentia, — alia intellectio potest esse rei secundum quod praesens est in exsistentia sua... Quod sit ponenda secunda cognitio in intellectu, patet: quod est perfectionis in potentia inferiore, est in superiore; sed hoc est perfectionis in potentia inferiore (ut in visu) quod potest cognoscere rem secundum suum verum esse exsistentiae; igitur similiter in intellectu hoc ponendum est, quod ipse potest cognoscere rem in exsistentia sua. Praeterea, prima istarum cognitionum, secundum quam intellectus intelligit rem abstrahentem ab omni exsistentia, dicitur esse cognitio 'abstractiva', — et alia, secundum quam videt rem in exsistentia sua, dicitur esse cognitio 'intuitiva' (non autem dicitur esse cognitio 'intuitiva' quia non est 'discursiva', sed prout distinguitur contra abstractivam qua per speciem cognoscitur res in se)". — Some years ago the Scotistic Commission supplied the author with this text reconstructed for its use from Codices V and F by Father Barnabas Hechich, O.F.M.

[28]*Ordinatio* II, dist. 3, n. 321 (VII, 553).

[29]*Lectura* I, dist. 3, n. 112 (XVI, 266): "Unde dico quod intellectus noster primo cognoscit accidentia, a quibus abstrahit intentionem entis, quod praedicat essentiam substantiae sicut accidentis; et tantum intuitive cognoscit de substantia, et non plus. Hoc sicut dixi, experitur quilibet in se, quod non cognoscit plus de natura substantiae nisi quod sit ens. Totum autem aliud quod cognoscimus de substantia, sunt proprietates et accidentia propria tali substantiae, per quas proprietates intuemur ea quae sunt essentialia substantiae". The "intuemur", perhaps, refers to the non-inferential way of applying substantive names, indicative of the "species specialissima", to objects in the sense perceptual field — a vague form of intellectual knowledge that precedes even the abstraction of the distinct notion of being, and is another form of the verbal skills he calls "habitus vocalis de substantiis" *Meta.* II, q. 3 (VII, 114). Cf. A. B. Wolter, "A 'Reportatio' of Duns Scotus' Merton College Dialogue on Language and Metaphysics", *Sprache und Erkenntnis im Mittelalter*, Bd. 13.1 *Miscellanea Mediaevalia*, hrgb. von Albert Zimmermann (Berlin/New York: Walter de Gruyter, 1981), 179-191.

[30]Scotus seems to have studied Henry's *Quodl.* 3, q. 1, extensively where Henry asks: "Utrum ab intellectu creato in vita beata videbitur deus per aliquam speciem mediam" *(op. cit.)*. What prompted the question is that in color vision light is insufficient to determine the organ but the species of color is needed to inform it. This suggests that the light of glory may be insufficient without some created species in the beatified intellect. Henry rejects the theory, as did Scotus, though not for the same reasons.

[31]*Lectura* II, dist. 3, n. 290 (Hechich text): "Ista autem duplex cognitio potest apparere in cognitione sensitiva, nam aliter cognoscit imaginativa quam visiva; visus enim cognoscit rem in exsistentia sua dum praesens est, sed imaginativa imaginatur res dum absentes sunt sicut quando sunt praesentes; nunc autem quae sparsa sunt in inferioribus, unita sunt in superioribus, et ideo intellectus quando cognoscit rem in exsistentia sua, tunc dicitur videri et esse visus, sed quando cognoscit rem abstrahendo ab exsistentia, tunc dicitur cognoscere sicut imaginativa".

[32]*Ordinatio* I, dist. 2, n. 139 (II, 211): "De differentia intellectionis intuitivae et abstractivae et quomodo intuitiva est perfectior, tangetur distinctione tertia et alias quando locum habebit". In addition to the references cited by the editors, Scotus could well be referring also to the question on the adequate object of the intellect.

[33]*God and Creatures* par. 6.19 (pp. 136-137): "Such knowledge of the existent *qua* existent and present is something an angel has about himself. For Michael does not know himself in the

way he would know Gabriel if Gabriel were annihilated, viz. by abstractive cognition, but he knows himself as existing and as existing in a way identical with himself. He also is aware of his intellection in this way if he reflects upon it, considering it not just as any object in which one has abstracted from existence or non-existence in the way he would think of another angel's knowledge, if such did not actually exist; rather he knows himself to be knowing, that is to say, he knows his knowledge as something existing in himself. This knowledge possible for an angel, therefore, is also simply possible for our intellective power, because we have the promise that we shall be like the angels. Now this sort of intellection can properly be called 'intuitive', because it is an intuition of the thing as existing and present".

[34] *Meta*. II, q. 3, nn. 23-25 (VII, 112-114).

[35] *Ordinatio* I, dist. 3, nn. 58-61 (III, 42-43); *Lectura* I, dist. 3, nn. 50-60 (XVI, 244-246).

[36] *Meta. ibid.*, n. 23 (pp. 112-113). There are indications the edited text includes an earlier version of the parallel between sense and intellectual knowledge in nn. 23-25, namely in n. 119 (p. 110) and there Scotus seems to deny categorically that we have such intuition in this life. "In intellectu notitia visionis vel intuitiva, quae est prima cognitio, non est in via possibilis". Day (*op. cit.* p. 97) has attempted to explain away both this and the later version as not indicative of Scotus' views or as referring only to the intuition of immaterial substances. Admittedly we could do with a critical edition of this question, but the manuscripts I have examined contain both versions. The way Scotus introduces paragraph n. 23 ("Ad pleniorem igitur solutionem...") suggests this revision may have been appended later and reflects his growing awareness of the fact that some intellectual reflection is required for "perceiving darkness" (the example he gives of *per accidens* vision) in n. 19. See for instance the note he added to the *Ordinatio* I, dist. 3, n. 140ff. (III,87ff).

[37] *Meta*. II, q. 3, n. 24 (p.113): "Si vero teneatur quod intellectus hic posset cognoscere intuitive, potest dici quod omnem actum distinctum sensus concomitatur aliquis actus intellectus circa idem obiectum; et ista intellectio est visio".

[38] In an interesting "reportatio" found in the Wadding-Vivès edition *(Opus oxoniense* II, d. 42, q.4, n. 10; XIII, 460) Scotus explains that "for every single perfect and distinct intellection existing in the intellect, there can be many indistinct and imperfect intellections existing there. This is evident from the example of vision, the field of which extends as a conical pyramid at the lower base of which one point is seen distinctly, and yet within that same base many things are seen imperfectly and indistinctly; but of these several visions, only one is perfect, that upon which the axis of the pyramid falls. If this is possible in the sense, all the more so is it possible in the intellect". The will can focus on any one of these peripheral intellections and "by taking pleasure in it, firms it up and intends it [directly] whereas one that is nilled or in which the intellect does not take pleasure is weakened and diminished". It is in this way the will controls the intellect.

[39] *Meta*. IV, q. 3, n. 7 (VII, 339).

[40] *God and Creatures* par. 6.19 (p. 136). See text n. 33 supra.

[41] *Meta*. II, q.3, n. 24 (VII, 113): "...sed saltem secundum primum gradum cognitionis, nulla substantia separata hic a nobis cognoscitur. Nec secundo modo, quia oportet quod species illa immediate originaretur ab illo obiecto, quod non fit; nullam enim speciem recipimus nisi vel per sensus vel quam intellectus facit ex receptis".

[42] *Ordinatio* II, dist. 3, pars prima, qq. 1-7 (VII, 391-516); *Lectura* II, dist. 3, nn. 1-229 (Hechich text); *Meta*. VII, q. 13 (VI, 402-426).

⁴³*Meta.* VII, q. 15, n. 3 (VI, 436).

⁴⁴*Ibid.* n. 4 (pp. 436-437).

⁴⁵*Ibid.* n. 5 (p. 437).

⁴⁶*De anima* III, ch. 4 429b15-17.

⁴⁷*Meta.* VII, q. 15, n. 8 (VI, 439).

⁴⁸A. B. Wolter, "An Oxford Dialogue on Language and Metaphysics", *Review of Metaphysics* 31 (June 1978), 639-640; *idem*, "A 'Reportatio'...", p. 189.

⁴⁹*Lectura* I, dist. 3, n. 70 (XVI, 251); *Ordinatio* I, dist. 2, n. 73 (III, 50).

⁵⁰Meta. VII, q. 15, n. 6 (VI, 438).

⁵¹*Ordinatio* III, dist. 13, qq. 1-4; Codex A f. 153va: "In commendando Christum malo excedere laudando quam deficere a laude, si propter ignorantiam oporteat in alterum incidere"; cf. Vivès, n. 9 (XIV, 463).

⁵²*Summa theologiae* III, q. 9, art. 3; q. 10, art. 2; q. 11, art. 1; q. 12, art. 1 & 2.

⁵³*Ordinatio* III, dist. 14, q. 3, Codex A, f. 155va-156ra; cf. Vivès ed. XIV, 521ff.

⁵⁴See note 12 *supra* for the Latin text of Codex A, which differs significantly from that of the Vivès ed.

⁵⁵*Ordinatio* IV, dist. 45, q. 2, Codex A, f. 267vb: "Talis autem cognitio, quae dicitur intuitiva, potest esse intellectiva, alioquin intellectus non esset certus de aliqua existentia alicuius obiecti"; cf. Vivès ed. *ibid.* n. 12, p. 305.

⁵⁶*Ibid.* q. 3; Codex A, f. 268rb; the translation was made from a transcript of this MS. Since the text differs only slightly from the edition (Vivès, nn. 4-6, XX, 326-327), it seems unnecessary to cite it in Latin. Prof. M. M. Adams and I plan to publish the MS text with a translation and commentary.

⁵⁷*Ibid.* nn. 17-18 (pp. 348-349); Codex A, fol. 269ra. Cf. Guillelmi de Ockham, *op. cit.*, pp. 44-46.

⁵⁸Bérubé, *op. cit.* p. 201.

⁵⁹Scotus believed that what was given primitively at the conceptual level was "commonness" or the *natura communis*, and what needed explanation was how it became singular in the concrete individual and how it became universal in the mind, Ockham believed that what was primitively given was the individual and what needed explanation was only how it became universal. Another difference is that referred to in note 61, *infra*.

⁶⁰Scotus postulated a different "mechanism" for perfect intellectual intuition and ocular vision; the former requires the direct interaction of a real object with the intellect; the latter is mediated in terms of how the "medium" functions in propagating light and the accidental form. See note 30 *supra*.

⁶¹Scotus never abandoned the position that the content of thought had the peculiar existential status of an *ens diminutum* or what Ockham called a *fictum*. Only something with real *esse* could

interact causally with the intellect, *Ordinatio* I, dist. 13, n. 4 (V, 81); only in a qualified sense could one speak of intentional object as a *passio animae*; cf. *Ordinatio* I, dist. 3, nn. 386-388; on *Ockham's* abandonment of the *fictum* theory, see *op. cit.* p. 30, note 3.

[62]Cf. the note Scotus added as a guideline in revising *Ordinatio* I, dist. 3 (Vat. ed. III. p. 137). Scotus put introspective certitude of internal acts *qua* acts on a par with self-evident propositions, "for even though there is no certitude that I see white located outside, either in such a subject or at such a distance (for illusion can be caused in the medium or in the organ or in a number of other ways), still for all that there is certitude that I see"; *ibid*. n. 339 (p. 145); for the English translation, see A. B. Wolter, *Duns Scotus: Philosophical Writings*, p. 112.

[63]Cf. *Lectura* I, dist. 3, n. 79, (XIV, 254); *Ord*. I, dist. 27, n. 74 (VI, 92), etc. for references to Aristotle's Physics I, ch. 1 (184a16-23); and to Avicenna's *Physics*, *Lectura* I, dist. 7, n. 55 (XVI, 493), etc.

[64]Confer note 38, *supra*, and the corresponding text. This "reportatio" is a report of Scotus' Paris lectures; it is missing from his Oxford *Lectura* II (confer the Vienna codex latinus 1449, Österreiche Nationalbibliothek), but is found in a more polished version in the early 14th Century Codex V (Vat. lat. 876, f. 308 rb), which Wadding tells us he used in his edition of the *Reportata parisiensia* (see his "Censura" in Vivès ed., XXII, 4-5; and XXIII, 220-221 for the corresponding text). Its absence from *Ordinatio* II (e.g. Codices A, P and S) can be readily explained, if this revision of the Oxford lectures on Book II was finished before Scotus left for Paris in 1302. By the same token, its inclusion in both the *Opus oxoniense* and *Reportata parisiensia*/ Codex V would attest to its authenticity in the minds of those charged with editing Scotus' works (after his early death). The *Opus oxon.* text may even be closer to the actual lecture than the more polished version of Wadding/ Codex V, since the MS (f. 310va) adds: "Expliciunt Additiones secundi libri magistri Ioannis de Duns, subtilis doctoris, extractae per magistrum Willelmum de Alnewykm de Ordine Fratrum Minorum, de Lectura Parisiensi et Oxoniensi praedicti magistri Ioannis, cui propitietur Deus". If the revision contained in *Ordinatio*, books I and II, was complete before Scotus went to Paris, it would explain why his socius and editor, William of Alnwick, thought it necessary to make major additions to these first two books, which we know as the *Additiones magnae* (Bk. I) and *Additiones in II Sententiarum*.

6.

THE SUAREZIAN PROOF FOR GOD'S EXISTENCE

John P. Doyle

I.

Francis Suarez, S.J. (1548-1617) was convinced that God's existence could be demonstrated. In the 29th Disputation of his famous *Disputationes metaphysicae* (Salamanca, 1597), his main question was in effect: "By what means, physical or metaphysical, could it be done?"[1]

By Suarez's time this question was already old. Centuries earlier it had divided the two greatest philosophers of the Muslim world, Avicenna and Averroes. Avicenna, to some degree influenced by the revelation of Islam[2], had favored a metaphysical means leading to a Creator God, the First Cause of being for all else.[3] Averroes, for whom creation was a religious notion foreign to philosophy, had preferred the more Aristotelian physical means of the eternal motion of the heavens leading to a Prime Mover.[4] Suarez, like other Christian scholastics before him, opted for the view of Avicenna over that of Averroes. [5]

In exercising this option, the Jesuit Suarez was motivated by religious considerations akin to those which had influenced Avicenna. For a believer in creation *ex nihilo*, it would not suffice to show the existence of a prime mover. Rather, what had to be demonstrated was the existence of a *prime being*, necessary and uncreated, the unique source of all else. [6]

II.

To clear the ground, Suarez first denied that any physical proof based on motion will show that there actually exists an immaterial substance, much less one which is primary and uncreated.[7] This is because the well known principle, "Everything that is moved is moved by another" *(Omne quod movetur ab alio movetur)*, upon which such proof will rest, cannot be shown to have universal validity. There are many instances of things which seem to change without the help of anything else, e.g. will and appetite, or, in a more material vein, water which is cooling. As regards local motion, something similar seems to occur, for example, in the case of a stone falling by its own weight.[8]

But even granting the principle, we still could not use it to reach beyond the plane of material things to an immaterial (let alone an uncreated) mover. For how could we infer from a consideration of even the heavenly movement that such a mover exists? Nor from the premiss that heavenly movement is eternal, since this is not true, says Suarez, and consequently it cannot ground an inference in actual fact — whatever Aristotle might have thought.[9]

Still less can we infer it from heavenly movement considered absolutely. If we assume the heavens to be moved by an external mover who impresses on them an internal impetus which would then be productive of their motion, we cannot demonstrate precisely from this motion that there is any substance superior to the heavens themselves. Instead, their motion as such would find sufficient explanation in the assumed internal impetus.[10] If, contrariwise, we assume that the heavens are moved immediately (i.e. without any impetus) by an extrinsic mover, we cannot show from their motion alone that this mover is immaterial. For, granted even that heavenly movement is perpetual and invariable, one need not further grant that its cause is immaterial. Perpetuity and invariability are not necessarily signs of immateriality. Witness the heavens themselves, which in this hypothesis would be perpetual and invariable, but which are obviously also corporeal.[11]

III.

Clearly, therefore, the motion of the heavens will not warrant a conclusion to the existence of an immaterial creator God. For such a conclusion, one must abandon the physical plane of motion and proceed on the wider and deeper plane of *entitative perfection* — the plane, in fact, of metaphysics.[12] To do this, says Suarez, it is necessary to substitute another principle for the questionable *omne quod movetur ab alio movetur*. This new principle will be: *Omne quod fit ab alio fit* — "whatever is made is made by another" or "Whatever comes to be come to be by another."[13] This principle is wider inasmuch as every *movetur* is obviously a *fit*;[14] but the reverse is not true. A becoming or a being-made can be without motion and, in fact, if we are dealing with a creation *ex nihilo*, that is what we will have.[15] Again, *omne quod fit* is deeper and more evident than *omne quod movetur*. Mere motion presupposes a subject in which there could conceivably be power to move itself. Becoming or being-made, however, supposes no such subject. On the contrary, what comes to be or is made is supposed not to be beforehand. Consequently, it is more evident that in it there cannot be power to make itself.[16] So what we now have is an evident principle, true on the metaphysical plane of being, rather than a questionable one restricted to the physical plane of motion.

Suarez's main argument then is as follows: "Every being is either made or not made, i.e. uncreated; but not all beings *in universo* can be made; therefore, necessarily there is some being which is not made but which is uncreated."[17] The major premiss is a perfect disjunction.[18] The minor is certain, for our principle states that whatever is made is made by another. Now this other will itself be either made or not made. If it is not made, then we have what we want: an uncreated being. If it is made, it must again, by our principle, be made by another — about which the question recurs: "Is it made or not made?" Ultimately, we will have to reach a being which is not made. Otherwise, we will have an infinite series of made makers, unless in some circular way they will make themselves.[19] Both of these alternatives, he goes on to show, are insufficient to explain the being-made from which we started.[20] Therefore, his conclusion stands: there must be some being which is not made, but which is uncreated.[21]

In the last two sections of the 29th Disputation, Suarez goes on to establish the unicity of uncreated being in two ways. The first of these, which is the concern of section 2, proceeds from the beauty and order of the whole universe to show that there is but one first being by whom all other things are governed and from whom they have their origin.[22] While this reasoning is said to be totally *a posteriori*[23], and is apparently outside the framework of the main argument from section 1, it does need to be buttressed by the second way,[24] which is exhibited in section 3, and which is called "proximately a priori, although remotely also a posteriori."[25] Having demonstrated, by the main argument that there is at least one God in the sense of an unproduced being, we can deduce *a priori* (i.e. from its nature) that there cannot be another. Suarez's preferred reasoning here is that if a nature is multiplied in different individuals, singularity must in some way be extrinsic to its essence. However, in the case of an unproduced being, it is necessary that existence itself *(ipsum esse existentiae)* be of its essence, since it has existence by virtue of its essence in such a way that it is essentially identical with that existence. But existence belongs only to what is singular and only insofar as it is singular. Therefore, it is necessary that the singularity of such a nature belong to it also of its essence and, consequently, that this nature not be multiplied.[26]

IV.

Now in all of this there are certain presuppositions. From the start, Suarez has assumed that the totality of beings — *tota collectio entium*[27] — is alike enough to give rise to a concept that may be split in a number of ways which will ultimately be equivalent to creatures and God.[28] Thus all beings are, in the 29th Disputation, either made or not-made. Earlier, in the 28th Disputation, he had adumbrated his explicit metaphysical proof by dividing all beings as either dependent or independent, contingent or necessary, participated or essential, potential or actual.[29] In each of these divisions, as in the case of made and not-made, the lesser member would require the existence of the greater member.[30] But the key is that both the member which would require and that which is required are alike as falling under the common concept of being.[31]

More exactly, the original requirement is not just in the lesser member of the division; it is in the dividend being itself. For, in a manner which recalls Duns Scotus,[32] Avicenna,[33] or even Parmenides,[34] Suarez tells us that being itself, however abstractly or confusedly it is conceived, of itself *(ex vi sua)* demands *(postulat)* that it primarily, essentially, and, as it were, fully, belong to God, and that it secondarily belong to other things.[35] In this way, the one common concept of being is a quasi-middle term through which one can demonstrate deductively[36] the being of God from that of creatures.[37] Because there is community in being between God and creatures, a community intrinsically tilted in the direction of God, we can argue from the made or dependent being of the one to the Not-made or Independent Being of the Other.[38]

Exploring this concept of being further, we find that Suarez has equated it with being which is the object of metaphysics. To clarify this he has used what was by his time the ordinary *(vulgaris)* distinction between formal and objective concepts.[39] Properly speaking, the objective concept is that which is known or understood through the formal concept.[40] What metaphysics deals with as its object is the common objective concept of being which includes all real beings insofar precisely as they are alike in being.[41]

Here we are introduced to another distinction current *(usitata)* in 16th century Scholasticism, namely, that between *being as a participle* and *being as a noun*.[42] Being as a noun, says Suarez, signifies whatever is or can be — that which has a real essence, prescinding from actual existence without excluding or denying it.[43] It designates, therefore, whatever is not a mental fiction or chimera but what is true and of itself *(ex se)* apt really to exist.[44] Over against this, being as a participle is restricted to actually existing things.[45] Since being as a participle is thus more contracted than being as a noun,[46] metaphysics, which studies all real beings insofar as they are alike in being, will have as its object the objective concept of being as a noun.[47] And it is this same objective concept which underlies the Suarezian proof for God's existence.[48]

V.

In line with his aim of reaching a Creator God, Suarez's approach at the level of being seems justified. However, his particular procedure based upon a comprehensive concept of being leaves something to be desired.

Among other things, the *origin* of such a concept is dubious. Suarez needs immaterial realities (and, I believe, even an uncreated immaterial reality) in order to have this concept and in order to have metaphysics as he envisages it.[49] At the same time, he has said that knowledge of the existence and nature of immaterial things can be attained only in a metaphysical way through such a concept.[50]

Then, there is question about the common concept of being precisely as it is *common*. What is the likeness which permits the inclusion of all beings under one objective concept? Is it extra-mental or is it something supplied by the mind? This question is complicated by the fact that God is in every way simple and therefore utterly diverse from all else.[51] Suarez's quandary is evident when he tries to prove, in a single convoluted paragraph, that simple realities can be at once diverse from and still similar to other (even other simple) realities. The only way in which he can do this is by using the notoriously ambiguous term *"ratio"* two times to mean "reason" in the sense of mind as contrasted with extra-mental reality, once in a sense between the mind and reality, and once more in the sense of "real characteristic", patently outside the mind — all, let me repeat, within a single paragraph![52] The result is at best perplexed. Suarez is between the sort of nominalistic conceptualism with which he has often been charged[53] and, what would be for him, an unwelcome ultra-realism,[54] such perplexity cannot but cast shadow upon his proof of God's existence.

Again, there is room to ask Suarez about the real counterpart of the concept of being, precisely as *being*. Why should there be in it the kind of demand in the direction of God which we have seen him posit? If creatures are somehow real essences, of themselves apt to exist, why at that level — which is exactly the level on which Suarez's proof proceeds — should they require a Creator? It would rather seem at that level there would be an equality between creatures and the Creator,[55] such that one might easily reason that the Creator requires creatures, as, for example, Plato's Demiurge might require Forms — for knowledge and action.[56]

Along a parallel line, there is room to ask how a proof which in its fundamental presupposition prescinds from actual existence can legitimately conclude to the actual existence of a not-made being which ultimately is God. Instead, it appears, dividing things precisely as they are apt to exist should leave us still with things apt to exist. To go on to the actual existence of anything at all would demand, at a minimum, some further reasoning which Suarez has not vouchsafed us.[57]

A final question is whether Suarez's metaphysical demonstration is not in truth a form of "ontological" argument. Does it not presuppose from its inception that God will be found within the total collection of beings, represented inasmuch as they are real essences apt to exist by the common concept of being as a noun? When the answer is "yes",[58] one must further ask how from the very outset of his proof could Suarez presume that God was real, even in the very pallid sense of apt to exist? Has he not in fact given himself too much, and is not the pattern of his reasoning already necessitated by this gift? Said another way, does not the foundation which Suarez has so meticulously laid already guarantee too much about the building it will support?[59]

Notes

[1] Cf. "Utrum esse quoddam ens increatum ratione physica vel metaphysica demonstrari possit." *Disputationes Metaphysicae*, disp. 29, sec. 1; in *Opera Omnia*, ed. C. Berton (Paris: Vives, 1856-1877), Vol. 26, p. 22.

[2] On this, see e.g. E. Gilson, *History of Christian Philosophy in the Middle Ages* (New York, 1955), pp. 210f.

[3] Cf.: "... an sit [Deus] non potest quaeri nisi in hac scientia. Manifestum est enim ex dispositione hujus scientiae quod ipsa inquirit res separatas omnino a materia." Avicenna, *Metaphy.* I, 1 (ed. Venice, 1508, fol. 70r, b); "... manifestum est quod necesse esse [i.e. Deus] unum numero est, et patuit quod quicquid aliud est ab illo, cum consideratur per se, est possibile in suo esse et ideo est causatum ... Unde quicquid est, excepto uno quod est sibi ipsi unum et ente quod est sibi ipsi ens, est acquirens esse ab alio a se per quod est sibi esse non per se." *ibid.* VIII, 3 (fol. 98v, b).

[4] Cf. "Divinus enim accipit prima principia moventia a Naturali et nullam habet viam ad demonstrandum esse primum motorem, nisi accipiat ipsum pro constanti a naturali." Averroes, *Physica* VIII, t. 3 (ed. Venice, 1562, fol. 349r 2); "Substantia enim aeterna declarata est in naturalibus in fine Octavi Physicae sicut declarata sunt principia substantiae generabilis et corruptibilis in Primo istius libri. ... Et ideo impossibile est declarare aliquid abstractum esse, nisi ex motu et omnes viae quae reputantur esse ducentes ad primum motorem esse praeter viam motus aequaliter sunt insufficientes." *idem, Metaphysica* XII, t. 5 (ed. Venice, 1574, fol. 293r 1). Note that Averroes is aware of the influence of Islamic doctrine upon Avicenna: "Via autem qua processit Avicenna in probando primum principium est via loquentium et sermo ejus semper invenitur quasi medius inter Peripateticos et Loquentes." *Physica* II, t. 22 (fol. 57r 1); cf. *idem, Destructio destructionis* IV (Venice, 1573, fol. 72v 2).

[5] Cf. *Disp. Metaphys.*, disp. 29, sec. 1, nn. 3 and 6 (Vol. 26, p. 22). In paragraph 3, Suarez mentions Albertus Magnus and Duns Scotus as following Avicenna. In paragraph 5, the opinion attributed to Soncinas and Javellus seems partially to follow that of Avicenna. In a connected context, Suarez further mentions St. Thomas, Alexander of Hales, Aegidius Romanus, and even Averroes in his role of Commentator on Aristotle: "Dicendum est ergo, ens in quantum ens reale esse objectum adaequatum hujus scientiae. Haec est sententia Aristotelis, 4 Metaph., fere in principio, quam ibi D. Thomas, Alensis, Scotus, Albert., Alex. Aphrod., et fere alii [sic] sequuntur, et Comment. ibi, et lib. 3, comm. 14, et lib. 12, comm. 1, Avicen., lib. 1, suae Metaph., c. 1; Sonc., 4 Metaph., qu. 10; Aegid., lib. 1, q. 5, et reliqui fere scriptores." *ibid.*, disp. 1, sec. 1, n. 26 (Vol. 25, p. 11).

[6] "Et ideo ad demonstrandum Deum esse, non satis est ostendere dari in rerum natura ens quoddam necessarium, et a se, nisi etiam probetur illud esse unicum, et tale, ut sit fons totius esse, a quo pendent, et illud recipiunt omnia, quae ipsum esse quoquo modo participant." *ibid.*, disp. 29, sec. 2, n. 5 (Vol. 26, p. 35).

[7] "Hoc autem medium per se ac praecise sumptum multis modis invenitur inefficax ad demonstrandum esse in rerum natura aliquam substantiam immaterialem, nedum ad demonstrandum primam et increatam substantiam ..." *ibid.*, sec. 1, n. 7 (Vol. 26, p. 23).

[8] Cf. "... principium illud in quo tota illa ostensio fundatur: *Omne quod movetur, ab alio movetur*, adhuc non esse satis demonstratur in omni genere motus vel actionis; nam multa sunt quae per actum virtualem videntur sese movere et reducere ad actum formalem ut in appetitu seu voluntate videre licet, et in aqua reducente se ad pristinam frigiditatem; idem ergo accidere potest in motu locali; ... sicut motus deorsum resultat in lapide ex intrinseca gravitate." *ibid.*

For discussions of virtual act as found in Suarez, see J. Owens, C.SS.R., "The Conclusion of the *Prima Via*," *The Modern Schoolman*, XXX (1952), esp. pp. 208-211; P. Descoqs, S.J., *Praelectiones Theologiae Naturalis* (Paris, 1932), I, 306-310; J. Hellín, S.J., "Sobre el transito de la potencia activa al acto según Suárez," *Razón y Fe*, número extraordinario (Madrid, 1948), pp. 353-407.

[9]"Deinde ponamus ut verum illud principium, *omne quod movetur, ab alio movetur* (est enim revera probabilius, recte intellectum), et ex consequente ponamus coelum ab alio moveri, qua, quaeso, necessaria aut evidenti consecutione inferri potest ex illo principio et motu coeli, dari substantiam aliquam immaterialem? Aut enim id colligitur ex motu aeterno aut ex motu tantum. Si primum, collectio imprimis fit ex falso principio, et ita nulla est demonstratio in re ipsa, quicquid Aristot. senserit." *Disp. Metaphys.*, disp. 29, sec. 1, n. 8 (Vol. 26, p. 23).

[10]Cf. "... duobus enim modis potest coelum moveri ab alio. Uno modo ut ab imprimente internum impetum proxime activum motus, sicut grave dicitur moveri a generante. Alio modo ut a proximo movente separato, sicut rota movetur a manu." *ibid.* n. 12 (p. 25), "Si ergo ponamus coelum moveri ab alio, priori modo, nihil inde probari potest; nam licet recte inde inferatur, esse aliam substantiam priorem coelo, tamen hoc non tam probatur illo modo, quam supponitur, nam ille motor coeli non aliter dicitur movere coelum, nisi quia impressit illi internum impetum intrinsecum et connaturalem, qui non imprimitur nisi a generante, seu ab auctore naturae; supponit ergo illa ratio coelum habere auctorem, a quo procreatum sit; hoc autem non demonstratur illo discursu, neque ex solo motu physico demonstrari potest, ..." *ibid.*, n. 14.

[11]Cf. "... etiamsi supponamus coelum moveri ab alio extrinseco, et proprio motore proximo; quid enim habet motus coeli, propter quod necessarium sit illum motorem esse immaterialem? Aut enim illud est perpetuitas motus seu diurnitas, quae de se potest perpetuo durare, et hoc non, quia ad illud non sufficit similis duratio et perpetuitas in motore, et in virtute ejus, quam posset habere, etiamsi esset corporeus, sicut coelum ipsum vel sol illam habet. Vel illud esset invariabilitas motus, quae indicat indefatigabilem virtutem in motore, et hoc ad summum declarat motorem esse incorruptibilem, ... posset autem esse incorruptibilis, etiamsi esset corporeus, sicut est coelum ipsum." *ibid.*

[12]"... constat ex vi solius motus coeli concludi non posse, dari aliquod primum ens immateriale, et increatum; ... ergo multo minus poterit ex motu coeli colligi esse aliquod primum ens, in quo perfectiones illae conveniant; sed oportebit semper aliquod medium metaphysicum adjungere, quo id concluditur." *ibid.*, n. 16 (p. 26).

[13]"Primo igitur, loco illius principii physici: *Omne quod movetur, ab alio movetur*, sumendum est aliud metaphysicum longe evidentius: *Omne quod fit, ab alio fit*, sive creetur sive generetur, sive quacumque ratione fiat." *ibid.*, n. 20 (p. 27). For the Aristotelian background of this new principle, cf. *Metaphysics*, VII, c. 7, 1032a 13; *ibid.*, c. 8, 1033a 24.

[14]For this thought, see J. Gomez Caffarena, S.J., "Suárez filósofo," *Razón y Fe*, número extraordinario (Madrid, 1948), p. 147.

[15]Cf. "Cum ergo creationis dependentia non supponat aliquod subjectum ex quo fiat, non potest veram rationem passionis aut mutationis habere." *Disp. Metaphys.*, disp. 20, sec. 4, n. 17 (Vol. 25, p. 774); also *ibid.*, n. 24 (p. 776).

[16]Cf. "... prius enim, quam res sit, non potest esse in actu formali vel virtuali ad faciendum se, et hac de causa est longe evidentius hoc principium: *Omne quod producitur, ab alio producitur*, quam de illo: *Omne quod movetur, ab alio movetur*; nam quod movetur, supponitur esse, in quo esse potest intelligi actus virtualis ad se movendum; quod autem efficitur, non supponitur esse, sed potius supponitur non esse, antequam fiat; in ipso autem non esse non potest esse virtus ad se efficiendum, et ideo est evidens illud principium proprie intellectum de prima

ac vera effectione, ..." *ibid.*, disp. 29, sec. 1, n. 20 (Vol. 26, p. 27). Between *Omne quod fit* and *Omne quod producitur* there is apparently no difference since Suarez uses them interchangeably here.

[17]Cf. "Hoc ergo posito principio, sic concluditur demonstratio: omne ens aut est factum, aut non factum, seu increatum; sed non possunt omnia entia, quae sunt in universo, esse facta; ergo necessarium est esse aliquid ens non factum, seu increatum." *ibid.*, n. 21.

[18]"Major est evidens, cum necesse sit ex duobus contradictoriis alterum cuilibet convenire." *ibid.*

[19]"Minor probatur, quia omne ens factum, ab alio est factum; vel ergo illud a quo factum est, est etiam factum vel non; si non est factum, datur ergo aliquod ens increatum, quod intendebamus; si vero illud etiam factum est, oportebit ab alio esse factum, de quo ulterius idem inquirendum erit, et ita tandem aut sistendum erit in ente non facto, aut procedendum in infinitum, aut circulus committendus: non potest autem aut committi circulus, aut in infinitum procedi, sistendum ergo necessario est in ente non facto." *ibid.*

[20]*Ibid.*, n. 22 (pp. 27-28) and n. 26 (p. 29). A circular production (e.g. A makes B, B makes C, C makes A) is patently impossible and violative of the principle *omne quod fit* just as evidently as if a single thing were to produce itself. An infinite series of made makers essentially subordinated one to another is insufficient mainly because it is impossible that the whole collection *(tota collectio)* of beings or efficient causes be dependent in their existence and operation. For if the whole collection of beings were dependent, it would have to depend on another being — since *omne quod fit ab alio fit* is equivalent to saying *omne quod dependet ab alio dependet*. Such dependence, however, is impossible inasmuch as outside the *whole* collection there is no other being. Therefore, within the collection there must be at least one being which is independent. As for an infinite series of accidentally subordinated made makers, Suarez thinks that even if this were possible (which he would deny: *ibid.*, n. 35 [p. 32]), such a series would still have an essential dependence on a superior cause, with regard to which the argument would then apply: "Quod licet admittamus, nihil obstat nostrae demonstrationi, quia in hoc processu supponitur superior causa, vel simpliciter non facta, vel saltem non tali modo, neque in tali serie generationum contenta, ex qua facile est pervenire ad causam simpliciter non factam, eadem argumentandi forma, ut saepe dictum, et factum est." *ibid.*, n. 34 (pp. 31-32). J. Leiwesmeier ("Zur Stellung der Gottesbeweise in der scholastichen Philosophie", *Theologische Quartalschrift*, 120 [1939] p. 192, and *Die Gotteslehre bei Franz Suarez* [Paderborn, 1938], p. 33) believes that Suarez's denial of an infinite series of accidentally subordinated causes is directly dependent upon his Christian belief in a temporal creation. This, however, is wrong. Suarez holds that creation *ab aeterno* was possible, although it did not in fact occur; cf. *Disp. Metaphys.*, disp. 20, sec. 5, n. 11 (Vol. 25, p. 782). At the same time, he maintains here (disp. 29, sec. 1, n. 35 [Vol. 26, p. 32]) that an infinite series of accidentally subordinated causes is impossible.

[21]*Ibid.*, n. 21 (p. 27), text in note 17 above. Also: "... ergo non potest in illo progressu in infinitum procedi, sed sistendum est in ente improducto quod etiam in causando sit independens." *ibid.*, n. 26 (p. 29); "... ergo si tota collectio etiam esse non potest dependens, ut ostensum est, necesse est esse in illa collectione aliquod ens omnino independens, et non factum." *ibid.*, n. 28.

[22]Cf. "... totius universi pulchritudo, omniumque rerum, quae in eo sunt, mirabilis connexio et ordo, satis declarant esse unum primum ens, a quo omnia gubernantur et originem ducunt." *ibid.*, sec. 2, n. 7 (p. 36).

[23]"Una est omnino a posteriori, et ex effectibus; ..." *ibid.*

[24]"... altera est proxime a priori, quamvis remote sit etiam a posteriori, ..." *ibid.*

[25] Cf. *ibid.*, sec. 2, n. 31 (p. 45); n. 37 (p. 47).

[26] Cf. "Quia ubicumque ratio communis est multiplicabilis secundum diversas naturas singulares, esto non sit necesse singularitatem in re ipsa distingui a natura communi, oportet tamen, ut aliquo modo sit extra essentiam talis naturae; nam si esset illi essentialis, revera talis natura non esset multiplicabilis, ... in ente autem improducto intelligi non potest, quod singularitas sit extra essentiam naturae ejus; ergo impossibile est, ut talis natura sit multiplicabilis. Minor probatur, quia in ente improducto necesse est, ut ipsum esse existentiae sit de essentia ejus; in eo enim consistit intrinseca necessitas essendi, quod ex vi essentiae suae habet esse, ita ut essentialiter sit suum esse; sed esse non est, nisi rei singularis, ut singularis est; ergo necesse est ut singularitas talis naturae sit etiam de essentia ejus, et consequenter ut talis natura non sit multiplicabilis." *ibid.*, sec. 3, n. 11 (p. 51). It is difficult to see how Suarez can find much comfort in this argument since for him, who denies any real distinction between essence and existence in creatures as well as in God (cf. *Disp. Metaphys.*, *disp. 31, sec. 6, n. 1* [Vol. 26, p. 241]), all essences might seem equally unique, on this, see A. Breuer, *Der Gottesbeweis bei Thomas und Suarez* (Freiburg in Schweiz, 1929), p. 30. On the question of God's unity, also see: *Disp. Metaphys.*, *disp. 30, sec. 10 (An tantum unum Deum esse demonstrari possit)*; Vol. 26, pp. 137 ff.

[27] On the totality of beings as Suarez understands it here, see *Disp. Metaphys.*, *disp. 29, sec. 1, n. 26 (Vol. 26, p. 29)*.

[28] This is clear from the very opening plan of Suarez's *Disputationes Metaphysicae*; cf.: "Deinde in priori tomo ejusdem objecti amplissima et universalissima ratio, qua, videlicet, appellatur ens, ejusque proprietates et causae diligenter expenduntur. ...In tomo autem altero inferiores ejusdem objecti rationes prosecuti sumus, initio sumpto ab illa entis divisione in *creatum* et *creatorem*, ..." *ibid.*, *Ratio et discursu totius operis ad lectorem* (Vol. 25); *ibid.*, disp. 28, prol. (Vol. 26, p. 1); *ibid.*, sec. 1, nn. 3-4 (pp. 1-2).

[29] Cf. *Disp. Metaphys.*, disp. 28, sec. 1, nn. 6-15 (Vol. 26, pp. 2-6).

[30] Cf. e.g.: "... oportebit totam speciem talis entis ab alio superiori trahere originem; ..." *ibid.*, disp. 28, sec. 1, n. 6 (p. 2); "... non potest tota aliqua collectio effectuum esse dependens, quin supponatur aliqua res, seu causa independens, ..." *ibid.*; "... necesse est, ens quod est tale per participationem, reduci ad aliud quod habeat esse absque tali participatione; ..." *ibid.*, n. 13 (p. 5); see also: "... Deus ita est causa suorum effectuum, ut illi ex intrinseca natura et intrinseca necessitate talem causam postulent ut sint, ..." *ibid.*, disp. 21, sec. 1, n. 9 (Vol. 25, p. 788).

[31] Cf. "... omnia entia realia vere habent aliquam similitudinem et convenientiam in ratione essendi; ergo possunt concipi et repraesentari sub ea praecisa ratione qua inter se conveniunt; ergo possunt sub ea ratione unum conceptum objectivum constituere; ... creatura etiam participat aliquo modo esse Dei, et ideo dicitur saltem esse vestigium ejus propter aliquam convenientiam et similitudinem in essendo; qua ratione ex esse creaturae investigamus esse Dei, ..." *ibid.*, disp. 2, sec. 2, n. 14 (Vol. 25, p. 74).

[32] Cf. Scotus' use of the *ratio Anselmi* within the context of proving the existence of *Ens Infinitum; Ordinatio* I, dis. 2, par. 1, q. 2 (ed. Vat. II, pp. 209-210, nn. 137-138), and also *Tractatus de primo principio*, c. 4 (ed. Muller-Roche [Madrid, BAC, 1950] pp. 686-687. See É. Gilson, *Jean Duns Scot: Introduction à ses positions fondamentales* (Paris, 1952), pp. 166-167.

[33] For this, cf. "Médite comment, pour établir l'existence du Premier, son unicité, son affranchissement de toute matière, notre explication n'a pas besoin de réfléchir sur autre chose que l'être même." *'Isārāt*, 146, as cited by A.-M. Goichon, *La distinction de l'essence et de l'existence d'après Ibn Sīnā* (Avicenne), (Paris, 1937), p. 336.

[34]Here I agree with A. Gnemmi (without accepting his favorable estimate of it) that Suarez's doctrine evokes the memory of Parmenides; cf. *Il fondamento* metafisico ... Capitolo settimo, "La via Parmenidea della ratio formalis entis: gli elementi", pp. 255-296; Capitolo ottavo, "L'Inferenza Parmenidea: bilancio", pp. 297-309; esp.: "Non fa uso la via parmenidea del principio di causa, non passa per esse l'inventio di Dio: la causalità, il principio è introdotto dalla o in forza della ratio entis ut sic, che, come impone l'esistenza di Dio, così impone la derivazione, la dipendenza, l'essere DA per la totalità dell' esperienza: impone la partecipazione verticale ontologico-teologica quale ragione ultima della partecipazione fenomenologica (gradi): impone per il mondo la *creazione*." p. 296.

[35]Cf. "... ipsum ens quantumvis abstracte et confuse conceptum, ex vi sua postulat hunc ordinem, ut primo ac per se, et quasi complete competat Deo, et per illud descendat ad reliqua, quibus non insit, nisi cum habitudine et dependentia a Deo; ..." *Disp. Metaphys.*, disp. 28, sec. 3, n. 17 (Vol. 26, p. 19); *ibid.*, n. 21 (p. 21). Just how far this demand in the very notion of being itself extends may be seen from the following: "... ergo ipsa ratio entis ut sic postulat ut secundum totam latitudinem perfectionis possibilem, aut vere excogitabilem, habeat in aliquo ente necessitatem essendi vel formaliter, vel eminenter; non potest autem habere hanc necessitatem quasi divisam et partitam in plura entia necessaria, ut supra probatum est; ergo necesse est ut illam habeat quasi congregatam totam in uno ente per se necessario, et hoc ipsum est illud ens esse infinitum." *ibid.*, disp. 30, sec. 2, n. 23 (p. 71).

[36]Cf. "... in illa collectione detur aliquod ens simpliciter independens, et non factum, quod nos deducere intendimus." *ibid.*, disp. 29, sec. 1, n. 26 (Vol. 26, p. 29).

[37]It should be remarked that Suarez does not always show the hesitation implied by our "quasi"; cf. "Denique jam supra ostensum est, ens uno conceptu dici de omnibus sub illo contentis, ideoque posse esse medium demonstrationis, et rationem entis in creaturis inventam posse esse initium inveniendi similem rationem altiori modo in creatore existentem." *ibid.*, disp. 28, sec. 3, n. 15 (Vol. 26, p. 18).

[38]*Ibid.*, disp. 2, sec. 2, n. 14; text in note 31 above.

[39]"Supponenda imprimis est vulgaris distinctio conceptus formalis et objectivi; ..." *Disp. Metaphys.*, disp. 2, sec. 1, n. 1. For examples of others using this distinction before and after Suarez, see John P. Doyle, "Suarez on the Analogy of Being", (Part I), *The Modern Schoolman*, XLVI (March, 1969), pp. 224-225, n. 29.

[40]"Conceptus objectivus dicitur res illa, vel ratio, quae proprie et immediate per conceptum formalem cognoscitur seu repraesentatur; ..." *Disp. Metaphys.*, disp. 2, sec. 1, n. 1 (Vol. 25, p. 65).

[41]Cf. "... simpliciter verius est dari conceptum objectivum entis, ... circa quem per se, et ut sic, potest aliqua scientia versari, ... hoc autem fit in hac scientia ..." *ibid.*, disp. 1, sec. 1, n. 23 (Vol. 25, p. 10); "In hac ergo disputatione praecipue intendimus explicare conceptum objectivum entis ut sic, secundum totam abstractionem suam, secundum quam diximus esse metaphysicae objectum, ..." *ibid.*, disp. 2, sec. 1, n. 1 (p. 65).

[42]Cf. "... utendum nobis est usitata distinctione entis, ... Ens ergo, ut dictum est, interdum sumitur ut participium ... interdum vero sumitur ut nomen ..." *Disp. Metaphys.*, disp. 2, sec. 4, n. 3 (Vol. 25, p. 88). For others using the distinction before and after Suarez, see John P. Doyle, "Suarez on the Analogy of Being", pp. 225-226, n. 30.

[43]"... ens enim vi nominis sumptum significat id, quod habet essentiam realem, praescindendo ab actuali existentia, non quidem excludendo illam, seu negando, sed praecisive tantum abstrahendo; ..." *Disp. Metaphys.*, disp. 2, sec. 4, n. 9 (Vol. 25, p. 90).

[44]"... si ens sumatur prout est significatum hujus vocis in vi nominis sumptae, ejus ratio consistit in hoc, quod sit habens essentiam realem, id est non fictam, nec chymericam, sed veram et aptam ad realiter existendum." *ibid.*, sec. 4, n. 5 (p. 89); "... solum dicere possumus, essentiam realem, eam esse quae ex se apta est esse, seu realiter existere." *ibid.*, n. 7 (p. 90).

[45]"... sumpto ente in actu, prout est significatum illius vocis in vi participii sumptae, rationem consistere in hoc, quod sit aliquid actu existens, seu habens realem actum essendi, seu habens realitatem actualem, quae a potentiali distinguitur, quod est actu nihil." *ibid.*, disp. 2, sec. 4, n. 4 (p. 89).

[46]Cf. *ibid.*, n. 9 (p. 90).

[47]Cf. "Rursus constat ex communi usu, *ens*, etiam sumptum pro ente reali (ut nunc loquimur) non solum tribui rebus existentibus, sed etiam naturis realibus secundum se considerata, sive existant, sive non; quomodo metaphysica considerat ens, et hoc modo ens in decem praedicamenta dividitur." *ibid.*, n. 3 (p. 88). On the objective concept of being as a noun as related to the universality and necessity required by the *science* of metaphysics, see John P. Doyle, "Suarez on the Analogy of Being," (Part I), pp. 229-231.

[48]Cf. "... de diviso hujus partitionis dictum est in prima et secunda disputatione, est enim ipsum ens quod est adequatum objectum Metaphysicae, ..." *Disp. Metaphys.*, disp. 28, prol. (Vol. 26, p. 1).

[49]Cf. "... hac substantia [i.e. immateriali] ablata, auferretur tam proprium quam adequatum objectum primae philosophiae, quia non solum auferretur immaterialis substantia, sed etiam omnes rationes entis vel substantiae communes rebus immaterialibus et materialibus, et data illa hypothesi, sicut nulla essent entia immaterialia, ita nullae etiam essent rationes entium abstrahentes a materia secundum esse, et ideo non esset necessaria alia scientia distincta." *ibid.*, disp. 1, sec. 1, n. 16 (Vol. 25, p. 7); *ibid.*, disp. 2, sec. 2, n. 31 (p. 80).

[50]Cf. "... scientia humana et naturalis vix potest attingere substantias immateriales, nisi incipiendo a rationibus quae communes sint illis substantiis, et aliis rebus." *ibid.*, disp. 1, sec. 1, n. 17 (Vol. 25, p. 8); *ibid.*, sec. 3, n. 10 (p. 25); *ibid.*, sec. 5, n. 15 (p. 41); *ibid.*, sec. 1, nn. 11 and 13 (pp. 5-6); *ibid.*, sec. 2, n. 16 (p. 17); also *ibid.*, disp. 35, sec. 2, n. 8 (Vol. 26, p. 439).

[51]For Suarez on the Divine Simplicity, see *Disp. Metaphys.*, disp. 30, sec. 3-6 (Vol. 26, pp. 72-95).

[52]Cf. "... si distinctio et convenientia sint diversorum ordinum, non repugnat in eodem fundari; sic enim una non involvit negationem alterius, imo quodammodo illam requirit. Ita vero est in praesenti; nam distinctio est realis, convenientia autem secundum rationem tantum, et ideo non repugnat ut duo simplicia, quae secundum rem sunt realiter primo diversa, secundum rationem habeant unitatem fundatam in reali similitudine vel convenientia, quam inter se habent. Ea enim, quae in re diversa sunt, in eo in quo distinguuntur, possunt esse similia: quin potius similitudo intrinsece postulat distinctionem secundum rem cum aliqua unitate rationis, seu formali, aut fundamentali, nam idem proprie non est sibi ipsi simile. Quod si haec convenientia vel similitudo sit imperfecta, qualis est in analogia entis, et similibus, facilius intelligitur quomodo possint res inter se, quantumvis primo diversae, habere nihilominus aliquam imperfectam convenientiam; non enim dicuntur primo diversae, quia nullo modo inter se similes sint, hoc enim in nullis rebus vel rationibus realibus reperiri necesse est, sed quia se ipsis primo distinguuntur; cum qua distinctione stat praedicta imperfecta convenientia. Cujus rei exemplum est in Deo, in quo nulla distinctio graduum ex natura rei excogitari potest; unde illa simplicissima natura per se ipsam est prorsus distincta a natura creata; et tamen simul est principium alicujus convenientiae analogae et secundum quid cum eadem: haec ergo duo non repugnant." *Disp.*

Metaphys., disp. 2, sec. 3, n. 16 (Vol. 25, p. 87).

[53] For the charge of nominalism (i.e. conceptualism), cf.: L. Mahieu, *Francois Suarez, sa philosophie et les rapports qu'elle a avec sa théologie* (Paris, 1921), pp. 283, 499-505, 522; C. Giacon, S.J., *Guglielmo di Occam: saggio storico-critico sulla formazione e sulla decadenza della Scolastica* (Milan, 1941), II, pp. 679-681, 689; and to some extent F. Peccorini ("Suarez's Struggle with the Problem of the One and the Many," *The Thomist*, 36 (1972), pp. 433-471) who is aware of Suarez's oscillation between conceptualism and realism. In defense of Suarez against the charge, see: J. Alejandro, S.J., *La gnoseología del Doctor Eximio y la acusación nominalista*, Comillas, 1948; J. Iturrioz, S.J., *Estudios sobre la metafísica de Francisco Suárez, S.J.* (Madrid, 1948), pp. 147-156, and esp. on the concept of being, pp. 201-277; P. Descoqs, S.J., "Thomisme et suarézisme," *Archives de Philosophie* IV (1926), pp. 82-192; E. Guerrero, S.J., "El 'Francois Suarez' de Leon Mahieu," *Razón y Fe*, número extraordinario (Madrid, 1948), pp. 313-351 — esp. pp. 323-325. J. Gomez Caffarena, S.J., whose own sympathies are definitely with Suarez, has in some degree admitted the charge: cf. "Sentido de la composición de ser y essencia en Suárez," *Pensamiento*, XV (1959), esp. pp. 149-149.

[54] For Suarez's rejection of any kind of ultra-realism, see *Disp. Metaphys.*, disp. 6, secs. 1-3 (Vol. 25, pp. 201-216).

[55] This inference may not daunt Suarez. For, in at least one place, he has told us that creatures, as non-repugnant in themselves, have in a certain negative way an independent necessity equal to that of God; cf. "Si autem posteriori modo concipiatur illa non repugnantia ex parte creaturarum, plane est tam necessaria in sua negatione, sicut Verbum in suo esse actuali, quia est sine dependentia ab alio in illa non repugnantia. Tota autem necessitas Dei est necessitas independentiae, ergo in hoc est aequalitas. Neque hoc est inconveniens, quia non est aequalitas in re positiva, sed in negatione quadam." Suarez, *De SS. Trinitatis Mysterio*, lib. 9, cap. 6, n. 19 (Vol. 1, p. 739). Among the Jesuits coming after Suarez in the 17th century, a similar doctrine can be found, e.g., in R. de Arriaga, S.J., *Cursus Philosophiae*, Metaphysica, disp. 2, sec. 1, subsec. 1 (ed. Lugduni, 1669), p. 958 and G. de Rhodes, S.J., *Philosophia Peripatetica, ad veram Aristotelis mentem*, lib. 4, disp. 2, qu. 2, sec. 3 (ed. Lugduni, 1671), p. 636.

[56] Cf. "Respondeo, ... non posse tolli illam possibilitatem ex parte creaturarum, quin tollatur a Deo positiva perfectio omnipotentiae, ac subinde scientia, et totius divini esse." Suarez, *De SS. Trinitatis Mysterio*, lib. 3, cap. 9, n. 13 (Vol. 1, p. 740). For this whole issue of the basic relationship in being between God and creatures, see John P. Doyle, "Suarez on the Reality of the Possibles," *The Modern Schoolman*, XLV (1967), esp. pp. 46-47; *idem*, "Suarez on the Analogy of Being (Part II)," *The Modern Schoolman*, XLVI (May, 1969), esp. pp. 329-340.

[57] On the need for some cross-over from being as a noun to the act of existence itself, not only for the Suarezian proof of God's existence, but also for the progression of Suarezian metaphysics itself, see John P. Doyle, "Heidegger and Scholastic Metaphysics," *The Modern Schoolman*, XLIX (1972), esp. pp. 208-209.

[58] Cf. "... in illa collectione detur aliquod ens simpliciter independens, et non factum, quod nos deducere intendimus." *Disp. Metaphys.*, disp. 29, sec. 1, n. 26 (Vol. 26, p. 29). Note also that from the very start of his *Disputationes* Suarez has included God as a "real being" under being insofar as it is being which forms the object of his metaphysics: *ibid.*, disp. 1, sec. 1, n. 26 (Vol. 25, p. 11); *ibid.*, n. 11 (p. 5); also cf. *ibid.*, n. 19 (p. 9) where, long before he has given any proof of God's existence, Suarez declares that He (God) is "an object naturally knowable in some way" *(objectum naturaliter scibile aliquo modo)* and that "He can fall under some natural science" *(potest cadere sub aliquam naturalem scientiam)*.

⁵⁹E. Gilson's comments in reference to Christian Wolff, when applied *mutatis mutandis* to Suarez, do not seem wide of the mark: "It is a widely discussed point to know if Kant was right in saying that all demonstrations of the existence of God involve in their texture the ontological argument. In point of fact, they do, at least if being is what Wolff has said that it is. Where being is identified with the pure possibility of essence, metaphysics finds itself confronted with the impossible task of finding a sufficient reason for actual existence in a world in which being as such, taken in itself, is essentially foreign to it. Not only the Anselmian argument, which can then rightly be termed 'ontological', but any proof of God's existence, nay, any demonstration of any actual existence is bound to be 'ontological' in such a philosophy. The whole doctrine of Wolff was ontological because it was suspended from an ontology which had defined itself as the science of being *qua* possible. A proof is 'ontological' wherever it looks at existentially neutral essence for the existential complement of its own possibility." *Being and Some Philosophers*, 2nd edition (Toronto, 1952), pp. 120-121. On Suarez as a precursor of Wolff, cf. *ibid.*, pp. 96-119; *idem, L'Être et l'essence* (Paris, 1948), pp. 141-183. Also on the relation between the metaphysics of Suarez and that of Wolff, see E. Conze, *Der Begriff der Metaphysik bei* Franciscus Suarez (Leipzig, 1928), pp. 64-70.

7.

REFLECTIONS ON DESCARTES' METHODS OF ANALYSIS AND SYNTHESIS

by

Richard J. Blackwell

The birth of science in the Seventeenth Century was the production of a set of twins. The first and better known of the pair was a new vision of the structure of the physical world and of man's place in it. Western man had come to see the world as much larger than he had suspected, as heliocentric in form, as governed by mechanical laws which were so exact and fixed that God need not intervene, at least not often, to keep it functioning smoothly, as devoid of purposes and secondary sense qualities which are properly the furniture of the human mind, and in short as a grand mechanical spectacle presented to man's scrutiny and amazement, but independent thereof.

The second and lesser known offspring, but in the long run the more influential of the two, was a new model of human understanding. What had previously counted as an adequate explanation of man and his world was discarded. In its place there gradually evolved in the seventeenth century a new view of how we acquire knowledge and a new set of criteria as to what was to count as adequate understanding.

Like any new process of generation and birth, the emergence of the new method did not occur in an instant, but developed slowly and was accompanied by some severe labor pains. And, of course, scientific method did not mean precisely the same thing to all of the major scientists of the period. But there was a general common denominator. At least at the verbal level, and very probably more fundamentally also, most of the prominent figures of the period talked methodologically in terms of the complementary processes of analysis and synthesis. This terminology was consciously borrowed from the early Greek mathematicians[1], although it was to be given newer and broader twists of meaning in the seventeenth century. On the negative side, dissatisfaction with the then contemporary status of Aristotelian logic was widespread. Aristotle's original spirit in logic had been lost, and along with it was lost the means of adding to the content of human knowledge; or as Bacon put it so well, what was needed was a new method for the advancement of learning. In more contemporary terms, some account was called for in the age of discovery to explain how we acquire new knowledge. The double method of analysis and synthesis, in its various versions in the hands of the creative minds of the period, was the response of the seventeenth century to fill this need.

One of the first scientists of the period to respond to this challenge was René Descartes (1596-1650). As a result we find in his writings, and especially in his earliest formal treatise, the *Regulae ad directionem ingenii*, a serious and sophisticated attempt to define the analytic-synthetic method. The spirit behind this excursion into methodology is perhaps to be found in Descartes' criticism of the work of Galileo as being piecemeal and unsystematic.[2] Descartes felt that the growth of the sciences would be best served by first formulating the new method as explicitly as possible, and then applying it carefully to various problem areas. It should be recalled, for instance, that his *Discourse on Method*, which we now improperly read in isolation, was intended by Descartes to serve as an introduction to the three explicitly scientific treatises which he viewed as his main contribution to mathematics and physical science at that time.[3] Be that as it may, the purpose of the present paper is to discuss and evaluate Descartes' version of the analytic-synthetic method as an account of the new science of the day.

The Background in the Greek Mathematicians

Rule IV of the *Regulae* bears the title "There is need of a method of finding out the truth." The method which Descartes envisions is not merely a protection against error; it is also to be a guarantee that our knowledge is not simply accidentally true but true with certainty and indubitability. He is confident that there is such a method from the evidence of what the Greek mathematicians were able to accomplish, even though they attempted to conceal their method of procedure. In an interesting passage Descartes remarks,

> Indeed I seem to recognize certain traces of this true Mathematics in Pappus and Diophantus, who though not belonging to the earliest age, yet lived many centuries before our own times. But my opinion is that these writers then by a sort of low cunning, deplorable indeed, suppressed this knowledge. Possibly they acted just as many inventors are known to have done in the case of their discoveries, i.e., they feared that their method being so easy and simple would become cheapened on being divulged...[4]

If this passage can be taken as Descartes' motif in the *Regulae*, it implies that he is antecedently confident that the method he seeks does exist, that it is a method of discovering new and certain truths, that it was already known to, and used by, the Greek mathematicians who jealously concealed it as more valuable than its products, and that this method of discovery is disarmingly simple. If so, the purpose of the *Regulae* is to reveal finally this method in all its power and simplicity.

The reference to Pappus of Alexandria in the above quotation is especially significant since the *locus classicus* of the analysis-synthesis distinction in Greek mathematics is to be found in his writings, and Descartes may well have had the following passage from Pappus in mind when he wrote his own Rule IV.

> *Analysis*, then, takes that which is sought as if it were admitted and passes from it through its successive consequences to something which is admitted as a result of synthesis: for in analysis we assume that which is sought as if it were already done, and we inquire what it is from which this results, and again what is the antecedent cause of the latter, and so on, until by so retracing our steps we come upon something already known or belonging to the class of first principles, and such a method we call analysis as being solution backwards.
>
> But in *synthesis*, reversing the process, we take as already done that which was last arrived at in the analysis and, by arranging in their natural order as consequences what before were antecedents, and successively connecting them one with another, we arrive finally at the construction of what was sought; and this we call synthesis.[5]

For example, we start with the question of whether a given proposition (e.g., the sum of the interior angles of a Euclidean triangle equals 180°) can be formally proven as true. Next we assume that it is true, and then reason by the reverse of the natural order of deduction to another higher proposition (e.g., a straight angle equals 180°) from which the first proposition would follow. We repeat this process as many times as is required to arrive either at a set of first principles (e.g., the axioms of Euclidean geometry) or at some theorem(s) previously proven by such axioms. At this point we have succeeded in proving the original proposition, and the analysis has been completed. In synthesis, on the other hand, we start with the axioms and derive their provable consequences according to the natural order of deduction. The "solution backwards" attributed to analysis by Pappus is the logical inverse of the natural order of deduction found in synthesis.

The logic involved in these processes had, of course, a long history prior to Pappus. Much earlier Aristotle in his *Prior* and *Posterior Analytics* had stated in detail the conditions to be met by synthesis, which results in an axiomatic, deductive system; and Euclid had succeeded in producing such a synthesis for geometry in his *Elements*. In this context the process of increasing knowledge within the system was seen as consisting of analysis as the logical inverse of deductive synthesis, or reasoning backwards, as Pappus put it.

Two qualifications must be noted. The methods of analysis and synthesis as described in Pappus' text must be applied to propositions which are simply convertible for the inversion of the reasoning process to be logically valid. This raises serious doubt about the applicability of this doctrine to the natural sciences. Secondly, and more importantly for our later argumentation, there is a difference between (1) generating an hypothesis as a tentative answer to a problem in the first place, and (2) showing that some line of argumentation constitutes a formal proof of a given hypothesis by derivation from a set of axioms. The latter, which is what is accomplished by analysis in Pappus' sense of the term, *discovers the proof by means of synthesis* of an already given proposition; the former, which antedates such an analysis, *formulates a proposition* which can become a candidate for later analytic consideration. In short, analysis in Pappus' sense does not generate the hypothesis; rather it discovers the proof of an already given hypothesis. This distinction is frequently blurred over in discussions of scientific discovery. The creative thinking involved in initially formulating an hypothesis is not the same thing as the subsequent determination of its truth by incorporating it into a deductive system of proof (nor is it the same as the inductive appeal to facts for verification, as happens in the natural sciences.) The inverse logical reasoning patterns attributed by Pappus to analysis apply only to the latter.

At this point let us formalize the above argument by distinguishing between P-analysis and G-analysis. P-analysis is Pappus' sense of *discovering the proof within a system* of an already given proposition by means of inverse deductive reasoning; G-analysis is the process of *generating a proposition as a solution to a question*. What we wish to argue in this paper is: (1) that Descartes was very much aware of this distinction; (2) that he focused primarily on G-analysis in the *Regulae* in his search for a new "method for finding out the truth"; and (3) that he failed in his attempts to lay down rules governing G-analysis.

Descartes on Analysis

When one examines Descartes' writings on method, one of the first impressions is that he is not very clear at all on the meaning of the term 'analysis.' This expression is used in a bewildering variety of ways. L. J. Beck, who has subjected the *Regulae* to a close and illuminating study, puts it thusly: "It is particularly the word 'analysis' which is used somewhat loosely. To be sure of the sense in which it is being employed, it is almost always necessary to look at the context."[6] Sometimes 'analysis' is used in the sense of a search for first principles, and sometimes in the more general sense of the discovery of new knowledge (G-analysis). In many places it is used in the reductionistic sense of breaking up a complex whole into its simple parts. At times 'analysis' refers to a general methodology which can be applied equally well in dealing with all kinds of subject-matter, while at other times it seems to be used in the more restricted sense of being a mathematical method. Especially in the latter context analysis is treated as a process of assuming that what is unknown is known, and then deriving its specific truth value from the relationships which can be designated between the unknown and the known (P-analysis). Still further, 'analysis' in other places, especially in applied contexts, can be interpreted as the method of hypothetical postulation in which one assumes a solution to an unanswered question and then proceeds to show that the consequences of this assumption are true, and thus the assumption is converted to a truth. This meaning of the term is well illustrated, for example, by Descartes' treatment of the nature of light in his *Optics*,[7] and is evidence for Olscamp's claim that Descartes deserves credit for being the modern founder of the hypothetical-deductive method.[8] This list of meanings for the term 'analysis' could be extended further, but need not be since Beck[9] and Buchdahl[10] have already sorted out these meanings with sufficient detail for our purposes.

Despite this embarrassing proliferation of specific meanings for the notion of analysis (which are not necessarily in conflict with each other), careful reflection on Descartes' discussion of the analytic method reveals a common pattern which is the core of the doctrine. Analysis for Descartes is always a method of solving a problem. This presupposes that we begin by being able to designate precisely what the problem is that is under examination. Then by a variety of routes, which differ apparently because of the nature of the problem, the mind moves to an understanding of the matter in question. Thus analysis culminates in discovering something new, something previously unknown (e.g., P-analysis discovers a new proof, G-analysis discovers a new idea), and hence it is that stage of methodology in general at which new content is added to our knowledge and a genuine advancement of learning has taken place.

The central difficulty, of which Descartes is quite well aware, is to define the question with enough precision to enable one to find its solution, i.e., to make the question "perfectly understood," as he puts it in Rule XIII. To this end, Descartes lays down the following conditions.

> Among the 'questions' whose meaning is quite plain, we must to begin with note that we place those only in which we perceive three things distinctly; to wit, the marks by which we can identify what we are looking for when it occurs; what precisely the fact is from which our answer ought to be deduced; and how it is to be proved that these (the ground and its consequent) so depend one on another that it is impossible for either to change while the other remains unchanged. In this way we shall have all the premises we require, and the only thing remaining to

be shown will be how to discover the conclusion.[11]

Imperfectly understood questions (to have been treated in the never written Rules XXV - XXXVI) apparently would have to be reduced to perfectly understood questions.[12] But how are these latter questions to be answered? In the above quotation Descartes talks about a deductive reasoning process which discovers the solution. But unlike P-analysis, in these unsolved questions we do not yet have a proposition which is a candidate to serve as a solution, but we must generate it (G-analysis). It is not an issue of finding a proof, but of generating a proposition. How is this to be done, and what are the "distinctly perceived marks" which identify the candidate solution if it were to appear somehow? This first requirement (which is the core of Meno's paradox) cannot be reduced to a set of rules, which Descartes apparently came to see and which may be the reason why the *Regulae* breaks off in the middle of this discussion and was never completed. In short, even if ideas are innate, their becoming available at the right time as problem solutions in the process of G-analysis is peculiarly rule-resistant.

Descartes seems to be reasonably clear and definite however on the two terminal points of the process of G-analysis; namely, the statement of the problem and the intuition of the solution. The ambiguity lies between these two extremes. This ambiguity should not be taken as a defect in Descartes' specification of his method, but rather as a sign that he knew from experience what it is like to do creative scientific work. This experience had taught Descartes that the interior of the process of G-analysis cannot be specified as occurring along only one route. Different types of question will require different methods of resolution. For the reasons just indicated, Descartes was forced to resist the temptation to formulate the interior of the process of G-analysis in terms of some kind of a set of determinate steps or procedures to be followed. Even though Descartes is a mechanist with a vengeance when it comes to his understanding of the physical world, he resolutely eliminates such an approach from his view of the human mind functioning in its analytic mode. Descartes' refusal to limit the interior of the process of G-analysis to only one route or procedure may well be the reason for the ambiguity in, and plurality of meanings of, the term 'analysis' in his writings.

Despite these caveats we can, however, be a bit more definite. In most cases Descartes views the process of analysis as a movement from the complex to the simple. Analysis for Descartes thus tends to be reductionistic, i.e., it assumes that large scale phenomena and problem areas are composed of parts, and that a grasping of these parts provides the means for the understanding of the whole. Thus, for example, Descartes' complex doctrine of enumeration[13] (which, by the way, has nothing to do with enumerative induction) tells us among other things to make a careful inventory of all the parts of the whole so that nothing essential is omitted and nothing extraneous included. His constant advice to repeat our enumerations in the process of analysis[14] (as well as in the process of synthesis, where they serve a different function[15]) is Descartes' attempt to prevent the finite inquiring mind from going astray by inadvertence or lack of attention.

However one gets from the initial problem to its solution, Descartes is very specific about the nature of the solution. It consists of an intuition into simple natures and their interrelations.[16] (The terminology of "simple natures" is dropped after the *Regulae* and is replaced in Descartes' later writings by a theory of essences, attributes, and modes—but this does not affect the methodological character of analysis.) This presupposes an ontology of ultimate entities or properties of some sort, whatever they may be called, and reinforces the reductionistic tone of Cartesian analysis. Epistemologically these simple natures are ultimate intelligibilities which cannot be analyzed into any more basic meanings, and thus the process of analysis comes to its termination. The act of intuition is, of course, non-discursive, and in several places Descartes indicates that intuition occurs spontaneously and instantaneously once the mind is directly presented with a simple nature.[17] The real work of the method of G-analysis consists then in clearing away all the obstacles and irrelevant parts of the complex whole so that all that remains is the relevant simple natures. At this stage intuition is automatic as well as absolutely certain, and the original problem is solved.

As we shall see in more detail later, the epistemological and ontological underpinnings of Descartes' theory of analysis are the sources of some serious difficulties within the Cartesian conception of science. But on the credit side Descartes has made a major step forward, indeed a genuine turning point in the history of scientific method, by formulating a methodology which is not merely a logic disputation or justification about already acquired views (i.e., P-analysis), but which instead is primarily designed to produce new knowledge (i.e., G-analysis). In short, Descartes conceives analysis as a methodology of discovery—which had the great advantage at the time of re-directing man's intellectual energies away from the arena of witty but fruitless debates and towards the much more serious and exciting business of advancing human learning.

Descartes on Synthesis

So far we have seen only half of the picture. When the process of analysis has been successfully completed, then the second phase of method, synthesis, is ready to begin. What we have from G-analysis to commence the process of synthesis is a set of first principles or axioms which can serve as the fountainhead for the deductive derivation of the content of a given science. The process of synthesis is, in effect, this method of deducing theorems from axioms in order to produce an axiomatization of the science.

To make this work Descartes is forced to introduce a number of stipulations. First the number of simple natures must be finite; in fact, Descartes declares that there are relatively few simple natures.[18] The reason for this stipulation is that one must possess all of the first principles of a science to be able to formulate it properly and completely, and this could not be done if the number of simple natures were infinite. Unfortunately, Descartes simply states that this is the case without giving anything that could count as a justification of this assumption. No doubt his confidence in the rationality of the universe and in the power of the human mind to know with certitude is operating here. But this is hardly a justification that simple natures constitute a small finite set.

A second stipulation Descartes makes about synthesis is that each step in the deductive chain, or each demonstration as he would put it, must be secured by another act of intuition.[19] Thus the mode of knowing involved in the grasping of simple natures cascades down the deductive chain (this is Descartes' own metaphor), and is repeated at each link in the chain. Descartes says this in order to guarantee that the same degree of full certitude which he claimed for the intuition of simple natures is carefully preserved throughout the entire deductive chain, no matter how long it becomes. Thus when he says in the *Regulae* that there are only two sources of certain knowledge: namely, intuition and demonstration,[20] he could have added that the latter actually reduces to the former. From the Cartesian point of view this strategy has great advantage since it in effect denies that there are any degrees of truth value within the sciences.

Descartes realizes that these chains of demonstrations can become exceedingly long—a fact which constitutes a problem because of the limited degree of attention and memory which the human mind can muster. In the ideal order he would add as a third stipulation on the process of synthesis that the whole deductive series be grasped as a unit in one intuition.[21] This is possible in relatively short sequences but becomes impractical in the more significant cases of elaborately developed sciences. Hence as an aid to the weakness of human memory and to the limited range of human attention, Descartes constantly advises us to review and enumerate the prior deductive steps as frequently as possible. In the *Regulae* this is called induction, and is indeed an unusual use of that term. Induction here does not mean the process of generalization from experienced particulars, but rather the complete enumeration of the individual demonstrations in a deductive chain. In pointing out this peculiar meaning of induction we do not mean to imply that Cartesian science is cut off from a basis in sensory fact. If the original problem to be resolved in the process of analysis was a physical question, then there is sensory input at the very beginning and it is preserved in the process of synthesis. The paradox in the terminology used is that analysis for Descartes is *not* inductive in character, but intuitional, while the *deductive* phase of synthesis does not involve induction but only in a special sense of that term.

The final stipulation about the process of synthesis can best be introduced by quoting Rule VI from the *Regulae* which is the rule defining synthesis.

In order to separate out what is quite simple from what is complex, and to arrange these matters methodically, we ought, in the case of every series in which we have deduced certain facts the one from the other, to notice which fact is simple, and to mark the interval, greater, less, or equal, which separates all the others from this.[22]

Descartes adds immediately that this rule at first seems quite innocuous but that actually "it contains, nevertheless, the chief secret of method, and none in the whole of this treatise is of greater utility." This comment is a clear clue that something quite important is being stated here. In order for either phase of method—analysis or synthesis—to work at all for Descartes, he must claim that "all facts can be arranged in certain series ... in so far as certain truths can be known from others."[23] Analysis proceeds from complex facts to simple ones, and synthesis reverses the direction of the movement of thought. But what is meant by a "fact" here? The term is conveniently ambiguous. Taken ontologically it refers to the properties possessed by objects, physical or immaterial, independently of our knowledge of them. Taken epistemologically the term refers to our concepts of these properties. Since facts come arranged in series, this in effect means that not all properties of objects and not all concepts are on a par. Rather they are both ordered in a non-mutual relation of independence and dependence, a fixed hierarchy of natural order. This is what guarantees success to the process of analysis which can now be seen as an exploration of the series from the dependent to the independent. The same could be said of synthesis except that the order is reversed.

If we are correct in giving such a double interpretation to the key notion of a fact, then another important consequence follows for Cartesian method. There is a one-to-one correspondence between the natural order of ontological properties and the logical order of concepts. Let us call this the principle of logical-ontological isomorphism. This is the essence of Cartesian methodology and the driving force behind Descartes' version of the analytic-synthetic modes of thought.

In summary, then, Cartesian method, modeled after the physical sciences and primarily mathematics, is a two-phase affair. G-analysis, which must come first, is fundamentally a methodology of discovery terminating in the certain intuition of simple natures as the resolutions of the problems initially presented for solution. Synthesis, which builds from the results of analysis, is a methodology of deductive proof of theorems from axioms. Both phases of method ultimately are grounded in the principle of logical-ontological isomorphism. The directions of the thought process in analysis and synthesis are the reverse of each other. But Descartes consistently resists the temptation to conclude from this that they have a common logical pattern. Synthesis is governed by standard deductive logic, but G-analysis (as distinct from P-analysis) is alogical since there are no rules leading one to the having of an intuition which is non-discursive. G-analysis and synthesis thus are distinctively different processes for Descartes and cannot be lumped together as simply the inverse of each other. Descartes seems to have felt that G-analysis is the more important of the two since it forces one to discover the truth for oneself. This at any rate is the reason he gives as to why he wrote the *Meditations* in the analytic mode.[24] The demand for a synthetic presentation of the same material was acknowledged three years later in the *Principia philosophiae*.

Later Cartesian Logic

Before we conclude this paper, it would be well to add a few comments on the curious later history of the notion of analysis within Cartesianism. Our discussion has been based primarily on the *Regulae* which Descartes wrote around 1628. This work was not published during his lifetime, and did not appear in print until 1701. However, Descartes' ideas in the *Regulae* were not unknown in the second half of the seventeenth century since some manuscript copies were in circulation. One of these was possessed by Antoine Arnauld (1612-1694) and was extensively used by him in writing the second edition of the famous *Port-Royal Logic*, which appeared in 1664. This book is extraordinary in many ways. The occasion for writing it was a bet by Arnauld that everything of value in logic could be taught in four or five days.[25] The book was a phenomenal success and became one of the main avenues through which Cartesianism gained and held its popularity for so long. It went through innumerable editions and reprintings, was translated into most European languages, and was still used as a text-book in logic two hundred years later. This latter was at least in part due to the almost total absence of advances in theoretical logic between the publication of the *Port-Royal Logic* and the appearance of Boole's *Mathematical Analysis of Logic* in 1847.

In Part IV of the *Port-Royal Logic* Arnauld discusses the Cartesian doctrine of analysis and synthesis, but the tone has changed. The method of analysis is discussed in only one short chapter (Chapter 2) while synthesis is given nine chapters (Chapters 3-11) in which detailed rules are set down for forming definitions, axioms, and demonstrations. The treatment of analysis is especially interesting. It is still a technique of solving problems and is described as follows:

> In every question there is something which is unknown, otherwise there would be nothing to look for. But this very unknown must be marked out and designated by certain conditions, directing us to search for one thing rather than another and enabling us to judge whether we have found what we seek. We must take careful account of the conditions placed on the unknown, adding no condition not included in the question and omitting no

condition which is included. Error is possible in either of these ways.[26]

The obvious question to ask again is how can all these conditions be so precisely designated *before* the problem is solved. For some mathematical questions this may be possible, and almost all of Arnauld's examples, like Descartes', are taken from this area. But what if the question is, for example, "What is the cause of gravity?" What do we do now to identify and evaluate all the possibly relevant conditions? Arnauld can give no reply other than to remind us that analysis "after all consists more of discernment and acumen than of particular procedures."[27] Apparently his view is that problem-solving follows no rules and is therefore a matter of individual psychology. Arnauld's de-emphasis on analysis may also be due to the fact that he maintains that analysis and synthesis have the same internal structure and differ only in the direction which our thinking pursues. He puts this very neatly when he says that analysis and synthesis "differ only as the road by which we ascend from a valley to a mountain differs from the road by which we descend from the mountain to the valley."[28] It is curious to note that exactly the same metaphor was used by N. R. Hanson in one of his later papers on the logic of discovery where he concedes that he had not been able to discern a logic of discovery which differs *as a logic* from the logic of verification.[29] The long use and influence of the *Port-Royal Logic* suggests that it may be one of the chief reasons why contemporary philosophy of science has largely neglected the discovery phase of science, preferring like Arnauld to list this as an issue relating to the individual psychology of the creative thinker.

Be that as it may, there is a substantive point at issue here. Is it possible to formulate a methodology of discovery? Descartes says "yes" and presents us with his method of G-analysis which is a bold attempt along these lines even though he failed to reduce such an analysis to a set of rules. Arnauld, along with many later writers, says "no" and leaves us with only an appeal to individual discernment and acumen. What are we to make of this disparity between Descartes and Arnauld? Has Descartes become scholasticized by his followers to the point where his own original and valuable contribution on this point has been lost in the formalism of a text-book? Or has Arnauld recognized and eliminated a major defect in his master's manuscript, a defect because the proposal of a methodology of discovery is impossible of attainment? If the latter judgment prevails, then Descartes' version of the analytic-synthetic method was an utter failure. If the earlier view is correct, then despite whatever internal deficiencies there may be in Descartes' theory of analysis, he is basically on the right track, and his views on method mark a significant advance in the philosophy of science. Our sympathies are with Descartes on this matter. For in our judgment he is correct in insisting that scientific method consists of two distinct phases which are structurally distinct and in insisting that the innovative thinking involved in the process of discovery or G-analysis is rational (even though not reducible to logical rules) and is not merely a matter of idiosyncratic discernment and acumen.[30]

Conclusions

Despite these plaudits, Descartes' version of the analytic-synthetic method is open to some serious criticisms. Looking at it from the easy wisdom of hindsight, one must conclude that the subsequent history of science has shown first that Descartes' claim for absolute certitude in science was excessive, and second that his notion that scientific methodology should culminate in ontological intuitions was mistaken. But judged from the perspective of his contemporaries, Descartes' position is less unusual. Galileo, for example, also had a doctrine of analysis which culminated in ontological commitments, albeit they were mathematical in character. In short, methodological discussions during the first half of the century were closely connected to the demand of arriving at ontological insights.

If we view Descartes' version of the analytic-synthetic method from the perspective of the second half of the century, then other emphases become prominent. Newton also had a doctrine of analysis and synthesis, but in his case analysis results in principles which are "accurately or very nearly true, notwithstanding any contrary hypotheses that may be imagined, till such time as other phenomena occur, by which they may either be made more accurate, or liable to exceptions."[31] The claim to absolute certitude has been dropped from this Newtonian version of the analytic method. And the reason for this is that Newton has also dropped the demand that scientific method terminate in ontological insights. He consistently resists attempts to force him to say what he thinks the "true nature" is of such things as gravity, light, etc. What we have rather is the more familiar scientific attitude of being comfortable and satisfied with less than absolute certitude. This change in Newton's version of the analytic-synthetic method strikes at the very heart of Descartes' version; namely, the principle of logical-ontological isomorphism.

Finally Descartes' frequent appeal to intuition is a sore point. Like any theory of intuition, it shares the double burden (1) of being potentially incommunicable, since one must experience the intuition personally, one cannot have it explained; and (2) of being unanalyzable in principle since there is nothing more basic to turn to for discussion. Serving thus as a last court of appeal, Descartes' doctrine of intuition threatens to become esoteric and dogmatic. In his favor it must be admitted that inferential knowledge must originate from some sort of non-inferential knowledge, and the appeal to intuition is a possible, but not the exclusive, way to deal with this aspect of how we know. Again this brings us back to the isomorphism in Descartes between the order of concepts and the ontological order in things outside the mind. The intuition is a simultaneous grasping of the meaning of the concept and of its ontological counterpart. On this basis everything is indeed clear and distinct, including the notion of intuition itself. But the waters become considerably muddied if the basic assumption of logical-ontological isomorphism is itself thrown into doubt, as the pressures from the later history of thought demand. The Cartesian conception of science and its method is then in serious straits indeed.

Despite the severity and fatal nature of these difficulties, one cannot help but greatly admire Descartes' attempt at formulating his version of the analytic-synthetic method. He is correct on much of what he has to say, especially his sharp distinction of the moment of discovery from the moment of proof in science, his strong insistence on the rigid deductive logical structure of the latter, and his equally strong insistence on the rational but non-logical structure of the former.

Notes

[1] For example, Descartes says this explicitly in *Regulae ad directionem ingenii*, Rule IV. *(Philosophical Works of Descartes*, translated by E. S. Haldane and G. R. T. Ross, New York: Dover, 1955, Vol. I, p. 10. Henceforth this edition will be referred to as "Haldane-Ross.")

[2] *Lettre à Mersenne*, 11 Oct. 1638, in Descartes, *Oeuvres*, eds. C. Adam and P. Tannery (1st edition, Paris: Cerf, 1897-1910), Vol. II, p. 380.

[3] All four of these works have been published together, as Descartes intended, in a complete English version: René Descartes, *Discourse on Method, Optics, Geometry, and Meteorology*, translated with an Introduction by Paul J. Olscamp (New York: The Bobbs-Merrill Co., Inc., 1965).

[4] *Regulae*, Rule IV (Haldane-Ross, I, 12).

[5] Pappus, *Synagoge*, Book VII, as translated in Sir Thomas Heath, *A History of Greek Mathematics* (Oxford: At the Clarendon Press, 1921), Vol. II, p. 400.

[6] L. J. Beck, *The Method of Descartes: A Study of the "Regulae"* (Oxford: At the Clarendon Press, 1952), p. 157.

[7] *Optics*, First Discourse.

[8] Cf. Olscamp's Introduction to *Discourse on Method, Optics, Geometry, and Meteorology*, cited above.

[9] L. J. Beck, *op. cit.*, Chapter XI.

[10] Gerd Buchdahl, "Descartes' Anticipation of a 'Logic of Scientific Discovery,'" in *Scientific Change*, ed. by A. C. Crombie (New York: Basic Books, Inc., 1963), pp. 399-417.

[11] *Regulae*, Rule XII (Haldane-Ross, I, 48).

[12] From Rule XIII to the end, the purpose of the *Regulae* was to spell out the methods of solving various types of questions. Descartes projected a total of thirty-six rules but the treatise breaks off after Rule XXI.

[13] For an excellent discussion on this very complex concept in Descartes, cf. L. J. Beck, *op. cit.*, Chapter VIII.

[14] *Regulae*, Rules VII and VIII.

[15] In this context "enumeration" refers to a repeated review of the individual steps in a deductive chain of reasoning so that all of the force of prior proofs can be brought to bear on the question at hand, thus resulting in one intuition of the whole series of deductive proofs (method of synthesis). Cf. *Regulae*, Rule XI.

[16] *Regulae*, Rule XII (Haldane-Ross, I, 40-45) gives a general summary of the analytic-synthetic method in which this point emerges very clearly.

[17] For example, cf. *Regulae*, Rule XII (Haldane-Ross, I, 46).

[18] *Regulae*, Rule VI (Haldane-Ross, I, 16).

[19] *Regulae*, Rule XI.

[20] *Regulae*, Rule III (Haldane-Ross, I, 7).

[21] *Regulae*, Rule XI specifies this requirement.

[22] Haldane-Ross, I, 15.

[23] *Ibid.*

[24] *Reply to Objections II* (Haldane-Ross, II, 49).

[25] This point is made in the Foreword. Cf. Antoine Arnauld, *The Art of Thinking: Port-Royal Logic*, translated with an Introduction by J. Dickoff and P. James (New York: The Bobbs-Merrill Co., Inc., 1964), p. 3.

[26] *Ibid.*, p. 304.

[27] *Ibid.*, p. 308.

[28] *Ibid.*, p. 307.

[29] N. R. Hanson, "Notes Toward a Logic of Discovery," in *Perspectives on Peirce*, ed. by R. J. Bernstein (New Haven: Yale University Press, 1965), pp. 42-65.

[30] For a further discussion of this point, cf. my *Discovery in the Physical* Sciences (South Bend: University of Notre Dame Press, 1969), Chapter I.

[31] This is the fourth of Newton's "Rules of Reasoning in Philosophy" which appears at the beginning of Book III of his *Mathematical Principles of Natural Philosophy*, Motte's translation revised by Cajori (Berkeley: University of California Press, 1962), Vol. II, p. 400.

8.

HOBBES AND SCEPTICISM

by Richard H. Popkin

Not too infrequently either Hobbes has been labeled a 'sceptic' by scholars, or some aspect of his thought has been claimed to be a form of scepticism. For instance, Dorothea Krook in her article on "Thomas Hobbes's Doctrine of Meaning and Truth" began by asserting, "It is generally acknowledged that Hobbes's radical scepticism is intimately connected with his nominalism."[1] A few lines later, she said: "The connection between Hobbes's scepticism and nominalism is indeed sufficiently attested by the pervasive influence of his nominalism in his whole doctrine of commonwealth in *Leviathan* ..."[2] The paper goes into great and careful detail about the character of Hobbes' nominalism. However, one can only speculate about the nature of his scepticism from remarks like, "The peculiar interest of Hobbes's scepticism for the philosophical reader is that it is the joint product of his radical nominalism in logic, in epistemology and in metaphysics."[3]

In Father Copleston's discussion of Hobbes in his history of philosophy, he devoted three pages to the question of whether Hobbes was a sceptic.[4] Copleston felt the answer was "no". He pointed out that many commentators have spoken of Hobbes's nominalistic scepticism. However, he contended, "If, therefore, we press the empiricist aspect of Hobbes's philosophy, it is possible to argue that his nominalism is not necessarily infected with scepticism."[5] The furthest Father Copleston would go was to suggest that perhaps Hobbes was a sceptic-nominalist.[6] However, Copleston maintained that anyone who reads all of Hobbes's philosophical writings is unlikely to consider that 'sceptic' is the most appropriate label for his view.

J. W. N. Watkins, in his *Hobbes's System of Ideas*, spoke of Hobbes's ethical scepticism, as contrasted with his ethical authoritarianism. The ethical scepticism is shown to be a fairly basic part of Hobbes's case. Watkins devoted a couple of pages to trying to show that ethical scepticism is not the proper result of finding out that there cannot be a proven or well-justified system of moral propositions.[7]

Hobbes is also sometimes called a religious sceptic, partly because of his view that Moses was not the author of the entire Pentateuch. (We will discuss this later on). One could easily multiply the free and easy way Hobbes has been labeled a sceptic, or has been saved from that label.

What I intend to do here is to try to delineate both historically and ideologically where Hobbes falls in the development of modern scepticism. Ten years ago I decided to start the next volume of my history of scepticism with Hobbes. The volume has yet to come to fruition, and I have turned my attention for some time to ascertaining Spinoza's position in seventeenth century scepticism.

Hobbes is historically most interesting. As we all know Hobbes spent many years in Paris, 1629-31, 1634, 1637 and 1640-1651.[8] What is not as well remembered is that he spent a great deal of his time, when most of his books were written, as a central member of a circle of Mersenne and Gassendi, both of whom were very interested in scepticism. I have tried to show that they were both "constructive or mitigated" sceptics, who were convinced that in a fundamental sense one could not establish the truth or falsity of any of our beliefs. Nonetheless, they each held in their own way that we are able to find adequate ways of dealing with the world. Gassendi called what he was doing, namely developing a modern atomic system of science, a via media between scepticism and dogmatism.[9] When Hobbes arrived in Paris in 1640, he stayed with a member of the Mersenne-Gassendi circle, Jacques Du Bosc, who was a close friend of Samuel Sorbière.[10] In the Mersenne-Gassendi circle were people far more sceptical, such as Guy Patin, Gabriel Naudé, Francois La Mothe le Vayer, and Samuel Sorbière.[11] The latter was at one time working on a French translation of Sextus Empiricus.[12] After he became one of Gassendi's chief disciples (who criticized Gassendi for not being sufficiently sceptical),[13] he was given the task by Mersenne of preparing a French translation of Hobbes's *De Cive*. Mersenne had told him that if he studied the work he would no longer be a complete sceptic.[14] Sorbière translated *De Cive*, remained a sceptic, and stayed in close relations with Hobbes. When Sorbière visited England, one of the main purposes of the trip was to see Hobbes again.[15]

Hobbes was a member of this avant-garde group in Paris for many years. Very little has been done about examining Hobbes's views in the context of Parisian philosophy of the time. Even the French Jesuit historian of philosophy, Gaston Sortais, who dug up so much material on other members of this group, did not delve deeply into Hobbes in the French scene.[16] The recently published manuscript of Hobbes's first philosophical work, his answer to Thomas White, was written in Paris, where Hobbes knew White. The manuscript was found about 30 years ago in the Bibliotheque Nationale in some papers of Mersenne.[17]

If Hobbes was deeply involved with the French new scientists, the new philosophers and the new sceptics, did he imbibe any of their views? He was definitely influenced by the mechanistic outlook that pervaded the scientific work of Mersenne, Gassendi, Descartes and others. But, if one compares how much scepticism is discussed by Mersenne, Gassendi and Descartes, with how much space is given over to it by Hobbes, the result is most striking. Mersenne wrote a thousand page book, *La verité des sciences contre les sceptiques* ou *pyrrhoniens*, of which the first quarter is a running commentary on Sextus Empiricus's ancient sceptical treatise, *The Outlines of Pyrrhonism*. Gassendi had written a sceptical attack on Aristotelianism, as well as the first part of his *Syntagma Philosophicum* which discussed the sceptical challenge to other epistemologies. Descartes, of course, devoted a good deal of his *Discourse on Method* and his *Meditations on First Philosophy* to developing a complete scepticism and then overcoming it.[18] Hobbes, we know, read Descartes' *Discourse* and *Meditations*, since he was one of the first persons to write an answer to Descartes.

In the light of the above, it is quite surprising that the index of the Molesworth edition of the *English Works* of Hobbes lists *one* entry under "Sceptics" or "Scepticism". It refers to a passage in *De Corpore* where Hobbes briefly chided the sophists and the sceptics for the way they denied and opposed the truth.[19] I have come across another reference to the sceptics in Hobbes's *Six Lessons to the Professors of the Mathematics*. In this work Hobbes twice cited points in Sextus Empiricus about mathematics. (And this seems to be the sole work in which Sextus is mentioned.) In discussing what he thought were inadequacies in Euclid's definitions, Hobbes said that Sextus used some of these definitions, "to the overthrow of that so much renowned evidence of geometry"![20] Later on Hobbes pointed out that Hobbes's mathematical opponent and Sextus had misunderstood Euclid's first definition. Sextus had then argued that geometry is no science. Hobbes's opponent by doing the same has "betrayed the most evident sciences to the sceptics."[21]

These two references hardly make it seem that Hobbes cared very much about scepticism and sceptics. He lived in an intellectual society in which one of the greatest issues of the time was whether or not there was any way of overcoming the sceptical doubts about man's ability to gain knowledge about the world. In my book on the *History of Scepticism*, I have traced the way the sceptical challenge dominated French intellectual life in the first half of the seventeenth century. In contrast to this, the works Hobbes wrote while in Paris, the center of the sceptical ferment, reflect practically nothing of what was going on. Had Hobbes been a recluse who never talked to anyone in the city at the time, then the detachment in his writings from the vital issues of the time would be understandable. However, since we know that, *au contraire*, Hobbes was involved all of the time with the leading figures who were discussing scepticism, some explanation is needed to account for what Hobbes wrote in Paris. Perhaps if a detailed study were made of Hobbes's actual relationships with the French and English intellectuals in Paris, we might see if there was something odd or different about Hobbes's reactions to the ideas being discussed around him from that of the others.[22]

Thus, if Hobbes does not seem to have been part of the sceptical crisis going on around him, he was nonetheless accused of being a sceptic, not in the sense of a Pyrrhonian sceptic, nor of a follower of Montaigne. Rather Hobbes, as soon as he began to publish, was accused of being a sceptic about religious convictions. At the time that *De Cive* was published, Descartes charged that the work contained dangerous maxims.[23] After *Leviathan* appeared, the charge of scepticism about religion became both more precise, and more forceful. One specific item which was brought up a great deal was the claim made in Part III, Chap. 33 concerning whether Moses wrote the Pentateuch. The chapter has an innocent enough looking title, "Of the number, Antiquity, Scope, Authority and Interpreters of the Books of Holy Scripture." At the outset Hobbes pointed out that it was of the greatest importance to know what God hath said. The Canon of the Church of England tells us what books to accept as biblical. But, "Who were the original writers of the several Books of Holy Scripture, has not been made evident by any sufficient testimony of other history, which is the only proof of a matter of fact; nor can be, by any arguments of natural reason; for reason serves only to convince the truth, not of fact, but of consequence. The light, therefore, that must guide us in this question, must be that which is held out unto us from the books themselves; and this light, though it show us not the writer of every book, yet it is not unuseful to give us knowledge of the time, wherein they were written."[24]

Starting with the Pentateuch, Hobbes argued that it is not enough to say that they were written by Moses because they are called the five books of Moses. In fact, the last chapter of Deuteronomy deals with the death of Moses. So Hobbes declared, "It is, therefore manifest, that those words were written after his interment".[25] If one then says Moses wrote all of the Pentateuch except the last chapter, Hobbes then pointed to other lines in Genesis and Numbers which appear to have been after Moses. From this excursus into biblical criticism, Hobbes concluded "But, though Moses did not compile these books entirely, and in the form we have them; yet he wrote all that which he is there said to have written."[26]

This less than shattering claim about the Mosaic authorship of the first five books of the Bible was enough to earn Hobbes a place in defenses of orthodoxy in the 17th century as a member of the unholy trinity of religious sceptics, Hobbes, Isaac La Peyrère and Spinoza, who had struck at the very foundations of religious knowledge. In later times up to the present Hobbes is usually listed in the histories of Bible scholarship as the first to publish a denial of the Mosaic authorship in 1651. We'll see that his "denial" is much less of a challenge than others being made at the time.

As early as the twelfth century, the Jewish scholar, Ibn Ezra (1092-1167), indicated that there were some lines that weren't by Moses, because they dealt with matters after his death. Ibn Ezra did not use this to suggest any scepticism about the Bible, but rather to suggest that there might be something special in these non-Mosaic lines. During the outburst of Bible study in the 16th century, several scholars saw the difficulty involved in claiming that Moses was the sole author. Suggestions were made that perhaps Ezra wrote some or all of the Pentateuch.[27] From Hobbes onward the actual denial that Moses was the author of the Pentateuch was definitely a key issue in developing a scepticism about revealed religion in the Jewish or Christian sense. At the end of the 17th century, the Catholic theologian Louis Ellies-du Pin, who put together various encyclopedias about religion and theology, declared that, "Of all of the paradoxes which have been advanced in our century, there is none more bold, in my view, nor more dangerous than the opinion of those who have denied that Moses was the author of the Pentateuch."[28] The dangerous religious sceptics who held this radical view were listed as Hobbes, La Peyrère, Spinoza and Richard Simon.[29] Du Pin made clear that the whole relation of the supposedly revealed document, the Bible, to the truth becomes problematical, and a person can doubt the veracity of the Bible. Moses provided the critical link of man to God, since supposedly God told him what is in the first five books. If the author or authors are not Moses, then the Bible becomes questionable as a source of truth.

Hobbes may have been classed with the other radical Bible scholars by those engaged in the hunting of Leviathan.[30] And for his views on the Mosaic authorship of the Pentateuch, Hobbes may have been considered a religious sceptic. However, if one compares him with La Peyrère or Spinoza, Hobbes hardly deserves to be considered a menace to established religion. Hobbes must have known La Peyrère, who was the secretary to the Prince of Condé, and a close friend of Mersenne and Gassendi and the other sceptical figures in the Mersenne circle.[31] In 1641 La Peyrère tried to publish his masterpiece, *Men before Adam*. He dedicated it to Cardinal Richelieu, who promptly banned it. A letter by Gabriel Naudé to Cardinal Barberini in the Vatican tells us that since the book was banned, everyone was trying to get a copy of it. The correspondence of the learned people of the time indicate that Mersenne and the author, La Peyrère, were showing everyone the work. The first refutation, by Hugo Grotius, appeared in 1643. The book itself was only published (in Holland, of course) in 1655, when it created a great stir.[32] It would seem likely that Hobbes knew the book and the author, since they moved in the same milieu. They had the same friends, and lots of common interests.

In La Peyrère's *Men before Adam* the case for doubting the Mosaic authorship is made much greater than Hobbes's. It is so much greater in fact that Hobbes's discussion of the issue looks like a truncated version of La Peyrère's. He pointed out a wide variety of Scriptural texts that most likely could not have been written by Moses. They included not only the lines about Moses's death, but also different inconsistent lines and a lot of discrepancies. From all of this the most that La Peyrère was willing to allow was that Moses probably made a diary, and part of the Biblical account is copied from this. In evaluating the evidence that he had set forth, La Peyrère enunciated his revolutionary theory — "I need not trouble the Reader much further to prove a thing in itself sufficiently evident, that the first five books of the Bible were not written by *Moses*, as is thought. Nor need any one wonder after this, when he reads many things confus'd and out of order, obscure, deficient, many things omitted and misplaced, when they shall consider with themselves that they are a heap of Copie confusedly taken." La Peyrère's denial of the Mosaic authorship was followed by still stronger cases developed by Spinoza and Richard Simon. In the light of what La Peyrère was saying before and after the publication of *Leviathan*, what Spinoza said in the *Tractatus* of 1670, and Richard Simon in his *Critical History of the Old Testament* of 1678, Hobbes hardly seems very sceptical or shocking. Simon himself told La Peyrère, "It seems to me that your reflections are going to ruin the Christian religion entirely."[34] An unsympathetic reader, the English jurist, Sir Matthew Hale, made a stronger claim. He said that the belief that La Peyrère's interpretations of the Bible "were true would necessarily not only weaken but overthrow the Authority and Infallibility of the Sacred Scriptures."[35]

The basic issue involved in the importance of the Mosaic authorship, is that it is through Moses's role as author and his role as direct recipient of the revelation, that the truth of Judeo-Christianity is secured. Questioning the Mosaic authorship opens the door to a powerful scepticism about the truth of accepted religion. After such questioning had done its work throughout the second half of the 17th century and throughout the Enlightenment, one of the leading sceptics with regard to religious knowledge, Tom Paine, could look back and see the monumental effects of doubting the Mosaic authorship. "Take away from Genesis the belief that Moses was the author, on which only the strange belief that it is the word of God has stood, and there remains nothing of *Genesis*, but an anonymous book of stories, fables, and traditionary or invented absurdities or downright lies."[36]

The importance of Mosaic authorship was, perhaps, made still clearer by one of Paine's opponents, the Jewish polemicist, David Levi of London. In his second answer to Joseph Priestley, he asserted that "if a Jew once calls in question the authenticity of *any part* of the Pentateuch, by observing that one part is authentic, i.e., was delivered by God to Moses, and that another part is not authentic, he is no longer accounted a Jew, i.e., a true believer." Every Jew, Levi insisted, is obliged according to the Maimonides thirteen principles, "to believe that the whole law of five books is from God" and that it was delivered by Him to Moses. Christians, Levi claimed, should be under the same constraints as Jews about accepting the divine origin of Scripture, for "if any part is once proved spurious, a door will be opened for another and another without end."[37]

The fantastic sceptical potential of the denial of the Mosiac authorship played a very important part in Western intellectual history. Of the four people who played the greatest roles in advancing the consideration of the denial of the Mosaic authorship in 17th century — Hobbes, La Peyrère, Spinoza and Richard Simon, I think one has to conclude either that Hobbes was the least sceptical and the most timid, or that he was trivializing the sceptical implications of the matter. La Peyrère denied that Moses was the author of any of the first five books of the Bible. He thereby opened the door to rewriting or reconstructing the document. Spinoza, following on La Peyrère's work, denied the supernatural status of the Bible, and portrayed it as a compendium of views of the early Hebrews. It thereby became essentially a secular document to be studied as part of the history of human stupidity. Father Richard Simon, who scandalized his fellow Catholics, insisted that he accepted many of the maxims of Spinoza but not their impious conclusions. Simon insisted, Spinoza and La Peyrère notwithstanding, that he believed that the Bible was an inspired document, whose content was revealed by God to man, or men. However, and unfortunately, no existent copy of the Bible is inspired. All are written by men, printed by men, read by men, in historical contexts. They have to be studied for what they are in the hopes of finding the real Bible behind or above, or under, all of the existent ones.[38]

Thus Simon made all exstant Bibles, copies or imitations of a real one. We were, on his terms, forced in a scepticism about the truth of any particular religious claim until we could reach knowledge about the real Bible. Spinoza, on the other hand, was a complete sceptic about any kind of revealed knowledge. Even if Moses wrote any of the Bible, is there any reason to believe that Moses had any genuine religious knowledge, rather than imagined religious ideas? La Peyrère, who was actually a Messianic mystic, cast doubt on the whole text of the Pentateuch, and reduced it to a "heap or copie of copie." When one gets back to Hobbes, in the light of what his three contemporary Bible critics set forth, the passage in *Leviathan* is very tepid. Hobbes went a few steps beyond what some of the earlier 16th and 17th century Bible scholars said about the problem of whether Moses could have written all of the Pentateuch. Hobbes accepted the negative evidence, that concerning the passage about Moses's death and about events thereafter. Then Hobbes opted for a conciliatory position (even though his contemporaries may not have seen it as such). All passages which are attributed in Scripture to Moses were actually written by him. This would preserve part of the crucial revelatory links between God, Moses, and man. A most significant part of the text could still be regarded as God's undoubted message to mankind. If one accepted Hobbes at his word, one might have to modify his claim in this chapter of *Leviathan* that he accepted the Scriptural Canon of the Church of England. Hobbes's Pentateuch would be a bit smaller than the Church of England's text. But, again taking Hobbes at his word, there would be no question or doubt, no scepticism with regard to religious knowledge about the Hobbesian Mosaic Pentateuch. Hence Hobbes, on this score, was hardly the sceptic that La Peyrère, Spinoza and Simon were. In spite of this he obviously went too far, in allowing any cuts in the text of the Pentateuch. His English clerical opponents went in for the hunting of Leviathan, and accused Hobbes of being an unbeliever, an atheist, a religious sceptic.[39]

Hobbes may have been caught up in what followed. La Peyrère was considered an interesting man with unusual ideas. As long as he just showed his manuscript to leading scholars and churchmen, nothing happened. As soon as he finally published it, at Queen Christina of Sweden's behest, the book was banned in Holland (a quite unusual event of the time), burned in Paris, published in England (where it was never banned), and the author was imprisoned. He only got out of prison by abjuring his many heresies, and turning from Calvinism to Catholicism and personally apologizing to the Pope.[40] Spinoza was excommunicated from the Amsterdam Synagogue in 1656. Some recent evidence indicates that part of the grounds for the excommunication was that Spinoza and two of his friends had started developing a critical Bible scholarship in the style of La Peyrère.[41] From then on Spinoza was a notorious figure. The publication in 1670 of his *Tractatus* led to its being banned and being treated as the most dangerous work of the time. Simon published his masterpiece, *The Critical History of the Old Testament* in 1678, a year before Hobbes died. The rest of Father Simon's life was spent defending himself, while losing one ecclesiastical post after another, until he was reduced to being a priest without a diocese or function.[42] In view of the persecutions of La Peyrère, Spinoza and Simon, their opponents may have read backwards and seen that the religious scepticism of the three followed after the timid initial questioning of the Mosaic authorship by Thomas Hobbes. Hobbes's questioning by itself might not have been enough to launch the Higher Criticism of the Bible. Followed by braver figures, La Peyrère, Spinoza and Simon, who could see much more drastic implications, Hobbes became the forerunner or the initiator of a key element involved in the development of religious scepticism, the question of the Mosaic authorship, the guarantee of the truth of the content of the Bible. Hobbes got blamed for the full-blown results of his successors. As Samuel Mintz has shown, Hobbes was often attacked together with Spinoza by thinkers in England and the Continent.[43] And the States General in Holland, which had banned La Peyrère's *Men before Adam* in 1655, banned both *Leviathan* and Spinoza's *Tractatus* in 1674.[44]

A significant effect within Hobbes's philosophical system, involving his denial that Moses wrote some parts of the Pentateuch, was his conclusion that the full truth of revelation cannot be known with certainty. Different interpretations of the biblical texts have and do lead to disagreements and to disturbances in the civil order. Therefore, in order to maintain civil peace, it must be left to the civil magistrate to interpret Scripture. Here Hobbes appealed to a view which in another form appeared in *De Cive*, which is, I believe, his real contribution to modern scepticism. Hobbes may have lived, eaten and drunk among French sceptics, but no influence appears in his works. The issues they worried about are hardly dealt with in his writings. Hobbes may have been a predecessor, and possibly a friend (in the case of La Peyrère) of the religious sceptics, but he did not suggest at all the line they were to develop, that if it is doubtful that Moses wrote the Pentateuch, it is doubtful that the content of those books constitutes religious truth. Instead Hobbes pointed to a radically different solution, that of a political rather than an epistemological criterion of truth.

John Watkins considered Hobbes to be an ethical sceptic for his holding that there was no absolute or independent criterion of moral truth, but only a political one.[43] Hobbes said in *De Cive* that, "Before there was any government, *just* and *unjust* had no being, their nature only being relative to some command; and every action in its own nature is indifferent; that it becomes *just* or *unjust*, proceeds from the right of the magistrate."[46] As Watkins pointed out, according to Hobbes, it is not due to the fact that the sovereign is in possession of some superior moral knowledge that his laws are 'just'. It is the same situation as with the sovereign's theological interpretations.[47] They are authoritative, not because the sovereign has any special superior theological knowledge. The sceptical element in both the moral and the religious case lies in Hobbes's conviction that there is no rational means for deciding between either competing moral or competing religious claims. Hence, Hobbes has denied that there is any rational criterion of knowledge in these areas. Since it is necessary for social reasons that moral and religious decisions be made, the sovereign makes the decision (arbitrarily from the point of view of rational evidence for the decision), and the decision is to be accepted by the populace as if it were true. Whether the sovereign decides that people should do one thing, or should do the opposite, either decision would be equally just. This kind of ethical and theological scepticism derives from two elements of Hobbes's thought. One is his nominalism that several of the commentators either identify with his scepticism or relate much more to 15th century Ockamites than to 17th century scepticism. The theory which seems to emerge from his *Elements of Law, De Corpore, De Cive* and *Leviathan* would restrict knowledge to names, and make names arbitrary. Names become more than individuals' private marks for elements in their experience, by becoming part of a socially acceptable language. This much of the Hobbesian account, oft-repeated in his works, suggests that there is no other standard by which to judge names, and propositions in which they occur. (Some commentators, to avoid endorsing the apparent results of this nominalistic theory, stress the instances where Hobbes appeared to point to some kind of self-evidence within the propositions whose truth was alleged to be beyond question, or to the logical relations of names as the standard of truth.)[48]

The second element has been mentioned above with regard to theological and religious propositions, namely that there are social consequences of naming that can cause social friction, civil war and so on. In Hobbes's day one did not need to produce any arguments to convince people that religious differences did and could produce social disturbances of great magnitude. After all, Hobbes's theory was published at the end of the Thirty Years War and during the English Civil War. The consequences of moral disagreements are objects in so many daily quarrels, crimes, etc. The social disorder that is constantly being produced by religious and moral disagreements is so divisive and so destructive of the public peace, that there is an overriding practical reason why these disagreements have to be resolved, even if they cannot be resolved in terms of rational criteria, procedures and evidence. Hence a political resolution is seen by Hobbes as the only way out of the endless turmoil and chaos that these kinds of disagreements could cause. The sovereign then decrees the solutions, not because he knows which solutions are right and wrong, or better or worse, but because he knows that for the social good there must be solutions.

If Hobbes had restricted his use of political solutions to moral and religious questions, his readers might have been willing to find his theory acceptable. Perhaps, however, Hobbes knew from his own case history, that scientific and mathematical disagreement could lead to social rather than intellectual difficulties. There are plenty of stories about how obnoxious Hobbes was as an arguer. We know he spent years trying to convince mathematicians of his method for squaring the circle. Dr. Wallis's remark that trying to explain mathematics to Hobbes was like trying to explain colors to a blind man, seems to reflect the extreme difficulties of dealing with Hobbes in intellectual society.[49] Hobbes obviously knew that intellectual views could cause a social uproar. Mintz's book ably documents that Hobbes had succeeded in accomplishing that.[50] And Hobbes was aware, at least in *De Cive*, when he indicated that purely intellectual disagreements can affect the public peace, and that the same political means had to be employed to eliminate these disagreements as were employed to terminate ethical and theological ones. This would seem to lead to a special kind of scepticism, a political scepticism, in which there are no intellectual standards of truth or falsity, only political ones. And the assessment of the political standards is pragmatic: do they work to preserve the polis? not, are they true or right?

To what extent did Hobbes hold such a view? I have found this political sceptical view only in the latter parts of *De Cive*. There Hobbes considered the question of what happens if people disagree about definitions. The context clearly indicates that Hobbes was talking about all kinds of definitions, not just moral or theological ones.

> "It is needful therefore, as oft as any controversy ariseth in these matters contrary to the public good and common peace, that there be somebody to judge of the reasoning, that is to say, whether that which is inferred, be rightly inferred or not; that so the controversy may be ended. But there are no rules given by Christ to this purpose, neither came he into the world to teach *logic*. It remains therefore that the judges of such controversies, be the same with those whom God by nature had instituted before, namely, those who in each city are constituted by the sovereign. Moreover, if a controversy be raised of the accurate and proper signification, that is the definition of those names or appellations which are commonly used; insomuch as it is needful for

the peace of the city, or the distribution of right, to be determined; the determination will belong to the city. For men, by reasoning, do search out such kind of definitions in their observation of diverse conceptions, for the signification whereof those appellations were used at diverse times and for diverse causes. But the decision of the question, whether a man do reason rightly, belongs to the city. For example, if a woman bring forth a child of an unwonted shape, and the law forbid to kill a man; the question is whether the child be a man. It is demanded therefore, what a man is. No man doubts but the city shall judge it, and that without taking an account of Aristotle's definition that man is a rational creature. And these things, namely, *right, policy,* and *natural sciences,* are subjects concerning which Christ denies that it belongs to his office to give any precepts, or teach any thing beside this only; that in all controversies about them, every single subject should obey the laws and determinations of his city."[51]

The quotation makes clear that Hobbes was talking about scientific propositions as well as moral and religious ones being assigned their truth values by the political authorities. Hobbes went on in *De Cive* to point out that observance of natural laws is one way people are led to salvation. These laws are taught as theorems by natural reason, or by divine authority. Drawing conclusions by natural reason involves employing human principles and contracts, and thus "is subject to the censure of civil powers." Hobbes expanded his point that whatever is not revealed, namely moral and political principles "and the examination of doctrines and books in all manner of rational science depends upon the *temporal right.*" Even the distinction of what is spiritual and what is temporal must be made by the temporal authorities "because our Saviour hath not made that distinction." The sovereign or sovereigns in each city thus are "the supreme authority of judging and determining all manner of controversies about *temporal* matters."[52]

If man followed their own opinions, they would dissolve society. There would be controversies that "should become innumerable and indeterminable."[53] Hobbes started from describing what would happen in the religious case. He next considered questions about human science, "whose truth is sought out by natural reason and syllogisms, drawn from the covenants of men, and definitions, that is to say, significations received by use and common consent of words; such as are all questions of right and philosophy."[54] Unless the common consents are accepted, all human society collapses.[55]

Richard Peters, who puts special stress on the passages quoted above, first spells out the import of what Hobbes was saying, namely that scientific disputes involving matters of public importance would have to be judged by political authorities.[56] Thus, and this is my example, not Peters', Velikovsky's astronomical theories, since they have stirred up a lot of controversy, and have produced ardent and forceful partisans amongst the scientific establishment and amongst other intellectual groups, and since this has resulted in public disputes, disruptive disagreements, nasty publications, and since this has also resulted in confusing a great many people about what is true and false in astronomy, and about how much the establishment astrophysicists can be trusted, the whole issue, which obviously has political consequences, is to be settled politically by the civil authorities. This has all of the earmarks of what the state legislature of Indiana was trying to accomplish when it passed a law making pi = 3, or what the state of Tennessee was trying to accomplish when they banned the teaching of Darwin's theory of evolution. Similarly, Hobbes's view smacks of what the Russian government was doing when it rejected Einsteinian physics and modern genetics for political reasons.

Peters commented on these passages in Hobbes by declaring, "It must be said, however, that this bizarre and authoritarian theory of truth is usually put forward when Hobbes is concerned to delimit the respective spheres of secular and ecclesiastical jurisdiction or when he is troubled about the kinds of disputes that provoke civil unrest."[57] This bizarre theory is certainly not unknown in our own day, and I will come back to this in a moment. First I should like to indicate that the theory seems to grow out of a fundamental kind of scepticism, that arises for Hobbes in the very attempt to distinguish the secular from the religious. Not only have we found no indubitable criteria to employ to make the distinction, we also realize the tremendous price that has to be paid if we are unable to make such a distinction, the price of the disintegration of our civil units. Our inability to live with any satisfaction under such circumstances leads us back to the acceptance of a sovereign and the acceptance of his judgment. Thus we apparently would not be led to this bizarre and authoritarian theory of truth if there were not ample sceptical grounds for disputing any human conclusions, and if these disputes were not corrosive of the public order. On the first point Hobbes (at least as he stated his view at the end of *De Cive*) saw that the sceptical attacks undermined any human being's claim to know absolutely or definitely any truth claim. Every alleged claim could be disputed. This would lead to the world being a debating society, except for the facts that some of the issues in dispute have important consequences in the social world. But the latter can lead to the dissolution of society. Therefore, the civil authority has to step in and announce who is right.

This political theory of truth, based on a total scepticism about an individual's ability to discover the truth, is a remarkable change in the pattern of sceptical thought in the 17th century. Various friends of Hobbes's were sceptics and fideists. They doubted man's ability to find truth, and therefore, by *non sequitur*, they accepted truth on faith from God or His Church. Hobbes, partly because of his analysis of what constitutes the Church, saw, at least in this chapter of *De Cive*, that fideism comes down to acceptance of a sovereign agency as the source of truth.

Father Mersenne, in a letter that is printed in the French edition of *De Cive*, told the translator, Samuel Sorbière, (who called himself on the title page one of Hobbes's friends) that Hobbes's noble philosophy is demonstrated as evidently as Euclid's geometry. Therefore, Mersenne went on, Sorbière will give up his suspense of judgment and all of the bagatelles of the sceptics, and become a dogmatist, whose foundations are unshakeable.[58] Neither Sorbière nor Mersenne seems to have commented on the scepticism that emerged at the end of the book.

Hobbes, who had apparently ignored the sceptical discussions of his French friends, opened the door to a new kind of scepticism. He might have been influenced by the Machiavellism of Naudé's *Considérations politiques sur les coups d'état*.[59] I have tried to show for 25 years that modern scepticism emerged from the religious quarrels of the Reformation and the Counter Reformation. One of its forms that flourished in Hobbes's day was fideism — a complete scepticism coupled with the acceptance of various principles on faith. It was only from Bayle to Hume that the fideism moved from a religious to an animal faith. Hobbes, at least once, realized that the so-called faith would have to be acceptance of authority, and the only recognizable authority was a civil one. Then truth became political truth as the only means of settling arguments and preserving the peace. This bizarre theory is, of course, closer to the character of modern scepticism than the views of Hobbes's friends and contemporaries. As we approach 1984 on the calendar, with its Ministry of Truth, we become more aware of government-generated truth in Russia and America. One could speak at length on the new version of Descartes' demonic scepticism developed by brainwashing, by propaganda, by classifying and falsifying records, etc.[60] Here I just want to mention a couple of points. In the 20th century world governments have taken the initiative and are now all entrenched in the business of declaring what is true, creating the evidence, and forcing people to accept it. Governments have also taken the initiative in declaring what is, and what is not a threat to peace. (Draft-card burning, speaking to foreigners, listening to Radio Free Europe, opposing any government policy, not filling out the administration's personnel efficiency card, etc.). The result is the totalitarian state with its helpless sceptical citizens.

So Hobbes, though almost oblivious to his contemporary epistemological sceptics, and far more cautious than his contemporary religious ones, did at one point lay the groundwork for a much more dangerous scepticism involved in making the sovereign the political arbiter of truth. From arbiter to creator of truth, the modern state then developed its Orwellian character. With no means of delimiting its power to create truth, and to maintain the peace, the citizen becomes helpless. Hobbes with his great concern to preserve the possibility of civil life in an extremely chaotic age, could not foresee what this state, the preserver of peace, could become with sufficient technological advances.

Notes

[1] Dorothea Krook, "Thomas Hobbes's Doctrine of Meaning and Truth", *Philosophy*, XXXI (1956), p. 3.

[2] *Ibid.*, p. 3.

[3] *Ibid.*, p. 13. See also p. 8.

[4] Frederick Copleston, *A History of Philosophy*, Vol. V, *Hobbes to Hume* (Westminister, Maryland: Newman, 1961), pp. 17-20.

[5] *Ibid.*, p. 17.

[6] *Ibid.*, p. 20.

[7] J.W.N. Watkins, *Hobbes's System of Ideas* (London: Hutchinson, 1973), pp. 110, 129-31.

[8] On Hobbes's trips to France, see Gaston Sortais, *La philosophie moderne depuis Bacon jusqu'à Leibniz*, Tome II (Paris: Lethielleux, 1922), pp. 272-285.

[9] Richard H. Popkin, *The History of Scepticism from Erasmus to Spinoza* (Berkeley: University of California Press, 1979), chap. 7, pp. 129-150. See also Arrigo Pacchi, *Convenzione e ipotesi nella formazione della filosofia naturale de Thomas Hobbes* (Florence: La Nuova Italia, 1965), on the connections of Hobbes's natural philosophy with that of Mersenne and Gassendi. Theodore Waldman sought to show that Hobbes used their type of constructive skepticism in his theory of liberty. See "Hobbes on Liberty: A Study in Constructive Skepticism", *Proceedings of the Seventh Inter-American Congress of Philosophy* (Quebec 1968); and Rudolf Ross, "Obligations: Science and Philosophy in the Political Writings of Hobbes," paper presented at the Hobbes Tercentenary Congress, University of Colorado, Aug. 6-8, 1979.

[10] See Perez Zagorin, "Thomas Hobbes's Departure from England in 1640: An Unpublished Letter", *The Historical Journal*, XXI (1978), pp. 157-160; and Samuel Sorbière, *Sorberiana ou les pensées critiques de M. de Sorbière*, 2nd ed. (Paris 1965), art. "Bosc" pp. 55-56, and in Graverol's Mémoire, p. ev.

[11] See Popkin, *op.cit.*, chap. V, pp. 87-109.

[12] *Ibid*, pp. 106-07.

[13] *Ibid.*, p. 107.

[14] Mersenne had said to Sorbière, "You will gladly renounce the suspension of judgment and the other idle talk of the Sceptics, when you will be forced to admit that dogmatic philosophy rests upon an unshakeable basis." Letter of Mersenne to Sorbière, 25 April 1646, printed in the preface to Thomas Hobbes, *De Cive* (Amsterdam 1647). See Popkin, *op.cit.*, p. 279-80, n. 34.

[15] See Vincent Guilloton, "Autour de la relation du voyage de Samuel Sorbière en Angleterre 1663-1664", *Smith College Studies in Modern Languages*, XI (1930), esp. p. 18; and J.J. Jusserand, *English Essays from a French Pen*, (New York 1895), p. 174.

[16] See sections in Sortais' book, cited in n. 8.

[17] See Jean Jacquot, "Notes on an Unpublished Work of Thomas Hobbes", *Notes and Records of the Royal Society of London*, IX (1952), pp. 188-195. The work is published as *Thomas Hobbes, Thomas White's De Mundo Examined*, (London: Beekman, 1976).

[18] On this, see Popkin, *op.cit.*, chaps. V, VII, and IX.

[19] Thomas Hobbes, *De Corpore, Elements of Philosophy. The First Section, Concerning Body*, in *The English Works of Thomas Hobbes* (London, 1839) Vol. I, p. 63.

[20] Hobbes, *Six Lessons to the Savilian Professors of the Mathematics*, in *English Works*, Vol. VII, p. 184.

[21] *Ibid.*, pp. 317-18.

[22] Professor John F. Wilson of the University of Hawaii, Manoa, Honolulu, has undertaken research into Hobbes's relation with sceptics, free-thinkers and the like in England and France. He has kindly let me see his results, which unfortunately do not throw much more specific light on Hobbes's relations with the philosophical sceptics in France.

[23] Descartes, *Lettre au Pere****, in *Oeuvres*, Adam-Tannery edition, Tome IV, p. 67. See also Sortais, *op.cit.*, p. 216.

[24] Hobbes, *Leviathan*, English Works, Vol. III (London 1839), pp. 267-268.

[25] *Ibid.*, p. 368.

[26] *Ibid.*, p. 369.

[27] Popkin, *op.cit.*, p. 218.

[28] Louis Ellies-du Pin, *Nouvelle Bibliothèque des Auteurs Ecclésiastiques*, (2nd edition), Tome I, (Paris 1690), p.4.

[29] *Ibid.*, p. 30.

[30] See Samuel I. Mintz, *The Hunting of Leviathan*, (Cambridge: University Press, 1962), pp. 57-59, 62, and 102.

[31] Cf. Popkin, *op.cit.*, p. 215.

[32] Popkin, "The Marrano Theology of Isaac La Peyrère", *Studi Internazionali di Filosofia*, V (1973), pp. 99, 103-107.

[33] Popkin, *History of Scepticism*, p. 217; Isaac La Peyrère, *Men before Adam*, (London 1656), Book III, chap. I, pp. 204-05.

[34] Popkin, *History of Scepticism*, p. 220. Letter of Richard Simon to La Peyrère, in *Lettres choisies de M. Simon*, Tome II, (Rotterdam 1702), pp. 12-13.

[35] Sir Matthew Hale, *The Primitive Origination of Mankind* (London 1677), p. 185.

[36] Thomas Paine, *The Age of Reason, Part the Second, being an Investigation of True and Fabulous Theology* (London 1795), p. 14.

[37] David Levi, *Letters to Dr. Priestley in Answer to his Letters to the Jews Part II, occasioned by Mr. David Levi's Reply to the Former Part* (London 1789), pp. 14-15.

[38] Popkin, *History of Scepticism*, pp. 226-227.

[39] Mintz, *op.cit.*

[40] See Popkin, *History of Scepticism*, p. 219 and 222-223.

[41] *Ibid.*, p. 227.

[42] Jean Steinmann, *Richard Simon et les origines de l'exégèse biblique*, (Paris: Desclee, 1960).

[43] Mintz, *op.cit.*, pp. 57-9, 62 and 102.

[44] Mintz, *op.cit.*, p. 62.

[45] Watkins, *op.cit.*, p. 130.

[46] Hobbes, *De Cive*, XIII, i, p. 151.

[47] Watkins, *op.cit.*, p. 111.

[48] See for instance, Richard Peters, *Hobbes* (Baltimore: Penguin, 1967), p. 58.

[49] On Hobbes's quarrels with the mathematicians and especially with Wallis, see Peters, *op.cit.*, pp. 37, 38 and 40.

[50] Mintz, *op.cit.*

[51] *De Cive*, chap. XVII, pp. 268-69. There are passages in *De Cive*, chap. ii, sec. 1, pp. 14-17, (esp. the note on p. 16); and *Leviathan*, I, chap. 4, pp. 21-29, that suggest this sceptical possibility. I am grateful to Professor Ezequiel de Olaso for pointing this out to me. I am also grateful to Professor Olaso for letting me see his unpublished paper on "Thomas Hobbes y la recta razón."

[52] *Ibid.*, p. 271.

[53] Hobbes, *De Cive*, chap. XVII, sec. 27, p. 293.

[54] *Ibid.*, sec. 28, p. 295.

[55] *Ibid.*, pp. 296-297.

[56] Peters, *op.cit.*, pp. 55-57.

[57] *Ibid.*, p. 57.

[58] Marin Mersenne to Samuel Sorbière, 25 April 1646, preface to Hobbes, *Le Citoyen* and *De Cive*, (Amsterdam 1647).

[59] Gabriel Naudé, *Considérations politiques sur les coups d'état*. Sur la Copie de Romo 1667 (Cologne 1744).

[60] See on this Harry M. Bracken, "Descartes, Orwell, Chomsky: Philosophers of the Demonic", *The Human Context*, IV, (1972), pp. 523-536.

# 9.

THE *DEUTSCHE METAPHYSIK* OF
CHRISTIAN WOLFF: TEXT AND TRANSITIONS

Charles A. Corr

A text in the history of philosophy can come to have significance of many sorts and for many different reasons. It might, for example, mark the emergence of a novel philosophic viewpoint, one that will influence developments in philosophizing for many years to come. Alternatively, it might reflect or sum up a specific line of thinking, serving as a kind of fulfillment or conclusion for the articulation of a particular perspective. As a third possibility, a philosophical text might play the role of an intermediary, functioning as a bridge from one thinker or viewpoint to another. Some texts have their greatest power only within the framework of their original composition and for their author or for contemporary thinkers. Other realize their full import in retrospect when they are examined and re-assessed by later judges. That import may be primarily philosophical in character or primarily historical; usually it involves elements of both. We see these points perhaps most clearly and can articulate them most precisely for texts of the highest rank, those that are the outstanding monuments in our historical surveys of Western thought. But for individuals who have sufficient opportunity and energy, it can also be profitable from time to time to re-evaluate the weight of some of the far more numerous second- and third-rank texts in the history of philosophy. I propose an undertaking of this latter sort in the present paper.

Specifically, I want to look at a relatively early work from the pen of a prolific but not overly admired author, Christian Wolff (1679-1754). For the most part, Wolff is known to general histories of philosophy as the stereotypical continuator of the so-called "Leibnitzian-Wolffian" philosophy and as one who was influential in a vague sort of way prior to Kant in eighteenth century German philosophy. It may surprise us to realize that nearly half a century passed between the death of Leibniz in 1716 and the first publication of his *New Essays Concerning the Human Understanding* in 1765. And another sixteen years followed until the appearance of Kant's *Critique of Pure Reason*. What was going on in German intellectual circles during this lengthy period? Leibniz was dead and in some important ways unavailable in terms of the body of writings that we now know, while Kant's critical philosophy had yet to arrive on the scene. How did philosophy achieve the transition from the harmonious metaphysics of Hannover to the transcendental critique of Konigsberg?

One way was through a text like Christian Wolff's *Vernünftige Gedanken von Gott, der Welt und der Seele des Menschen, auch allen Dingen überhaupt*, a book which is not well known today. What is this work like? What is its own background and position in the over-all body of its author's published writings? What sort of reception did it receive? How did it happen to be or to become so influential during the period in question? What are the kinds of internal and external transitions in which it is involved? In particular, how does it stand as a prominent example of Wolff's thought looking simultaneously backwards to Descartes and Leibniz, and forwards to Kant? And not incidentally, what did it contribute to the emergence of a specifically German mode of philosophizing in the midst of the numerous French and Latin texts which continued to appear even through the middle years of the eighteenth century?

We cannot answer all of these questions in a single essay. And in any event, I am not suggesting that any one text defines the entire history of more than half a century of German philosophizing. But conventional wisdom is correct in acknowledging that Wolff was one of the most influential thinkers on the Continent during the years in question. And the work we are to consider here—commonly referred to as Wolff's *Deutsche Metaphysik*—has a special prominence among his many writings for a number of reasons. Few of Wolff's works have been available in English, and only within the last 20 years have new editions appeared in Wolff's *Gesammelte Werke*, the first of its kind since the eighteenth century.[1] It is the preparation of a new edition of the *Metaphysik* that makes possible this paper and suggests opportunities for other similar initiatives in the future. I begin by describing this text itself and the particular context in which it first appeared, as a prelude to exploration of some of the historical and doctrinal transitions within which it can profitably be seen.

Text and Context

Wolff's *Deutsche Metaphysik* was both an early and a relatively mature work, a book that was enormously popular and influential during his lifetime and yet one that for readers in the latter part of the 20th century is largely overshadowed by later events and texts. These somewhat paradoxical remarks will become clear if we see the work in its biographical and bibliographical context.[2] The *Deutsche Metaphysik* was completed toward the end of 1719 and published probably in the very last days of that year though it is usually dated as appearing in 1720. Prior to this time, Wolff had not published much in what might now be seen as the primary areas of philosophical concern. He was, after all, Professor of Mathematics and the Natural Sciences at the University of Halle, and it is in the areas defined

CHRISTIAN WOLFF: THE *DEUTSCHE METAPHYSIK* 151

by the title of his *Lehrstuhl* that he had most distinguished himself between his appointment in 1706 and the time in question. Hitherto, Wolff's published works mainly consisted of numerous small treatises in natural philosophy, several large volumes on aspects of mathematics, and some short works on specialized philosophical topics.[3]

The significant exception to this pattern of Wolff's writings prior to 1720 is the publication of his *Vernünftige Gedanken von den Kräften des menschlichen Verstandes* in 1713.[4] This is an introductory handbook on logic for a fairly broad educated readership. In many ways it is like the *Metaphysik* in scope, style, and aims. Both works provide Wolff's "rational thoughts" on their respective subjects, and that prefix will continue to appear in the titles of most of the later German volumes that are to follow during the early 1720s. Certainly, the *Deutsche Logik* as it is commonly called was the most popular of all of Wolff's works. It appeared and reappeared in 14 separate editions and reprintings prior to Wolff's death in 1754. A Latin translation was published in 1730 and the book was translated into English in 1770. Two points might particularly be noted about the *Logik*. First, it was the only one of Wolff's central philosophical works to appear while Leibniz was still alive. And second, as its common part-title and themes might indicate, in this book Wolff is signalling his interest in moving more directly into the mainstream of philosophical issues. That rather natural development was facilitated by the departure from Halle in 1709 of another faculty member whose presence had somewhat preempted those areas, and it is reflected in 1718 in the publication of a book describing the plan of Wolff's lectures in both mathematics and philosophy in general.[5] The *Logik* prepared the groundwork and the instrument for the philosophical treatises that were to follow. Apparently Wolff had intended to move from the former to the latter more quickly than he actually did. But as his plans for philosophical writing were delayed, by 1718 he is evidencing concern that his views not be distorted through inaccurate student reports. The *Metaphysik* is the first substantial realization of Wolff's intentions following the lengthy interval since 1713.

We view the *Metaphysik* today in the light of Wolff's subsequent German publications on ethics, politics, physics, teleology, physiology, scientific experimentation, and an over-all retrospective, and in terms of the much larger Latin volumes appearing regularly from 1728 to 1754 in which Wolff re-worked this same ground and moved forward into such areas as practical philosophy, natural law, international law, and economics. Thus, we may not fully appreciate the impact of the book that was the proximate initiation of such relentless writing and publishing. The *Deutsche Metaphysik* was, after all, a metaphysics, it was written in German, and it was clearly a success for Wolff. By this I mean, first, that the *Metaphysik* goes beyond specialized, instrumental, or partial expositions to set forth Wolff's basic views on being, world, man, and God. There is more to come now that the way has been opened by this first staking out of positions, but that achievement is neither tentative nor provisional. That is, although the *Metaphysik* is an "early" work in the senses indicated, it is also the product of years of teaching and reflection, a work which comes to us from an author who is already forty years old. We do not have here a youthful piece nor one whose main outlines will be much altered in the years to come.

A second sort of significance applies to the *Metaphysik* (together with the *Logik*) because it was composed in the vernacular. Although occasional lectures had previously been given in German—by, for example, Christian Thomasius—Wolff seems to have been the first university professor to announce a regular course of lectures in that language.[6] In this he broke with the regular use of Latin, the traditional language of the intellectual world of his time. The *Logik* and *Metaphysik* carried this practice into print in the areas central to philosophy and what we would now call undergraduate education. They and the German titles that followed were essentially textbooks for students and educated lay or professional persons. In these textbooks, Wolff took particular care to define his technical vocabulary and to relate the new German terms to their older Latin counterparts. He thus gave substantial impetus to the development of the German language and to its establishment as an instrument of scientific discourse. To this extent, Wolff has rightly been called (curiously enough, still in a Latin phrase) the "preceptor Germaniae," the man who taught the Germans to think.[7]

The success of the *Metaphysik* is its third feature to remark, one which led equally to calamities and reversals. A total of 12 editions of this book were published before Wolff's death. They are spread rather evenly throughout the third (1720, 1722, 1725, and 1729), fourth (1733, 1736, 1738), and fifth (1741, 1743, 1747) decades of the century, and even extend into the sixth (1751, 1752) while he was still alive. Clearly, the book was in demand and served a steady readership. Moreover, the basic doctrine of the text remains unaltered throughout its history. Even though the last edition is nearly 100 pages longer that the first (672 vs. 576 pages), most of the new material came in the second and third editions, and those following the fourth are essentially reprintings rather than new editions.[8] Further, additions to the text are mainly intended to clarify Wolff's positions or to defend them against his critics.

Mention of criticism is the other side of the coin of success for this book. During the time when Wolff had remained within the relatively safer areas of mathematics, natural philosophy, and logic, and as long as he did not bring the full scope of his philosophical views into print, his work did not generate much opposition. But the detailed and prominent positions of the *Deutsche Metaphysik* became unavoidable bones of contention for some theologians and other academic critics. To them, Wolff's confidence in reason undercut claims as to the sinfulness of human nature and left insufficient room for faith. In this, Wolff served as a model figure of the early German Enlightenment and his opponents played an equally classic role. Wolff gave no ground to opposition as the manuscript of the *Metaphysik* reveals, and his determination (some would say arrogance) only fueled the fire. An undiplomatic public speech commending the heathen Chinese for achieving a responsible code of morality (without the help of faith)—given on June 12, 1721, at the transference of the pro-rectorship of the university from Wolff to his principal opponent, Joachim Lange—became the occasion for bitter intrigue that eventually led to Wolff's expulsion from Prussia in 1723.[9] Though welcomed at Marburg in Hesse-Cassel, Wolff did not take this disgrace lightly and he soon renounced the vernacular as a vehicle for his philosophical writing, turning instead to Latin as the language of a broader (and hopefully more appreciative) intellectual community and beginning anew with volumes on logic and metaphysics. As is often the case, expulsion did not diminish Wolff's popularity. The *Logik* and *Metaphysik* continued to be reissued quite regularly; new German works were published until 1726, including a volume of *Annotations* (later designed as the second Part) to the *Metaphysik* which took up its own history of six editions through 1760[10]; and Wolff was returned to Halle in triumph by Frederick the Great in 1740. His personal prominence may have somewhat passed by that time and other thinkers like Johann Heinrich Lambert and Christian August Crusius had also come onto the German philosophical scene, but the influence of Wolff's philosophy continued for many years through a stream of books by himself and his partisans, and through the prominence of his followers the ''Wolffians'' as occupants of teaching posts in numerous German universities and educational institutes.

Some Historical and Doctrinal Transitions

We have already observed several internal Wolffian historical transitions that relate to the *Deutsche Metaphysik*. For example, in the publication of this work, Wolff successfully moved beyond his *Logik* and other previous publications to carry into print a full-scale statement of his views in the central field of speculative philosophy. He was sufficiently satisfied with this achievement to rest content with amplifying and embroidering his positions without altering them in any fundamental way throughout the extensive printing history of this book and of its subsequent companion volume of *Annotations*. One suspects that developments which occurred in the restatement of Wolff's metaphysics in the later Latin volumes may be of somewhat more significance, but to say that with confidence would require a full scale study of these latter texts of the sort that has not previously been available and will only now be most easily undertaken as the last of the Latin metaphysical works has just come into print in the new edition prepared by Professor Jean Ecole.[11] In the meantime, we can usefully consider some external transitions of both a historical and a doctrinal character between Wolff and some other thinkers and authors. These may be both retrospective and prospective, though both are equally selective and illustrative rather than comprehensive.

Retrospective Transitions

As mentioned above, Wolff is most frequently depicted as little more than a systematizer and popularizer of Leibniz's thought. Not unexpectedly, he did not care much for this way of viewing his achievements.[12] Apparently with some justice, he noted that Leibniz saw him mainly as a teacher of mathematics and did not know much about his more specifically philosophical interests of the sort represented by the *Metaphysik*. Nevertheless, like most stereotypical characterizations, the label "Leibnizian-Wolffian" philosophy does rest on a basic core of truth. Leibniz was a diverse and stimulating figure in late seventeenth and early eighteenth century German intellectual circles; rather like a grinding wheel sending off sparks in many directions at once, as he was once described to me. Often incomplete and undeveloped, these ideas—insofar as they were known to other thinkers —must have been stimulating to his contemporaries. Surely Wolff drew upon Leibniz in important ways, just as he obtained help from the older man in securing his professorship in 1706 at the young University of Halle. But Wolff rightly observes that his own philosophical education at Breslau and Jena took place a few years earlier in a milieu as much Cartesian and Aristotelico-Scholastic as anything else. Leibniz does not necessarily stand apart from or in opposition to such a milieu, but four doctrinal examples from the *Deutsche Metaphysik* will show how Wolff moved away from Leibniz's philosophy on some key points while holding on to others and to his own rather unique interpretations of some Cartesian positions. These examples include simple substances vs. monads, pre-established harmony, a revised version of the *cogito* argument, and Wolff's over-all program for a systematic philosophy especially as it is given in the *Metaphysik*.

In describing the ultimate constituents of all reality, Leibniz advocates simple substances (later called "monads") which are essentially spiritual or non-physical entities. Wolff knows this doctrine, but does not accept it.[13] The stumbling block seems to be a concern that Leibniz has failed to respect the distinctive nature of physical beings. To that end, Wolff repeatedly praises what he takes to be a more satisfactory account of irresolvable metaphysical differences between soul and body or mind and nature that he finds in Descartes. It may be said that Leibniz is more consistent, explicit, or subtle than either Descartes or Wolff on this issue. But Wolff is clearly unhappy with the Leibnizian tendency to pan-psychism and is determined to draw back from such commitments.

This lays the ground for a need to find some theoretical account for involvement between these two sorts of entities that make up the universe, and in particular for the experienced fact of mind/body interaction within the human being—a classic problem for the whole rationalist tradition. Curiously enough, although Wolff addresses this problem at great length in the *Metaphysik* and elsewhere, he notes that originally he had not intended to do so, but found himself drawn into the question and believes that he has now set it in a proper light.[14] I believe this reflects his awareness of the importance of the issue, his sensitivity to its implications for a variety of philosophical and theological concerns involving man, God, and freedom, and what must have been some embarrassment for a thinker like Wolff over evident inability to resolve the issue in a demonstrative or certitudinal manner. Wolff sets out the issue and putative solutions in familiar fashion, beginning with an experienced fact and proceeding to "explanations" by way of direct physical interaction ("physical influx"), indirect involvement via God's present intervention ("occasionalism"), and indirect involvement via divine prescience and the working out of the natures in question ("pre-established harmony").[15] The first of these positions (attributed to Aristotle!) is criticized as providing no proper account of how one mode of being can actually influence another; the second (attributed to Descartes!) as calling for a perpetual series of miracles unfitting to God. Beyond this argument by exclusion, pre-established harmony (attributed properly to Leibniz) is recommended as fittingly respecting the divine and the two finite modes of being which are drawn together in this issue. But—and Wolff is careful to insist on this qualification repeatedly—even in this third account we achieve only a hypothetical explanation of the existential or contingent fact, not a conclusive demonstration of its essential necessity. Despite the elegance of the Leibnizian position, this point is crucial to Wolff and leads him to carefully qualify anything that might depend upon this doctrine.[16] The importance of this in Wolff's mind has to do with the next two examples selected for discussion.

Wolff opens the *Deutsche Metaphysik* with a very short five-page first chapter centering on a quasi-Cartesian *cogito* argument.[17] It asserts that whatever is conscious of itself and of other things outside itself must exist, that we are so conscious, and that therefore we must exist. The syllogistic framework is Wolff's own, the premise of a plurality of subject-knowers resembles what Leibniz might have said, and the over-all argument despite distortions is of course broadly Cartesian. That last point is confirmed when we are told that the goal of this chapter is to establish a standard of demonstrative certitude from the outset whereby all that follows can be measured. In other words, the content of this argument is not so important—perhaps less so than for Descartes who is more threatened by the spectre of skepticism than Wolff and who wants to draw more richly upon his *cogito* assertion in an immediate and many-faceted way. After all, as Wolff says, who would deny his own very existence? The aim is not merely to re-affirm the obvious, but to put it in into proper logical form and to show that in metaphysics, as well as in mathematics and geometry, one can attain to demonstrative certainty. Once that is accomplished, Wolff almost begins afresh in the second chapter of the *Metaphysik* and in a way which does not directly depend upon his initial argument. Once the methodic point has been made, Wolff makes no return to the balance of the argument until his chapter on rational psychology when he comes back to the existence and nature of the human soul.[18] And in the Latin metaphysical works, there is no counterpart to this opening gambit.[19]

The appearance of an argument *cogitamus ergo sumus* in the first chapter of the *Deutsche Metaphysik* is one reflection (later somewhat adjusted in this particular detail) of a broad and enduring conviction throughout Wolff's writings that philosophy must be both certitudinal and systematic. The one serves the other. Philosophy for Wolff employs a demonstrative method to achieve the certitude that is reflected in a systematic order.[20] The *Logik* laid out the principles of this method, and the *Metaphysik* put them to work. Thus, arranging the parts of metaphysics carefully, establishing individual doctrines firmly, and building them upon each other in an interdependent way is of great concern throughout the *Metaphysik*. In different ways, this is illustrated in both the mind/body discussion and the distinctive *cogito*-like first step in the *Deutsche Metaphysik*. It is also evident in the careful exposition of general ontological concepts and principles in the second chapter of the book, especially in Wolff's demand that the principle of sufficient reason be derived from the principle of non-contradiction—though again he knows that this last point differs from Leibniz's practice.[21] Even in *Logik* and *Metaphysik*, which are relatively informal and unsophisticated by comparison with their later Latin counterparts, Wolff's goal for philosophy is *system*, something that he found neither in practice nor in principle in Leibniz's thought.[22] In this he is again somewhat closer to his own perception of Descartes,[23] though probably only in some general ideals and not as an individual guide, since Wolff's sense of the history of philosophy is unlikely to be sufficiently strong or precise to support the latter point and his proximate sources are more likely to be in the school text traditions. The import of all this and the previous examples is not to trace in detail all of the tangled influences on Wolff's philosophizing—even merely in the *Metaphysik*—but to illustrate just a few of the more prominent lines of succession that are implicated in the way in which that work came from Wolff's pen.

Prospective Transitions

When we look forward from 1720 to select some transitions from the *Metaphysik* to other writers and thinkers, two examples spring immediately to mind: the "Wolffians" and Kant. The Wolffians are a diverse group of largely third-level teachers and writers. With one or two exceptions on selected points, they are even less well known today despite their rather large numbers and extensive influence in the German *Hochschulen* right up to and through Kant's critical philosophy. These people were mainly concerned to achieve two goals: 1) to translate Wolff's philosophy from one language to another; and 2) to synthesize and to some extent to simplify his thought for pedagogic uses. Because Wolff wrote his principal philosophical treatises first in German at a time when Latin was still the main language of instruction and study, the first wave of Wolffian texts was concerned to render this thought into Latin. This began with the *Institutiones philosophiae Wolfianae* (2 vols.; 1725-1726)[24] of Ludwig Philipp Thümmig (1697-1728) and continued for many years with a series of texts on Wolff's thought in general or on a specific field of philosophy. Later, when Wolff abandoned German for Latin, many of the Wolffians also reversed direction. At that point German was becoming an ever-more acceptable vehicle for professional philosophical expression and the process gained some momentum as time went on. Johann Christoph Gottsched's popular *Ersten Gründe der gesamten Weltweisheit* (2 vols., 1733-1734; eight editions by 1778) is a good example of this second wave of Wolffian texts. Carl Günther Ludovici and Georg Volckmar Hartmann have provided extensive histories of the development of this philosophical viewpoint which they openly call "Leibnizian-Wolffian"— through the mid-1730s.[25] For later readers, these histories are the principal contemporary sources for our knowledge of the many individuals and publications that take up a position of advocacy or criticism towards what they view as Wolff's philosophy.

From this plethora of text and countertext, I want to select just one example to illustrate a quite diverse genre. The *Metaphysica* (1739; seven editions by 1779, plus a German translation in 1766) of Alexander Gottlieb Baumgarten (1714-1762) is in many ways a late "first wave" Wolffian text. It directly parallels the structure of Wolff's *Metaphysik* (with the Thümmig revisions) and it achieved a popularity and influence that is evident in its publishing history. Kant used this book as a text and called it "the most useful and most well-grounded among all the manuals of its kind."[26] For our purposes, two instances will serve to identify Baumgarten's relative independence within a broadly Wolffian outlook. First, his account of simple substances which underlie all compounds makes them out to be non-spatial entities without qualification.[27] Thus, he does not display Wolff's concern to keep apart the fundamental natures of physical and spiritual entities. Secondly, perhaps in keeping with this, Baumgarten is more willing to accept direct interaction between substances than Wolff was. That is, both as a general principle and specifically in relationship to the mind/body problem, Baumgarten merges pre-established harmony with the older doctrine of physical influx.[28] As Giorgio Tonelli has written, "Baumgarten was thus less Leibnizian than Wolff in accepting physical influence and more Leibnizian in his panpsychism."[29] Perhaps for this reason, and because he structures his *Metaphysica* according to a series of predicates or categories, Max Wundt characterizes the book "as a bridge between Scholasticism and Kant."[30]

In this way, we are brought quite naturally to a further and final case linked (though certainly not exclusively) to Wolff's *Deutsche Metaphysik*, which might be introduced by asking: how did all of this come out in Kant? I leap over the complexities of Kant's own historical development in his pre-critical period (which would require extensive discussion in its own right) to consider some remarks pertaining to Wolff in the Preface to the second edition of the *Critique of Pure Reason* and what they entail about some quite fundamental aspects of Kant's thought. In mentioning "the strict method of the celebrated Wolff, the greatest of all the dogmatic philosophers," Kant has the following to say:

> He was the first to show by example (and by his example he awakened that spirit of thoroughness which is not extinct in Germany) how the secure progress of a science is to be attained only through orderly establishment of principles, clear determination of concepts, insistence upon strictness of proof, and avoidance of venturesome, non-consecutive steps in our inferences. He was thus peculiarly well fitted to raise metaphysics to the dignity of a science, if only it had occurred to him to prepare the ground beforehand by a critique of the organ, that is, of pure reason itself.[31]

English-speaking readers of Kant often pay special attention to his remarks in the introduction to the *Prolegomena* and elsewhere about the role of David Hume in waking him from his dogmatic slumber and inspiring his critical philosophy. It does not detract one bit from the importance of this to observe that it is not and cannot be the whole story. The Humean influence is but one side of a complex genesis, and it does not stand unrevised at the hands of Kant.

Kant did not simply set aside dogmatic philosophy *tout court*; he subsumed what he regarded as its best and enduring features in his own new viewpoint. Nor did he rest content with Hume who, in Kant's words, "ran his ship ashore, for safety's sake, landing on scepticism, there to let it lie and rot."[32] Kant's aim is to disengage himself from dogmatism, preserve and reinforce what is sound in mathematics and physics, lay the base for an effective moral philosophy, and avoid the pitfalls of skepticism. In so doing, he defines dogmatism as "the dogmatic procedure of pure reason, *without previous criticism of its own powers.*"[33] It is the lack of previous self-criticism that perverts the dogmatic procedure of pure reason into an undesirable dogmatism. Were the former present, the latter might not be so misled. In Kant's language: "This critique is not opposed to the *dogmatic procedure* of reason in its pure knowledge, as science, for that must always be dogmatic, that is, yield strict proof from sure principles *a priori.*"[34] However disparaging Kant will be of the pretentions of traditional, transcendent metaphysics, he never abandoned a deep-seated conviction that philosophy is and must continue to be a scientific discipline. In this, for all their differences, he shares something quite fundamental with Wolff and Baumgarten.

For this reason, Kant can praise Wolff honestly and without irony, and he can uphold a relatively tolerant attitude towards those who philosophized in a pre-critical era. In fact, Kant's harshest words are aimed in a direction quite other than Wolff's.

> Those who reject both the method of Wolff and the procedure of a critique of pure reason can have no other aim than to shake off the fetters of *science* altogether, and thus to change work into play, certainty into opinion, philosophy into philodoxy.[35]

As Hans Saner has said, Kant "would ask whether and how metaphysics could be scientific, but never whether it ought to be scientific. . . .Instead, he always presumes that if metaphysics should turn out to be possible at all, it would be a metaphysical science. We note here an unquestioned point in Kant's radical critical questioning."[36] However this last point may be, surely the commitment in Kant to scientific philosophy is unwavering, just as it was earlier in Wolff's *Deutsche Metaphysik*. This is why Kant can speak favorably of Wolff and Baumgarten even though he is no longer an adherent of many of their conclusions. And it also explains Kant's remark in 1790, in the course of a sharp dispute with a latter-day, self-styled Wolffian, that "the *Critique of Pure Reason* can thus be seen as the genuine apology for Leibniz, even against his partisans whose eulogies scarcely do him any honor. ...they are incapable of recognizing beyond what the philosophers actually said, what they really meant to say."[37]

Implications

In this investigation, I have undertaken to explore some aspects of one work by a particular writer in the context of some of that author's other writings and in the light of some relationships with other thinkers. My aim has been to soften some harsh characterizations, to revise at least in a limited way some rigid stereotypes, and to contribute to increased appreciation of the actual historical and doctrinal currents alive in the flow of German philosophy during the early and middle years of the 18th century. I do not profess to have radically shaken previous interpretations of the history of philosophy. That was not my goal. Rather, what I have sought to suggest is the value of increased sensitivity to textual and contextual historical realities as one means toward more astute assessment of philosophical value and significance.

Historians of philosophy construct "from-to" spans as devices for synthesizing the flow of thought from one thinker, period, or movement to another. Devices of this sort are both necessary and useful for philosophical interpretation. Such thematizations link together thinkers and texts that might otherwise have seemed discrete and disconnected. In so doing, they permit new and instructive comparisons and contrasts. It would be naive and counterproductive to attempt to overthrow all such interrelationships. But it is not at all misplaced to acknowledge their limitations. These are, after all, human interpretative constructs. As such, in James Collins's felicitous phrase, they are "porous in principle."[38] Thus, "the essential revisability of every schema is the historian's way of affirming the principle of fallibilism in his own domain." We need to keep before us at all times a sense of our own limitations. That entails a willingness to re-open and re-formulate "from-to" spans as the evidence guides us and as we find value in new ways of surveying the historical landscape in philosophy. If we do not do so, thinkers and texts that are still actually or potentially vital will ossify into dry bones that have nothing new to offer to us. Only by seeing the history of philosophy in a proper light and by asking more rather than less of ourselves can we expect to benefit from an on-going and instructive dialogue with our philosophical predecessors.

Christian Wolff is a thinker whom we have firmly entrenched in a particular set of categories and who has not yet excited much widespread revisionary interest. One could offer many reasons to explain why that is the case. But when curiosity nibbles at the edge of such stubborn categories some interesting results can emerge. In this essay, I have focused attention on just one of Wolff's publications, chosen for its centrality, influence, and—not least of all—very ambitious full title. Thereby, I have attempted to bring the *Metaphysik* itself and its position in Wolff's early writings into clearer perspective. If nowhere else, in its own time it certainly was a fairly substantial landmark in the history of philosophical publication. More importantly, it lets us see how Descartes appeared to a rather well-educated German professor some 70 years after his death, and how some of the ideas of Leibniz were regarded by that same schoolmaster who had published his eulogy just three years earlier in the *Acta eruditorum* and who would write the preface for the German translation of the *Leibniz-Clarke Correspondence* which appeared in the same year as the *Metaphysik*. Finally, I have sought very briefly to suggest some ways in which Wolff's thought was represented by the Wolffians—a diverse group whose advocacy, as it is for most followers, was always balanced by their own insight, concerns, and personal viewpoints—and how it was received by the mature Kant. The case of Kant is certainly the most important of all the relationships that we have addressed and notwithstanding all his criticisms of dogmatism it is instructive to see where Kant can be most accommodating toward Wolff and most comfortable in joining hands with his Prussian colleague at Halle.

Notes

[1] Christian Wolff, *Gesammelte Werke*. Edited by Jean École, H. W. Arndt, C. A. Corr, J.E. Hofmann⁺, & M. Thomann. Hildesheim: Georg Olms Verlag, 1962. This edition is being published in three series: I. Abteilung, Deutsche Schriften; II. Abteilung, Lateinische Schriften; & III. Abteilung, Ergänzungsreihe: Materialen und Dokumente. The *Deutsche Metaphysik* will be Bd. 2 in I. Abt.

[2] The principal contemporary biographical documents—including biographical sketches by Baumeister and Gottsched, Wolff's own incomplete autobiography, and the 19th century introduction to this last essay by Heinrich Wuttke— are now conveniently available in Wolff's *Gesammelte Werke*, I. Abt., Bd. 10. For his German writings, the reader should also consult the retrospective *Ausführliche Nachricht von seinen eigenen Schriften die er in deutscher Sprache von den verschiedenen Teilen der Welt-Weisheit heraus gegeben*, auf Verlangen ans Licht gestellet (*Ges. Werke*, I, 9).

[3] The only full-length general study of Wolff's thought in the last half-century is Mariano Campo, *Cristiano Wolff e il razionalismo precritico* (2 vols.; Milano: Società editrice "Vita e Pensiero", 1939; reprinted 1980 in *Ges. Werke*, III, 9). A valuable examination of Wolff's position in 18th century German philosophy has been provided by Max Wundt in *Die deutsche Schulphilosophie im Zeitalter der Aufklärung* (Tübingen: Mohr, 1945; reprinted Hildesheim: Georg Olms Verlag, 1964).

[4] *Ges. Werke*, I, 1.

[5] *Ratio praelectionum Wolfianarum in mathesin et philosophiam universam* (*Ges. Werke*, II, 36).

[6] Cf. Eric A. Blackall, *The Emergence of German as a Literary Language*, 1700-1775 (Cambridge: at the University Press, 1959), esp. 26-48.

[7] Wolff himself is proud to cite Voltaire's comment, "Wolfio docente, Rege Philosopho regnante, Germania applaudente Athenas invisi." See *Eigene Lebensbeschreibung* (*Ges. Werke*, I, 10), p. 185.

[8] Cf. Charles A. Corr, "Christian Wolff's German Metaphysics Volumes, Their Revisions, and Leibniz," *Akten des III. Internationalen Leibniz-kongresses, Hannover, 12. bis 17. November 1977* (3 vols.; Wiesbaden: Franz Steiner Verlag, 1980), III, 231-239.

[9] Wolff's *Oratio de Sinarum philosophia practica* was first published in an authorized edition in 1726. It is now available in his *Meletemata mathematico-philosophica* (*Ges. Werke*, I, 35), Sec. III, #4. A German translation appears in Wolff's *Gesammelte kleine philosophische Schriften*, ed. G. F. Hagen (6 vols.; Halle 1736-40), VI, A, 1-322 (*Ges. Werke*, I, 21.6). The story of Wolff's expulsion is capably told by Eduard Zeller in "Wolffs Vertreibung aus Halle; der Kampf des Pietismus mit der Philosophie," *Preussische Jahrbücher*, 10 (1862), 42-72. The principal documents in the controversy are available in *Ges. Werke*, I, 17 & 18, & II, 9.

[10] The full title of this work is *Anmerkungen über die vernünftigen Gedanken von Gott, der Welt und der Seele des Menschen, auch allen Dingen überhaupt, zu besserem Verstande und bequemeren Gebrauche derselben*. In the second edition of 1727, it was changed to *Der vernünftigen Gedanken von Gott, der Welt und der Seele des Menschen, auch allen Dingen überhaupt, anderer Teil, bestehend in ausführlichen Anmerkungen*. This book will be Bd. 3 in the I. Abt. of the *Ges. Werke*.

[11]*Ges. Werk*, II, 3-8 (1962-1980).

[12]For an investigation of Wolff's relationships with Leibniz, see: Walter Arnsperger, *Christian Wolffs Verhältnis zu Leibniz* (Weimar: Felber, 1897), and my two articles, "Did Wolff Follow Leibniz?", in *Akten des 4. Internationalen Kant-Kongresses* (3 vols.; Berlin: Walter de Gruyter, 1974-1975), II. 1, 11-21, and "Christian Wolff and Leibniz," *Journal of the History of Ideas*, 36 (1975), 241-262.

[13]See *Deutsche Metaphysik*, ##598-599 & 900, together with *Anmerkungen*, ##215, 251, & 298. Cf., Jean Ecole, "Cosmologie wolffienne et dynamique leibnizienne. Essai sur les rapports de Wolff avec Leibniz," *Les études philosophiques*, 19 (1964), 3-9, and my article, "Cartesian Themes in Christian Wolff's German Metaphysics Volumes," forthcoming in the Proceedings of the Wolff Symposium, Wolfenbüttel, Nov. 1979.

[14]*Deutsche Metaphysik*, Preface to the 1st edition (p. vii), and Preface to the 2nd edition (pp. xx-xxii).

[15]*Deutsche Metaphysik*, ##527-539 & 760-791. Cf. Richard J. Blackwell, "Christian Wolff's Doctrine of the Soul," *Journal of the History of Ideas*, 22 (1961), 339-354, and my "Christian Wolff's Distinction Between Empirical and Rational Psychology," *Studia Leibnitiana*, Supplementa, Bd. XIV, 114-134.

[16]*Deutsche Metaphysik*, Preface to the 2nd edition (pp. xvi-xvii), and *Anmerkungen*, ##1 & 55.

[17]*Deutsche Metaphysik*, ##1-9.

[18]*Deutsche Metaphysik*, ##722ff.

[19]The parallel passage there is in *Psychologia empirica*, #16 (*Ges. Werke*, II, 5), p. 12.

[20]On method in Wolff, cf., Giorgio Tonelli, "Der Streit über die mathematische Methode in der Philosophie in der ersten Hälfte des 18. Jahrhunderts und die Entstehung von Kants Schrift über die 'Deutlichkeit'," *Archiv für Philosophie*, 9 (1959), 37-66, and Nicolao Merker, "Christiano Wolff e la metodologia del razionalismo," *Rivista critica di storia della filosofia*, 22 (1967), 271-293, & 23 (1968), 21-38.

[21]*Deutsche Metaphysik*, ##30-31.

[22]For Wolff's own account of his conception of philosophy, see *Discursus praeliminaris de philosophia in genere* (*Ges. Werke*, II, 1. 1); translated into English by Richard J. Blackwell as *Preliminary Discourse on Philosophy in General* (New York: Bobbs-Merrill, 1963). Among the secondary sources, see: Hans Lüthje, "Christian Wolffs Philosophie-begriff," *Kantstudien*, 30 (1925), 39-66; Richard J. Blackwell, "The Structure of Wolffian Philosophy," *The Modern Schoolman*, 38 (1961), 203-218; and my "Certitude and Utility in the Philosophy of Christian Wolff," *Southwestern Journal of Philosophy*, 1 (1970), 133-142.

[23]For what are essentially the pre-Leibniz origins of Wolff's thought on this point, see H. J. de Vleeschauwer, "La genèse de la méthode mathématique de Wolf. Contribution à l'histoire des idées au XVIIIe siècle, *Revue Belge de philologie et d'histoire*, 11 (1932), 651-677.

[24]It appears to have been Thümmig who influenced Wolff to abandon the approach of the short first chapter of the *Metaphysik* and to shift its argument to the realm of his psychology, and also to place his discussion of general cosmology before both empirical and rational psychology. Cf. *Ausführliche Nachricht*, #79, (*Ges. Werke*, I, 9), pp. 230-232.

[25]Carl Günther Ludovici, *Ausführlicher Entwurf einer vollständigen Historie der Wolffischen Philosophie. Zum Gebrauche seiner Zuhörer heraus gegeben* (3 vols.; Leipzig 1737-1738); *Sammlung und Auszüge der sämmtlichen Streitschrifften wegen der Wolffischen Philosophie* (2 Parts in 1 vol.; Leipzig 1737-1738); & *Neueste Merckwürdigkeiten der Leibnitz-Wolffischen Weltweisheit* (Frankfurt & Leipzig 1738). George Volckmar Hartmann, *Anleitung zur Historie der Leibnitzisch-Wolffischen Philosophie und der darinnen von Hn. Prof. Langen erregten Controvers, Nebst einer Historischen Nachricht vom Streite und Übereinstimmung der Vernunfft mit dem Glauben, oder Nutzen der Philosophie in der Theologie . . .Mit Anmerckungen erläutert* (Frankfurt & Leipzig 1737). All of these titles are now reprinted in *Ges. Werke*, III, 1-4.

[26]Kant, "Neue Anmerkungen zur Erläuterung der Theorie der Winde," in *Kant's gesammelte Schriften* (22 vols.; Berlin: Königlich Preussischen Akademie der Wissenschaften, 1900-1938), I, 503: "Das Handbuch des Herrn Prof. Baumgarten . . . dieses nützlichste und gründlichste unter allen Handbüchern seiner Art."

[27]Baumgarten, *Metaphysica* (reprinted Hildesheim: Georg Olms Verlag, 1967), ##230-245.

[28]*Ibid.*, ##733-739 & esp. 761-769.

[29]Tonelli, "Alexander Gottlieb Baumgarten," *The Encyclopedia of Philosophy* (8 vols.; New York: Macmillan, 1967), I, 256.

[30]Wundt, *op. cit.*, 222.

[31]Kant, *Kritik der reinen Vernunft*, Vorrede zur zweiten Auflage, Bxxxvi-xxxvii (*Kant's gesammelte Schriften*, III, 22): ". . . der strengen Methode des berühmten Wolff, des grössten unter allen dogmatischen Philosophen, folgen, der zuerst das Beispiel gab (und durch dies Beispiel der Urheber des bisher noch nicht erloschenen Geistes der Gründlichkeit in Deutschland wurde), wie durch gesetzmässige Feststellung der Principien, deutliche Bestimmung der Begriffe, versuchte Strenge der Beweise, Verhütung kühner Sprünge in Folgerungen der sichere Gang einer Wissenschaft zu nehmen sei, der auch eben darum eine solche, als Metaphysik ist, in diesen Stand zu versetzen vorzüglich geschickt war, wenn es ihm beigefallen wäre, durch Kritik des Organs, nämlich der reinen Vernunft selbst, sich das Feld vorher zu bereiten."

[32]Kant, *Prolegomena zu einer jeden künftigen Metaphysik, die als Wissenschaft wird auftreten können*, Vorwort (Kant's gesammelte Schriften, IV, 262): "...sein Schiff, um es in Sicherheit zu bringen, auf den Strand (den Scepticism) setzte, da es denn liegen und verfaulen mag."

[33]Kant, *Kritik der reinen Vernunft*, Vorrede zur zweiten Auflage, Bxxxv (III, 21): "Dogmatism ist also das dogmatische Verfahren der reinen Vernunft *ohne vorangehende Kritik ihres eigenen Vermögens*." (Kant's italics.)

[34]*Ibid.*: "Die Kritik ist nicht dem dogmatischen Verfahren der Vernunft in ihrem reinen Erkenntniss, als Wissenschaft, entgegengesetzt (denn diese muss jederzeit dogmatisch, d. i. aus sichern Principien *a priori* strenge beweisend, sein)."

[35]*Ibid*, p. 22: "Diejenigen, welche seine Lehrart und doch zugleich auch das Verfahren der Kritik der reinen Vernuft verwerfen, können nichts andres im Sinne haben, als die Fesseln der Wissenschaft gar abzuwerfen, Arbeit in Spiel, Gewissheit in Meinung und Philosophie in Philodoxie zu verwandeln."

[36]Saner, *Kant's Political Thought: Its Origins and Development*. Translated by E. B. Ashton (Chicago: University of Chicago Press, 1973), pp. 94 & 226. Cf. my "Analytic and Synthetic Method in Kant," *Proceedings of the Ottawa Congress on Kant* (Ottawa: Ottawa University Press, 1976), 382-390.

[37] Kant, *Über eine Entdeckung, nach der alle neue Kritik der reinen Vernunft durch eine ältere entbehrlich gemacht werden soll* (VIII, 250-251): "So möchte denn wohl die Kritik der reinen Vernunft die eigentliche Apologie für Leibniz selbst wider seine ihn mit nicht ehrenden Lobsprüchen erhebende Anhänger sein...vernachlässigt und über dem Wortforschen dessen, was jene gesagt haben, dasjenige nicht sehen kann, was sie haben sagen wollen." Translated by Henry E. Allison, *The Kant-Eberhard Controversy* (Baltimore: The Johns Hopkins University Press, 1973), p. 160.

[38] Collins, *Interpreting Modern Philosophy* (Princeton, NJ: Princeton University Press, 1972), p. 229. The quotation in the following sentence of the text is from p. 40 of the same work. Cf. my article, "Toward an Improved Understanding of the History of Philosophy," *Metaphilosophy*, 6 (1975), 54-71.

10.

KIERKEGAARD, ABRAHAM AND THE MODERN STATE

John W. Elrod

Almost everyone with even a passing acquaintance with Kierkegaard's writings is familiar with his interpretation of the Biblical story about Abraham and Isaac. There is perhaps no book by Kierkegaard that is more widely known and discussed by scholars and students than is his *Fear and Trembling*. This book has provided both undergraduates and scholars with a set of issues that are as intensely discussed today as they were when the book first appeared in its English translation forty years ago. The philosophical and theological background of this book is the Hegelian and Kantian reductionist program by which the distinction between ethics and religion is collapsed so that religion becomes merely the narrative or symbolic form of ethics. Under the pseudonym, Johannes de Silentio, Kierkegaard sets out polemically to reconstitute logically and existentially the separation of ethics and religion through his imaginative recasting of Abraham's intention to sacrifice Isaac in order to demonstrate his faith in Jahweh, the god of Israel.

The imaginative form of the book, its polemical intention, as well as its being pseudonymously authored have led many justifiably to be concerned with whether this book represents any of Kierkegaard's own positions on the many issues that are raised in it. I do not intend to probe this problem here, although it is my purpose to show that much later in Kierkegaard's authorship, the Abraham and Isaac story re-appears and is given a very different emphasis from the one that it receives in *Fear and Trembling*. Late in his authorship, Kierkegaard published a book with the title *For Self-Examination*. This book also has a sharply polemical tone, although its object is not the misrepresentation of Christianity by philosophical idealism but rising Danish liberalism and the acculturation of Christianity by the prevailing political, economic, and social priorities of the new liberalism. Kierkegaard called this symbiotic relation between Christianity and culture "Christendom," and most of the books that he published after 1846 constitute an attempt to separate logically and existentially Christianity and Danish culture.[1] The two are neither identical nor complementary as many nineteenth century Danes believed, and Kierkegaard perceived his task as a writer after 1846 as one of re-establishing a distinction between the two in his readers' public and private lives. Toward this end *For Self-Examination* leads the individual reader to see that the Bible and the ethical imitation of Christ are the proper forms of Christian *self understanding* and *action* and that together both reward the individual with the true life of the spirit. Kierkegaard's discussion of these three issues in the Christian life is set against his contemporaries' belief that proper self-understanding and action and their rewards are to be found in the politics and economics of Christendom.

Kierkegaard's attack on Christendom does not begin, as is generally believed, in the last eighteen months of his life with the series of articles published first in *The Fatherland* and later in his own journal, *The Instant*. These articles directly attacked the institutional church and many of its ecclesiastical procedures and practices, but the attack had begun much earlier in his writings and had taken the form of encouraging the inward transformation of the individual. This inward transformation, Kierkegaard believed, would itself set the individual in opposition to Christendom so that the attack would proceed from the inside out, which is the way Kierkegaard thought all genuine reform must proceed. This strategy for the inward transformation of the individual prominently included a program of clarifying categories that had a value in the Christian community. One of its central problems was that categories such as love, faith, freedom, equality, God, and hope had been appropriated by Christendom so that their meanings were seriously distorted by its language. In the third part of *For Self-Examination*, Kierkegaard's attempts to rescue three of these categories from their distortions in the vernacular of Christendom. It is in this context that the Abraham and Isaac story reappears in Kierkegaard's writings. Here the story is not employed to clarify the relation of ethics and religion but to help clarify the meaning and value of faith, love, and hope for Christian inwardness.

Category confusions important to the life of the spirit and their clarifications are never merely, or even essentially, technical matters. That is to say, these confusions are not of the sort that they can be clarified by clear-headed and analytically minded philosophers and theologians or by historically astute biblical scholars. Thinkers and historians are not irrelevant to the task, but their contributions are vital only when they are Socratically employed. The existential connection between character and beliefs/values is the arena for category clarification and only the Socratically minded teacher is capable of analyzing and correcting confusions about categories important to the life of the spirit. Kierkegaard understood this fact as well as anyone has in the modern period. Hence, in order to correct prevailing misunderstandings about Christianity, he launched an attack on Christendom. This attack was in fact, however, an attack which took the form of enabling his individual readers to understand that each individually was *himself*, to the extent that he called himself a Christian in Christendom, a confusion or a distortion of Christianity. The category confusion was not essentially a technical one to be clarified by clear-headed thinking but an existential confusion to be clarified by existentially changing one's life. Kierkegaard nowhere more explicitly states this view than in *For Self-Examination*. "There is absolutely no definition of Christian truth given without the subordinate determinant which is posited at the outset of Christianity, namely, death, this thing of dying — by which it would secure Christian truth against being taken in vain" (*FSE*, 95).[2] There is no greater life change for any individual than that of death, and here Kierkegaard claims quite simply that the only access to an understanding of Christian truth is the way through death. Thus, category confusions within Christendom can be corrected only by dying to that way of life which is itself a distortion of Christianity. Our task here is to explore this claim and to uncover the significance of the Abraham and Isaac story for it.

In writing about the individual in Christendom, Kierkegaard frequently uses the term "natural man." The term does not have its conventional connotations of referring to the human self in some pre-historical or pre-social/political sense. Kierkegaard rather uses the term to capture both a philosophical sense of the self as teleological in nature and a sociological sense of the contemporary Dane as one who is actively participating in the political, economic, social, and cultural life of nineteenth century Denmark. The term "natural man" refers to the self that is teleologically seeking its completion in the public life of Denmark. It is the self that has broken free of medieval Europe and is confidently *remaking itself by remaking Denmark* in the institutions and practices of the constitutional monarchy, laissez-faire economics, experimental science, the Golden Age of literature, freedom of the press, the ecclesiastical reform of the religious establishment, the urbanization of much of Denmark, the conversion of agriculture from a communal to a profit-making activity and the elevation of the rural peasant class from the position of political and economic powerlessness to one of power. While Kierkegaard was clearly not a trained sociologist, he certainly astutely observed not only these profound changes transforming Denmark from a feudal to a modern state in the century from 1750 to 1850 but also, and more significantly, the spiritual significance of these changes for the individuals who confidently participated in them.

According to Kierkegaard, their spiritual significance had to be measured in terms of some understanding of the nature of the self. The political, economic, and social significance of democracy and liberalism were important and plain for all to see. Yet Kierkegaard believed that the deeper and more important spiritual significance of these events was not readily apparent for all to see since an appreciation for the teleological character of the self was essential for grasping this deeper aspect of these changes. Following Aristotle and Hegel, Kierkegaard maintained that the self was not characterized by an innate essence. The self does not appear in human history as a finished product. On the contrary, the self appears within history as an unfinished subject with a natural inclination or drive toward self-completion in and through its own activity. In his earlier pseudonymous writings, Kierkegaard works out this conception of the self in terms of his famous stages of existence. The self's striving for completion carries it through the stages of pleasure and duty until it finds its resting place in faith. In the second literature, Kierkegaard comes to appreciate the social component of the self's search for completion and the significance of this fact for understanding the modernization of Denmark.

Kierkegaard believed that human beings in their *natural state*, unlike other species of living beings, require "the other" for their own completion. This fact applies in both the private and public domains of social life. Describing the individual in his natural state, Kierkegaard claims that "in order to be himself, a man must first be expertly informed about what the others are, and thereby learn to know what he himself is — in order to be that" (*CD*, 42).[3] Since it is not possible to be human fully without the other, "it seems as though he must constantly wait for the others in order to learn to know what he is now, at this moment" (*CD*, 43). Existing for the natural man "lies in existing only before others, in not knowing of anything else but the relationship of others" (*CD*, 44). Therefore, "he is what the others make of him, and what he makes of himself by only being for others" (*CD*, 47). The point here is that the individual acquires an identity in and through a relationship with another subject.

Kierkegaard understood the potential of this fact for struggle and conflict within human relationships. If the individual finds his completion in and through the other, it follows that the other will in some sense be instrumentally perceived by the becoming subject. If the other is a necessary condition for my completion as a becoming subject, then the other must exist in a manner that is consistent with my own sense of what constitutes my completeness. Kierkegaard's second literature is filled with examples and discussions of his own version of the war of all against all, and I shall only briefly discuss four of these examples in order to fill out this important point.

This negative self-seeking scenario is nowhere more thoroughly analyzed in Kierkegaard's second literature than in his discussion of love in *Works of Love*. In this book, Kierkegaard argues that most expressions of love are in fact expressions of self-love. Kierkegaard relies heavily on Aristotle to make this point. In the *Nichomachean Ethics*, Aristotle argues that craftsmen and poets love their handiwork and poems more than they would love their producers if they were to come alive (*EN*, IX, 7).[4] This is true also of benefactors who love those whom they have helped more than the benefited love their benefactors. "The cause of this," explains Aristotle, "is that existence is to all men a thing to be chosen and loved, and that we exist by virtue of activity (i.e. by living and acting), and that the handiwork *is* in a sense, the producer in activity; he loves his handiwork, therefore, because he loves existence. And this is rooted in the nature of things; for what he is in potentiality, his handiwork manifests in activity" (*EN*, IX, 7, translator's italics). Here Aristotle claims that the object of love is loved, because it represents the lover as actualized.

Kierkegaard sees in Aristotle's observations a principle governing the behavior of the natural man. Love within nature is a mode of self-production through which each individual attempts to pass from a state of potentiality to one of actuality by creating himself in and through the other. Self-love is then the basis of all love for the natural man. "In [erotic] love and friendship one's neighbor is not loved, but one's self, or the first I once again, but more intensely" (*WL*, 69).[5] In *eros* and friendship, self-love "selfishly unite[s] the two in a new selfish self" (*WL*, 69-9). "The one whom self-love in the strictest sense loves is also basically the other-I, for the other-I is oneself, and this is indeed self-love" (*WL*, 69). In his discussion of *eros* and friendship for the natural man, Kierkegaard argues that even the commitment of "devotion" and the feeling of "boundless abandonment" toward the other are modes of self-constitution in and through the other (*WL*, 67). A similar view is expressed in the journals. "The basis for erotic love is a drive, the basis of friendship is inclination, but drive and inclination are natural qualities, and natural qualities are always selfish...therefore there is still a hidden self-love in erotic love and friendship..." (*JP*, IV, 4447).[6] *Eros* and friendship do not include *essentially* the dimension of selfless concern for the well-being of the other. For the natural man, both are *essentially* opportunities for self-discovery and self-completion in and through instrumentally relating to the other in the sense that the other makes it possible for the becoming subject to have a concrete and tangible sense of himself as an "I."

A second example of how the becoming subject may instrumentally relate to others is offered much later in *Works of Love*. Here the scenario of self-completion is not innocently played out in *eros* and friendship but is expressed in the harsher form of domination. The important issue here in this example for Kierkegaard is that domination is essentially a spiritual striving for identity and self-completion rather than a play for power for its own sake. Such striving ignores the individuality of the other in the subject's own quest for his completion. Kierkegaard correctly claims that "only true love loves every man according to his individuality. The strong and domineering person lacks flexibility, and he lacks a sense of awareness of others; he demands his own with everyone; he wills that everyone shall be recreated in his own image, be trimmed according to his pattern for human beings...if the strong and domineering individual cannot create, he wants at least to remodel; he seeks his own so that wherever he points he can say: see, this is my image, this is my ideal, this is my will. Whether the strong and domineering individual is allotted a great sphere of activity or a small one, whether he is a tyrant in an empire or a house-tyrant in a little attic room, the essence is the same: domineeringly unwilling to go out of himself, domineeringly wanting to crush the other person's individuality..." (*WL*, 252-53). The passage's tone is a bit too strident and bombastic to describe what I think Kierkegaard actually has in mind. Tyranny in both public and private life is rarely quite so overt and self-conscious as this passage here implies. It is rather more subdued, discreet, indirect, well-meaning, and hidden from both the tyrant's and victim's consciousness. The result is nevertheless the same as Kierkegaard states, *viz.* disregarding the individuality of the victim by the tyrant's striving to recreate himself in the other.

The third example is from *Christian Discourses* where Kierkegaard analyzes this struggle in terms of class conflict for economic and political power. But in these discourses, Kierkegaard's analysis of class conflict does not settle on its economic and political dimensions but on the spiritual basis of the struggle. Kierkegaard views class conflict in the same way that he views natural love and tyranny, *viz.* as a struggle for identity. While it is true that economic and political issues are genuinely at stake in class conflict, Kierkegaard sees underlying these tangible struggles a more fundamental struggle for identity. Since one's identity is dialectically constituted in relation to the other, the conflict between classes is nothing less than an identity struggle. From Kierkegaard's perspective, it is seriously mistaken to distinguish radically the struggle for political and economic power from the spiritual struggle to become a complete self. Since all natural human relations are grounded in self-love, political and economic power becomes the means whereby members of the ruling class establish their identity through the domination of the lower class.

Moreover, "the lowly man...sinks under the prodigious weight of comparison which he lays upon himself" (*CD*, 48). He is "tortured by the thought of being *nothing*, tortured by the fruitlessness of his efforts to be something" (*CD*, 48, Kierkegaard's italics). His "anxiety is to become something in the world... To be [simply] a man...is not to be anything — that is in fact to be nothing, for in this there is no distinction from nor advantage over all men... But to be Councillor of Justice — that would be something" (*CD*, 47).

To have power is to be something; to be powerless is to be nothing. And since one cannot be powerful unless there is powerlessness, one must have the other *qua* powerless in order to be. Maintaining these class distinctions between the powerful and the powerless, the wealthy and the poor, is essential for the natural man if there is to exist any possibility of gaining identity, being, in the world. Thus, it is not ironic for members of the lower class to cling to the system that suppresses them, for without it there would be no possibility of becoming a complete self. Therefore, the lowly man "desires to belong to the temporal...he will not let it go, he clings tighter to being nothing, tighter and tighter as he seeks in vain to be something..." (*CD,* 48).

While this struggle for identity may be carried out publicly in the struggle for economic and political power, it may also be present in social and cultural conflict. Here we find our fourth and final example of Kierkegaard's analysis of the teleological character of the subjectivity within the natural man's realm. In *Works of Love*, he describes as "small-minded" those persons who band together and prejudicially exclude all those who do not share in some common trait or characteristic that they regard as peculiarly distinguishing. Small-mindedness has fastened itself tightly to a very particular shape and form which it calls its own; only this does it seek, and only this can it love. If small-mindedness finds this, then it loves. Therefore small-mindedness sticks together with small-mindedness; they grow together like an ingrown nail, and spiritually speaking it is just as bad. This association of small-mindedness is then praised as the highest love, as true friendship, as true steadfast, sincere harmony" (*WL*, 254). Such prejudicial and cowardly small-mindedness "feels...a damp unpleasant anxiety upon observing another person's [or group's] individuality and nothing is more important that to get rid of it" (*WL*, 254). All those not possessing this trait or characteristic are excluded, yet feared, for their individuality stands as a constant threat to the identifying and valuing trait of such a closed society.

This impetus toward becoming a self in and through the other naturally insinuates itself into every form of human life. In analyzing the relations between persons in this way, Kierkegaard gives an entirely different character to our most basic social relations and institutions. Within the realm of the natural man, these relations and institutions have to be understood as a function of the individual's pursuit of self-identity. In the individual's relation to the other, he comes to an awareness of himself as somebody, as an identity which stands out from all other things and persons, as ontologically distinct, unique, and worthy.

We should not understand these four cases as *a priori* deductions from the theological premise that human beings are inherently evil. Kierkegaard did not believe that self-love is an evil, although he did view it as requiring an ethical-religious mediation if it is not to result in its own contradiction. The realization of self-love, the fulfillment of the drive to be a complete self, requires its ethical-religious transformation. Otherwise, the individual's self-love will necessarily result in contradicting its own objective. We should also not understand these four cases as ones that are hypothetically concocted in Kierkegaard's imagination to illustrate an equally hypothetical way of life. As I indicated above, these examples of the natural man's self-love are intended by Kierkegaard to explain the basic dynamic underlying the multiplicity of changes transforming Denmark from a feudal to a modern liberal state. In Kierkegaard's view, liberalism, with its emphasis on an understanding of freedom that is derived from a conception of the individual as naturally endowed with political and economic rights, paved the way for the emergence of this form of self-love as a dominant historical force in modern western history. The society that Kierkegaard describes in these four cases will inevitably emerge when the following three ingredients are blended as Kierkegaard believed that they were in the formation of the modern Danish state: (1) the teleological nature of the self; (2) the social character of the self's completion; (3) a conception of freedom that is exclusively derived from the concept of natural rights. Kierkegaard accepted (1) and (2) as axiomatically true and (3) as the view of freedom that contingently entered western history during the Enlightenment. The result was the emergence of what Kierkegaard called selfish self-love as the basic principle underlying the appearance of the modern state.

What remained to be accomplished was to give this new form of life a mythic legitimation, and in Kierkegaard's view this role is the one that the Danish state religion, Lutheranism, came to occupy in the nineteenth century. There is not time here to rehearse in detail the roles played by key Danish religious leaders like Mynster, Grundtvig, Rudelbach, Adler, and others. Nor is there time to review Kierkegaard's criticisms of each of these figures in relation to their uniting Lutheranism and the modernized Denmark. All that can be said here is that from Kierkegaard's perspective Christianity in nineteenth century Denmark failed to distinguish being a good Dane and being a Christian. In a variety of subtle and not so subtle ways, the Christian church came to stand for everything that typified the modern liberal state. In Kierkegaard's words, "the lust for power and human ambition...turned its attention to Christianity to see if it could cunningly take possession of it and then with respect to other men play our Lord, who rules with the help of eternity as background. The really great attempt in this direction is the Pope... The other effort in this direction is that of the state" (*JP*, IV, 4504). Thus, once Christianity is "spavined and decrepit and on its last legs, spoiled and muddle-headed, then the state said: see, now I can begin on it; and smart as I am, I can see very well that I can use it and profit from it enough so that I can properly see my way to spending a little to polish it up" (*JP*, IV, 4232). Kierkegaard could also discuss this alliance between the state and Christianity in strictly theological terms. "Throughout Christendom the dialectical element has been abolished. The doctrine 'grace' is moved a whole stage too high. Christianity had demanded the genuine renunciation of the world, had demanded the voluntary, and then, on top of this, one is to acknowledge that he is nothing, that all is grace. Christendom removes the former entirely—and then lets grace move up; it grafts 'grace', if thou will, directly onto the secular mind" (*JP*, I, 763).

This homogenization of Christianity and the modern Danish state is Kierkegaard's chief concern throughout his second literature. In this connection, two questions continually preoccupy him. More visibly present in the second literature is Kierkegaard's struggle to separate logically and existentially Christianity and the modern state. Less visibly present, but as essential to his general goal, is his concern with the issue of how to channel self-love, i.e. the self's desire for completion, in a constructive direction. Kierkegaard believed that in Danish life only Christianity was equipped to channel properly the self's natural desire for completion. But, unfortunately, it had become entangled with the modern liberal state, which, as we have seen, Kierkegaard understood as a selfish expression of the self's teleological striving for completion.

Kierkegaard viewed as his task one of identifying this fact and then proceeding to correct it first by making this separation and then by pointing the way toward an ethical-religious channeling of self-love within the context of the modern state. In order to accomplish this goal, Kierkegaard believed that a specific action was necessarily required of each individual, *viz.* that he die to the way of life that Kierkegaard called Christendom. Just what this action requires of each individual is implied in his reference to the Abraham and Isaac story in *For Self-Examination*.

Referring to the individual, Kierkegaard asks: "What does he more strongly crave and more vehemently than to feel keenly the pulse of life in himself?" (*FSE*, 96). This "pulse of life" is felt most intensely when it comes into relation with an object that is the "eyes' delight and his heart's desire" (*FSE*, 96). But the relation to this object is one of selfishness, for "his selfishness would be wounded very deeply indeed by being deprived of the object..." (*FSE*, 98). If the individual is required by himself or by God to let go of the object, "we have an example of what it is to die (*afdø*)" (*FSE*, 98). Now Kierkegaard fully addresses the meaning of this Biblical story.

> For not to see his wish, his hope, fulfilled, to be deprived of the object of his desire, his beloved—that may be very painful, selfishness is wounded, but that does not necessarily mean to die. No, but to be obliged to deprive oneself of the object of desire of which one is in possession—that is to wound selfishness at the root, as in the case of Abraham, when God required that Abraham himself, that he himself—frightful!—with his own hand—Oh, horror of madness!—must sacrifice Isaac, the gift so long and lovingly expected, and the gift of God, for which Abraham conceived that he must give thanks his whole life long and would never be able to have thanks enough—Isaac, his only son, the son of his old age, and the son of promise (*FSE*, 98).

Kierkegaard adds a paragraph later: "This is what it means to die" (*FSE*, 99).

To die is to wound selfishness at its root, and this action must be a voluntary one. In Abraham's case, what is required of him is that he cease thinking of Isaac as in his being the fulfilment of God's promise to him and, hence, his own fulfilment. For this reason, to sacrifice Isaac is to sacrifice himself since his own identity is essentially related to Isaac's destiny. Isaac *is* Abraham's desire, his hope, the fulfilment of God's promise to him. This relation of father to son is the foundational spiritual bedrock of Abraham's understanding of himself as a person, and this relation no doubt conditioned the public and external dimensions of their relation in the political, economic, and social domains of their lives. Kierkegaard characterizes this spiritual relation as one of selfishness, because Isaac appears to Abraham as his own identity in its publicly actualized form. Kierkegaard's observation about the natural man's love in *Works of Love* is appropriate here: "The one whom self-love in the strictest sense loves is basically the other-I, for the other-I is oneself, and this is indeed self-love" (*WL*, 69). Thus, "what is sought after is not the other's good or not that alone" (*FSE*, 103).

It is very important to notice the religious form of Abraham's selfishness. We can hear him saying to his god: "But Isaac is *your promise to me*." The relation of Abraham to Isaac is neither blatantly tyrannical nor manipulative. It does not appear to be one in which an imbalance of power is subtly concealed in the political practices or social conventions of the day. It is, or at least it appears to be, a highly ethical-religious relation in which a father provides and cares for the promised son of his old age. Yet within this ethical-religious relation, there lies concealed at its core the selfishness of a father who sees in his son only God's promise to him. It does not take much imagination to imagine how this perception of his son readily and necessarily translates into certain political, social, and economic arrangements not necessarily of Isaac's own choosing. Yet who is Isaac to object to the working out of God's divine plan for both his father and himself? Thus, God requires of Abraham that his religious vision be sacrificed in the interest of both Abraham's and Isaac's own freedom. Neither is free so long as both are caught in the ethical and secular imbalances of this religiously justified father-son relation.

So long as one lives only within the realm of nature, religious categories will be interpreted in its terms. This was the case with Abraham as with all human beings who exist religiously this side of death. But "this bestowing of life in the spirit is not a *direct* increment of the natural life of man, *immediately* continuous with it..." (*FSE*, 101, Kierkegaard's italics). When the life of the spirit is directly continuous with the life of the natural man, "love is selfishness" (*FSE*, 102), faith is "confidence in oneself, in the world, in mankind, and (among other things) in God" (*FSE*, 101), and hope is a "spontaneous (immediate)" belief that death is only an illusion and that the eternal life expected by the natural man will in fact arrive (*FSE*, 101). In all three cases, these religious categories are grounded in "an immediate apprehension" of God as a being whose intentions for us are consistent with our own natural inclinations and desires to become a completed self in and through others. "Therefore, first death, first thou must die to every merely earthly hope, to every merely human confidence, thou must die to thy selfishness or to the world; for it it only through thy selfishness that the world has power over thee; if thou hast died to thy selfishness, thou hast died also to the world" (*FSE*, 97). This act of dying to the world is Abraham's act in his journey to Moriah and back.

Kierkegaard's reference to this story in the midst of his attack upon Christendom is very significant, because he has selected an ancient religious narrative to dramatize the fundamental problem of Christendom. By referring to a narrative about persons in relation to God, Kierkegaard illustrates clearly his belief that the central problem of Christendom is a spiritual one. The story is, as we have seen, about a person whose central concern is a religiously legitimated realization of his search for identity, selfhood, being-in-the-world and of his despair in having to give up that subject in whom he experienced this realization. Thus, the spiritual nature of the fundamental problem of Christendom is located in its personal dynamic. As with Abraham, the driving principle within Christendom is the individual subject's self-seeking; the object of its satisfaction is another subject; and the authoritative justification of this subject-object relation is derived from yet another, albeit divine, subject. This dynamic within Christendom has been set in motion, as I have already suggested, by the emergence of liberalism in western history, and it is skillfully played out in the institutions, social conventions, and cultural forms governing the nineteenth century Dane's public and private life.

Just as this story dramatically illustrates the personal and religious nature of the problem of Christendom, it also clearly points toward its equally, and necessarily, personal and religious resolution. In encountering God, Abraham is confronted with the possibility of letting Isaac go, yet it is a letting go that must be of his own choosing. It is a relationship that cannot be reconstituted by political, economic, or even divine action. Clearly, this letting go involves yet to be determined implications for the public dimensions of this relationship, but this public dimension can be essentially transformed only when Abraham chooses to undergo the despair that follows from letting go that subject in and through whom he is who he is. The relation is changed, then, when Isaac, the object, comes to be viewed not from Abraham's subjective but from God's point of view. Isaac is no longer only God's promise to Abraham but also a being who, like Abraham, is loved by God. And to be viewed as an object of God's consciousness is to be viewed essentially as an object of responsibilities and obligations rather than as an object of desire and inclination. Thus, this religious re-orientation of one's relation to the other involves quite simply moving in one's relation to the other from the aesthetic relation of inclination to the ethical relation of obligation.[7]

Kierkegaard believes that the religious resolution of the problem of selfishness in Abraham's relation to Isaac, whereby it is elevated from the aesthetic to the ethical stage of life, is the same resolution that is required for the central problem of Christendom. Its dilemma is the problem of the selfishness of inclination which has found new life in the liberalism of the modern state. The individual's inclination or drive to complete himself in and through his relations to others cannot, in Kierkegaard's view, be denied. Self-love is an unalterable fact of our nature. Kierkegaard views the modernization of Denmark as offering institutional, social, and cultural conduits for the realization of selfish self-love. A religious resolution of this problem is no less necessary that it was in Abraham's case. This being the case, there is no task more important than the clarification of those categories essential for the Christian life. And, as we have seen, the clarification of these categories is essentially an existential process. They can only be clarified by the individual's coming to exist in them as Christ did. Hence, becoming a Christian in Christendom should be the central aim of all individuals committed to resolving its central problem.

Notes

[1] Prior to 1846, Kierkegaard published his books almost exclusively under pseudonyms and after 1846 hardly at all. Those books published after 1846 shall here be referred to as the second literature.

[2] Søren Kierkegaard, *For Self-Examination*, translated with introduction and notes by Walter Lowrie (Princeton: Princeton University Press, 1968).

[3] Søren Kierkegaard, *Christian Discourses*, translated with introduction by Walter Lowrie (London: Oxford University Press, 1952).

[4] Aristotle, *Ethica Nicomachea*, trans. W. D. Ross in *The Basic Works of Aristotle*, edited with introduction by Richard McKeon (New York: Random House, 1941).

[5] Søren Kierkegaard, *Works of Love*, translated with introduction and notes by Howard V. Hong and Edna H. Hong (New York: Harper and Row, 1962).

[6] *Søren Kierkegaard's Journals and Papers*, translated and edited by Howard V. Hong and Edna H. Hong, 7 vols. (Bloomington: Indiana University Press, 1967-78).

[7] This move from the aesthetic to the ethical-religious stage of existence does not mean that the individual forgoes the prospect of fulfilling his natural desire to become a self in relation to other selves. In a long argument in *Works of Love*, Kierkegaard tries to show that loving the other as a neighbor is a necessary condition for fulfilling the desire to become a self so that love for the other as a neighbor and self-love are dialectically related. I have discussed this argument in detail in *Kierkegaard and Christendom* (Princeton: Princeton University Press, 1981), pp. 123-63.

11.

PEIRCE ON 'SIMPLICITY' AND THE CONDITIONS OF POSSIBILITY OF SCIENCE

By C. F. Delaney

Given the fact that during his formative years as an undergraduate at Harvard Peirce "devoted two hours a day to the study of Kant's *Critic of Pure Reason* for more than three years until I knew almost the whole book by heart and had critically examined every section of it" (1.4), it is not surprising that the projects (if not the conclusions) of the First Critique would become central to his own philosophical investigations. Such was clearly the case with regard to the project of exhibiting the conditions of possibility of science. However, as in most instances of genuine inspiration, there was a marked difference between the execution of the master and that of his creative pupil, a difference in this case which had its ultimate ground in the centrality of the notions of *history* and *community* in Peirce's over-all philosophical orientation. This general orientation disposed Peirce to what might be termed a concrete as opposed to an abstract conception of science. In contrast to the conception of science as a static set of propositions, he conceived of it as a socio-historical process of inquiry. This fundamental shift in perspective gave a quite different tonality to his project of exhibiting its conditions of possibility.

In this paper I would like to make clear the general contours of Peirce's project, and my point of departure will be his account of the criterion of 'simplicity' as it functions in scientific methodology. The emphasis in the paper is not at all on a detailed analysis of Peirce's account of the simplicity criterion, but rather on using his account of simplicity as an opening wedge into the exploration of his over-all conception of science as a general method of inquiry. This having been secured, I will move on to an exploration of his two pronged account of the conditions of possibility of science so construed.

*I. Simplicity, the Economics of Research
and the Structure of Science*

Pierce's general characterization of scientific method as involving an abductive, a deductive and an inductive phase is reasonably well known. The abductive stage of inquiry is concerned with the original generation and recommendation of explanatory hypotheses; the deductive phase has to do with the logical elaboration of the hypothesis and the derivation from it of specific predictions; and the inductive phase bears on the confirmation or falsification of the hypothesis by future experience. The movement of thought is from experience, through rational elaboration, back to experience.

In his more fine-grained account of the abductive phase of scientific inquiry Peirce distinguishes two moments. The first moment is simply the origination of those conjectures which will make up the list of possible explanations of the phenomena under consideration. This discovery moment is a function of the creative imagination of some people. Peirce talks of it in terms of a natural instinct and does not think it can be reduced to strict formulae or rules of procedures. The second moment takes its rise from the fact that there may well emerge many suggested hypotheses that equally 'explain' the facts. Accordingly, if we are to get on with the task of scientific explanation we must single out from the list of possible explanations those we are seriously to consider, and, furthermore, effect a preference ordering of these. This moment of the abductive process is rule-governed, and it is here that Peirce situates the functioning of simplicity as a criterion of theory choice. It is important to emphasize that this moment of theory choice is in the abductive phase of inquiry and thus is prior to all confirmation considerations. It is the choice as to which on the list of possible explanations to take as serious candidates and in what order to take them.

The first such regulative principle that Peirce articulates for this moment of the abductive phase of inquiry is that we should "follow the rule that that one of all admissible hypotheses which seems the simplest to the human mind ought to be taken up for examination first" (6.532). The operative phrase here is "seems simplest to the human mind" and much needs to be said to clarify the precise meaning of this phrase. In a comment on Galileo's use of this notion, Peirce pins down what he himself means by "simple" much more firmly:

> That truly inspired prophet had said that, of two hypotheses, the *simpler* is to be preferred, but I was formerly one of those who, in our dull self-conceit fancying ourselves more sly than he, twisted this maxim to mean the *logically* simpler, the one that adds least to what has been observed, in spite of three obvious objections: first, that so there was no support for any hypothesis; secondly, that by the same token we ought to content ourselves with simply formulating the special observations actually made; and thirdly, that every advance of science that further opens the truth to our view discloses a world of unexpected complications. It was not until long experience forced me to realize that subsequent discoveries were every time showing I had been wrong, while those who had understood the maxim as Galileo had done early unlocked the secret, that the scales

fell from my eyes and my mind awoke to the broad and flaming daylight that it is the simpler hypothesis in the sense of the more facile and *natural*, the one that instinct suggests, that must be preferred; for the reason that unless man have a natural bent in accordance with nature's, he has no chance of understanding nature at all...I do not mean that logical simplicity is of no value at all, but only that its value is badly secondary to that of simplicity in the other sense (6.477).

The hypotheses that should be initially preferred, then, are those that "naturally recommend themselves to the mind, and make upon us the impression of simplicity — which here means facility of comprehension by the human mind, — of aptness, of reasonableness, of good sense" (7.220). In the first instance, then, Peirce maintains tht we should prefer those hypotheses that seem most natural to us, those with which we feel comfortable.

What justification can there be for accepting such a rule of procedure, a rule which amounts to the assumption that we have a natural instinct for guessing right in this investigative situation? Peirce brings three considerations forward in support of this assumption. First, in view of the survival instincts prevalent in the rest of the animal kingdom, it seems not inappropriate that we too have those instincts necessary for the continuance of our distinctive mode of life (6.476); secondly, given the infinite number of possible explanations for any configuration of phenomena, it certainly behoves us to hope that we have such an ability and to act accordingly (7.219); thirdly, the history of science seems to lend support to the belief that we do have such a natural ability to guess right in virtue of the incommensurability between the explanatory success we have experienced to date and the low probabilities that would have been involved in antecedent theory selection without such a natural instinct (7.220). For these reasons Peirce concludes it reasonable to assume that we do have this natural instinct. It remains for him to render a full philosophic explanation of this instinctive ability to guess right, an explanation which will move him from the claim that we have such an ability to an account of how we come to have it. But this dimension of the issue is a part of his exploration of the conditions of possibility of science.

This, however, is not the only *kind* of justification Peirce offers for the acceptance of this criterion of simplicity. He immediately adds the following consideration?

> This rule has another advantage, which is that the simplest hypotheses are those of which the consequences are most readily deduced and compared with observation; so that, if they are wrong they can be eliminated at less expense than any others (6.532).

The point here is that the simplest hypotheses are the easiest ones for us to work with and so enable us to get on with the inquiry most efficiently. Inasmuch as they encapsulate the views with which we feel comfortable, it is usually the case that we can quickly see what each entails and imagine how to go about testing them. Accordingly, should they prove promising, we may well be on the road to the true explanation; if they prove to be false starters, at least they can be eliminated with less trouble than other alternatives and so speed us on our way down other avenues. In this line of justification of the criterion of simplicity, we can see the seeds of a *dynamic* (as opposed to a static) and a *social* (as opposed to an individual) notion of simplicity functioning in Peirce's view of science. Simplicity is not a logical feature of a theory at a time. It is, rather, a property a theory has in virtue of certain roles it can play at given historical stages of the inquiry process. Moreover, the justification of simplicity is not in terms of the individual scientist but in terms of the over-all functioning of the community of inquirers.

These points are brought out much more clearly in Peirce's immediate movement from this narrow formulation to the much broader rule it suggests?

> This remark [above] at once suggests another rule, namely, that if there be any hypothesis which we happen to be well provided with means for testing, or which, for any reason, promises not to detain us long, unless it be true, that hypothesis ought to be taken up early for examination (6.533).

What Peirce is doing here is situating the criterion of simplicity in the broader context of what he called the "economics of research," an area of investigation that he carved out in his 1876 paper entitled "A Note on the Theory of the Economy of Research."[1]

It is under this general rubric of *economy* that Peirce proposes to organize the several regulative principles that bear on this second moment of the abductive process:

> What really is in all cases the leading consideration in Abduction is the question of Economy — Economy of money, time, thought, and energy (5.600).

It is important to take note of the broad scope of the term "economy" here before moving on to examine some of the concrete regulative principles in terms of which this general maxim is specified. The term ranges over the various human resources that are invested in our cognitive endeavors and suggests that our principal concern ought to be to realize the best possible cognitive return on our investment.

The various rules Peirce articulates for employment in this initial moment of theory choice can be seen to emanate from this general statement of the principle of economy. (1) The first rule is a straightforward application of the general maxim: "If any hypotheses can be put to the test of experiment with very little expense of any kind, that should be regarded as a recommendation for giving it precedence in the inductive procedure" (7.220). In the same vein is the recommendation that that hypothesis should be preferred which "can be the most readily refuted if it is false" (1.120). (2) A second rule, which could be seen to be a corollary of the first, recommends that one hypothesis should be preferred over another if one could not test the latter without doing almost all the work required to test the former but not vice versa (7.93). (3) A third rule expressed in the jargon of the game of billiards maintains that that hypothesis should be preferred which, if false, would give the best "leave," that is, whose residuals would be the most instructive with reference to the next avenue to be explored (7.221). In the same vein Peirce invokes the party game of Twenty Questions and recommends the preference of that hypothesis which would halve the number of possible explanations (7.220). (4) A fourth rule that he suggests enjoins us on the basis of economy to prefer (all else being equal) the broader of two hypotheses on the grounds that the illumination it will shed on the general inquiry will be greater whether it is true or false (7.221).

Taken together these rules amount to the injunction that at the abductive stage of inquiry the investigator should do a cost-benefit analysis of the various paths along which he can proceed. The reason for this Peirce thinks is obvious.

Proposals for hypotheses inundate us in an overwhelming flood while the process of verification to which each one must be subjected before it can count as at all an item, even of likely knowledge, is so very costly in time, energy and money — and consequently in ideas which might be had for that time, energy and money, that Economy would override every other consideration even if there were any other serious considerations. In fact, there are no others (5.602)[2]

The various rules provide guidelines for this cost-benefit analysis. The decision procedure is far from automatic or simple, however, because the various rules are not only difficult to apply in concrete cases but also are often in conflict one with the other. In concretely deciding what line of investigation seriously to pursue, a kind of practical rationality is involved which cannot be reduced to a mere following of rules.

The point I would like to emphasize is that in this account of the criteria of antecedent theory choice in terms of a general theory of the economics of research, Peirce clearly construes these criteria both *historically* and *socially*. One hypothesis is to be preferred over another not in terms of its intrinsic merits or its likelihood of being true but in terms of the role it can play in a process of inquiry which is aimed toward truth in the long run. An hypothesis is recommended to the degree that its pursuance at this point in time would move the inquiry along most efficiently. Peirce's invocation of the game of Twenty Questions is instructive. In playing this parlor game, a line of questioning recommends itself not in terms of the likelihood it will "hit upon" the correct answer immediately but in terms of the role this line of questioning will play in definitely hastening the convergence on truth of the line of inquiry in general. Secondly, the justification of these abductive rules is not in terms of the individual investigators but in terms of the community of investigators of which he is a member. The hypothesis recommended to any individual may not at all be the one most likely to enable him to attain the truth but rather the one which will most efficiently ensure the eventual attainment of truth. Given the state of the inquiry, an individual investigator may be rationally constrained to spend his days eliminating some unlikely possibilities. It seems that in the cognitive order the individual's good is secondary to the good of the community. Accordingly, even in his account of the abductive phase of inquiry we can see Peirce moving from an abstract propositional conception of science toward a construal of science as a concrete socio-historical process of inquiry.

This emphasis is even more pronounced in his account of the inductive phase of the inquiry process. "Induction" as Peirce is here using the term is to be understood not simply in terms of the relation of individual cases to the general law but in terms of the *role* such a logical relationship plays in the inquiry process in general:

> The only sound procedure for induction, whose business consists in testing an hypothesis already recommended by the retroductive procedure, is to receive its suggestions from the hypothesis first, to take up the predictions of experience which it conditionally makes, and then try the experiment to see whether it turns out as it was virtually predicted in the hypothesis that it would. Throughout an investigation it is well to bear prominently in mind just what it is that we are trying to accomplish in the particular stage of the work at which we have arrived. Now when we get to the inductive stage what we are about is finding out how much like the truth our hypothesis is, that is, what proportion of its anticipations will be verified (2.755).

The principal role of the inductive relationship in the cognitive process is that of confirmation or falsification. The role of the relationships between propositions describing individual instances to the relevant laws or theories is not that of the latter being derived from them, but rather of these instances, having been predicted by the theory, functioning either to confirm or to falsify it. It is through this inductive phase that the speculative flight of scientific inquiry is continually monitored by experience.

Much more needs to be said about this "monitoring" because it is in virtue of the role in inquiry of this inductive phase as a constant check on speculation that Peirce sees himself as able to construe science as a *self-regulating* and *self-corrective* process.

Induction is the experimental testing of a theory. The justification of it is that, although the conclusion at any stage of the investigation may be more or less erroneous, yet the further application of the same method must correct the error (5.145).

The point is that the method of testing which this inductive phase of inquiry involves is such that "if it be persisted in long enough it will assuredly correct any error concerning future experience into which it may temporarily lead us" (2.769).[3]

A little more needs to be said to appreciate the picture Peirce here has in mind. When we commit ourselves to the program of testing our hypotheses by the deliverances of experience, we are aware of the fact that any given hypothesis will range over many more cases than can possibly come under scrutiny. Peirce's contention is that so long as we are careful to predesignate the cases that will count and follow the procedure of fair sampling we can be assured that the continued application of the inductive procedure will reliably eliminate the false theories and thus by indirection recommend the true one. We will eventually discover whether or not reality has those characteristics our theory ascribes to it. And the "we" here does not refer to any specific individual. The logical subject of the inquiry is *the scientific community over time* and it is in its ultimate success that Peirce has confidence. The self-corrective feature of its method ensures its convergence on the truth. Reality must have some character; so, given that new hypotheses are forthcoming, the continued application of this process of elimination "must lead to a result indefinitely approximating to the truth in the long run" (2.781). His picture of science culminates in the view that "science is foredestined to reach the truth of every problem with as unerring an infallibility as the instincts of animals do their work" (7.77). The ultimate justification for this belief that scientific inquiry is self-monitoring and, consequently, truth-guaranteeing in this way involves Peirce's theories of *truth* and *reality* which emerge in his explorations of the conditions of possibility of science.

Our philosopher, then, is not looking at the confirmation process (the inductive phase of inquiry) in terms of the degree of warrant any specific theory has in terms of specific test results but rather in terms of the long-run effect of continued empirical testing. The self-correctiveness of science is to be understood in terms of the role of the inductive phase in monitoring the process of inquiry. The inductive phase if not self-corrective in the sense that it automatically provides better hypotheses; it only functions to eliminate. Better hypotheses are provided by the whole process of inquiry over time; it is a matter of promising suggestions continually subjecting themselves to the process of elimination. The individual scientist is seen as a member of this historical community whose bond of unity is the employment of this self-corrective method. The abductive phase provides the creative thrust with the inductive phase continually adjusting the direction in terms of nature's cues. And it is important to underline that concretely it is the total inquiry process that is both creative and self-corrective through these various phases.

The socio-historical picture of science that emerges from Peirce's account of scientific inquiry in terms of abduction, deduction, and induction receives its untimate generalization in his over-all construal of science as "a mode of life." Applauding Bacon's vision of science (while demurring at many particulars), Peirce puts forward the following general "definition" of the word:

> For him man is nature's interpreter; and in spite of the crudity of some anticipations, the idea of science is in his mind inseparably bound up with that of a life devoted to single-minded inquiry. That is also the way in which every scientific man thinks of science. That is the sense in which the word is to be understood in this Chapter. Science is to mean for us *a mode of life* whose single animating purpose is to find out the real truth, which pursues this purpose by a well-considered method, founded on thorough acquaintance with such scientific results already ascertained by others as may be available, and which seeks cooperation in the hope that the truth may be found, if not by any of the actual inquirers, yet ultimately by those who come after them and who shall make use of their results. It makes no difference how imperfect a man's knowledge may be, how mixed with error and prejudice; from the moment that he engages in an inquiry in the spirit described, that which occupies him is *science*, as the word will here be used.
>
> By a specific science will be meant a group of connected inquiries of sufficient scope and affinity fitly to occupy a number of independent inquirers for life, but not capable of being broken up into smaller coexclusive groups of this description. For since we are to consider science in general as a mode of life, it is proper to take as the unit science the scientific mode of life fit for an individual person. But science being essentially a mode of life that seeks cooperation, the unit science must, apparently, be fit to be pursued by a number of inquirers (7.54 - 5).

The contrast here is with the German handbook conception of science as a body of doctrine. Peirce does not deny that this sense of the term (science as an organized body of knowledge) has its appropriate uses but simply insists that his use represents what he calls "a deeper cut." Given the static and doctrinaire picture that the former usage tends to encourage, Peirce thinks it behoves us rather "to consider science as living, and therefore not as knowledge already acquired but as the concrete life of the men who are working to find out the truth" (7.50).

This concrete characterization should also carry over to our conception of the particular branches of science. He views a particular branch of science, for example, chemistry or biology, as "no mere word manufactured by some academic pedant but as a real object, being the very concrete life of a social group constituted by real facts of inter-relation" (7.52). From Peirce's perspective, then, when we speak of science in general or of some particular science, what we are concretely talking about is a community of inquirers extended over time with a unity of purpose and method which enables the product to be much more than just the sum of the individual contributions. The classical conception of science as an organized set of propositions freezes this process at a time and thus abstracts from its life, whereas it is Peirce's inclination "always to look upon those aspects of things which exhibit whatever of the living and active there is in them" (7.53). It is in this spirit that Peirce returns to the question of definition and maintains that "If we are to define science, not in the sense of stuffing it into an artificial pigeon-hole where it may be found again by some insignificant mark, but in the sense of characterizing it *as a living, historic entity*, we must conceive it as that about which such men as I have described busy themselves" (1.44).

II. *The Conditions of Possibility of Science*

It is against the background of this conception of science that we should examine Peirce's attempt to exhibit the conditions of possibility of science. As I will attempt to reconstruct it, the project has two facets: first, the articulation of certain qualities of the inquirers necessary to sustain the process; and secondly, the articulation of certain features of the world necessary to guarantee its objective reach. Together these will constitute the conditions of possibility of science as we know it.

It should be recalled that science, as Peirce understands it, is only one model of a cognitive mode of life; and, furthermore, it is one which has not always been dominant and whose continuance is by no means inevitable. Peirce himself has spelled out three other models of cognitive inquiry (the methods of tenacity, authority, and self-evidence) that have had historical periods of dominance and which continue to vie with science for our allegiance. The continuance of science as we understand it depends on the persistence of certain inter-related social practices which in turn depends on certain *virtues* being embodied in the individual members of the community of investigators. So it is to these sustaining virtues that Peirce turns his attention in his initial exploration of the conditions of possibility of the scientific mode of life.

The tone of the discussion is set by the following remark:

> The most vital factors in the method of modern science have not been the following of this or that logical prescription — although these have had their value too — but they have been *the moral factors* (7.87).

The case Peirce wants to argue is that the continual development of science as we know it, is grounded in certain dispositions which mark its individual practitioners. The specific moral factors on which he focuses are *the love of truth, the sense of community,* and *the sense of confidence.*

The first appears completely uncontroversial: "The first of these has been genuine love of truth and the conviction that nothing else could long endure" (7.87). Appearances, however, can be deceiving. The contrast Peirce has in mind here is that between the scientific mind and the teaching mind; that is, the mind of the inquirer and the mind of the pedagogue. Peirce envisions the scientist as one whose dominant, driving force is the unfettered search for truth which results in his following the inquiry wherever it may lead; whereas he sees the mind of the teacher as one whose dominant orientation is that of organizing and communicating what he already knows. This dichotomy is recapitulated within philosophy itself in Peirce's distinction between laboratory philosophy and seminary philosophy with the former embodying the spirit of the scientists and the latter the spirit of the teachers (1.129). The contrast is between the quest for truth and dissemination of belief, a contrast which runs deep into the human character. Moreover, Peirce regards this perennial character difference as being "writ large" in the difference between the spirit of the Middle Ages and that of modern times. In the earlier era, the dictates of an authoritative faith were dominant and the direction of the inquiry was formed by the intention of rationalizing this faith; while in the latter day the quest for a presently unattained truth became the overriding intention with specific "faiths" playing their roles within that framework.[4] Peirce sees this shift in cognitive orientation as a principal part of the story of the historical emergence and continuing foundation of modern science.

The second moral factor, the sense of community, is more complicated and attracts more of Peirce's attention. Having made some initial remarks about the requirement of intersubjectivity of evidence imposed by the social character of science, he focuses on this social character itself and the conception of self that it both presupposes and engenders. Science as a way of life is seen to demand an overcoming of self-interest in favor of the long-range goals of the investigating community:

> The method of modern science is social in respect to the solidarity of its efforts. The scientific world is like a colony of insects in that the individual strives to produce that which he cannot himself hope to enjoy. One generation collects premises in order that a distant generation may discover what they mean. When a problem comes before the scientific world, a hundred men immediately set all their energies to work on it. One contributes this, another that. Another company, standing on the shoulders of the first, strikes a little higher until at last the parapet is attained (7.87).

The life of science is essentially that of an historical community that is teleological in structure. Its continuance depends on this social sense coming to assume a dominant role in the lives of the individual investigators so that proximate attractions are constrained by long-range goals. The comparison to a colony of insects can be instructive because Peirce does think that there is a kind of social instinct that sustains man in matters cognitive as well as in the broader spheres of human conduct. Science as we know it is grounded in this social sense.

It is most important to note that for Peirce this sense of community is not merely an extrinsic support of the life of science but is essentially tied to the very logic of scientific method. It will be recalled that the rationality of both the abductive and the inductive phases of inquiry required one's looking beyond the individual inference to the role it played in the over-all inquiry process. Its rationality was bound up with viewing it from this perspective:

> It can be shown that no inference of any individual can be thoroughly logical without *certain determinations of his mind* which do not concern any one inference immediately; for we have seen that that mode of inference which alone can teach us anything or carry us at all beyond what was implied in our premises — in fact, does not give us to know any more than we knew before; only, we know that, by faithfully adhering to that mode of inference, we shall on the whole approximate to the truth (5.354).

Hence, the rationality of the abductive and inductive procedures of science is, from the point of view of the inquiring subject, grounded in certain determinations of his mind which enable him to view his inferences as part of an ongoing inquiry, the full logical subject of which is the historical community. It is with this in mind that Peirce can make the strong claim that "he who recognizes the logical necessity of complete self-identification of one's own interests with those of the community, and its potential existence in man, even if he has it not himself, will perceive that only the inferences of that man who has it are logical, and so views his own inferences as being valid only so far as they would be accepted by that man" (5.356).

It is in the spirit of this general sense of community that Peirce introduces his discussion of the three logical sentiments. His point is that the justification of particular abductive and inductive inferences is proximately grounded in three logical sentiments:

> I should put forward three sentiments, namely, interest in an indefinite community, recognition of the possibility of this interest being made supreme, and hope in the unlimited continuance of intellectual activity, as indispensable requirements of

logic (2.655).

The life of science, then, demands the transcendence of both selfishness and skepticism through the active hope that cooperative effort will in the end prevail. After a passing comparison of these three logical sentiments to the classical triad of Charity, Faith and Hope, Peirce draws the somewhat flamboyant conclusion that "he who would not sacrifice his own soul to save the whole world is, as it seems to me, illogical in all his inferences collectively" (2.654). The rationality of scientific inquiry is rooted in the social principle.[5]

The discussion of these three logical sentiments merges into Peirce's account of the third moral factor undergirding the continuation of science, namely, the sense of confidence. Peirce thinks that a sense of confidence is particularly crucial in an inquiry that proceeds by the method of conjecture and refutation. The opportunities for discouragement will be plentiful. In our specific hypotheses we are clearly going to be wrong more often than we are right, so it is important that we continue to view our proximate failures in terms of their contributions to the long-range effort, and our motivation to persist in doing this is grounded in the confidence that the long-range effort will be successful. When Peirce looks at the history of modern science, he sees this disposition of its practitioners manifest in science as a whole: "Modern science has never faltered in its confidence that it would ultimately find out the truth concerning any question to which it could apply the check of experiment" (7.87). From the point of view of the individual scientist this confidence is simply the action-guiding hope that the indefinite application of these methods will lead to the attainment of truth in the long run. From the metaphysical perspective, however, we shall see that this confidence can have an even deeper foundation.

While the grounding of scientific inquiry in these virtues may well account for the historical development of science as a mode of life, it doesn't seem to speak at all to the question of science's objective validity. To complete the exploration of the conditions of possibility of science, this inquiry into the question "What must people be like that science may continue?" must be supplemented by an inquiry into the question "What must the world be like that science may be cognitively successful?" It is to Peirce's reflections on this issue that I now turn.

It will be recalled that the distinctive features of science as a cognitive mode of life were the regulative principles embodied in the abductive and inductive phases of scientific inquiry. It seems reasonable to assume, then, that it is on these that we should focus if we are to get clear about science's objective reach. In Peirce's account of simplicity in particular and the abductive principles in general, the presence in man of a natural instinct to guess right played a crucial role. Can any account be given of such a cognitively reliable natural instinct that will render our belief that we have it not unreasonable? Can the existence of such an instinct be rendered intelligible by our metaphysical view of the world? Secondly, we saw in Peirce's account of the inductive phase of science the important role played by an abiding confidence that the continued application of those procedures would lead to the attainment of truth in the long run. Is there any metaphysical basis for this confidence and thus for the ultimate objectivity of science?

In the earlier discussion of the abductive phase of inquiry and the role therein of this natural instinct to guess right, I brought to the fore several of the methodological considerations Peirce put forward in support of this assumption. These, however, seem to fall short of making the complete case. The notion of natural instinct has a nagging subjectivity about it that is not eradicated by Peirce's methodological considerations, a subjectivity which gives pause to the objective construal of science. Inasmuch as the truth of this assumption is one of the conditions of possibility of the objective success of science as we know it, it remains for Peirce to put forward a methaphysical picture of the world in terms of which this assumption is at least rendered plausible.

The picture Peirce puts forward is broadly evolutionary and the first thing he points to is the tremendous evolutionary advantage that would accrue to creatures possessing the ability of ampliative reasoning of either the abductive or the inductive sort. Raising the question as to how we can explain such a general ability, he responds in terms of natural selection: "Since it is absolutely essential to so delicate an organism as man's, no race which had it not has been able to sustain itself" (5.341).

Focusing specifically on the natural instinct to guess right that functions in the abductive process, Peirce very specifically ties it to certain organic practices necessary for survival:

> If you carefully consider with an unbiassed mind all the circumstances of the early history of science and all the other facts bearing on the question, I am quite sure that you must be brought to acknowledge that man's mind has a natural adaption to imagining correct theories of some kinds, and in particular, to correct theories about forces, without some glimmer of which he could not form social ties and consequently could not reproduce his kind. In short, the instincts conducive to the assimilation of food, and the instinct conducive to reproduction, must have involved from the beginning certain tendencies to think truly about physics on the one hand and psychics on the other (5.591).

Peirce spells out this last point a little more fully in an earlier passage: "The instincts connected with the need of nutrition have furnished all animals with some virtual knowledge of space and force... and the instincts connected with sexual reproduction have furnished all animals at all like ourselves with some virtual comprehension of the minds of other animals of their kind" (5.586). The point is that those organisms that have the most reliable ability to guess right in the areas that Peirce labels physics and psychics, given the role played by such beliefs in fundamental organic practices, would clearly be advantaged in the process of natural selection. And it must be emphasized that the ability Peirce is talking about is the ability to guess *right*, because he thinks that it is only correct beliefs that are likely to have staying power given ever changing circumstances: "As that animal would have an immense advantage in the struggle for life whose mechanical conceptions did not break down in a novel situation (such as development must bring about), there would be a constant selection in favor of more and more correct ideas of these matters" (6.418). This being the case, it is not surprising that we, the survivors, should have this ability to guess right to a considerable degree.[6]

But can anything more be said about how we come to have this ability in the first place? Peirce's next suggestion is that if we adopt a broadly anti-Cartesian picture of the relation of man to nature the presence of this instinct becomes even more intelligible:

> General considerations concerning the universe, strictly philosophical considerations, all but demonstrate that if the universe conforms, with any approach to accuracy to certain highly pervasive laws, and if man's mind has been developed under the influence of those laws, it is to be expected that he should have a *natural light*, or *light of nature*, or *instinctive insight*, or genius tending to make him guess those laws aright, or nearly aright (5.604).

The point is that if we assume that the mind of man is outside nature looking in and trying to guess at the laws which describe its structure, its high apparent success rate seems mysterious or occult. But, if we assume that the mind of man is constituted by nature's evolving development, its affinity with its object becomes less mysterious. Since the presence of this instinct does seem to be borne out by the history of science, and since this anti-Cartesian conception of the world seems necessary to render it intelligible, Peirce feels justified in adopting this metaphysical picture as one of the conditions of possibility of science. He makes the point specifically with regard to mechanics: "Our minds having been formed under the influence of phenomena governed by the laws of mechanics, certain conceptions entering into these laws become implanted in our minds, so that we readily guess at what the laws are" (6.10). Being nature's products, we have privileged access to her secrets.

There is one more chapter to this metaphysical account geared to rendering intelligible the success rate of the abductive moment of science. The evolutionary point makes the case for a continuity between the realms of mind and nature, but it doesn't specify which categories are going to be basic. In an inversion of the standard evolutionary accounts, Peirce suggests that from an explanatory point of view it is more reasonable to take the psychical laws as basic and treat the physical laws as derived and special than the other way around. That is, it is easier to explain physical laws on the model of habits than to account for psychological phenomena on the model of mechanical processes. Given this ultimately idealistic derivation of the laws of matter from the laws of mind, clearly the existence of such a natural abductive instinct would be far from an anomaly. The affinity of man's mind with the structure of the natural order would have been given the strongest possible reading.[7]

Having thus worked from the most distinctive feature of the abductive process to a view of the world which grounds its objective reach, Peirce now turns to the most distinctive mark of the inductive phase of science in order to explore the same issue of metaphysical grounding. Is our confidence that the continued application of induction procedures will lead to the attainment of truth in the long run merely a hope or can it be shown to have a deeper metaphysical foundation? Can our metaphysical picture of the world be extended to render intelligible the success of this self-monitoring feature of scientific inquiry and thus the long-run objectivity of science as a whole? Although concretely this is a question about the self-corrective feature of scientific inquiry, logically it is simply the question of the justification of induction. For, if the confirmation procedures of science are going to be viewed as playing this crucial role in the movement toward truth over time, then we must have reason to believe that the inductive sampling that functions in the confirmation stage is a reliable guide to the structure of the real.

Peirce's first move in response to this problem of induction is to dismiss all responses framed in terms of "the uniformity of nature." At best, these would tie the validity of inductive procedures to the particular consititution of this world thus leaving open the possibility of other worlds in which inductive procedures would not have held. He feels that this kind of contingent foundation is too weak for induction and for scientific inquiry in general. The validity of induction and the reliability of the self-monitoring feature of science seem to rest on more than a contingent fact.[8]

Peirce finds it difficult to imagine a world in which inductive procedures would not be reliable:

> If men were not able to learn from induction, it might be because as a general rule, when they had made an induction, the order of things would then undergo a revolution... But this general rule would be capable of being itself discovered by induction; and so it must be a law of such a universe that when this was discovered it would cease to operate. But this second law would itself be capable of discovery. And so in such a universe there would be nothing which would not sooner or later be known; and it would have an order capable of discovery by a sufficiently

long course of reasoning. But this is contrary to the hypothesis; and therefore that hypothesis is absurd (5.352).

Hence his view is that the justification of induction is not tied to any facts about this particular world but rests rather on the fact that it is a procedure "which if steadily persisted in must lead to true knowledge in the long run of cases of application whether to the existing world or to any imaginable world whatsoever" (7.207).

To appreciate the reasons for this belief we must move in the direction of Peirce's fundamental theory of "reality." Inductive inference is basically an inference from part to whole and its validity depends simply on the fact that the parts do make up and constitute the whole. We are involved in drawing samples from a population, and if the frequency with which some relevant property is distributed over the individuals of the sample does not correspond to its frequency of distribution over the population, the discrepancy is sure to become apparent as the sampling process is extended over the long run. To resist this line of thinking is to entertain a conception of the population or the whole which will never manifest itself in the samples or the parts. But to entertain this is to conceive of reality as possibly incognizable, as a thing-in-itself; and this Peirce thinks he has good reason to reject.

The only adequate conception of reality for Peirce is one in terms of the ultimately settled opinion of the inquiring community, and he tries to capture what seems right about the phenomenal-noumenal distinction in terms of the contrast between those representations of the world which include features peculiar and idiosyncratic to the individual inquirers and that ultimate representation where all these are corrected. But this is a conception of reality in terms of characters that are eventually manifested, and this conception of reality enables Peirce's justification of induction to go through without pause:

> An endless series must have some character; and it would be absurd to say that experience has a character which is never manifested. But there is no other way in which the character of that series can manifest itself than while the endless series is still incomplete. Therefore, if the character manifested by the series up to a certain point is not that character which the entire series possesses, still, as the series goes on, it must certainly tend, however irregularly, towards becoming so; and all the rest of the reasoner's life will be a continuation of this inferential process. This inference does not depend on any assumption that the series will be endless, or that the future will be like the past, or that nature is uniform, or upon any material assumption whatever (2.784).

In this way, Peirce effects a purely conceptual justification of inductive procedures, a justification cryptically embedded in his claim to the effect that "that the rule in induction will hold in the long run may be *deduced* from the principle that reality is only the object of the final opinion to which sufficient investigation would lead" (2.693) With this metaphysical grounding, science as a whole can be viewed as reliably self-corrective; the monitoring of the inductive phase occasions continual conceptual revision through the abductive phase with the total process of inquiry resulting over time in a more and more adequate picture of the world.

Thus it is that Peirce's rethinking of the Kantian project is brought to a conclusion. The task of a philosophical understanding of science begins with a characterization of science as a socio-historical process of inquiry having a distinctive methodological structure. This concrete as opposed to abstract conception of science gives direction to the project of exhibiting the conditions of its possibility. The focus is on the long range stability and objectivity of a specific kind of socio-historical inquiry. The distinctive features of both the abductive and the inductive phases of science are viewed as calling for a philosophical grounding both in a theory of man the inquirer and in an over-all theory of reality; and, in its final stages, the project of exhibiting the conditions of possibility of science melds into the broader project of laying down the conditions of possible objects of experience.

Notes

[1] Cf. (7.139-161). Peirce generously alluded to Ernst Mach's much later "The Economical Nature of Physical Inquiry" (1895) as the principal impetus to this area of investigation (5.601). For the most complete treatment of this strand of *Peirce's Philosophy of Science*, see Chapter IV of Nicholas Rescher's *Peirce's Philosophy of Science* (Notre Dame: University of Notre Dame Press, 1978).

[2] This emphasis on economy should not be read as implying a totally instrumental view of knowledge. Peirce is here talking about a principle of economy that functions within the cognitive sphere:

> The value of knowledge is, for the purposes of science, in one sense absolute. It is not to be measured, it may be said, in money; in one sense that is true. But knowledge that leads to other knowledge is more valuable in proportion to the trouble it saves in the way of expenditures to get that other knowledge. Having a certain fund of energy, time, money, etc., all of which are merchantable articles to spend on research, the question is how much is to be allowed to each investigation; and *for us* the value of that investigation is the amount of money it will pay us to spend upon it. *Relatively*, therefore, knowledge even of a purely scientific kind has a money value (1.122).

[3] Peirce draws many of his clearest examples of a self-corrective reasoning process from the area of mathematical computation (cf. 5.574), but he clearly sees it as a feature of scientific reasoning

in general. For the most complete discussion of this feature of Peirce's philosophy of science in its historical context, see L. Laudan "Peirce and the Trivialization of the Self-Correcting Theses" in R. Giere (ed.), *Foundations of Scientific Method in the Nineteenth Century* (Bloomington: University of Indiana Press, 1973).

[4] Peirce's attitude toward the difference between the medieval and modern minds is much more complicated than this point might incline us to believe. On many other specific issues, he sided with the medieval mind (realism versus nominalism) and even on this one he felt that the medieval attitude was reasonable at that point in time:

> The schoolmen however, attached the greatest authority to men long since dead, and there they were right, for in the dark ages it was not true that the later stage of human knowledge was the most perfect, but on the contrary. I think it might be said then that the schoolmen did not attach too much weight to authority, although they attached much more to it than we ought to do or than ought or could be attached to it in any age in which science is pursuing a successful and onward course (1.32).

[5] Peirce points out that this emphasis on the social sentiment should not come as a surprise. Reminding us of his earlier discussion of the four different methods of fixing belief, he remarks that since "the other methods of escaping doubt fail on account of the social impulse, why should we wonder to find social sentiment presupposed in reasoning" (2.655).

[6] It is interesting to note that the same general kind of account of our abductive principles (specifically "simplicity") is argued on the contemporary scene in W. V. Quine and J. S. Ullian *The Web of Belief*, second edition (New York: Random house, 1978), p. 73:

> Considering how subjective our standards of simplicity are, we wondered why we should expect nature to submit to them... Are we to conclude that the favoring of simplicity is entirely our doing, and that nature is neutral in the matter? Not quite. Darwin's theory of natural selection offers a casual connection between subjective simplicity and objective truth in the following way. Innate subjective standards of simplicity that make people prefer some hypotheses to others will have survival value insofar as they favor successful prediction. Those who predict best are likeliest to survive and reproduce their kind, in a state of nature anyway, and so their innate standards of simplicity are handed down.

[7] This metaphysical idealism of Peirce is a long and complicated story. Cf. 6.24-25; 6.264; 6.268 and 6.277.

[8] For the development of this point, see my paper "Peirce on Induction and the Uniformity of Nature," *The Philosophical Forum*, 4 (1973), pp. 438-448.

PART II

PROBLEMATIC OPENINGS TO QUESTIONS OF TODAY

...Recurrency...Creative Adaptation of Sources...Theories of Interpretation...Religion within Philosophy...In a Wittgensteinian Perspective?...A Concrete Historical Ideal...the Future of Philosophy

12.

ARE THERE RECURRENT PROBLEMS IN PHILOSOPHY?

Frederick C. Copleston, S.J.

I.

It is both a pleasure and a privilege to contribute to a *Festschrift* in honour of Professor James Collins. The theme which I have selected is obviously not a novelty, but the questions whether there are recurrent philosophical problems and, if so, how this recurrence is to be explained arise out of reflection on the historical development of philosophical thought, a field of study in which Dr. Collins has done outstanding work. I have indeed touched on this theme elsewhere,[1] but I wish to treat it rather more thoroughly, so far as available space permits.

Most people who are acquainted with the history of philosophy are probably inclined to regard it as obvious that the concept of a recurrent problem has been exemplified. For example, the problem of human freedom (in a psychological sense, that is to say) has been discussed at various times in the past, not only in Western philosophy but also in early Islamic thought, and it is still with us today. Again, the nature of the human being and the relation between the human being's physical and psychical activities have been discussed by many philosophers, not only in the West but also in India and China. Similarly, the problem of the existence of God has recurred in Indian philosophy as well as in Western thought. Is it not obvious that it has been a recurrent theme from early Greek thought up to the present day? Another example is the question whether or not the concept of sense-data is required, it we are to give an adequate account of perception.

Although it is probably true to say that most people who have some knowledge of the history of philosophy are prepared to accept the idea of there being recurrent philosophical problems, it by no means follows that all those who reflect on this phenomenon would agree to accept the same explanation of it or to draw the same conclusions. Some would doubtless be inclined to argue that if a question recurs, this is because it has not been answered, not at any rate adequately. Others would argue that what we call the recurrent or perennial problems of philosophy are in fact unanswerable, at any rate in the forms in which they have been expressed, and that it is for this reason that they recur. But the claim that certain problems are unanswerable can be understood in more than one way. It can be argued, with Immanuel Kant, that though certain questions are important for life and certainly merit serious reflection, they cannot be answered in the way in which most philosophers of the past have tried to answer them, and that a new approach is needed. It can also be maintained, as Bertrand Russell sometimes did, that there are certain questions which are unanswerable in a stronger sense than Kant would allow but of which it is important that human beings should be aware, it being therefore one of the tasks of philosophy to keep alive awareness of these problems.[2] There are also of course those who have argued that unanswerable questions are pseudo questions, problems without any real meaning, and that it is for this reason that they cannot be answered. On this view, the relevant problems should be suppressed, dissolved, shown up for what they are, not kept alive.

The foregoing lines of explanation do not exhaust the possibilities. It can be argued, for example, that it is essential to distinguish between proof and persuasion, and that the fact that a question recurs does not show that it has not been answered. Thus a Thomist may argue that St. Thomas proved the existence of God in the thirteenth century, and that if the Five Ways (or one or more of them) have failed to convince all philosophers, this is because they have not been properly understood. He might however wish to argue that St. Thomas, writing in the historical context of medieval Christendom, made certain presuppositions which cannot be taken for granted nowadays and which stand in need of reasoned support.[3] It is also possible to argue that the world as we experience it is of such a kind or has such features that doubt about the existence of God is pretty well bound to arise in many minds, and that even if proofs given centuries ago were good arguments, they need to be re-expressed in terms which can be more easily understood and appreciated by people living at a different period of time. In other words, the recurrence of problems or questions does not prove that they are unanswerable, nor even that they have not in fact been answered. It does however show the need for rethinking and re-expressing lines of thought in the light of the outlook of the relevant culture, society or period.

All these lines of explanation have a common presupposition, namely that there are recurrent philosophical problems. As has already been remarked, this is indeed what most of us are probably inclined to regard as true. It has however been argued that there are no recurrent problems in philosophy, and that it is a mistake to think that there are.[4] In this case of course the *explicandum*, what is to be explained, disappears. What stands in need of explanation is not the existence of recurrent philosophical problems but why people should think that there are. To a good many minds this contention probably seems to fly in the face of the historical evidence and to be an eccentric point of view. But it merits examination. For reflection on the reasons adduced to support it may draw attention to a factor in the situation which it is important to bear in mind and which should be allowed for, even it we decide to stick to the idea of recurrent philosophical problems.

II.

In the first place let us consider, though perforce very briefly, the question of understanding the past. It might be argued that we, living in the twentieth century and reconstructing the past from a twentieth-century perspective, are unable to understand the problems of a past society or of a culture other than our own as they were understood by the people in question. What we think of as problems of the past or of other cultures are really our own constructions which we then proceed to read back into the past. We are confined to our own perspective. We cannot adopt the perspective of another society or culture. When we believe that we are doing so, we are simply creating a twentieth-century conception of the past. In a real sense we are confined to understanding ourselves. The problems of the past therefore do not recur. They are so linked to past outlooks and frameworks of thought, to past perspectives, that they cannot, properly speaking, recur.

This point of view is obviously an application to the history of philosophy of the general contention, defended, for example, by Professor Charles Beard,[5] that we cannot know the past as it actually was. I cannot treat here of the general contention. It needs too much analytic examination and criticism for this to be possible. Besides, it has been discussed at some length by others.[6] I must content myself with a few remarks relating to the history of philosophy.

There are obviously some philosophical questions which presuppose states of affairs or situations which have emerged only in the course of the temporal development of the human being's intellectual life. For example, the philosophy of science as we know it today is parasitic on science, in the sense that questions about, say, the assumptions, if any, of empirical science or about the basic concepts employed by scientists presuppose the development of empirical science as a recognizable discipline or set of disciplines. Similarly, what is commonly described as critical philosophy of history presupposes the development of serious historical studies, as distinct from mere chronicling. But there are also questions which presuppose permanent states of affairs or a permanent human situation. One need not assume of course that such questions were discussed from the beginning of the human race. But given the development of a certain degree of reflection, they could in principle be raised at any time and in any culture. For example, human beings, wherever they are, and to whatever culture they belong, exercise both physical and mental activities. Hence in any culture it is possible in principle for questions to be raised about the relation between these activities, about the relation between mind and body. Again, in any society human beings are born and die, and it is possible to raise questions such as whether the human being is a purely this-worldly being or is oriented to a reality beyond the visible world. In point of fact such questions have been raised in a variety of cultures, and as they arise out of reflection on permanent states of affairs or on a lasting human situation, it is natural to believe that they can be understood by members of a culture other than the one in which we are thinking of them as having been raised and discussed. We are indeed members of a given society, living in a particular historical situation; but we are also all human beings, and we can understand problems arising out of reflection on situations which affect human beings in general, and not simply those living at a particular period or in a particular culture. It is indeed true that the concept of a permanent or abiding human situation is an abstraction, in the sense that it is never found in a pure state, so to speak, and has to be conceived by abstraction from particular situations. But we are presupposing philosophical reflection, which is capable of performing such abstraction.

The contention that one cannot understand the thought of a culture other than one's own seems to assume that cultures are self-contained units, each of which runs its life-course quite independently of positive influence by other such units. This was the thesis maintained, for example, by Oswald Spengler, though he found himself forced to make certain concessions, which he tried to reconcile with his theory of cultural units. In the first place however it is very difficult to identify separate cultures, historical periods and so on in a definitive manner. In the second place the claim that what we ordinarily think of as distinct cultures have passed through completely separate life courses seems to conflict with historical facts, at any rate as a general claim. In the third place the conclusion that we cannot understand the thought of another culture neglects the fact that in all cases we are considering the thought of human beings. To be sure, it may be extremely difficult, for a variety of reasons, to appreciate the thought of this or that society other than one's own. This is undeniable. None the less, there is a common unifying element, namely human nature, which makes understanding possible in principle, even it if is often difficult to achieve in practice. It is of course true that we cannot *be* Greeks of the sixth century B.C. or Chinese of 1000 B.C. This is obvious. But it does not necessarily follow that understanding is impossible, provided that sufficient historical evidence is available and that linguistic barriers can be overcome.

To my mind at any rate it seems that the implications of the truism that we look at the past from the standpoint or perspective of twentieth-century Westerners can be greatly exaggerated. Obviously, if we are using the thought of Plato as a springboard for philosophical reflection today, we naturally emphasize those themes and lines of thought which seem to us important in the light of contemporary philosophy. But this does not prevent us from understanding that problems or themes which seem to us of little significance today may well have seemed important to Plato himself. Moreover, it is not impossible to identify reasons why this or that idea seemed important to Plato. And analogous remarks can be made in regard, say, to early Chinese philosophy, even if difficulties in understanding are in this case considerably greater.

III.

My conclusion therefore is that the claim that talk about the recurrence of problems which were discussed in the past is unwarranted, on the ground that we cannot understand the past, should be rejected. It can however be argued that there are no recurrent philosophical problems not so much because we cannot understand the past at all as because talk about recurrent problems is a slipshod way of speaking, which passes over differences and confuses distinct problems or questions. This, it seems to me, is a much stronger objection against acceptance of the idea of recurrent problems in philosophy than the claim that we cannot understand the fact. And I wish to say something about it.

A simple example, which I have mentioned elsewhere,[7] is talk about the recurrence problem of human freedom (freedom of the will, as it is often expressed). In early Islamic thought this problem was raised in a theological context. The doctrine of reward and punishment in the Koran seems to imply that human beings are personally responsible for their actions, and that they are free to obey or to disobey the divine commands. But there are also passages in the Koran which seem to imply that God is the universal cause, causing even human decisions. The problem, it can be argued, was therefore this. If God is the universal cause, how can man be free? Now consider the problem of freedom as it arose in the post-renaissance Western world, and as it presented itself to Immanuel Kant. If the world is a system of bodies in motion, motion being transmitted according to mechanical laws: if, that is to say, the world is a mechanical system, how can the human being, who is in the world and a member of it, constitute an exception? Obviously, it may be said, this problem is different from the problem which arises in a theological context, whether Islamic or Christian. Again, the problem as it presented itself to Kant must be distinguished from the problem of freedom as it presents itself in the context of depth psychology. How do we know that the so-called free decisions of human beings are not the effects of infraconscious determining causes? To group all these distinct problems together and speak of the recurrent problem of human freedom is to neglect differentiating factors. It is a case of distinct problems rather than of one recurrent problem.

Let me take another example. Buddhist thinkers rejected the concept of *atman*, of a permanent, substantial, unchanging inner self, and analyzed the self into a series of states, asserted by a number of Buddhist thinkers to be momentary. The mind, no less than the body, was a series of transitory states. In the West Hume defended the same sort of reductive analysis of the concept of mind. It seems natural therefore to say that both the Buddhist thinkers and Hume were concerned with the same problem, the nature of the mind, a problem to which they offered similar solutions. If however we pay attention to the relevant contexts, the situation appears in a rather different light. According to his general programme, Hume should have been concerned with the limits of what we can be said to know, rather than with making ontological statements. But it is true that in the case of the mind he did make an ontological statement, namely that the mind is nothing but a succession of psychical states. He may thus seem to be saying precisely the same as the Buddhists had said centuries before. It is arguable however that the Buddhists were primarily concerned with the attainment of Nirvana and with promoting the detachment required for reaching this goal. If we assume that they were primarily concerned with an ontological question, difficulties immediately arise in regard to the compatibility between their analysis of the self and their acceptance of the theory of transmigration. For what is it of which it can be said that it is reborn? If however we see the Buddhists as addressing themselves to the question 'what interpretation of the self will best promote detachment from it?', it is clear that their problem was rather different from Hume's. To be sure, it is by no means everyone who would accept the idea that Buddhist analysis of the self had a purely pragmatic function.[8] But if the idea is accepted, it is then misleading to claim that the Buddhists thinkers and Hume were concerned with the same recurrent problem.

What are we to say about this line of thought? In the first place it is obviously true that if we wish to understand the thought of a past philosopher we have to understand the context in which certain problems or questions arose in his mind, the context including of course the thought of his predecessors and contemporaries. For the problems to which a given philosopher devotes his attention are often suggested by previous or contemporary philosophical discussion. Anyway, it is essential to bear the context in mind. For example, the illuminating power of the statement that Plato, Aristotle, St Augustine, St Thomas Aquinas, Hobbes, Locke, Rousseau, Hegel, Bradley, Nietzsche and others all reflected on political society, the State, is pretty limited. To receive further illumination we have to consider the relevant historical contexts and the forms taken by the questions which arose in the minds of such thinkers. It would be absurd to claim that the approaches of St Augustine, Hegel, Marx and Nietzsche to reflection on political society were the same. Nor indeed were the questions asked by St Augustine precisely the same as those asked by Nietzsche.

It may therefore seem very misleading to say that the thinkers named, plus others, were all concerned with 'the problem of the State', as though there were one single problem, which has recurred many times. For the matter of that, has not political society changed its form in the course of history? Plato and Aristotle thought in terms of the Greek city-State, medieval thinkers in terms of feudal society (or sometimes of the empire), Hegel in terms of the national State as it had emerged in the post-renaissance world, Chinese thinkers in terms of the Chinese empire or of the warring feudal states. Does not this fact make it difficult to claim that they were all concerned with the same problem, with one recurrent problem?

There is clearly a lot of truth in this contention. If we were invited to discuss 'the problem of the State' or 'the problem of God', we would naturally want to know first of all what particular problem or problems the person had in mind. For example, in the case of 'the problem of God', we might well ask how the person understood the word 'God', unless of course we knew him or her so well that we could be reasonably sure of the answer without having to ask. Did the person want to discuss arguments to support the belief that the empirical world is ontologically non-self-sufficient and depends on a transcendent reality? Or was he or she asking how belief in God as conceived by Christians can be reconciled with certain features of human life and history? After all, the phrase 'the problem of God' is pretty vague; and before discussion could be profitably pursued, we would have to have a clearer idea of the point at issue. Similarly, if someone asks what one thinks about the problem of war, it is natural to ask for a clearer indication of the question which the person has in mind.

At the same time, when we reflect on the historical development of philosophical thought, we undoubtedly find similar general themes recurring, such as philosophical anthropology, the attempt to answer the question 'what is the human being?' It is obviously true that this theme has been approached in a variety of ways. The Chinese Confucianists approached it primarily from a socio-ethical point of view, conceiving the human being primarily as a moral agent in a social context. Aristotle approached the matter in what we might describe as a biological context, reflecting both on the features which human beings can be regarded as having in common with other living things and on those which differentiate human beings from plants and animals. Sometimes the approach has been markedly religious in character, emphasis being placed, as in the Vedanta philosophies, on the idea of the inner self as being one with or oriented to the divine reality.[9] In modern Western philosophy since Descartes the approach has tended to be by way of reflection on the relation between mind and body in the human being. Evidently, we can envisage these different approaches as finding expression in rather different questions, proposed for consideration. None the less, questions relating to human nature or to the psycho-physical constitution of the human being obviously have a closer relation of similarity to one another than any of them have to the question whether a proposition can be self-referring or to questions in the philosophy of mathematics. We need to be able to refer to this similarity, to this family likeness; and the natural way of doing so is by speaking of a common theme. This theme can be seen as recurring, though admittedly in different contexts. The different contexts and approaches give rise to distinguishable questions; but these questions form, so to speak, a related cluster, distinguishable from other clusters. The phrase 'recurrent problem' is doubtless open to criticism, but it is a way of grouping together questions or problems which are interrelated. In other words, while the reaction against the idea of recurrent philosophical problems is, or can be, the expression of advertence to facts which ought to be borne in mind, it does not follow that the phrase is useless. Differences are important, but so are similarities. Each can be real.

IV.

So far we have been thinking of problems stated in a very broad and pretty vague way, such as 'the problem of freedom', 'the problem of the State', 'the problem of God', and so on. And I suppose that some critics would argue that if we allow ourselves to formulate problems in this sort of way, it is natural to think of them as recurring, whereas if we abandon vagueness and substitute particularity for generality, we can then abandon the concept of recurrence.

But is this true? Is it only vaguely stated problems, stated in portmanteau phrases, which can be thought of as recurring? This seems to me highly doubtful. The question whether a proposition can be self-referring was raised in the Middle Ages,[10] and it has also been raised in modern times. Again, the nature of relations has been discussed on temporally successive occasions. I once asked a well known philosopher whether he could mention even one philosophical question which had been answered in a final and definitive manner to everyone's satisfaction and which could therefore be regarded as settled. He thought for a moment or two and then replied that nobody now believes in the theory of internal relations. I mentioned the name of Brand Blanshard and asked my colleague whether he was prepared to prophesy that the question of internal relations would never recur. As this interchange occurred in more or less casual conversation, it would not be fair to mention my colleague's name and ascribe to him a definite position. But my impression was that he was not prepared to state that the question of internal relations would not recur, in spite of attacks on the theory.

It might perhaps be argued that all philosophical problems are potentially recurrent, in the sense that it is possible in principle for them to recur. All that is required for actual recurrence is either that later philosophers should be unaware that a given problem had been raised, discussed and answered at an earlier time or that, if they are in fact aware of this, that they should be dissatisfied with the answer previously given or with the arguments advanced in support of a certain answer or with both. In other words, the mere fact of recurrence is not sufficient to show that the question which recurs in unanswerable, still less that it is meaningless. The point however which I wish to make at the moment is that even if we are prepared to talk about recurrent problems or questions, it is none too easy to distinguish between recurrent and non-recurrent problems. For, given certain conditions, any problem can recur. Nor is recurrence necessarily a sign that a problem has been stated in such a general and vague way that it cannot be dealt with unless it has been broken up into more particular questions. This may indeed be the case on occasion. I have no intention of denying this. But it should be clear to all that even a quite definite question can recur, if philosophers are dissatisfied with a previously given answer, or if they are unaware that the question or problem has been discussed and given a sensible solution at an earlier date.

There is often no great difficulty in assigning reasons for the reopening of a question or for renewed discussion of a certain theme. I suppose that not so long ago it was taken for granted by a large number of philosophers that it had been shown that a clear distinction could be made between statements of fact and judgments of value, a belief which seems to be required by the 'no ought from an is' thesis. For my own part, I am inclined to accept the 'no ought from an is' thesis, though for various reasons I think that its practical importance has been exaggerated at times.[11] The fact remains however that the belief that we can make a clear distinction between factual statements and judgments of value has been challenged. The obvious reason is that the challengers are convinced that there are aspects of the situation which were not taken into account, or at any rate not sufficiently, by the defenders of the belief mentioned. It certainly does not follow that the question whether there is a sharp distinction between statements of fact and judgments of value is an unanswerable question, simply on the ground that discussion of it has recurred.

V.

Reference has been made above to the recurrence of questions such as whether a proposition can be self-referring. It seems to me that in such cases the phenomenon of recurrence can be explained, at any rate sometimes, without much difficulty, in terms, for example, of the interlocking of questions. Let us suppose that a philosopher has adopted a position which implies that a proposition can refer to itself. He asks himself whether this thesis is really tenable. He may not be aware that the question was raised some centuries before. But even if he is, it does not follow that he is satisfied with what was said on a former occasion. He may think that though the question was indeed raised, no adequate answer was given and that it needs fuller consideration. It by no means follows that the question is unanswerable. All that follows, if the philosopher is right, is that it received no adequate answer when it was raised at an earlier date.

It seems safe to say however that when people talk about the recurrent problems of philosophy, they are generally thinking of problems which are known by all philosophers to have been frequently discussed up to the present day but in regard to which reputable thinkers have adopted and still adopt different, even incompatible positions, and which one is therefore tempted to regard as unanswerable. Why should such questions go on recurring, if they are answerable? Surely they ought to have been answered by now in such a way that all philosophers can see the truth of the answer.

One possible reason for the recurrence of a problem is the emergence or appearance of factors, advertence to which or reflection on which demands the reopening of a question or reconsideration of a given problem. Let me illustrate what I mean by referring to the problem of human freedom. As we have already noted, it can be argued that it is a mistake to talk about one recurrent problem of human freedom. There have been a number of distinct problems or questions, which have been raised successively. To ask, for example, whether human beings can reasonably be described as free agents if nothing happens without being caused by God is not the same thing as to ask whether discoveries relating to the dependence of mental activities on physical states and processes do or do not warrant the conclusion that human choices are determined and not free. While however this line of argument reminds us of the need to take note of differences, there is another aspect of the situation which should be borne in mind. Left to themselves, so to speak, human beings believe (some might wish to say 'know by experience') that at least on some occasions they are free to act or not to act, to act in this way or in that, to accept a post or not to accept it, to propose marriage to someone or not to do so. Even if after a choice has been made, a person may doubt whether he or she was really free to make any other choice, at the time of choice human beings, left to themselves, sometimes think of themselves as free to choose between alternatives.[12] This initial belief can be challenged by a succession of objections on a variety of grounds. But as these objections are directed against a recurrent initial belief, to speak of a recurrent problem of freedom is hardly unreasonable. Is the initial belief justified or not?

The objections which successively arise can be, as just noted, of different kinds. Given acceptance of certain theological doctrines, it follows or may seem to follow that the initial belief is unjustified, and that human choices are caused by God. In other words, it may follow or seem to follow that Spinoza was right in asserting that the persuasion of freedom or the belief that one is free is the result of ignorance of the determining causes.[13] The question then arises whether the initial belief can be reconciled with the relevant theological doctrines or whether it has to be sacrificed. As we all know, no final universally accepted solution of the problem was actually arrived at by all the participants in the discussion. But even if one had been reached, to quote it would hardly satisfy those people at a later date for whom the objection against the initial belief was not so much theological doctrines (in which they might not even believe) as objections arising out of modern physiology and psychology. To Aristotle it seemed clear that, whereas the exercise of sight was dependent on the possession and proper functioning of certain organs, the eyes, intellectual activity was not tied to any particular organ in the same way. If however it is argued that intellectual operations or activities are in fact dependent on physical states and processes, especially in the brain, this thesis is certainly relevant to the problem of human freedom and requires further consideration of what I have called the initial belief. If therefore the problem recurs, it is for a very good reason, namely the emergence or appearance of a fresh relevant factor, to which attention has been paid. To claim that this recurrence shows that the problem is unanswerable would be an over-hasty conclusion. What has happened is that attention has been drawn to an aspect of the problem which has not been seriously taken into consideration before, largely because the relevant empirical studies had not taken place. We might perhaps speak of a developing problem.

Obviously, we cannot exclude in advance the possibility that in the future other factors may appear, reflection on which will result in further discussion of the problem of freedom. Indeed, the phenomenon of recurrence might continue pretty well indefinitely. It is therefore understandable if a philosopher tries to put an end to the process. He can hardly do so simply by claiming that freedom is intuited, that it is an immediate datum of consciousness. This may be true, but if factors emerge which seem to cast doubt on the validity of the claim, their significance will have to be discussed, even if the claim is true. For anyone who feels sure that human beings have intuitive knowledge of their freedom, that they are free agents, it will be a question of showing that facts which seem to conflict with this position do not in fact do so. But he would have to show this. There would have to be discussion. And in this sense the problem would recur. It would certainly recur for those who did not accept the claim that the initial belief in freedom expressed intuition of the truth.

Perhaps however one might attempt to prevent the sort of recurrence of which I have been speaking by so defining freedom, the object of the initial belief, that this belief would not be affected by any further empirical discoveries which might be made or by any scientific hypotheses. But this procedure is open to objection. If, on the one hand, the definition is at variance with the initial belief, it can be objected that the problem of freedom is being solved once and for all by an arbitrary decision. On the other hand, a philosopher may claim that in his definition he has simply made explicit the content of an initial belief, a content which, as far as the initial belief is concerned, finds expression in the concrete utterances of ordinary language, and not in any abstract concept or theory. What he has done is to reflect on the concrete utterances in question and make explicit the underlying or implicit concept of freedom. Though however I have no wish to question the utility of this procedure,[14] there is certainly ground for objection if the philosopher assumes that so-called ordinary language is a criterion of truth. For it is precisely the implications of ordinary language which critics of belief in human freedom call in question. If they are true, they cannot be shown to be true without discussing the grounds which successively arise for doubting whether they are true. It is therefore not clear to me that recurrence of the problem of human freedom can be successfully arrested by defining freedom in a certain way.

What I have been saying should not be understood as implying that in my opinion the phenomenon of recurrence can be explained in the same way in regard to all those philosophical problems of which it can be said that they have recurred. Granted that there is an initial belief in freedom, it seems clear to me that a variety of factors, from theological doctrine to scientific findings and hypotheses,[15] can help to explain recurrent discussion of the validity of the initial belief. I cannot however think of any empirical discovery or scientific hypothesis which would be relevant to determining whether a proposition can be self-referring. If this question has recurred, we must look for another explanation. As we have seen, there are several possible explanations. My intention has been to show, by considering a particular example, that the phenomenon of recurrence need not be considered a scandal or as indicative of some defeat in philosophy. Recurrence of the problem of freedom is easily understandable. Belief (or, if preferred, awareness) of freedom occupies the field in the first instance. But grounds for doubt can arise successively, and then the validity of the initial belief has to be discussed again in the light of the relevant factors. There is also of course the difficulty in stating exactly what we mean by freedom, in clarifying the point or points at issue. This is certainly a matter of some importance. For if people are not clear about the nature of the issue, discussion of it is likely to recur. However, I have not said anything about this aspect of the situation, except to make a few remarks about attempts to cut the discussion short by means of a definition of freedom. What I had in mind was the attempt, by means of a definition, to make belief in freedom immune from possible objection. I doubt whether such a policy can be successful. But I did not of course intend to condemn attempts to clarify the concept of freedom.

VI.

Let me try to pull together the various reflections expressed in the foregoing sections. It seems to me that we cannot make a clear distinction between recurrent and non-recurrent philosophical problems, of such a kind that the members of the class of recurrent problems can be known by the possession of certain distinguishing characteristics which are not found in members of the class, if there is one, of non-recurrent problems. Any philosophical problem is potentially recurrent, in the sense that discussion of it may be renewed. The reasons for recurrence can be varied. There is no one single explanation. Discussion of a problem may be renewed simply because the philosopher or philosophers concerned are unaware that it has been treated at an earlier date, or because, even if they are aware of this fact, they are dissatisfied with the solution already given or with the arguments advanced to prove the truth of a certain conclusion. Again, a problem may recur because new relevant factors appear, reflection on which demands further discussion, or because factors which originally gave rise to the problem are still with us.[16] I have illustrated the sort of thing which I have in mind by reference to the problem of freedom. Again, the problem of the existence of God has peculiar features of its own. If the word 'God' is understood in terms of the Christian conception of God, as a loving Father, I think that this analogy is accepted by Christians on the authority of Christ, as recorded in the gospels, and that it is a matter of the response of faith, not of metaphysics. This point apart however, it is clear that aspects of the world and of human life and history which tell against the conception of God as a loving Father are always with us, perennially recurrent so to speak. If we regard the metaphysical question as being whether or not the empirical world of plurality depends ontologically on a transcendent One, we have to remember that, to perpetrate a tautology, the transcendent transcends. It cannot be an object before our eyes, nor can it be neatly caught in a conceptual web expressing an experience of empirical reality. There remains room both for affirmation and negation, both, as Karl Jaspers might put it, for Kierkegaard and for Nietzsche. By saying this I do not mean to imply that no reasonable argument can be developed for the existence of a transcendent One. But arguments have premises. And though attempts have been made to establish a presuppositionless metaphysics (sometimes in the interests of religious apologetics), I have my doubts about their success. Referring to the search for the ultimate reality, F.H. Bradley postulated what he described in various ways, as a presupposition or an assumption or even as an initial faith.[17] If metaphysical arguments for the existence of a transcendent One involve some presupposition or presuppositions, this would be relevant to explaining recurrence of philosophical discussion of the question at issue. It is all very well to claim that the existence of God can be demonstrated. No doubt it can, given certain premises. But the premises can be questioned, unless we are prepared to claim that there is a presuppositionless metaphysics, developed by strict logical deduction from an unquestionable point of departure. As I have my doubts about this, I feel no great surprise at periodic renewed discussion of the problem of God's existence.

Though I have been speaking of recurrent problems, I am not altogether happy with this phrase. It is perfectly reasonable, in my opinion, to speak about recurrent themes, such as human freedom or human knowledge. For there are similarities or family likenesses which make this way of speaking pretty well unavoidable. But we have to allow for the fact that the actual questions asked at a given time may differ somewhat from the actual questions asked at an earlier date, questions, that is to say, which fall within the same general area on each occasion. Still, a theme would not give rise to philosophical discussion unless it were seen as generating questions or problems of some kind. So if it is convenient to speak of recurrent themes, it is also convenient, I suppose, to speak of recurrent problems.

Is what I have been saying equivalent to asserting that no philosophical problem or question can be answered finally and definitively? It was not my intention to make any such dogmatic assertion. But I do not accept the idea of philosophy as a discipline in which entirely separate questions can be answered successively, in the sense that having finished with one question philosophers can then proceed to tackle and polish off another. Gilbert Ryle drew attention to the way in which philosophical questions or problems have a habit of interlocking.[18] What is said about one issue may well affect what is said about another issue. I suspect that this feature of philosophical thought may have a good deal to do with the phenomenon of recurrence. For reconsideration may be demanded.

Notes

[1] In *Philosophers and Philosophies* (London: Search Press, and New York: Barnes and Noble, 1976), pp. 24-5, and *Philosophies and Cultures* (Oxford and New York: Oxford Univ. Press, 1980), pp. 120-124.

[2] See, for example, *Unpopular Essays* (London: Allen and Unwin and New York: Simon and Schuster, 1950), p. 41, and *A History of Western Philosophy*, (London: Allen and Unwin, and New York: Simon and Schuster, 1945), p. 10. I say 'in a stronger sense than Kant would allow', inasmuch as Russell would not accept Kant's moral arguments for God and immortality.

[3] It might be argued, for example, that the 'transcendent metaphysician' seeks a One and will be satisfied with nothing else as an explanation of the existence of the Many, thus manifesting an implicit presupposition, that to make the existence of our pluralistic world intelligible is to relate the Many to a One as their ultimate source. I have referred to this topic in *Religion and Philosophy* (Dublin and New York: Barnes and Noble, 1974), pp. 8f, 126, 141 ff, 172f.

[4] I have heard an historian of philosophy maintaining precisely this thesis. But as I have to rely on my memory of what he said, I prefer not to mention his name.

[5] In his articles 'Written History as an Act of Faith' and 'That Noble Dream' (*American Historical Review*, 1934, pp. 219-31; and 1935, pp. 74-87). Both articles have been reprinted, the first in *The Philosophy of History in Our Time*, edited by H. Meyerhoff (New York: Doubleday, 1959), the second in *The Varieties of History*, edited by F. Stern (New York: Meridian, 1956) and *Ideas of History*, edited by R. Nash, vol. 2 (New York: Dutton, 1969).

[6] See, for example, *Perspectives on History* by William Dray (London and Boston: Routledge and Kegan Paul, 1980), pp. 27-46. I have made some remarks about the subject in my book *On The History of Philosophy* (London: Search, and New York: Barnes and Noble, 1979), pp. 40-65.

[7] *Philosophers and Philosophies*, p. 24.

[8] This idea has been proposed as one line of reply to accusations that Buddhist thinkers maintain incompatible positions. For my own part, while I agree that apparently ontological statements made by Buddhist philosophers do have a pragmatic function, I doubt whether this is their only function.

[9] While the Advaita philosophers maintained that the inner self is not-different from Brahman, the Dvaita philosophers, such as Madhva, insisted on the difference between the human self and God. Both groups however belonged to the Vedanta tradition or school.

[10] The question arose in connection with the liar paradox. For example, Occam maintained that in the case of a statement such as 'every proposition is false' the subject-term must refer to all *other* propositions, inasmuch as a proposition cannot refer to itself.

[11] For example, a theological or metaphysical system may include, explicitly or implicitly, one or more judgments of value. Such judgments can obviously function as premises in reasoning leading to normative conclusions or to other value-judgments without the 'no ought from an is' thesis being infringed.

[12] I am talking about an initial belief, the existence of which was admitted even by Spinoza. It seems to me to be presupposed by such statements as 'I had no choice: I could not have acted in any other way'.

[13] *Ethics*, part I, appendix. Cf. part 2, proposition 49, scholium. Spinoza is indeed primarily concerned with denying that there are any uncaused actions. And there are of course senses in which he affirms freedom. But so-called 'liberty of indifference' does not fare well at his hands.

[14] It seems to me to constitute a natural and sensible approach to discussion of freedom. Insofar as determinism involves raising objections to an initial belief which precedes philosophical reflection, it is obviously important to obtain a clear idea of what the belief is. Further, if objections are brought against an explicit philosophical theory upholding freedom, it is at any rate relevant to ask whether the theory in question reflects or distorts what people spontaneously believe.

[15] We obviously have to beware of passing off as established scientific truth some questionable hypothesis or speculation proposed by a scientist. But to find precise criteria for distinguishing between scientific 'facts' and questionable theories is not altogether easy.

[16] In 'Sense Data Revisited' (included, pp. 98-112, in *Perception and Identity. Essays Presented to A.J. Ayer with his Replies to them*, edited by G.F. Macdonald [London: Macmillan, 1979]) Professor Charles Taylor maintains that Kant developed an argument sufficient to dispose of the theory of sense data. Taylor sees subsequent defense and criticism of the theory as telling us 'something about the endlessness of philosophical debate'. It seems to me probable that modern defenders of the theory either did not know that Kant had said anything relevant to the theory or, if they did, disagreed with what Kant said. In any case there are features of perception which understandably give rise to theories of this kind, features which Kant could not of course have eliminated, even if he had wished to do so.

[17] *Appearance and Reality* (2nd edition, 1897), pp. 553-4; *Essays on Truth and Reality*, pp. 15, 200.

[18] In his essay 'The Theory of Meaning', contributed to *British Philosophy in the Mid-Century. A Cambridge Symposium*, edited by C.A. Mace (London: Allen and Unwin, 1957), p. 264.

13.

METAPHYSICS AND THE HISTORY OF PHILOSOPHY: THE CASE OF WHITEHEAD

Albert William Levi

The chief purpose of James Collins' *Interpreting Modern Philosophy* was to provide a comprehensive description of how past or historic philosophical materials achieve present use—how the intrinsic insistence of the major sources is transmuted into the creative acts of present philosophizing. This paper is only a footnote to Collins' fine book, for it seeks in the case of Whitehead— the most original metaphysician in the modern world— to show how he supports the recondite metaphysics of *Process and Reality* by constant appeal to the classics of the Western philosophic tradition.

It should be noted at the beginning that this mode of procedure which Collins' book takes for granted is not universally applied, and that there is some serious current disagreement as to the validity of authenticating contemporary philosophic positions by appeal to the giants of our philosophic history. It is, of course, not surprising to find disdain for the tendency of some philosophers to create a doctrine of their own out of an ingenious dialectical combination of the doctrines of others, and a thoroughgoing empiricism has always counseled philosophy to turn away from the opinions of philosophers and turn toward the facts of experience for its data. Yet historical caution urges that we must consider the views of the great philosophers in considerable detail (and with some attention to their sequential placement) as we pass in review the major metaphysical positions of our contemporaries.

One party sees inseparable connection between the history of philosophy and the present growing edge where contemporary metaphysicians do their work. The other espouses the cult of "the new beginning" where tradition hampers and the past had best lie buried. In this conflict my own sympathies (and I take it, Collins' also) lie with the first. Our philosophic training proclaims that all philosophers speak a common language in which the great texts of Plato and Aristotle and St. Thomas, of Descartes and Locke, of Berkeley and Hume, of Kant and Hegel, create a vocabulary and a terminology constitutive of our heritage. We are all the creatures of this philosophic tradition and we turn our backs upon it at our peril. Descartes purposely forgets the Augustinianism and the Thomism upon which he was raised and this forgetfulness takes its revenge in some very bizarre aspects of his mature system. Wittgenstein in his senseless passion for originality and the new beginning purposely keeps us in ignorance of his indubitable debts to Schopenhauer, Augustine, Kierkegaard, and Tolstoy and the result is the patent incongruity of the last six pages of the *Tractatus* with all that has gone before. Thus it requires Gilson's act of reminder in the case of Descartes[1] and S. Morris Engel's in the case of Wittgenstein[2] to restore a just perspective.

The majority of philosophers are, of course, not so forgetful. For it seems an essential part of their concern to maintain continuity between their own work and the tradition. This is evident even in such profoundly different fields as contemporary semantics and phenomenology. Bertrand Russell in *An Inquiry into Meaning and Truth* goes out of his way to criticize the unconcern of the logical positivists. He states in the Preface: "As will be evident to the reader, I am, as regards method, more in sympathy with the logical positivists than with any other existing school. I differ from them, however, in attaching more importance than they do to the work of Berkeley and Hume. This book results from an attempt to combine a general outlook akin to Hume's with the methods that have grown out of modern logic." And this concern is later repeated in the body of the work itself:[3] "There is a tendency—not confined to Neurath and Hempel, but prevalent in much modern philosophy—to forget the arguments of Descartes and Berkeley. It may be that these arguments can be refuted, though, as regards our present question, I do not believe they can be. But in any case they are too weighty to be merely ignored." And Edmund Husserl, always anxious to relate his brain-child to the continuity of the philosophical generations, can affirm:

> It is therefore not surprising that phenomenology is as it were the secret longing of the whole philosophy of modern times. The fundamental thought of Descartes in its wonderful profundity is already pressing towards it; Hume again, a psychological philosopher of the school of Locke, almost enters its domain, but his eyes are dazzled. The first to perceive it truly is Kant, whose greatest intuitions first become quite clear to us after we have brought the distinctive features of the phenomenological field into the focus of full consciousness. It then becomes evident to us that Kant's mental gaze rested on this field, although he was not yet able to appropriate it and recognize it as the centre from which to work up on his own line a rigorous science of Essential Being. Thus the Transcendental Deduction of the first edition of the *Critique of Pure Reason*, for instance, already moves strictly on phenomenological ground; but Kant misinterprets the same as psychological and therefore eventually abandons it of his own accord[4].

Russell's appeal to Descartes, Berkeley and Hume, Husserl's invocation of Descartes, Hume, and Kant are already lesser examples of a procedure which *Process and Reality* is to render classic.

Whitehead's Gifford Lectures of 1927-28, *Process and Reality*, one of the really seminal works in Western metaphysics, is unusual for the sense which it projects of having been written less *sub specie aeternitatis* than *sub specie philosophiae perennis*. Its Preface begins:

> These lectures are based upon a recurrence to that phase of philosophic thought which began with Descartes and ended with Hume. The philosophic scheme which they endeavour to explain is termed the "Philosophy of Organism." *There is no doctrine put forward which cannot cite in its defence some explicit statement of one of this group of thinkers, or of one of the two founders of all Western thought, Plato and Aristotle*. But the philosophy of organism is apt to emphasize just those elements in the writings of these masters which subsequent systematizers have put aside. *The writer who most fully anticipated the main positions of the philosophy of organism is John Locke in his Essay, especially in its later books*.[5]

"That phase of philosophic thought which began with Descartes and ended with Hume" — in short, the age of classical rationalism and classical empiricism has a peculiar significance for Whitehead for two reasons. *Science and the Modern World* had already alluded to the great group of philosopher-scientists of the seventeenth century: Bacon, Harvey, Kepler, Galileo, Descartes, Pascal, Huyghens, Boyle, Newton, Locke, Spinoza, and Leibniz, and had appended its author's conviction that the intellectual life of European culture during the succeeding centuries up to our own times has been lived upon the accumulated capital of ideas provided by these men.[6] Whitehead is not merely a metaphysician: he is also a cosmologist—one whose "coherent, logical, necessary system of general ideas in terms of which every element of our experience can be interpreted" is inspired by the progress of scientific thought no less than the insights of pure philosophy. *Therefore* the additions of Plato and Aristotle and of Berkeley and Hume. For Plato and Aristotle are the giants of Greek scientific cosmology. Descartes and Leibniz codify the advances of Galileo; while Locke, Berkeley and Hume supply an epistemology thought to be adequate to the insights of Newton. The metaphysical accreditation of classical rationalism and classical empiricism thus hinges upon two unstated but implicit presuppositions: (1) that science undergirds metaphysics and (2) that metaphysics is inseparable from epistemology. It is therefore understandable that Plato, Aristotle, Descartes, Leibniz, Spinoza and Locke, Berkeley and Hume should constitute ammunition for the philosophy of organism and that "some explicit statement of one of this group of thinkers" can always be cited in its defense.

This conclusion is perhaps not immediately obvious. Even though this group of philosophers has formed "the complex texture of civilized thought" in the Western world, even though "they give a general presentation which dominates the development of subsequent philosophy," Whitehead, by his own admission, began with an initial intuition of incongruence. "I started the investigation with the expectation of being occupied with the exposition of the *divergencies* from every member of this group." But the endeavor to point out the exact points of agreement and of disagreement eventuated in a paradoxical consequence— a recognition that the tendency of subsequent thought has been to abandon just those elements in *their* thought upon which the philosophy of organism bases itself. An appeal to Locke will illustrate this perfectly.

When Whitehead asserts that "the writer who most fully anticipated the main positions of the philosophy of organism is John Locke in his *Essay*" the reader is stunned. And this is because the most celebrated of Locke's doctrines— the famous distinction between primary and secondary qualities outlined in Book II, Chapter VIII of *An Essay Concerning Human Understanding* — is precisely the one which Whitehead inveighs against in Chapter II of *The Concept of Nature*, "Theories of the Bifurcation of Nature." Singling Locke out as the father of this bifurcation theory, Whitehead proceeds to excoriate this doctrine as one of the chief obstacles to the formation of an adequate metaphysics of nature. But when Whitehead comes to write his Gifford Lectures, then he is most appreciative of Locke particularly in relation to the later and more metaphysical sections of the *Essay* almost totally neglected by historians of the empirical philosophers. Thus in the Preface to *Process and Reality* he singles out for particular approbation the long passage in Book IV, Chapter VI, Section 11 where Locke repudiates the doctrine of simple location (the independent self-subsistence of the material object with its determinate spatio-temporal reference within the extensive continuum) in favor of a concept of internal relations and universal relatedness.[7] It is for Whitehead a privileged moment in the history of philosophy in which "the relationship" emerges as the ontological primitive to replace the self-subsistent and independent material objects of the Newtonian world.

But to do it this way is a quixotic, not to say perverse, use of the givens of the philosophic tradition. To forget the customary prominence given to the Lockean distinction between primary and secondary qualities in order to elevate into prominence an obscure passage insisting upon universal relatedness is not merely to use Locke, but also to abuse him. But such abuse is a conscious element in Whitehead's historical methodology. "The depositions," he says, "of Plato, Aristotle, Thomas Aquinas, Descartes, Spinoza, Leibniz, Locke, Berkeley, Hume, Kant, Hegel merely mean that ideas which these men introduced into the philosophic traditions must be construed with limitations, adaptations, and inversions, either unknown to them, or *even explicitly repudiated by them.*"⁸ That adaptations be made of the philosophic ideas of other men is standard practice, but that such adaptations or "inversions" be made even though *explicitly repudiated by them* seems a questionable procedure indeed.

Some idea of the kind of adaptation or inversion which Whitehead makes in the case of Locke can be envisaged from the long section devoted to him in Part II, Chapter I, Section VI of *Process and Reality*. "A short examination of Locke's *Essay on Human Understanding*," says Whitehead, "will throw light on the presuppositions from which the philosophy of organism originates. These citations from Locke are valuable as clear statements of the obvious deliverances of common sense, expressed with their natural limitations. They cannot be bettered in their character of presentations of facts which have to be accepted by any satisfactory system of philosophy."⁹ But it soon becomes clear what price Locke's text has to pay for this applicability. "The merit of Locke's *Essay Concerning Human Understanding* is its adequacy, and not its consistency. He gives the most dispassionate descriptions of those various elements in experience which common sense never lets slip. Unfortunately he is hampered by inappropriate metaphysical categories which he never criticized. He should have widened the title of his book into 'An Essay Concerning Experience.' His true topic is the analysis of the types of experience enjoyed by an actual entity."¹⁰

This may well be the topic which Whitehead *wished* Locke to have had. It was, however, decidedly *not* Locke's topic. Following not the metaphysical objectivism of the ancient and medieval worlds, but the new pathway of Cartesian subjectivism, Locke was less a metaphysician than an epistemologist and that in the classical sense of being devoted to the process of human knowing. His title discloses his topic as *human* understanding and his epistemic vocabulary is devised to cover the exigencies not of physical bodies, or molecules or atoms or protons but of high grade human cognition. Whitehead, on the contrary, wants the paradigm of human perception to serve as a model for the universal interaction of the most primitive of actual entities. He thus transforms Locke's "ideas" or atoms of mentality into "feelings" and considers that these ideas or feelings express how other things are components in the construction of these actual entities. Thus Whitehead is forced to find fault with Locke's epistemic vocabulary, no matter how adequate it was for Locke's avowed purpose. "Locke talks of 'understanding' and 'perception'. He should have started with a more general neutral term to express the synthetic concrescence whereby the many things of the universe become the one actual entity. Accordingly I have adopted the term 'prehension' to express the activity whereby an actual entity effects its own concretion of other things."¹¹

This intransigent cognitivity of Locke is in marked contrast to the procedure of Francis Bacon. In a famous passage of *Science and the Modern World* Whitehead quotes a long section from the latter's Natural History

(Silva Silvarum).

> It is certain that all bodies whatsoever, though they have no sense, yet they have perception; for when one body is applied to another, there is a kind of election to embrace that which is agreeable, and to exclude or expel that which is ingrate; and whether the body be alterant or altered, evermore a perception precedeth operation; for else all bodies would be like one to another. And sometimes this perception, in some kind of bodies, is far more subtle than sense; so that sense is but a dull thing in comparison of it: we see a weatherglass will find the least difference of the weather in heat or cold, when we find it not. And this perception is sometimes at a distance, as well as upon the touch; as when the loadstone draweth iron; or flame naphtha of Babylon, a great distance off. It is therefore a subject of a very noble enquiry, to enquire of the more subtle perceptions; for it is another key to open nature, as well as the sense; and sometimes better. And besides, it is a principal means of natural divination; for that which in these perceptions appeareth early, in the great effects cometh long after.[12]

And to underline its relevance Whitehead comments: "In the first place, note the careful way in which Bacon discriminates between *perception*, or *taking account of*, on the one hand, and *sense*, or *cognitive experience*, on the other hand. In this respect Bacon is outside the physical line of thought which finally dominated the [seventeenth] century." And indeed the Newtonian ambience of Locke. Whitehead is in this contrast only requiring that Locke write not *An Essay Concerning Human Understanding* but *An Essay Concerning the Mutual Relations Between the Ultimate Entities of Nature*!

Whitehead's entire and considerable use of Locke in *Process and Reality* is founded upon this requirement. Yet it would be false to say that Whitehead misunderstands what in fact Locke has intended. Only, he is concerned that Locke should be *improved* so as to be metaphysically available. In the chapter "From Descartes to Kant" in *Process and Reality* (Part II, Chapter VI) Whitehead expresses his ultimate evaluation of Locke's contribution to his process philosophy: "Locke explicitly discards metaphysics...But his *Essay*, however, does contain a line of thought which can be developed into a metaphysics."

> In the first place, he distinctly holds that ideas of particular existents...constitute the fundamental data which the mental functioning welds into a unity by a determinate process of absorption, including comparison, emphasis, and abstraction. He also holds that 'powers' are to be ascribed to particular existents whereby the constitutions of other particulars are conditioned.

Correlatively, he holds that the constitutions of particular existents must be described so as to exhibit their 'capacities' for being conditioned by such 'powers' in other particulars. He also holds that all qualities have in some sense a relational element in them.[13]

It is now possible to discern the strategy by which Whitehead transforms Locke from a sensationalist in epistemology to an organicist in metaphysics. And it is by inserting a formidable wedge between Books I and II and Books III and IV of Locke's *Essay*—by extolling the fertility of Locke's thought at the expense of its coherence.

> Nothing can make the various parts of his *Essay* consistent. He never revises the substance-quality categories which remain presupposed throughout his *Essay*. In the first two books of the *Essay*, he professes to lay the foundations of his doctrine of ideas. These books are implicitly dominated by the notion of the ideas as mere qualifications of the substrate mind. In the third book of the *Essay* he is apparently passing on to the application of his established doctrine of ideas to the subordinate question of the function of language. But he tacitly introduces a new doctrine of ideas, which is difficult to conciliate with the sensationalist doctrine of the preceding books. Hume concentrates upon the doctrine of Locke's earlier books; the philosophy of organism concentrates upon that of the later books in the *Essay*. If Locke's *Essay* is to be interpreted as a consistent scheme of thought, undoubtedly Hume is right; but such an interpretation offers violence to Locke's contribution to philosophy.[14]

But in precisely what does "Locke's contribution to philosophy" consist? Careful attention to Whitehead's continual citations of Locke's text find them to be primarily three in Number. And they are: (1) the reference to Book IV, Chapter VI, Section 11 which Whitehead reads as the doctrine of universal relatedness, (2) the reference to Book II, Chapter XXIII, Section 7 where Locke asserts that 'power' is 'a great part of our complex idea of substances' which Whitehead reads as a primitive statement of his "ontological principle" (all reasons are reducible to the behavior of actual entities) and (3) the reference to Book II, Chapter XIV where Locke refers to time or duration as "the fleeting and perpetually perishing parts of succession" and which Whitehead literally appropriates as the doctrine that time is recorded merely in the perpetual perishing of actual entities. Thus universal relatedness, the ontological principle, and time as a perpetual perishing are the metaphysical confirmations which Whitehead discovers in the interwoven tapestry of Locke's *Essay*!

Whitehead's reading of Locke is surely eccentric (off center), and it seems clear that these doctrines which he appropriates have become available to him only at the cost of a singular distortion of what *An Essay Concerning Human Understanding* is really all about. But this needs to be understood as servicing rather a prior emotional commitment; namely that Whitehead's two philosophic heroes originally were and have remained Plato and Locke, and that his history of philosophy finds them playing analogous roles in the ancient and in the modern world.

> The philosophy of organism in its appeal to the facts can thus support itself by an appeal to the insight of John Locke, who in British philosophy is the analogue to Plato, in the epoch of his life, in personal endowments, in width of experience, and in dispassionate statement of conflicting intuitions.[15]

Whitehead's reverence for Plato is permanent and pervasive. It stretches from *The Concept of Nature* of 1920 through the *Dialogues* recorded by Lucien Price in June 1943.[16] It reached its apogee in *Adventures of Ideas* of 1933 in the chapter "Science and Philosophy" where he outlines the indispensable "seven main notions" which Plato bequeathed to Western science and philosophy.[17] *Process and Reality* records it with almost equal enthusiasm. Its Preface refers to the abiding importance of the cosmology of Plato's *Timaeus* and Chapter I of its second part contains the now famous apotheosis of Plato and the Gifford Lectures' debt to it.

> The safest general characterization of the European philosophical tradition is that it consists of a series of footnotes to Plato... His personal endowments, his wide opportunities for experience at a great period of civilization, his inheritance of an intellectual tradition not yet stiffened by excessive systematization, have made his writing an inexhaustible mine of suggestion. Thus in one sense by stating my belief that the train of thought in these lectures is Platonic, I am doing no more than expressing the hope that it falls within the European tradition. But I do mean more: I mean that if we had to render Plato's general point of view with the least changes made necessary by the intervening two thousand years of human experience...we should have to set about the construction of a philosophy of organism. In such a philosophy the actualities constituting the process of the world are conceived as exemplifying the ingression (or 'participation') of other things which constitute the potentialities of definiteness for any actual existence. The things which are temporal arise by their participation in the things which are eternal.[18]

The eulogy is enormous and it is couched in much the same language as the tribute to Locke instanced above. The unusual "personal endowments" and "width of experiences" are cited for both men and the identical turn of phrase in the two cases shows how in Whitehead's mind there is a like admiration and appreciation of the two philosophers, never to my knowledge elsewhere similarly associated. For Whitehead Plato is the Greek Locke, while Locke is the close to home, the quintessentially English, Plato!

In fact the *Timaeus* is more related to Whitehead's purposes than Locke's *Essay*. *Process and Reality* is subtitled "An Essay in Cosmology," and whereas *An Essay Concerning Human Understanding* is chiefly epistemological in its concern, the *Timaeus* is pure cosmology. Whitehead is well aware of this. He has gone so far as to assert that "the history of philosophy discloses two cosmologies which at different periods have dominated European thought, Plato's *Timaeus*, and the cosmology of the seventeenth century, whose chief authors were Galileo, Descartes, Newton, Locke."[19] And, while he suggests that a present day cosmology might well be a fusion of the two previous schemes, careful attention to what he in fact does in *Process and Reality* shows it to be rather a repudiation of the "materialism," "mechanism," and "simple location" of the seventeenth century cosmology and what might be termed its *correction* by an appeal to the *Timaeus*, bringing the latter up to date and rendering it congruent with contemporary relativity physics and quantum theory.

The two chief notions here are those of the Platonic "forms" and "the receptacle." And their Whiteheadian analogues are the "eternal object" and "the extensive continuum." Whitehead says explicitly: "I use the phrase 'eternal object' for what in the preceding paragraph of this section I have termed a 'Platonic form.' Any entity whose conceptual recognition does not involve a necessary reference to any definite actual entities of the temporal world is called an 'eternal object.' "[20]

Whitehead appropriates the Platonic "receptacle" and renames it "the extensive continuum." It is for him the coordination of all individual standpoints, the mother of becoming, the "one relational complex in which all potential objectifications find their niche."[21] Its properties are very few and do not include the relationships of metrical geometry, but it does imply both indefinite divisibility and unbounded extension and that is why it is the matrix of the becoming (and also the "perishing") of all actual entities. Whitehead interprets the *Timaeus* as connecting the behavior of things with the formal nature of things and thus with the ultimate molecular character of actual entities.[22] And therefore the *Timaeus* which interprets the process of the actual world as the coalescence of forms of potentiality into that real togetherness which is an actual thing,[23] is the historical precedent for that *process* which lies at the heart of Whitehead's metaphysical system.

Whitehead's appeal to the history of philosophy in *Process and Reality* is a dialectic of acceptances and repudiations. Locke and Plato are his major acceptances. But his repudiations merit equal attention. Doctrinally they are the subject-predicate logic, the substance-attribute metaphysics, the doctrine of simple location, the sensationalist theory of perception.[24] And the philosophers whom he primarily takes as representative of these doctrines are Descartes and Hume.

Whitehead's relentless panpsychism results in an endless revolt against dualism and the chief historical offender here is certainly Descartes. Moreover Descartes compounds this error by also accepting the dogma of independent existence. "Incoherence is the arbitrary disconnection of first principles. In modern philosophy Descartes' two kinds of substance, corporeal and mental, illustrate incoherence. There is, in Descartes' philosophy, no reason why there should not be a one-substance world, only corporeal, or only mental. According to Descartes, a substantial individual 'requires nothing but itself in order to exist.' Thus this system makes a virtue of its incoherence."[25] But this is only the beginning. All modern philosophy, Whitehead believes, hinges around the difficulty of describing the world in terms of subject and predicate, substance and quality, particular and universal. "The current view of universals and particulars inevitably leads to the epistemological position stated by Descartes...His unquestioned acceptance of the subject-predicate dogma forced him into a representative theory of perception."[26]

Whitehead critizes Descartes for his metaphysics ("the substance-quality metaphysics triumphed with exclusive dominance in Descartes' doctrines"), for his logic ("Descartes allowed the subject-predicate form of proposition...to dictate his subsequent metaphysical development"), and especially for his "presupposition...of the individual independence of successive temporal occasions," but his total treatment of Descartes in *Process and Reality* is not without ambivalence. Thus, in two sections at least (pp. 116-126 and pp. 239-243 respectively) he praises Descartes for his pluralism ("an extensive plenum of actual entities") and for his subjectivism ("the famous subjectivist bias which entered into modern philosophy through Descartes"). For although he is clear as to the doctrines he repudiates and the philosophers who hold to these doctrines, he is more than generous in finding historical antecedents for his philosophy of organism even when they occur in these same philosophers.

Already in *The Principle of Relativity* (1922) Whitehead referred to Hume as having "made short work of the theory of the relatedness of nature as it existed in the current philosophy of his time," and he indicated the major failure of that philosopher in no uncertain terms: "If you once conceive fundamental fact as a multiplicity of subjects qualified by predicates, you must fail to give a coherent account of experience."[27] And in *Science and the Modern World* he continued this critique in two areas. In the first place he repudiated Hume's attack on "the order of nature" as denying the possibility of the rationality of science. And in the second place he attacked the doctrine of the entirely arbitrary connections within nature implied by the contingency of Hume's account of causation. A proper theory of induction, he insisted, presupposes metaphysics. It rests upon an antecedent rationalism.[28]

Process and Reality continues the same line of argument which *The Principle of Relativity* and *Science and the Modern World* had initiated. Hume is criticized for having assumed "the radical disconnection of impressions." His theory of causation is rejected as resting upon the irrationality of "repetition" and "habit." He is seen as radically in error in finding in "an individual independence of successive temporal occasions." And he is criticized as having "explained away the obvious facts of experience in obedience to the a priori doctrine of sensationalism inherited from the mediaeval philosophy which [he] despised."[29] Here again, as in the case of Descartes, Whitehead is ambivalent. Hume is for him one of the very greatest of modern philosophers. The Hume citations in *Process and Reality* (48 in number) are even more numerous than the references to Locke (43). Only—he happened on most of the crucial issues to be mistaken!

Whitehead's appeals to the history of philosophy in *Process and Reality* gravitate about the figures of Plato and Locke, Descartes and Hume. Aristotle and Kant are also referred to but almost cursorily. Aristotle, as might be expected, is dismissed as the author of the substance metaphysics and the subject-predicate logic. But the treatment of Kant is particularly disappointing in view of the earlier testimony of Bertrand Russell. "His philosophy," said Russell,[30] "was very obscure, and there was much in it that I never succeeded in understanding. He had always had a leaning toward Kant, of whom I thought ill, and when he began to develop his own philosophy, he was considerably influenced by Bergson." If Whitehead ever had "a leaning toward Kant," it is not discernible in *Process and Reality*, and even the explicit acknowledgment to Bergson in the Preface (as also to James and Dewey) is but sparsely underwritten in the body of the text.[31]

The real enigmas in the relationship of the history of philosophy to the development of the metaphysics of *Process and Reality* occur, however, in the cases of Berkeley, Leibniz, and Hegel. For here is where one should have expected his debts to be greatest. As Hocking has remarked,[32] it was Berkeley "who first felt the scandal of bifurcation, and to cure it reunited the primary with the secondary qualities on the same ontological plane," who attacked materialism and the vices of abstraction, who implied not only that to be is to be perceived, but also that to perceive is to be, and in this latter respect is also a primitive panpsychist. It was Leibniz who emphasized that each substance (actual entity) mirrors the entire universe from its own point of view, that our inner experience is our most immediate contact with reality, that the essence of individual being is effort or endeavor, energy or power, and that nature is one vast continuum with infinite gradations of monads differing only in their powers of perception. While in Hegel is to be found par excellence the dominance of "relatedness" over "quality" and a cosmological picture of universal and infinite relationship.

The Concept of Nature applauds Berkeley's polemic against matter,[33] and in *Science and the Modern World* he is praised for criticizing the notion of simple location and for its "intuitive refusal seriously to accept the abstract materialism of science,"[34] but in *Process and Reality* Berkeley has become totally forgotten. The prevalence of Leibnizian phraseology in Whiteheadean formulations cannot but be obvious to those who have read both philosophers. Consider this passage from *Science and the Modern World*.

> I will not repeat myself now, except to remind you that my theory involves the entire abandonment of the notion that simple location is the primary way in which things are involved in space-time. In a certain sense, everything is everywhere at all times. For every location involves an aspect of itself in every other location. Thus every spatio-temporal standpoint mirrors the world.

Clearly this is but the metaphysics of the *Monadology* in the language of modern mathematical physics. *Process and Reality* does specifically refer to the *Monadology* at least six times, but each of the references is unfavorable. Why should this be?

It is, I think, because Whitehead's general picture of Leibniz has been totally influenced (and probably distorted) by Bertrand Russell's influential book of 1900, *A Critical Exposition of the Philosophy of Leibniz*. Russell found Leibniz' metaphysics to be a direct outgrowth of his logic and that logic to be of the subject-predicate variety. Whitehead shared with Russell an antipathy for that brand of logic and he uncritically followed Russell in a rejection of the *Monadology* as well—blind to how clearly it resembled his own deepest metaphysical insights. Some proof of this is to be found in *The Concept of Nature* where Whitehead says:

> Some schools of philosophy, under the influence of the Aristotelian logic and the Aristotelian philosophy endeavour to get on without admitting any relations at all except that of substance and attribute. Namely all apparent relations are to be resolvable into the concurrent existence of substances with contrasted attributes. It is fairly obvious that the Leibnizian monadology is the necessary outcome of any such philosophy.[35]

Although in every context in which Hegel is mentioned, Whitehead repudiates him by loudly confessing his ignorance,[36] his knowledge of the idealist tradition is far from negligible. The Preface to *Process and Reality* mentions a debt to Bradley: "Finally, though throughout the main body of the work I am in sharp disagreement with Bradley, the final outcome is after all not so greatly different." The final outcome is not so greatly different from Hegel either, and in most of his mentions of Hegel Whitehead is somewhat disingenuous. For, if he did not know the Hegelian text directly, he had indirect knowledge of it through his close early friendship with McTaggart. Not enough has been made of the educative results of Whitehead's *conversations* in his approach to the history of philosophy.

F.S.C. Northrop has cited the Bergsonian influence, which came to Whitehead through his personal friend, the late H. Wildon Carr. During those impressionable war years when Whitehead's philosophy of science was taking shape, Carr was writing a book on Bergson and continuously conversing with Whitehead concerning the French philosopher. From this source came the doctrine of the primacy of process, which is as basic to Whitehead's philosophy of science as it is to his metaphysics.[37]

And in answer to a question of mine about Whitehead's systematic presentation of the history of philosophy in his courses at Harvard, Professor Harold N. Lee of Tulane University, who took Whitehead's seminars in Metaphysics and Logic at Harvard in 1929-30, has provided valuable information:

> His seminars were conducted on an historical base, but not on any systematic study of the history of philosophy. The year I was a student, he spent the first month on Locke, but it was not Locke "scholarship": it was metaphysics, taking the point of departure from Locke's philosophy and Whitehead's criticism thereof. He assumed that we all knew the classical picture of Locke and emphasized doctrines which I had never heard of before such as Locke's doctrine of perishing...I doubt that he ever made a systematic study of the history of philosophy. He was not interested primarily from that point of view. I think that he studied those figures in the history of philosophy who interested him from the point of view of science and general culture. Of course, I do not know anything about his course of studies when he was a student. He picked up a great deal from his friends. I heard him say once that McTaggart had prepared a list of readings in Hegel for him, but that he never got past the first page, because he could not make out what Hegel was talking about. But he discussed Hegel a great deal with McTaggart. He was a close friend of his. I know first hand that he was thoroughly acquainted with the work of Leibniz. Bertrand Russell's first book was on Leibniz, and he published it when he and Whitehead were closely associated.[38]

The lack of specific acknowledgement in *Process and Reality* is therefore no proof of a lack of influence by some crucial figures in the history of philosophy. From Wildon Carr Whitehead knew Bergson, from McTaggart he knew Hegel, and from Russell he knew Leibniz, and the influence of all these figures, however subliminal, was continuous and pervasive in the formation of Whitehead's metaphysics!

Of course, Plato and Locke, Descartes and Hume, were the chief citations in *Process and Reality* and Victor Lowe in his very useful "Whitehead's Gifford Lectures"[39] has given us some of the reasons why. Whitehead came to Harvard in 1924 and he published *Science and the Modern World* in 1925. One year later he was giving special attention to Locke and to Descartes.[40] "He discussed Locke and Descartes in *Science and the Modern World*, but in 1926 he re-read Locke's *Essay* (of which he had inherited his father's copy), and Descartes (his wife gave him the Haldane and Ross translation of the *Philosophical Works* on his sixty-fifth birthday)." Whitehead's Gifford Lectures (the mature metaphysics of *Process and Reality*) were written between the summer of 1927 and the summer of 1928. About three months into this task, in a letter of August 22nd, 1927 to his son, North, Whitehead wrote:

> I think that I have got my metaphysics into capital order now. I have managed, to my own satisfaction at least, to make quite plain where I agree and disagree with the big seventeenth century men, especially Descartes, Spinoza, John Locke, and (later) Hume. The upshot of my studies is to "boost up" John Locke as the best of the lot of them—not the most consistent.[41]

This letter indicates the unique and very interesting method utilized by Whitehead in the elucidation of his metaphysics—that of constant reference to the seminal figures in the history of philosophy in a dialogue of congruence and disagreement. In an earlier essay on Whitehead this "historical bent" did not exactly please Victor Lowe.

> Another effect of his historical bent is his piety toward the great philosophers. There is ample reason for expounding a new philosophy in connection with their depositions, but I sympathize with those critics who call Whitehead's piety toward them excessive...Whitehead has read philosophy all his life. But possibly we can see in the excessive space devoted to Descartes and Locke in his essay on cosmology a bad effect of his philosophical professorship. Whitehead's comparisons of his doctrines with theirs are helpful to students of philosophy. But, since the future rests with the scientists, was it not far more important to emphasize the utilization of scientific and theoretical conceptions in the philosophy of organism, and to emphasize the importance of philosophy for such conceptions, than to gain the authority of Descartes and Locke?[42]

But here, I think, Lowe misses the point and is essentially mistaken. Science has its claims, to be sure, but the history of culture has its rights and its necessities no less. What is unique and infinitely valuable in Whitehead's metaphysical method is precisely its deeply humanistic intent.

This becomes clearest if we attend to Whitehead's own words. He begins the first chapter of Part II of *Process and Reality* thus:

> All human discourse which bases its claim to consideration on the truth of its statements must appeal to the facts. In none of its branches can philosophy claim immunity to this rule. But in the case of philosophy the difficulty arises that the record of the facts is in part dispersed vaguely through the various linguistic expressions of civilized language and of literature... In this second part of these lectures, the scheme of thought which is the basis of the philosophy of organism is confronted with various interpretations of the facts widely accepted in the European tradition, literary, philosophic, and scientific. So far as concerns philosophy only a selected group can be explicitly mentioned... What is important is that the scheme of interpretation here adopted can claim for each of its main positions the express authority of one, or the other, of some supreme master of thought—Plato, Aristotle, Descartes, Locke, Hume, Kant. But ultimately nothing rests on authority; the final court of appeal is intrinsic reasonableness.[43]

Two things are important here. One is that the appeal to authority is less evidential than corroborative, and this search for corroboration is the result of a quasi-Hegelian perception that the history of philosophy is in fact an element in the general history of culture. And the other is that Whitehead understands with exquisite tact that the great body of texts created by the great philosophers—those worthy of credence and consideration—is a specific cultural repository of right thinking and of apt expression.

This is what is most original in the creation of Whitehead's metaphysics—the attempt to reconcile the history of thought with thought itself. Such a metaphysical effort represents not only a triumph of the speculative impulse but of *the historical sense*. About this T.S. Eliot had something important to say: "Tradition...cannot be inherited, and if you want it you must obtain it by great labour. It involves, in the first place, the historical sense... and the historical sense involves a perception, not only of the pastness of the past, but of its presence..."[44]

Whitehead felt the insistent and palpable *presence* of Plato and Locke, of Descartes and of Hume, and this is why they loom so large upon the pages of *Process and Reality*.

Notes

[1] Étienne Gilson, *Études sur le rôle de la pensée médiévale dans la formation du système cartésien* (Paris: J. Vrin, 1930).

[2] S. Morris Engel, "Schopenhauer's Impact upon Wittgenstein," *Journal of the History of Philosophy* VII, No. 3 (July, 1969), pp. 285-302.

[3] Bertrand Russell, *An Inquiry into Meaning and Truth* (New York: W.W. Norton and Co., 1940), pp. 179-80.

[4] Edmund Husserl, *Ideas: General Introduction to Pure Phenomenology* (London: George Allen and Unwin, 1952), p. 183.

[5] Alfred North Whitehead, *Process and Reality* (New York: The Macmillan Co., 1930) p.v. Emphasis mine. All further references to *PR* are to this edition.

[6] Alfred North Whitehead, *Science and the Modern World* (New York: The Macmillan Co., 1925), pp. 55-57. All further references to SMW are to this edition.

[7] The entire section is relevant but I quote a part of it as characteristic. "We are then quite out of the way, when we think that things contain *within themselves* the qualities that appear to us in them; and we in vain search for that constitution within the body of a fly or an elephant, upon which depend those qualities and powers we observe in them. For which, perhaps, to understand them aright, we ought to look not only beyond this our earth and atmosphere, but even beyond the sun or remotest star our eyes have yet discovered. For how much the being and operation of particular substances in this our globe depends on causes utterly beyond our view, is impossible for us to determine. We see and perceive some of the motions and grosser operations of things here about us; but whence the streams come that keep all these curious machines in motion and repair, how conveyed and modified, is beyond our notice and apprehension: and the great parts and wheels, as I may so say, of this connexion and dependence in their influences and operations one upon another, that perhaps things in this our mansion would put on quite another face, and cease to be what they are, if some one of the stars or great bodies incomprehensibly remote from us, should cease to be or move as it does" (*An Essay Concerning Human Understanding*, ed. Fraser [New York: Dover, 1959], II, pp. 261-262).

[8] *PR*, p. 16. Emphasis mine.

[9] *Ibid.*, p. 80.

[10] *Ibid.*, p. 81.

[11] *Loc. cit.*

[12] *SMW*, pp. 58-9.

[13] *PR*, pp. 220-23.

[14] *Ibid.*, p. 223.

[15] *Ibid*, p. 94.

[16] A.N. Whitehead, *The Concept of Nature* (Cambridge: At the University Press, 1955), pp. 16-18. *Dialogues of Alfred North Whitehead*, as recorded by Lucien Price (New York: Mentor Books, 1956), pp. 177, 187.

[17] Alfred North Whitehead, *Adventures of Ideas* (New York: The Macmillan Co., 1933), pp. 187-93.

[18] *PR*, p. 63.

[19] *Ibid.*, p. ix.

[20] *Ibid.*, p. 70.

[21] *Ibid*, p. 103.

[22] *Ibid.*, p. 144.

[23] *Ibid.*, pp. 146-7.

[24] *Ibid*, p viii.

[25] *Ibid.*, pp. 9-10.

[26] *Ibid.*, p. 77.

[27] A.N. Whitehead, *The Principle of Relativity* (Cambridge: At the University Press, 1922), p. 13.

[28] *SMW*, pp. 5, 62.

[29] Relevant citations are: *PR*, pp. 127, 172, 205-208, 220-21.

[30] Bertrand Russell, *Portraits from Memory and other Essays* (London: George Allen and Unwin, 1956), p. 93. Russell's statement is underscored by Whitehead himself in "Autobiographical Notes" in Paul Arthur Schilpp, *The Philosophy of Alfred North Whitehead* (New York: Tudor Publishing Co., 1951), p. 7.

[31] He approves of the Bergsonian theory of intuition (*PR*, pp. 49, 65, 4) and to some extent his doctrine that the intellect "spatializes" the universe (*ibid.*, pp. 74, 319, 336).

[32] Schilpp, *op.cit.*, p. 398.

[33] *The Concept of Nature*, p. 28.

[34] *SMW*. pp. 93-96, 120.

[35] *The Concept of Nature*, p. 150.

[36] See the remarks in "Autobiographical Notes" in Schilpp, *op.cit.*, p. 7, and William E. Hocking, "Whitehead as I Knew Him," *The Journal of Philosophy* Vol. LVIII, No. 19 (Sept. 14, 1961), p 512.

[37] Schilpp, *op.cit.*, pp. 168-9.

[38] In a letter to me of 12/23/80. Quoted by permission.

[39] *Southern Journal of Philosophy* (Winter, 1969), pp. 329-338.

[40] *Ibid.*, p. 330.

[41] *Ibid.*, p. 333.

[42] "Whitehead's Philosophical Development" in Schilpp, *op.cit.*, pp. 117-18.

[43] *PR*, pp. 62-63.

[44] In his essay "Tradition and the Individual Talent". Reprinted in *T.S. Eliot: Selected Prose*, edited by John Hayward (Penguin Books, 1953), p. 23.

14.

COLLINS AND GADAMER ON INTERPRETATION

James L. Marsh

One of the bonds among different philosophical schools is the concern with language; within Thomism, analytic philosophy, phenomenology, hermeneutics, and critical social theory, for example, there is reflection on the meaning and import of language.[1] Among the sub-disciplines of philosophy of language is hermeneutics or theory of interpretation. What is one doing when one interprets a text? How can such interpretation be described and justified as a form of knowing? What are the implications of hermeneutics for theory of knowledge, metaphysics, philosophy of religion, and social theory?

In such a context it is useful to reflect on two theorists of interpretation from two different schools of philosophy, James Collins from Thomistic, theistic realism and Hans-Georg Gadamer from phenomenological hermeneutics. Such reflection contributes to assessing the achievement of each and also to building bridges between different philosophical methods. For one result of such a study is the profound affinity between two thinkers working in relative independence of one another.

Also, insofar as differences emerge between the two, that dialogue so important to each about the unfinished business of philosophy can begin, develop, and become yet another bridge. Such results are not insignificant in an age dominated by multiplicity and conflict of philosophical methodologies. Consequently this paper will have four main parts: an initial exposition of Collins's theory, a treatment of Gadamer, a section on affinities between the two, and finally some concluding reflections on some of their differences and on Habermas's criticism of hermeneutics. In this paper I will focus primarily, but not exclusively, on *Interpreting Modern Philosophy* and *Truth and Method*. Other works will be consulted only to further develop themes and answer questions arising from these two works.

James Collins

In the preface to *Interpreting Modern Philosophy* Collins states that his aim is "to illuminate the methodology and epistemology of modern philosophy, by reflecting upon the concrete ways of historians in the field."[2] To achieve this end he proposes a hypothesis for understanding their procedures, a schema outlining and relating the main components in their pattern of interpretation. The method used for the inquiry is one of functional reflection operating within three specifying limits. (1) Such reflection hugs as closely as possible to the actual working procedures and conditions in the history of philosophy. (2) The source materials considered are those found in the three centuries of classical modern European philosophy, 1600-1900, with the usual overlaps at either end. (3) The historians of philosophy whose procedures come under examination are, for the most part, men of the twentieth century.[3]

The activity of interpreting modern philosophy involves three main factors: (1) the insistent modern sources; (2) the art of historical questioning; and (3) the interpreting present in its several modes. These factors are essentially related to each other; the texts only become effective sources through historical questioning and reference to our own present concerns, historical questioning arises only as a response to difficulties arising in the sources, and questioning depends for its drive and relevance on a present generation of students. Finally these three factors are unified only in the philosopher engaged in a study of the modern sources. Consequently there are "the three co-factors of ingrediency" and the contemporary philosopher himself as a unifying agent.[4]

In approaching the insistent modern sources, one needs to cultivate four different attitudes. First, he should have a dissatisfaction with previous schemas, for instance, the automatic placing of Descartes, Leibniz, and Spinoza under a rationalist and Locke, Berkeley, and Hume under an empiricist paradigm. Second, there should be skepticism about any monistic usage, "the philosophy of Leibniz" or "the rationalism of Descartes", in discussing the work of a particular philosopher. One has to distinguish here among an originative relationship to the thinker taking into consideration the context of his work, the development of his work from early to late, and differect forms of expression his work took; a continuative relationship developing in a school devoted to the thinker in question; and a recurrent relationship to the thinker that is often polemical and related to the thinker's actual work only in a very abstract, remote way. The goal of interpretation is to facilitate an originative relationship.

Third, the illusion of mastery must be given up. A text must be read vigorously and critically, but any attempt to barge in upon a philosopher and wrest his meaning away on our terms is based on an illusion and distorts our understanding. When we read a thinker such as Nietszche this way, he only becomes more elusive and subject to misinterpretation. The text always remains inexhaustible and suprising, continually demanding reinterpretation. Fourth, we must behave towards the source men and their works as we would towards a company of critical inquirers. The relationship of interpreter to thinker is analogous to an interpersonal relationship in which I treat the other with respect, with openness for new revelations, and with a sense of his mystery and profundity.[5]

Corresponding to the opening of philosopher to text is the opening of text to philosopher, its insistence on being taken seriously in itself and at the same time illuminating the interpreter's own present. In reflecting on the Cartesian theme of order, for example, one reaches a depth of insight in Descartes that both resists easy schemes of mastery and yet is pertinent to contemporary philosophical questions about the relationship between method and metaphysics. The text expresses fundamental or basal acts of philosophizing, grounding the philosopher's basic arguments, permeating all his different works and forms of expression, and calling forth corresponding acts in the interpreting philosopher. The relationship between text and historian is not like that between clay and potter, but like a marriage "between two distinct but intertwining and mutually adapted partners... The relationship is not proprietal in nature, but closer to that of a discerning friendship."[6] The resulting history of modern philosophy is a marriage to which both the source text and historian contribute.

The second ingredient of functional reflection, historical questioning, reveals itself as openness to the "open yet inovert page." To open up the source texts themselves, the historian has various means at this disposal: new editions and translations, biographies and autobiographies that the historian uses to illumine the text, not to reduce it psychologistically to merely an expression of the author's individuality; genetic and systematic accounts that avoid false dichotomies such as that between the humanistic, young Marx and the positivistic, old Marx; and synoptic, synthetic accounts emerging after initial romantic encounter and rigorous analytic work on the philosopher in question. Here the goal is not either to transport ourselves totally into the mind of Descartes or Hegel nor to transport them totally into a dehistoricized present, but to interpret the text in such a way that the temporal difference between text and interpreter is preserved. Neither total identity nor mere difference but identity-in-difference is the reality, in which we do not have total lucidity about either pole and in which each pole bites into the other.[7]

Not only is the historian in historical questioning related to the primary text of the philosopher but he takes into account the from-to relationship of this thinker to other thinkers; Descartes links up with Spinoza and Leibniz, and Hegel with Kierkegaard and Marx. The originative philosopher himself recognizes his indebtedness to others and is continually commenting on problems they raise. Leibniz, for example, is very explicit about his relationship to Pascal, Spinoza, Descartes, and Malebranche. A historian can write a study on a particular from-to span or construct a problem-centered study. When he does so, he has to employ his own art of historical questioning to achieve a well-turned synthesis. In selecting texts, choosing problems and topics to emphasize, and ordering philosophical arguments, he is like the composer Penderecki, whose *Passion According to Saint Luke* unifies into a harmonious whole sacred texts from Psalms and Gospels, hymns and sequences from the Roman Missal and Breviary, and a whole range of musical techniques and forms from Gregorian chant to the twelve tone method.[8]

Classical texts do not speak to us by themselves, but rather demand the interpreting present. The present with its unceasing novelty is the source of the revisionary process that leaves us dissatisfied with present interpretations and motivates us to look for a new Spinoza or Marx. Present and past, rather than excluding one another, include one another in dynamic relationship. There is an intention towards futurity in the classical texts that demands to be completed by the interpreting present itself. When Descartes and Leibniz present their methodic proposals about positions merely sketched by them and Kant presents his *Prolegomena to Any Future Metaphysics*, these thinkers solicit the collaboration of later readers and thinkers. In such collaboration the experience and questions of the interpreter play a major role and prevent his interpretation from being a mere playback. What enables the historian to avoid fanciful constructions and achieve meaningful interpretation is the bond of language between himself and the text. Here Hegel's sensitivity to the nuance, creativity, and universality of language is a good model for historian and philosopher alike and is one of the indices of Hegel's greatness as a philosopher.[9]

Because of questions arising from his own situation, therefore, the interpreter will approach the classical texts in certain ways. He can reform from-to perspectives, such as the Hegel-Marx relationship; he can come to new appreciations of middle-range philosophers or paraphilosophers, such as Feuerbach or Kierkegaard; or he can engage in interpretations serving current theoretical aims, such as Husserl's reflections on Descartes and Kant. In such efforts as Husserl's the interpreting present has the primacy, but he also motivates the historian to scrutinize more closely Descartes' *Meditations* or Kant's *Critique of Pure Reason* on the issues—of certainty, method, reflection, and the meaning of the ego.[10]

For the contemporary philosopher serving as the unifying center of the three modes, a text is not there merely to be contemplated passively; rather interpretation is necessary if he is to gain access to the meaning of the text. Drawing on Peirce's theory of interpretation, Collins argues that interpretation is actional, both in the sense of the text's influence on the interpreter and his active response to it. Interpretation involves effort, intellectual, imaginative, and even muscular, to improve our historical understanding. There is a necessary openness to the plural forms which historical understanding takes, excluding any one privileged access or text. To achieve understanding, one must have a certain feeling of being at home with the text in its own context; one is comfortable with "our friend John Locke" in his milieu of modern philosophy. Finally only in this context of feeling and action is logic brought in, but only as presuming and incorporating these and only as conditional. Logic arises in questioning, is dynamic, is linked with personal growth, and grounds habits of understanding and judging. The interpreter must conjecture, interpret, and judge but not in such a way as to impose in a violent way his interpretation on the text. Every interpretation must be somewhat tentative in that it respects the gap between the limited interpretation and the ideal to be arrived at by a community of interpreters.[11]

The general aim animating the interpreter, therefore, is to do justice to the historical sources. There is a hermeneutical categorical imperative analogous to Kant's ethical categorical imperative.

> Just as Kant takes pains to qualify each such statement with the general directive: *Act in such a manner that*, so the reflective historian qualifies every procedural statement with the general direction: *Interpret in such a manner that*.[12]

He is guided by the sense of the text's historical imperativity, its capacity always to say something new. Because the historian shares that modern philosopher's passion for truth, there is a generous-mindedness towards the sources combined with rigor of appraisal, and a justice towards the present bearing of the sources combining veracity with relevance and avoiding the extremes of a deadening literal accuracy and a false contemporaneity. Because the historian is sensitive towards the various modes of historical inquiry, he avoids complacency and keeps open to the contributions of others in the discipline. Finally the interpreter of modern philosophy is oriented towards an interpretation that will illumine our sense of humanity in its historical and contemporary reality. Like Chagall in his *Paris Opera Ceiling* depicting composers from every period and culture, the historian of modern philosophy interrelates the key modern philosophers, creatively interprets in the light of the insistent historical present, and constructs an image of man contributing to the self-understanding and evolving of humanity.[13]

Hans-Georg Gadamer

Gadamer begins his discussion in *Truth and Method* by stating that he is "concerned to seek that experience of truth that transcends the sphere of the control of scientific method wherever it is to be found, and to inquire into its legitimacy."[14] Along with the human sciences, there are modes of experience outside of science such as art, history, and philosophy that resist the positivist model. Through a use of phenomenological method, understood as a reflexive, descriptive self-grounding, Gadamer uncovers eidetic structures in experience that transcend positivism. One result will be the falsity of the absolute mastery over being present in the positivist model of knowing. Primary influences in such an attempt are Heidegger, Dilthey and Husserl.[15]

Art, for example, is not reducible to the subjectivism postulated by Kant. Because objective knowing for Kant is achieved only through science, art cannot be a form of knowing. As a form of play, however, art reveals itself as disinterested, as a unity of form and content, subjective and objective; and consequently as a form of knowing. If one takes Aristotle's "imitation" not as mere reduplication of the surfaces of things but as a manifestation of their inner essence, then art is imitation. A Shakespeare play, a Rembrandt portrait, and even a cubist still life reveal something about their subject matters that would otherwise remain hidden. In such representation a work of art increases the being of the original.[16]

Moving to the historical knowing in social science as another kind of interpretation, Gadamer rejects Dilthey's romantic hermeneutics. It is a fallacy to think that I can transport myself back into the mind of thinker and know him better than he knew himself. Such an approach incorrectly ignores the difference between present and past and the necessary rootedness of interpretation in the present. Interpretation is grounded unavoidably in prejudice, and that dependence is a good thing. Because of the interpreter's own questions, values, and presuppositions, an access is gained to the text that would otherwise be closed. For example, current questions about freedom can make us more sensitive to Kant on this issue, and current social-political alienation can cause us to rediscover certain aspects of Marx and Hegel. The Enlightenment attempt to be totally free from prejudice is misguided and reveals itself in a self-contradictory way as a prejudice against prejudice.[17]

Interpretation is involved in a hermeneutical circle in which one starts with preconceptions about the text and has these tested in a self-correcting process. One moves from a conception of the whole to the parts of the text and emerges with deepened, qualified, corrected sense of the whole. If, for example, I have bought the dichotomy between the humanistic, early Marx and the scientistic, later Marx, then a reading of Marx's *Grundrisse* or the section in *Capital* on commodity fetishism will help correct such a misconception. Present research interests motivate our research into the past; the past puts our own biases into question and helps us to distinguish between legitimate and illegitimate bias. The result is a fusion of past and present with their differences maintained. There is an interplay between past and present in such a way that the interpreter does not dominate. "Hermeneutics in the sphere of literary criticism and the historical sciences is not knowledge as domination, but rather a subordination to the text's claim to dominate our minds."[18]

Interpretation, therefore, is a form of service; this fact is especially obvious in legal and theological hermeneutics where there is a long, highly regarded, normative, historical tradition. But just as the judge interpreting the law cannot prescind from the present circumstances that call for an interpretation affecting the meaning of the law itself, so also any historian understands himself in the text he interprets. The literary critic who tries to flee such self-involvement by escaping into the classics forgets his own commitment to them as classics and the norms in the light of which he sees them as classics. Such self-forgetfulness is absolutized and legitimized in the positivist model of science.[19]

Hermeneutical experience is dialectical in that it involves an encounter of consciousness with a text that is other and is a constant source of surprise. "Every experience worthy of the name runs counter to our expectations."[20] Experience is radically undogmatic insofar as it challenges and reveals the limits of any interpretation. Because of such negativity, the thinker or interpreter becomes aware of his own finitude and must commit himself to interpretation as a continual, self-correcting process. Fruitful interpretation is rooted in an openness to this experience of negation, finitude, and surprise. The truly experienced man is aware of this negativity and conscious that he is master neither of the past nor of the future. "The dialectic of experience has its own fulfillment not in definitive knowledge, but in that openness to experience that is encouraged by experience itself."[21] Interpretation is rooted in a readiness for experience that joyfully renounces the illusion of mastery and commits itself to the playfulness and surprise of experience.

To experience tradition in this way is to encounter it as we would a "thou" in a situation of mutual questioning. The experience of finitude and negativity grounding interpretation finds its most appropriate expression in questioning. The "thou" presents himself neither as an object to be known by science nor a slave to be dominated but as an equal who to some extent transcends me and is the source of his own initiatives. Through questioning, we both open up the matter to be illumined and allow ourselves, as in a Socratic dialogue, to be guided by the question. False or ungrounded opinion is banished by insight arrived at through questioning. Dialectic becomes the art of conducting the conversation in such a manner that dogmatic opinion does not suppress questions and one does not merely outargue the other. One focuses on the strength of the other's opinion and strives to let that emerge.[22]

Conforming to the logic of question and answer, then, the text asks a question of the interpreter and brings him into question. At the same time the interpreter opens up and illumines the text with questions coming from his perspective, experience, and presuppositions. The encounter between text and interpreter is dialectical in that the point is neither to submit uncritically to the text nor to win an argument. Rather a genuine fusion of horizons occurs in which the text finds its own meaning developed and clarified and the interpreter alienates himself and returns to himself with fuller self-knowledge. Such a fusion occurs through language as the common bond between interpreter and text. The text is part of a linguistic tradition, and the interpreter's thought is completed only through linguistic expression. To think is to experience oneself in the language of a particular national and cultural tradition. This language is not initially experienced as an object, but as the context in which one comes to experience objects and persons. Any particular linguistic statement means more than itself because of this relation to context. To discuss with someone Plato's theory of forms, for example, presupposes that we share common, unexpressed, implicit presuppositions about Greek philosophy, culture, and history.[23]

What is apparent finally is that language reveals being; Gadamer's theory of interpretation expands to become a theory of being. Language is not about itself but about the world, and strives to allow its meaning to emerge. Like Socrates and his friends, the interpreter and philosopher allow the meaning of truth, piety, and justice to shine forth. As the colors and shapes of a beautiful painting reveal something of beauty to the beholder, so the uses of language reveal something of being to the thinker. Language is truly speculative insofar as there is the thing distancing itself from itself and the thinker distancing himself from his own dogmatic preconceptions. In such thinking the dogmatism of the thing-in-itself passes over into the relationship of the thing to us. In the activity of thought reflecting upon the thing and mirroring it, there is an overcoming of false oppositions between opposites and the dialectical play of language turns into the play of being. Here Gadamer returns full circle insofar as the concept of play used in describing aesthetic experience now becomes a hermeneutical and ontological category. The play of language is the play of being, and the beautiful is the self-manifestation of being.[24]

Comparison Between Collins and Gadamer

What emerges first of all is substantial agreement about the method of interpretation, which may be described as dialogal, receptive, and interrelational questioning of the text. For both thinkers questioning opens up the text by highlighting themes and perspectives and leading to insights that would otherwise not emerge. For both thinkers the inexhaustibility of the text makes questioning the most appropriate approach to it. Questioning initiates the process of inquiry leading to interpretations, whose limits are revealed by further questioning.

Such questioning emerges in a context of dialogue. Both thinkers use the "I-thou" model for their explanation of interpretation. Descartes, Kant, and Hegel are not objects to be mastered, but friends and collaborators in a common enterprise of philosophy. Consequently, there is for Collins a hermeneutical, categorical imperative always "to interpret in such a manner that" this community is respected and for Gadamer the necessity of remaining always open to the novelty of experience. Because the text is a "thou" with its own initiatives and capacity to say more to us, one must give up any idea of total control and domination. Instead one must become receptive to the text. The text is not an object to be manipulated but a "thou" to be reverenced, listened to, and served.

Interpretation in theory and practice is always interrelational. Both Collins and Gadamer affirm the necessary relationship of texts to other texts written by the same author, to other thinkers, to the historical context of the source philosopher, and finally to the interpreting present. For Collins, using notions of Leibniz, there is a radial presence of the text beyond itself to what is other; for Gadamer no one text or relationship gives the whole story, and the text is always part of a larger tradition leading from the past to the present.[25]

One such interrelationship, that between the interpreting present and interpreted past, merits special comment. Both Collins and Gadamer reject as naive and dogmatic the notion of a text in itself able to speak for itself, because the remarkable fact is that Plato and Aristotle, Kant and Hegel, Marx and Nietzsche keep speaking for themselves in remarkably different and even contradictory tongues and accents. Consequently, one must use all available techniques of edition, translation, biographies, genetic and systematic accounts, and synoptic treatments to unlock the meaning of the text; and Dilthey's romantic project of understanding the thinker better than he did himself by transporting oneself totally into his mind and epoch must be renounced. Once the text becomes a reality it has a certain independence, not only from the interpreter but from the individual psychology of the philosopher who wrote it. For these reasons Collins warns that one should use biographies and autobiographies not in any project of psychological reductionism but in illumining the text itself in its historical context.

Likewise both thinkers insist on the importance of the interpreting present. The relationship between thinker and text is a marriage or fusion in which both have a role, but such a fusion is an identity-in-difference in which the difference of past from present is respected. One uses his own prejudices or presuppositions to open up the meaning of the text, and these prejudices are in turn put into question by the text in a playful back-and-forth movement. Any Enlightenment attempt to be free from prejudice only reveals itself in a self-contradictory way as a prejudice against prejudice. One's preconceptions, which lead him to reform from-to perspectives or engage in research into the *a priori* are not obstacles but positive aids. "To interpret means precisely to use one's own preconceptions so that the meaning of the text can really be made to speak for us."[26]

For both thinkers language is essential for achieving this fusion between past and present. Language grounds the difference between arbitrary and true interpretations and provides the context within which the interpretation goes on. The text is part of a linguistic tradition that stretches towards the future, and the interpreter thinks out of a linguistic tradition that reaches back towards the past. In language and in reflection on its use, the philosopher overcomes false dichotomies of inner and outer, thought and expression, public and private.

In such overcoming of false oppositions lies the final similarity between Collins and Gadamer, the dialectical character of their thinking. Both have learned from Hegel that philosophy, and consequently philosophical reflection on interpretation, is a reflective overcoming of one-sidedness. Thus we see both thinkers refusing the false oppositions of subjectivity or objectivity, archaicized past or detemporalized present, activity or passivity, history of philosophy or philosophy. Such dialectical thinking emerges not only in what the two say about interpretation but in the form of the argument itself, not only their theory but in their practice. For example, Collins and Gadamer both use insights from the history of philosophy in their theorizing. As I have already shown, Collins uses Leibniz's notion of radiality and Peirce's theory of interpretation, and Gadamer employ Hegel's notion of dialectic and Plato's model of dialogue. Both thinkers exemplify in their practice the internal relationship between history of philosophy and philosophy, past and present.

Contrary to Hegel, however, both thinkers refuse closure; theirs is a finite dialectic emphasizing the open-endedness, plurality, and inexhaustibility of texts to be interpreted. Consequently all claims to total comprehension must be given up, and all attempts at total control must be renounced. If Merleau-Ponty argues that the phenomenological reduction shows the impossibility of a complete reduction,[27] reflection on interpretation shows the impossibility of a complete interpretation. The most illusory, destructive prejudice of all is the prejudice against prejudice. Interpretation is not the sober work of mastery but the playful dialectic of a game. In such playfulness lies the more profound seriousness.[28]

Concluding Reflections

When one reflects upon the relationship between Collins and Gadamer, he discovers that there is a sense in which each complements the other. Insofar as Collins's is a theory of interpreting modern philosophy, he may be taken as a confirmation of Gadamer's universal theory.[29] Insofar as Collins confines his theory to interpreting modern philosophy, Gadamer's may be taken as the universal account of interpretation towards which Collins's account points. Collins verifies Gadamer, and Gadamer universalizes Collins.

There are three qualifications to the above claims, two that Collins himself makes and one that I develop below. First of all, Collins argues that there is an intellectual continuity between present and past in modern philosophy absent from other kinds of interpretation; we are closer to Descartes, Kant and Hegel than to Plato, Aristotle, or Aquinas. Second, the theme of humanity is central in modern philosophy is a way that it is not in other epochs. The problem of man is important in all periods, but serves as the primary organizing principle and teleological aim in modern philosophy. Consequently, the theme of humanity is a "sur-teleology" for the historical study of modern philosophy. "Our inquiry into the modern source philosophers aims at *such* an interpretation of their thought as will illumine and improve the meaning of humanity among us."[30]

Second, insofar as both thinkers show interpretation to be a form of legitimate knowing, they deal a death blow to positivism. which claims that only logic or empirically verifiable scientific propositions are true. In contrast to the positivist model of mastery and control, interpretation is receptive and open-ended. In contrast to attempts at reducing all knowing to knowing objects, interpretation understands a "thou-text," to which one cannot claim access by merely barging in. Positivism is quantitative and monologal; dialogal and qualitative accents prevail in interpretation. Positivism is oriented to dominance and predictability; surprise and submission are the values sought by interpretation.

There are some possible, false, related either-ors that beckon and tempt us here and that Collins avoids more successfully than Gadamer: the dichotomies between truth and method, science and understanding, analytic philosophy and interpretation. That positivism overstates its case does not mean that science, kept within its own proper boundaries, cannot contribute to understanding reality; "it is unfortunate that anyone should be permitted to pit the values of dialogal existence against the truths about nature as embodied in a scientific ordering." Indeed Habermas criticizes Gadamer for not recognizing that adequate social theory is itself a science and requires not only hermeneutics but also empirical, positive science, because there are certain social structures hidden from hermeneutical reflection that only an explanatory, theoretical empirical science can uncover; and Collins argues that there are questions within philosophy, such as those concerning causal proofs for the existence of God, that cannot be treated dialogally or hermeneutically. Philosophy has an explanatory as well as a descriptive moment. Also Gadamer correctly argues that all social science, because it involves a relation to a tradition and a language, necessarily involves a hermeneutical moment; but it may also be argued that even the physical sciences, because of their dependence on the ordinary, pre-scientific life world and ordinary language of the community of scientists, are hermeneutical at their roots.[31]

That analytic philosophy has often fallen into an overly aggressive approach to the text is no reason for saying that all analytic attempts at interpretation necessarily miscarry. More recent analytic philosophy has loosened up in its approach to texts, and Collins is very careful to include such analytic efforts as Strawson's work on Kant within the realm of fruitful interpretation.[32]

Third, interpretation of a text and reflection upon such interpretation are only parts of philosophy for both thinkers, not the whole; and here the third qualification mentioned above must come in. Both thinkers take differing positions on wider methodological, and metaphysical issues. Collins manifests increasing sympathy for the phenomenological, transcendental approach in philosophy and the relation between his philosophy and modern thinkers becomes progressively more internalized. Nonetheless he stops short at taking the transcendental turn in philosophy.[33] Gadamer, on the other hand, is frankly phenomenological in orientation while avoiding the subjectivistic excesses of earlier efforts.

On the question of being, Collins adopts an approach that he variously describes as "realism", "realistic theism", "Thomism", or "theistic realism";[34] things within the world have a metaphysical structure of matter, form, and existence, and God is the transcendent cause of the world. Gadamer, on the other hand, moves towards a Heideggerian conception of being as hermeneutical, expressive, and playful; being is the total context within which interpretation takes place and which reveals itself partially through particular interpretations. Two issues, then, arise between Collins and Gadamer. Is Thomistic realism or phenomenological hermeneutics the more appropriate method to critically ground and expand such a theory of interpretation?[35] Is Thomistic, theistic realism or hermeneutical being the more appropriate, metaphysical expansion of hermeneutics?

Finally, one critical issue raised by Habermas concerns the value and limits of hermeneutics itself. Habermas argues that hermeneutics justifies an uncritical abandonment to tradition and is, therefore, unable to distinguish between the tradition as truth-bearing and as ideologically justifying class difference and class domination. Is not the respectful approach to the text as a "thou" excessively passive? Is not the model of dialogue inappropriate when the tradition is implicitly ideological and, therefore, violates the conditions of fruitful dialogue? What is necessary is ideology critique in which the repression hidden in various forms of historical communication is articulated and seen through.[36]

What can be said in response to such a criticism? First of all, Gadamer argues that even criticism is bound to tradition in such a way that it cannot be totally thematized or transcended. Any attempt to do so is to place oneself tacitly outside the tradition in a false position of omniscience and domination.[37] Second, both Collins and Gadamer endorse and practice various kinds of criticism within the interpretive context. As I have already shown, Collins criticizes a one-sided approach of mastery to the text, positively evaluates Hegel as a major, radial philosopher, rejects as one-sided any univocal approach to interpretation, and judges that various philosophers such as Feuerbach are secondary figures. He also accepts as legitimate reflection on historical figures serving current theoretical aims. Gadamer rejects Kant's aestheticism, Dilthey's romantic hermeneutics and the Enlightenment model of knowing present in such thinkers as Descartes and Husserl. If criticism in general is possible within the hermeneutical model, then ideology critique as one kind of criticism is certainly possible. Indeed the whole of *Truth and Method* may be taken as a critique of the dominant ideologies in late capitalism—according to Habermas, positivism and scientism.[38]

Third, the opposition between a hermeneutics of respect and a hermeneutics of suspicion is false, because such a dichotomy rests upon a false disjunction of activity or passivity, total capitulation or total domination.[39] The model of dialogue developed and defended by both thinkers overcomes such oppositions. Even though the context is given in a way that is not totally thematizable, Socrates can criticize Thrasymachus on justice and Glaucon can tell Socrates that his belief in justice is naive. The dialogue reveals itself as a unity of activity and passivity, openness and critique, faith and suspicion in such a way that none of these moments is absolutized. "In other words, philosophical discussion involves argument as well as dialogue, clash as well as openness, evidence as well as personal respect."[40]

Fourth, Habermas in other works endorses a dialogal model for critique, in which four validity claims, comprehensibility, truth, sincerity, and appropriateness, are employed. To say that anything is true implies that my statement is comprehensible and true and that I am sincere in making the claim; otherwise the dialogue could not go on. Also it must be appropriate for me to make the statement; any claims to authority or expertise must be and can be tested and justified in the dialogue itself. As initially present these validity claims are not thematized, nor is the speech situation as such ever totally open to explicit inspection. Habermas in this model seems to affirm that the opposition between dialogue and critique is false.[41]

Fifth, hermeneutical reflection in answering Habermas engages in another overcoming of false oppositions; Habermas's criticism brings out the strength of the hermeneutical position. Interpretation can be understood in either a broad or a narrow sense. Understood broadly, it includes criticism as a moment of itself. It is in this sense that Ricoeur includes ideology critique as a part of hermeneutics.[42] Understood narrowly, interpretation is completed and complemented by criticism. Understanding and judgement, interpretation and critique, hermeneutical openness to tradition and ideology critique require one another. Critique without interpretation is willful and blind; interpretation without critique is naive and irresponsible.

Notes

[1]Bernard Lonergan, *Insight: A Study of Human Understanding* (New York: Longmans, Green, and Co., 1957), pp. 562-94. *Method in Theology* (New York: Herder & Herder, 1972), pp. 153-73. J. L. Austin, *How to Do Things with Words* 2nd ed., eds. J.O. Urmson and Marina Sbisa (Cambridge, Massachusetts: Harvard University Press, 1975). Maurice Merleau-Ponty, *The Phenomenology of Perception*, trans. Colin Smith (London: Routledge & Kegan Paul, 1962), pp. 174-99; *Phénoménologie de la perception* (Paris: Librarie Gallimard, 1945), pp. 203-32. Paul Ricoeur, *Interpretation Theory: Discourse and the Surplus of Meaning* (Fort Worth, Texas Christian University Press, 1976). Jürgen Habermas, *Zur Logik Der Sozialwissenschaften* (Frankfurt: Suhrkamp Verlag, 1970), pp. 188-285.

[2]James Collins, *Interpreting Modern Philosophy* (Princeton, New Jersey: Princeton University Press, 1972), p. viii. Hereafter this text will be referred to as *IMP*.

[3]*IMP*, pp. 28-29.

[4] *IMP*, pp. 30-31.

[5] *IMP*, pp. 38-44, 54-56.

[6] *IMP*, pp. 44-71, quotation on p. 52.

[7] *IMP*, pp. 99-154, 203-204. For the notion of identify-in-difference, see Hegel's *Science Of Logic*, trans. A. V. Miller (New York: Humanities Press, 1969), pp. 409-43; *Wissenschaft der Logik*, II (Frankfurt: Suhrkamp Verlag, 1969), pp. 35-80.

[8] *IMP*, pp. 154-85. See Collins's *The Emergence of Philosophy of Religion* (New Haven: Yale University Press, 1967), for an example of a from-to study: and his *God in Modern Philosophy* (Chicago: Henry Regnery Company, 1959), for an example of a problem-centered study.

[9] *IMP*, pp. 188-200, 381-84.

[10] *IMP*, pp. 212-266.

[11] *IMP*, pp. 359-77.

[12] *IMP*, pp. 353.

[13] *IMP*, pp. 390-417.

[14] Hans Georg Gadamer, *Truth and Method*, trans. and ed. Garrett Barden and John Cumming (New York: The Seabury Press, 1975), p. xii, hereafter referred to as *TM*; "ihr Anliegen ist, Erfahrung von Wahrheit, die den Kontrollbereich wissenschaftlicher Methodik übersteigt überall aufzusuchen, wo sie begegnet und auf ihr eigene Legitimation zu befragen." *Wahrheit und Methode*, 2nd ed. (Tübingen: J. C. B. Mohr, 1965), pp. xxv-xxvi, hereafter referred to as *WM*.

[15] *TM*, pp. xxi-xxvi; *WM*, pp. xix-xxiv.

[16] *TM*, pp. 91-150; *WM*, pp. 97-161.

[17] *TM*, pp. 192-274; *WM*, pp. 205-290.

[18] *TM*, pp. 235-278, quotation on p. 278; "Die Hermeneutik im Bereich der Philologie und der historischen Geisteswissenschaften ist, überhaupt nicht, Herrschaftswissen, d. h. Aneignung als Besitzergreifung, sondern ordnet sich selbst dem berherrschenden Anspruch des Textes unter." *WM*, pp. 250-95, quotation on p. 295.

[19] *TM*, p. 278, pp. 289-305; *WM*, p. 295, pp. 307-323.

[20] *TM*, p. 319; "Jede Erfahrung, die diesen Namen verdient durchkreuzt eine Erwartung." *WM*, p. 338.

[21] *TM*, p. 319; "Die Dialektik der Erfahrung hat ihre eigene vollendung nicht in einem abschliessenden Wissen, sondern in jener Offenheit für Erfahrung, die durch die Erfahrung selbst freigespielt wird." *WM*, p. 339.

[22] *TM*, pp. 325-41; *WM*, pp. 344-60.

[23] *TM*, pp. 333-97; *WM*, pp. 351-415.

[24] *TM*, pp. 397-447; *WM*, pp. 415-65.

[25] *IMP*, pp. 155-65; *TM*, pp. 358-59; *WM*, pp. 375-76.

[26] *TM*, p. 358; "Auslegen heisst Gerade: die eigenem Vorbegriffe mit uns Spiel bringen, damit die Meinung des Textes für uns wirklich zum Sprechen gebracht wird." *WM*, p. 375.

[27] Merleau-Ponty, *Phenomenology of Perception*, p. xiv; *Phénoménologie de la perception*, p. viii.

[28] *TM*, pp. 91-92; *WM*, pp. 97-98.

[29] Gadamer's own hermeneutical studies, of course, also exemplify his theory of interpretation. See *Hegel's Dialectic*, trans. P. Christopher Smith (New Haven: Yale University Press, 1976). *Hegels Dialektik* (Tübingen: J. C. B. Mohr, 1971). "Hegels Dialektik des Selbstbewusstseins," *Materialien zu Hegels "Phenomenologie des Geistes,"* ed. Hans Friedrich Fulda and Dieter Henrich (Frankfurt: Suhrkamp, 1973). *Dialogue and Dialectic: Eight Hermeneutical Studies on Plato*, trans. P. Christopher Smith (New Haven: Yale University Press, 1980). *Kleine Schriften*, III (Tübingen: J. C. B. Mohr, 1972), pp. 50-63, 27-49. *Platons Dialektische Ethik* (Hamburg: F. Meiner, 1968), pp. 181-204, 207-20, 224-47, 251-68. "Die Unsterblichkeitsbeweise in Platons Phaidon," *Wirklichkeit und Reflexion—Walter Schulz zum Geburtstag* (Pfullingen: 1971), pp. 145-61. *Idee und Wirklichkeit in Platons "Timaios"* (Heidelberg, 1974).

[30] *IMP*, pp. 406-407.

[31] Edmund Husserl, *The Crisis of European Sciences and Transcendental Phenomenology*, trans. David Carr (Evanston, Ill.: Northwestern University Press, 1970), pp. 103-89; *Die Krisis der Europäischen Wissenschaften und die Transzendentale Phenomenologie*, ed. Walter Beemel, vol. VI, *Husserliana* (The Hague: Martinus Nijhoff, 1954), pp. 105-93. Karl-Otto Apel, *Towards A Transformation of Philosophy*, translated Glyn Adey and David Frisby (London: Routledge and Kegan Paul, 1980), pp. 225-300; *Transformation der Philosophie* II (Frankfurt: Suhrkamp Verlag, 1973), pp. 358-435. Habermas, *Zur Logik der Sozialwissenschaften*, pp. 281-89. Collins, *Three Paths in Philosophy* (Chicago: Henry Regnery Company, 1962), pp. 379-82, quotation from p. 381; *God in Modern Philosophy*, pp. 381-83.

[32] *IMP*, pp. 314-27.

[33] See especially James Collins, *God in Modern Philosophy*, pp. 377-409; *Three Paths in Philosophy*, pp. 85-131, 225-397; *The Emergence of Philosophy of Religion*, pp. 350-491.

[34] *God in Modern Philosophy* p. 380; *Three Paths in Philosophy*, pp. 321-47, 376-97; *The Emergence of Philosophy of Religion*, pp. 423-25.

[35] See Lonergan, *Insight*, pp. 562-94; *Method in Theology*, pp. 153-73, for a transcendental approach that integrates Thomism and hermeneutics.

[36] Jürgen Habermas, "A review of Gadamer's Truth and Method," *Understanding and Social Inquiry*, editors Fred Dalmayr and Thomas McCarthy (Notre Dame: Notre Dame Press, 1977), pp. 335-63. *Hermeneutik und Ideologie Critik*, ed. Karl Otto Apel (Frankfurt: Suhrkamp Verlag, 1971), pp. 45-56. In their other essays in this book continuing the debate, Habermas and Gadamer seem to come closer together by qualifying initially more extreme positions. See pp. 57-82, 120-59, 283-317.

[37] *TM*, pp. 495-98. *Philosophical Hermeneutics*, trans. and ed. David E. Linge (Berkeley: University of California Press, 1976), pp. 18-42. *Kleine Schriften*, I (Tübingen: J. C. B. Mohr, 1967), pp. 113-30.

[38] Habermas, *Towards a Rational Society*, trans. Jeremy Shapiro (Boston: Beacon Press, 1970), pp. 81-122; *Technik und Wissenschaft als 'Ideology'* (Frankfurt: Suhrkamp Verlag, 1971), pp. 48-103.

[39] Paul Ricoeur, "Ethics and Culture: Habermas and Gadamer in Dialogue," *Philosophy Today* 17 (1973), pp. 153-56, 164-65.

[40] Collins, *Three Paths in Philosophy*, p. 380.

[41] Habermas, *Theory and Practice*, trans. John Viertel (Boston: Beacon Press, 1973), pp. 17-19. *Theorie und Praxis* (Berlin: Hermann Luchterhand Verlag and Suhrkamp Verlag, 1963, 1966, and 1971), pp. 23-26. *Zur Logik der Socialwissenschaften*, pp. 281-89.

[42] Ricoeur, "Ethics and Culture": 156-64.

15.

RELIGION WITHIN THE SCOPE OF PHILOSOPHY

John E. Smith

James Collins, in his illuminating and demanding book, *The Emergence of Philosophy of Religion*, has done an immeasurable service to philosophers engaged in interpreting religion, and to theologians of a philosophical bent. Not only has he traced with great care, through the medium of representative thinkers—Hume, Kant and Hegel—the novel development of a philosophical treatment of religion from standpoints not initially rooted in theological traditions, but he has helpfully focused six issues (pp. 350 ff.) to which, as he says, "every present day philosopher of religion should give careful consideration" (p. 351). I believe that these issues are illuminating because they make clear the aims of the philosophy of religion and the problems anyone engaged in the enterprise must face. Each question provides material for an extended discussion; unfortunately, that is not possible under present circumstances. I propose to consider an aspect of the second issue cited by Collins which he calls "religionizing the theory of God" (pp. 359 ff.). If I understand him correctly, he is claiming that when an analysis of religion becomes a major task for an autonomous philosophy, the relation between this analysis and the theory of God must be of central importance. By "religionizing" the theory of God, Collins means a study of this relationship focusing on its importance for evaluating "our philosophical reasoning about God" (p. 359). The special point I wish to consider in connection with this process is raised in the interpretation of Hegel and is expressed by Collins in this intriguing question: "'What would happen to the religionizing theme, however, if some sort of metaphysical knowledge were restored to good standing?'" (p. 368). As I shall suggest, this same question could be transposed so as to apply to the first issue mentioned, namely religion within the scope of philosophy. The *sort* of philosophy involved, not just the standpoint, realism, idealism, materialism, etc., but the conception of the *role* of philosophy envisaged, has much to do with the philosophy "within" which religion comes to be situated. Before proceeding, however, some background is required.

In view of the exhaustiveness of Collins' analysis, I cannot simply presuppose the long discussion that precedes his treatment of "the common issues," nor on the other hand can I undertake to summarize it. What is possible, however, is a statement of Collins' conception of the distinctive features of the philosophy of religion that emerged as a novel enterprise in the period 1730-1830 spanning the philosophies of Hume, Kant and Hegel. To begin with, Collins is acutely aware of the peculiar situation of these modern thinkers; they were professional philosophers approaching religion chiefly in the form of the Judeo-Christian tradition (although they were not unaware of other religious traditions) and treating it from their own philosophical standpoints without the presence of any explicitly theological purpose. That their thought had enormous repercussions for theology is, of course, true, but that fact must not obscure the initial point about the novel enterprise in which they were engaged. Collins, moreover, correctly points out the error of those who suppose that the treatment of religion by Hume, Kant and Hegel represents no more than an appendix to their thought; on the contrary, in each case, their account of religion had a decidedly "retroactive" effect on their philosophical doctrines. This influence may seem to be more obvious in the case of Kant who aimed at showing the limits of knowledge in order "to make way for faith," or of Hegel who insisted that his philosophy of Absolute Spirit was the translation of the content of the revealed religion into the form of the Notion, than in the case of Hume. There is no question, however, that the study of religion played a large part in the thought of the author of *A Treatise of Human Nature* for whom the knowledge of man was the central concern.

In a remarkably rounded and judicious account of Hume's thought, Collins shows how Hume "naturalized" religion in the twofold sense of a natural theology philosophically elaborated and a view of nature shaped in accordance with the argument from design. In opposition to the usual view that Hume's treatment of natural religion is entirely negative because of the severe criticism of the theistic proofs dictated by his sense-bound epistemology, Collins shows that Hume had another aim, namely the endeavor to find a new foundation for religion in his theory of human nature. On this new basis religion does not depend on the proofs of natural theology or even on moral reasoning but instead represents an irreducible response of the total human being to his situation in the world. Hume's constructive philosophical aim was to induce people to elevate themselves from popular theism and its corresponding religious forms to critical or genuine theism and true religion informed by a critical philosophy. As the concluding remark of Philo in the *Dialogues* shows, Hume saw the skeptic as superior to the dogmatist, for whereas the latter assumes the adequacy of philosophy for erecting a solid system of theology and thus "disdains any farther aid," the skeptic knows the imperfections of human reason and is thus in a position to seek a revealed truth.

Collins' treatment of Kant's philosophy of religion must rank with the very best that has been written on the subject. Not only does he call attention to the full range of Kant's writings on religion, but he deals in a straightforward way with Kant's conception of revelation, a topic often neglected by those who take it for granted that Kant was reducing religion to the proportions of moral faith. Much of the ground here is familiar although it has not always been covered in such detail. The pivotal idea is, of course, Kant's removal of the speculative foundation for religion through his criticism of the theistic proofs as the necessary preliminary to the establishing of a practical or moral basis for religious faith. Collins shows that Kant's philosophical position, including his philosophy of religion, is basically humanistic in the sense that it focuses ever and again on the bearing of some dimension of experience—science, morality, etc.—on human life in the world and its significance. In the case of religion, Kant's task was to show how religion, meaning especially Christianity, can be combined with "the purest practical reason." In carrying out that task, Kant was led to an analysis and interpretation of revealed religion to a far greater extent than has generally been emphasized. As Collins points out, Kant's *Religion innerhalb der Grenzen der blossen Vernunft* must not be understood as a synthetic attempt to construe religion from the concepts of reason alone for that would mean excluding the empirical element represented by the revelations to be found in the world religions. Consequently Kant could not and did not avoid a direct confrontation with Scripture and its view of the relation between God and man. Unlike other Enlightenment thinkers who regarded the historical element in religion as just so many occasions for the disclosure of rational truths that might have been discovered by reason left to itself, Kant saw biblical revelation as a distinctive message of its own, which, however, is addressed to man via his practical reason. Revelation, on his view, concretizes or brings down to earth the pure moral religion consonant with Kant's moral theism. The biblical narrative is essential because if fulfills man's basic need for a visible representation of what is by nature invisible, and Collins rightly calls attention to Kant's "remarkable comparison" between the incarnation of meaning in biblical revelation and the schematizing of the categories through the transcendental imagination (p. 164). Collins concludes this discussion with what I think is an illuminating and novel interpretation. According to this view, Kant's theory of religion cannot be uniquely situated in either the pure moral religion or the explication of the Scriptural revelation, but rather in the transition and mutual interplay between the two. The moral religion controls or furnishes the key to interpretation, but without revelational embodiment in an historical constellation of meanings we would be left merely with empty ideas.

Despite the massiveness of Hegel's philosophy, what is significant for our purposes in Collins' interpretation of it can be stated quite succinctly. It would, I think, be fair to say that Collins finds Hegel's pan-logism a greater threat to the autonomy of religion and especially of revelation than the "critical" philosophies of Hume and Kant. Hegel, by contrast, had recovered a form of the ontological standpoint that prevailed in Western philosophy throughout the period extending from Plato to Leibniz, and he was well aware of the long history of intellectual exchange that led to the development of the metaphysical theologies within Christendom. Collins' chief uneasiness in confronting Hegel stems from the all-inclusiveness of the speculative system within which religion, and especially Christianity, is to be encapsulated. This uneasiness, moreover, is not diminished but rather increased by Hegel's determination of Christianity as the absolute religion, and for at least two reasons. One has to do with the ground of this determination as something necessitated by Hegel's conception of the philosophical development of Absolute Spirit. The other concerns Hegel's conception of religion as a limited dimension that must ultimately give way to philosophy, so that even if Christianity is absolute in this sphere, the sphere itself is not absolute because, in having to rely on pictorial thought, religion falls short of the notional form in which Absolute Spirit is totally at home with itself.

Both reasons can be seen in Collins' treatment of the revelational character of Christianity as understood by Hegel. Moreover, as should now be obvious, this feature is regarded by Collins as the essential one throughout the entire discussion, presumably on the ground that any eclipse of revelation from the standpoint of the philosophy of religion would mean not only that religion is "within" the scope of philosophy, but that it is "wholly within" those boundaries. The crux of Collins' contention against Hegel on this point is that in arguing for the *necessity* of revelation in the absolute religion, Hegel finds this not in that religion itself but rather in the philosophical demand, based on the doctrine of essence, that Absolute Spirit must manifest itself in existence which means that it must reveal itself to finite spirits in a community able to receive and respond to the disclosure. And since this disclosure overcomes every gap between infinite spirit and man, the mystery of God is eclipsed. Revelation, then, though a culminating chapter in the autobiography of Absolute Spirit, is not the final chapter. Philosophy speaks the last word.

The foregoing, truncated and condensed as it is, must serve as a background for further consideration of the issue mentioned earlier on—"religionizing the theory of God." Collins' raising of the question of the repercussions for this issue and, as I indicated, for "religion within the scope of philosophy" as well, of a return of metaphysics to "good standing" in Hegel has more wide-reaching significance than I think he realizes. To begin with, both Hume and Kant are essentially "critical" philosophers representative of what I call the "reflexive turn" calling into question that correlation of thought and being which was the hallmark of the Western metaphysical tradition.[1] Since I maintain that metaphysics of some sort, explicit or not, is inescapable for any philosophy, I cannot go so far as to deny that Hume and Kant had a "metaphysics," but it is clear that as thinkers acknowledging the primacy of epistemology they did not intend to elaborate a metaphysical position in the sense in which Hegel clearly did. What fulfills the metaphysical role in Hume is his theory of human nature in all its aspects, and what performs the same function in Kant is the theory of morality and the conditions for its possibility. In neither case are we dealing with a theory of being in the classical mode, and yet it seems clear that Hume's theory of knowledge and of man's passional nature determines his conception of both God and religion as does Kant's reversal of the speculative tradition in favor of the primacy of practical reason. The difference of both from Hegel, however, is not to be underestimated because the latter had an explicit theory of being articulated as an ontology of Spirit, something for which there is, strictly speaking, no counterpart in either Hume or Kant. Another way of putting this point is in terms suggested by Collins' valid insistence that the "philosophy of" disciplines presuppose a substantive philosophy. In Hegel's case that philosophy is his ontology of Absolute Idealism; in the cases of Hume and Kant we find that it is more of a philosophical anthropology, dictated to a large extent by the results of a prior critique of knowledge. It is for this reason that they are led to conceive of God and of religion as essentially bound up with man and the dimensions of human experience, whereas Hegel recaptures the ancient theme that God is Truth in a sense that far transcends the anthropological plane. What do these fundamental differences between Hume and Kant on the one side and Hegel on the other mean for all three themes— religion within the scope of philosophy, the religionizing of the theory of God, and the emergence of the philosophy of religion?

Even if we allow, as I believe we must, that Collins is right in describing these thinkers as treating religion within the scope of philosophy, much depends on the scope of the philosophy involved. May it not be said that the critically oriented philosophies, being clearly of lesser scope than that of Hegel, can provide for religion a greater measure of autonomy precisely because they do not seek to contain it within a metaphysical system nor do they envisage religion as "passing over" into philosophy as Hegel's triad of Absolute Spirit requires. While it remains true that the three philosophies of religion are developed from the standpoint of autonomous philosophies, the resources and ambitions they embody differ vastly. The skeptical strain in the critical philosophies which reduces the theoretical content of philosophy and at the same time pushes in the direction of a "practical" interpretation of religion ultimately fosters a basic fideism in religion and a resolute denial of any cognitive status to religious insight.[2] One can see this at the present time in the approach of the analytic philosophers whose debt to Hume is obvious, even if that to Kant is less so. Apart from those who regard all religious utterance as meaningless, many analytic philosophers manage to combine a philosophy confined largely to clarification of religious language in use with a positivized faith virtually devoid of conceptual sophistication because derived directly from the Bible or the Creeds. This extreme actually deprives religion of the benefits of philosophical interpretation underlined by Collins as among the positive fruits of the philosophy of religion. Understanding is not achieved merely by leaving everything as it was before. I do not suggest that either Hume or Kant are to be identified with such an extreme view, but it does represent an outworking of critical philosophy wherein knowledge is assimilated to science with the result that philosophy no less than religion is ultimately deprived of a cognitive basis. In short, the greater autonomy allowed to religion from the critical standpoints as compared with a philosophy like Hegel's is not an unmixed blessing. On the other hand, it is certainly to be preferred to the eclipse of religion by a system of speculative contemplation.

With regard to the religionizing of the theory of God especially as it concerns not so much the understanding but the evaluation of reasoning about God, the contrast between a critical and anthropological position and that of a substantive metaphysics once again makes a great difference. Hume's sense-bound conception of knowledge sharply curtails the scope of such reasoning and leaves him with but faint analogies based on the design argument that he, like Kant, took to be the argument closest to the ordinary understanding of mankind. Kant is on more solid ground especially if one takes seriously (as is not always done) the derivation of the transcendental Ideas so that they have such tenure as is bestowed upon what we must necessarily *think* even if the "objects" of these Ideas cannot be *known* in a theoretical way. Since, however, Kant opted for the primacy of understanding and denied to reason a full cognitive reach, he had to fall back on the practical standpoint and moral faith. The result is that God enters only as a postulate required for the intelligibility of pure practical reason. The situation of Hegel, however, is quite different. Leaving aside the undoubted problems raised by the transcendence of religion in his system, he did nevertheless reach back, as it were, to recover the metaphysical standpoint at the foundation of the thought and reasoning about God represented as the ontological and cosmological approaches. Consequently, he was able to reinterpret the theistic arguments as ways of elevating the mind to the thought and the presence of God. In this way of thinking one can see both a promise and a peril. The promise consists in the transcendence of the anthropological context and the establishment of a theological vantage point so that attention is again focused on God, thus decreasing the possibility that religion itself and the human pole of the religious relationship will become the central concerns. The peril is, of course, the engulfing of religion, including the absolute religion, within the speculative system so that the religious truth is all "understood," made transparent to reason, and the reality and the risk of all faith are submerged or subordinated in a completed self-consciousness to which is already present the whole of reality in its truth.

Turning now to the special import of the difference between Hume and Kant on the one hand and Hegel on the other for the emergence of the philosophy of religion, I wish to make one central point which, in addition to being paradoxical, has far-reaching implications for religion, philosophy and the relations between the two. There is no question that Collins is right in his description and interpretation of the process whereby there developed a "philosophy of" religion on the basis of philosophical standpoints free of specific theological motives. Moreover, he rightly points to the integral relation between the treatment of religion and the total philosophical outlook to be found in the three representative thinkers. The point I would stress is that in virtue of not having constructed a commanding, even "threatening," ontological system, Hume and Kant were in a position to let religion "be" in its own nature and actual form. True, both thinkers construed religion in mundane terms and in relation to its human context; like all philosophers they were not without their interpretative "filters." But in being critical, somewhat skeptical as regards metaphysics, and anthropologically oriented, they had no tendency to absorb religion or to transform it into another dimension. Hegel, by contrast, and with paradox as well, could not really let religion "be" because he had to incorporate it into a total transcending vision. The philosopher of *being* who, in all fairness, must be acknowledged as a thinker who labored very hard at the task of having the subject matter *manifest itself*, nevertheless cannot let things—including religion—be, for the simple reason that the higher attitude for him is the transformation necessary for *being known*. Even if we allow, as I believe we must, that the knowing involved is of the richest and most profound sort, that *knowing* demand remains, and even religion which has always understood itself as an *ultimate* standpoint, comes to be incorporated in one that claims a greater ultimacy. It is for this reason that Hegel, while he has a "philosophy of religion," does not have it in the same sense as Hume and Kant. He borrows a content from the absolute religion and transforms this into a spiritual ontology that encompasses the borrowed content itself. If religion informs his philosophy, as indeed it does, his philosophy transforms religion to a far greater extent than was possible for either Hume or Kant.

And yet, having said all this, one cannot deny that Hegel had a far greater sympathy with and penetrating understanding of the meaning of classical theology than was possible for the two Enlightenment thinkers. This fact, is, of course, due to his ontological orientation and his deep understanding of the histories of both philosophy and theology. Richard Kroner, in his lectures on Hegel of many years ago, was fond of saying, in just this connection, that the danger of Hegel's thought lies precisely in the extent to which he actually accomplished his program. For if there are reasons to believe that his entire enterprise was *mistaken*, the awesome completeness with which he pursued it must leave us as far from the truth as we could possibly be!

The final question emerging from this discussion is this: is a more fruitful exchange between religion and philosophy possible when the philosophy in question is largely critical or when it is of a substantially metaphysical character? I can do no more here than point to two important developments on the contemporary scene. While we have learned much from the critical, analytic and linguistic philosophies in the clarification and assessment of religious insight, the only two points of contact in recent decades allowing for that sort of dialogue between philosophy and religion represented in the past by the Platonic-Augustinian and Aristotelian-Thomist traditions are to be found in existentialism and in the process philosophy of Whitehead. And the reason is clear—neither position is essentially "critical" but seeks to raise and illuminate from the philosophical side the same sort of metaphysical concern that was at the heart of classical theology. Augustine could have a creative *dialogue* with the Neo-platonic tradition, and Thomas with the philosophy of Aristotle. But is such a dialogue possible with Wittgenstein, Austin, or Quine, or indeed any of the representatives of a philosophy purporting to eschew the problem of being in any sense other than that of determining the mode of existence in logical terms?

Notes

[1] That correlation was still upheld by Leibniz and Spinoza; cf. the latter's: "the order and connection of ideas is the same as the order and connection of things." *Ethics*, Second Part, Prop. VII.

[2] Cf. Wittgenstein's remark that if there is for any statement even the smallest scrap of "empirical" evidence, that statement is *not* religious.

16.

WITTGENSTEIN AND PHILOSOPHY OF RELIGION: AN APPLICATION OF *EMERGENCE* THEMES

John W. Carlson

After detailing the emergence of philosophy of religion[1] among the classical moderns James Collins turns, in his final chapters, to synthetic and programatic concerns. Three themes come to the fore. First, a philosopher's treatment of religion must be consistent with, and indeed an organic outgrowth of, his foundational views on method and human reality. This, says Collins, is "the essential maxim" for researchers in this field.[2] Second, in spite of their marked differences in method and specific doctrine, the great originators in philosophy of religion—Hume, Kant and Hegel—together determined a "common fund of topics" for investigation; these topics provide later theorists with a "reliable guide for securing balance and rigor."[3] Third, it is to be hoped that philosophers in the tradition of realistic theism will engage the classical modern treatments of religion. This can be expected to produce "definite repercussions" upon the field—at the very least to "widen the range of effective positions open."[4] On the other hand an encounter with the problems and views of the classical moderns will affect realistic philosophers themselves, as they seek to develop their own accounts of religion.[5]

In the present study I apply and extend these *Emergence* themes. I do so by bringing them to bear on the philosophical work of Ludwig Wittgenstein and certain of his followers. The writings prepared for publication by Wittgenstein himself contain no organized treatment of religion. But his interest in the subject is attested to by his students,[6] and can be seen in scattered remarks in the published works. Further, during the period in which he was developing his mature philosophy Wittgenstein gave a set of Lectures on Religious Belief. Student notes from these lectures have been edited and published,[7] and a number of their ideas have been elaborated upon by Wittgenstein's close followers. Even at this, however, what may be termed Wittgensteinian philosophy of religion is very much in the process of formation, and, as we shall see, subject to internal criticism and development in a variety of ways.

I apply Collins' themes to this body of material as follows. I begin with a sketch of Wittgenstein's views on philosophical method and (insofar as

[255]

he has them) on human reality. Then I arrange and critically examine Wittgensteinian discussions of religion in terms of topic areas identified in *Emergence*. Finally, I consider the possibility of realistic theism having an impact on the thus developing Wittgesteinian account.

I. Wittgenstein's Approach to Philosophy

Let us begin, then, in Collins' words, with a discussion of the "distinctive methods and conception of man" developed in the philosophy of Wittgenstein.[8] Even a casual acquaintance with his works reveals that Wittgenstein was, throughout his career, preoccupied with methodological issues. And while they contain major differences in both style and substance his writings also express common themes. Philosophy is primarily an activity rather than a doctrine. Its aim is to introduce clarity and dispel confusion. The clarity philosophy seeks requires an investigation of the functioning— of the "logic" or "grammar"— of language.

In Wittgenstein's early book, the *Tractatus Logico-Philosophicus*, these themes were bound up with the "picture theory." According to that theory all meaningful language serves a single purpose—that of saying "how things stand" (T, 4.022, 4.5). How things stand ultimately means how the objects of the world are combined with one another to form facts (T, 2.15, 3.21, 4.1). And the picturing of facts can take place because our language can have a "projective relation to the world" (T, 3.12). Such a relation is established, in a manner not clarified by Wittgenstein, when we "think of the sense of the proposition" (T, 3.11). In doing this we somehow enable the proposition to "reach right out" to reality (T, 2.1511).

Because language mirrors the world there are, corresponding to the possibilities of combination among objects, rules of combination among linguistic signs. These rules comprise what Wittgenstein calls "logical grammar" or "logical syntax" (T, 3.325). Their precise features, however, are not easy to discern, for they are disguised by the "outward form" of our everyday propositions (T,4.002). Thus it is possible—and often happens in philosophy—that one should run afoul of the rules, and fall into confusion and nonsense (T, 3.324, 4.003). The proper philosophical method must, accordingly, be that of "analysis," in which one attempts to discover the real logical forms beneath the merely apparent ones (T, 4.0031). Insofar as one achieves this one gains a clear view of the forms of any "correct" language, and—given language's pictorial nature—the "form of reality" as well (T, 3.343, 2.18).

As mentioned above, the *Tractatus* did not attempt to clarify the act of thinking by which a proposition has its relation to the world. As he moved into his mature period Wittgenstein undertook a radical questioning of the manner in which our language acquires its sense. In the end he came to reject the theory of a special mental act, and also the idea that all meaningful language functions in some single way. The latter idea, he points out in *Philosophical Investigations*, was not a result of taking a close look at language; rather it was a supposition or requirement (PI, 107). Further, the line-up of generalized notions "Thought"—"Proposition"—"World" represented not our common use of these words but rather a "super-order" among "super-concepts"—concepts which, since they were purely philosophical inventions, had no genuine application (PI, 96-97). Instead of relying on a priori suppositions philosophers must investigate the actual functioning of language. When we do so we discover a great variety of types of meaning, from that involved in reporting an event to those involved in practices like thanking and greeting. Indeed, says Wittgenstein, "there are countless different kinds of use of what we call...'words' [and] 'sentences' " (PI, 23). Even "saying how things stand," or "fact-stating" uses of language, will manifest internal diversity (see PI, 23.) Thus a term like "fact" or "statement" is a "family resemblance" term—one whose various applications, like the members of a family, display a mix of similarities and differences (PI, 67). Further, it should be noted that a single word or sentence may have a number of uses or dimensions of use (PI, p. 200; Z, 180); and that a concept's employment may involve a number of strands which overlap and intertwine with one another (PI, 67).

Concerning the question of how language acquires meaning Wittgenstein refers to the human practices in which the use of words is rooted. These he often calls "language-games," which he says are among the "forms of life" (PI, 23). Included in the latter category are the manifold facets of human existence which give our language stability and sense: e.g., shared interests and concerns, judgments, perceptions and modes of action (PI, 241-42; Z, 545; C, 124, 156, 168). Like the linguistic uses themselves forms of life display great diversity. "Language," says Wittgenstein, "is variously rooted; it has roots, not a single root" (Z, 656).

These changes in the account of the functioning of language entail changes in the notion of logic or grammar. Rather than consisting of a neat, unified system of rules corresponding to the relations among objects, grammar is now seen to include many different kinds of convention: concerning the criteria for the correct application of a term; the kinds of thing it makes sense to say or think about a type of object; the consequences of saying one thing rather than another; etc. Further, these conventions have varying degrees of strictness and they operate within their respective language-games rather than universally. A rule or convention which functions in one linguistic context may have no counterpart—or a very different counterpart—in another (see PI, 100, 164, 206, p. 228).

Regarding philosophy itself the aim remains clarity and the corresponding elimination of confusion (PI, 122, 133). But if we continue to speak of "analysis" (PI, 91), or of seeking a grasp of "depth grammar" (PI, 664), we must remember that the philosopher's task is not to "penetrate phenomena," but rather to produce descriptions of things which are in principle already available—the various features of our language-games and forms of life (PI, 109, 122). Thus philosophy can be seen as an ongoing exercise in "natural history" (PI, 25, 415; Z, 469)—an exercise which gains its point from the perceived need for greater clarity about the phenomena in question. These phenomena, of course, are, broadly speaking, linguistic phenomena. Here it is important to note that, given Wittgenstein's mature account of language and meaning, it makes no sense to speak, as he had in the *Tractatus*, of philosophical analysis revealing the "form of reality," or of a particular type of language being, without qualification, either "correct" or "incorrect." This suggests questions about the ultimate justification of our language-games, and about how we should respond if we come across people whose forms of life are very different from our own. Wittgenstein turns to such questions often in the later writings, and his answers are complex and somewhat tentative. He recognizes the possibility of our meeting people whose practices we do not understand or appreciate (Z, 338-39, 387-90). In some such cases we may wonder whether they are genuine practices at all, i.e., whether they have coherence or point; or we may suspect that they are merely mistaken or inferior versions of our own— e.g., primitive forms of science. But the differences may run deeper than this, to fundamentally different ways of viewing things. And there is no completely general standard of reasonableness—one residing, so to speak, outside all language-games—by means of which language-games as a whole may be assessed (C, 336, 559). Thus in the end we might simply have to say of the others' practices, "We don't join in here" (Z, 330). We might have to recognize that we are "intellectually very distant" from them (C, 108). With regard to our own practices it may to some extent be possible to produce reasons or grounds or justifications. All of these, however, "come to an end," revealing our most basic modes of action, judgments, suppositions, assumptions and even decisions (PI, 217, p. 179; C, 146, 166, 168, 253, 559, 612). And thus, if someone balks at one of our language-games we may finally have to resort to simple persuasion (C, 612); or perhaps to a suggestion that with greater learning and experience the other might come to appreciate what we do (C, 206). It is not possible to say a priori at what points, if ever, such impasses will be reached; nor whether we or others might come to change certain fundamental perceptions. Such is the unpredictability of forms of life.

Insofar as Wittgenstein has an account of human nature it is to be gathered from the foregoing. It might be suggested that in his notions of language-games and forms of life (including their diverse foundational elements) Wittgenstein offers us the general *form* of an account, rather than one having definite *content*. Further, the type of account which would emerge from applying his views would be non-normative in character. Wittgenstein does speak of the "common behaviour of mankind" (PI, 206); and he says that there are certain "very general facts of nature," including, we may presume, human nature (PI, p. 230). But he also says that the concept of a human being has a measure of "indeterminacy" (Z, 326); and he does not see it

WITTGENSTEIN AND PHILOSOPHY OF RELIGION 259

as his philosophical role to attempt to set limits on the concept. The task of Wittgensteinian philosophy is, accordingly, simply to say "These language-games are played"(PI, 654); that is, to note and clarify—but not to judge—the variety of linguistic practices, along with their distinctive roots and grammars. In this way there might progressively be built up an accurate picture of human reality. It may be noted in this connection that investigations of religious phenomena can contribute to, as well as draw from, Wittgensteinian reflections on our nature.

II. Religious Belief: Elements of a Wittgensteinian Account

In *The Emergence of Philosophy of Religion* Collins urges that we maintain the classical modern philosophies "at full strength," so as to provide a set of stable reference points for further reflection on religion.[9] As we noted at the outset Wittgenstein did not himself produce a comprehensive treatment of this subject matter; the present essay, accordingly, can be seen as exploring steps toward the development of a full-strength philosophy of religion in this tradition. I focus on three closely related topics identified by Collins: A) the status of philosophical speculation concerning God, B) the nature of religious faith, and C) the significance of theological mysteries.[10] In each case I begin by setting out remarks made by Wittgenstein and his followers. Then, keeping in mind the "standard of evidential connectivity" between philosophy of religion and general methodology, I undertake a critical assessment of their various points in light of the religious phenomena, as well as the resources of Wittgensteinian method.[11]

A. *Speculative Theories of God.* Throughout the history of interaction between Western philosophy and religious belief people have speculated concerning God. One task for philosophy of religion is to assess the resulting theories. According to Collins the classical moderns employed two lines of critique: one measuring internal validity by "epistemological and metaphysical means" and the other measuring "religious relevance."[12] Let us consider the contributions of Wittgenstein and his followers along these two lines.

Regarding the question of validity, it will be recalled that the *Tractatus* held all meaningful language to picture objects and their relations within the world. On any traditional understanding the term "God" does not refer to such an object. This meant that religious concerns, as indeed all concerns about what lies "beyond," relate to the realm of the "Mystical"—a realm about which we cannot speak, let alone develop theories. A correct philosophy must respect the limits of language and thus pass over God in silence (T, 6.522, 7).

In his mature philosophy Wittgenstein expands the concept of meaning; thus language about God is in principle possible. This does not mean, however, that *metaphysical theorizing* about God must be accepted at face value. For while Wittgenstein, as a philosopher, is not concerned to judge genuine linguistic practices he does raise important questions about this alleged practice. The author of the *Investigations* suspects *all* forms of metaphysics (not just the metaphysics of the *Tractatus*) of being mere oversimplifications of grammar, and thus of having no real point (PI, 116). Further, Wittgenstein is in particular unable to appreciate reasoning of the cosmological sort. Norman Malcolm tells us that Wittgenstein could understand a number of ideas of God—e.g., as Judge or Redeemer—"but the notion of a being making the world had no intelligibility for him at all."[13]

Wittgenstein's followers extend these lines of thought. According to Rush Rhees metaphysics is a "confusion;" and a question like "Where does the world come from?" contains an elmentary mistake—for "the world" is not the name of a specific collection, and it is only concerning objects or specific collections that questions about origins make sense.[14] Similarly, D. Z. Phillips says that while we inquire about the reason for the existence of this or that, it is difficult to know "what meaning could be given to 'a reason-for-the-existence-of-the-world.' "[15] Paul L. Holmer adds that concepts like "first cause" are "not genuine concepts," that they have little or no "working significance." For they depend, for example, on a completely generalized concept of "cause," whereas in fact concepts of "cause"—which are diverse among themselves— occur "only within specific domains." Thus the concepts of cosmological thinking, and indeed all speculative theory, are a matter of "philosophical creation," about which "we do not know how to argue." Such concepts have every appearance of being "arbitrary" and "gratuitous."[16]

When tested for religious relevance speculative theories of God again receive low marks. In the Lectures on Religious Belief Wittgenstein presents his subject matter as having a radically distinctive character. He says that a question about the existence of God will be "entirely different" from such a question about "any person or object" (LRB, 59): and that in spite of superficial similarities a picture of God (e.g., Michelangelo's picture of God as Creator) "has to be used in an entirely different way" from pictures of people and events (LRB, 63). Further he remarks that children are often told that they have to believe in God, that not to believe is "something bad;" this would hardly be expected in connection with the existence of an object of experience or theory (LRB, 59).

Remarks such as these are developed by a number of recent Wittgensteinians. Malcolm asks what a purely theoretical belief in God would be. Would a belief that was "completely non-affective" really be a belief in *God*?[17] Phillips adds that while one might say "So what?" regarding the idea of a first cause, one cannot say this regarding the idea of one's Creator.[18] Further, both Phillips and Rhees remark that it is misguided to speak of God as an "object;" for this obscures the fact that, in Phillips' words, "there is no theoretical understanding of the reality of God."[19] Seeing the world as God's world is not a matter of reaching a speculative conclusion or explanation. Rather it is, primarily, "dying to the world's way of regarding things," and thus coming to possess a distinctive "love of the world" and a distinctive "relationship to people and things."[20] Holmer too suggests that "there is little obvious connection, if any" between cosmological language and the language of religious faith.[21] Indeed such is the irrelevance of speculative schemes of all sorts that "denials of theism—even conceptual atheisms—are not necessarily denials of Christianity and Judaism."[22]

Let us now consider what may be said concerning these various points. It is certainly understandable that Wittgenstein, recalling the empty theorizing of his earlier period, should be suspicious of metaphysical speculation. It should be asked, however, whether all speculative theory is on a par with that of the *Tractatus*. In this regard it is striking that the present Wittgensteinian discussions contain many pronouncements but few actual examples. Indeed there does not appear to be a single adequately detailed critique of a theistic metaphysical scheme. This is, to put it mildly, rather extraordinary in a philosophical tradition which emphasizes taking a close look, rather than relying on suppositions. Thus in spite of present claims may it not turn out that theorists of God can develop concepts of "cause," "existence," and the like which do have working significance—a significance which is distinctive, but no poorer for that, by reason of those concepts' purpose, mode of formation, susceptibility to argumentation, etc? And if Wittgenstein or some of his followers find that the resulting schemes of thought have "no intelligibility "for them, may this not indicate not that speculative theorists are engaging in an inept form of science, but rather that there is an unbridged "intellectual distance" between those who do and those who do not think metaphysically? May there not here be, that is to say, a fundamental difference in forms of life? This is not to deny that the present tradition raises issues of great importance concerning the meaning and validity of speculative theories. But the possibilities just mentioned show that Wittgensteinians should be open to a reconsideration of the matter.

What now of the religious significance of speculative theories? The present writers argue persuasively that religious notions of God cannot be reduced to theoretical elements. Concepts which did not engage our affective and conative dimensions would indeed be religously irrelevant. But if this shows that language about God must be *partially* non-theoretical it does not show that it must be wholly so. It does not show, for example, that speculative schemes must be totally irrelevant to religious belief; nor that seeing God as Creator must be solely a matter of adopting certain attitudes and relations; nor again that the use of religious statements must be entirely different from the use of statements about people and events. Here one has a sense that Wittgenstein and his followers are perhaps presenting the grammar of their own faith—or what they can personally appreciate in faith— but not necessarily what such grammar must be for all. To consider this matter we need to undertake a fuller investigation of religious forms of life. This effort corresponds to another element in philosophy of religion as identified by Collins.

B. *The Natural History of Religious Faith*. This title is taken directly from *Emergence*. It is strikingly appropriate in the present context, for, as we have seen, Wittgenstein often refers to his own philosophical work as investigations in "natural history." Like Hume, Kant and Hegel before him, Wittgenstein eschews any goal of producing a "uniform and exhaustive definition of religion."[23] Indeed, he points out that there may be cases in which we do not know whether to call a belief religious or not (LRB, 58). However, his principal examples are familiar ones from the literature and practices of Christianity. In considering his discussion let us focus on two kinds of points, the first concerning the character and roots of religious belief, and the second concerning religion's foundational judgments.

According to Wittgenstein salient features of the grammar of religious belief—e.g., Creation, Resurrection and Last Judgment—reveal that they have a distinctive character. By comparison with ordinary and scientific beliefs religious ones have "entirely different connections" and "consequences" (LRB, 58, 59). For one thing we don't find the sort of disagreement in religion "where one person is *sure*...and the other says: 'Well, possibly' " (LRB, 56). Nor is it appropriate to say of a matter of faith,' "You only believe—oh well...' " (LRB, 60). That is, religious beliefs are not in the same realm as well confirmed or not so well confirmed matters of opinion. Hence the use of special terms in religion, terms like "faith" and "dogma" (LRB, 57). Connected with this is the fact that reasoning in religion "is an entirely different kind of reasoning" (LRB, 58). (Wittgenstein perhaps has in mind the practice of appealing to the authority of the Bible or one's church.) Again, religious "evidence" relates to religious beliefs in an entirely different way from the way in which scientific evidence relates to scientific beliefs (LRB, 56-57). In fact, anything that might be called scientific evidence for religion, and in particular for Christianity, must be regarded as "extremely flimsy" (LRB, 58). However, even if evidence of the scientific sort—e.g., the results of historical research—turned out to have the character of "indubitability," this would not convert the nonbeliever; for when it comes to matters of faith "the best scientific evidence is just nothing" (LRB, 56-57). The reason for this, says Wittgenstein, is that religion asks me to "change my whole life," and to "base enormous things" on its proposals (LRB, 57-58). Doing this is not the same as dispassionately accepting a hypothesis; rather, elements like fear, hope and trust—absent from scientific ways of thinking—are "part of the substance of the belief" (LRB, 56).

In light of the above it is not surprising to find that the roots of religious practices are also distinctive. In Wittgenstein's view these mainly include a range of profound human experiences. He does not speak of these so much in the Lectures on Religious Belief as in a lecture formally devoted to ethics. There he mentions the following: "wonder at the existence of the world," the experience of "feeling *absolutely* safe," and a sense of "guilt" (LE, 8, 10). These and similar experiences give rise to religious ways of thinking. Malcolm adds that Wittgenstein also "regarded religious belief as based on qualities of character and will."[24] Conspicuously absent from this account is any mention of an interest in grand-scale explanation or theorizing. Concerning the experience of wonder just noted a recent commentator remarks, "It is not an intellectual attainment but a stance of gratitude and joy before all there is."[25] And while Wittgenstein in the Lectures does speak of religious people seeing events as rewards or punishments (LRB, 54), he regards such explanations as products of individual and personal concerns, rather than as things for which there might be common intellectual warrant.

The above and related points are developed by recent Wittgensteinians. Regarding the nature of faith D. Z. Phillips continually stresses its difference from ordinary and scientific belief.[26] He acknowledges that a search for evidence in the scientific sense is sometimes appropriate in religion—e.g., when the authenticity of a holy relic is in question; but apart from such special cases we go wrong when a "religious belief is taken to be a hypothesis."[27] As earlier noted Phillips says that religious faith requires a profound change in one's life—a dying to the world—and also that it is bound up with love. The roots of such faith come in experiences and attitudes one has in relation to key aspects of human existence—e.g., "birth, death, joy, misery, despair, hope, fortune and misfortune."[28] However, "the man who construes religious belief as a theoretical affair distorts it."[29] Rush Rhees and Paul L. Holmer contribute similar points. Rhees says that to think religiously is "to have a certain view of human life" and all to which one is related. It is to turn all of this "from the temporal to the eternal."[30] And for Rhees as for Wittgenstein the eternal is bound up with "wonder at the world," a wonder "which easily passes into reverence" and into "gratitude"—but not into efforts at conceptual knowledge.[31] For Holmer a "religious life... consists of all kinds of things, from prayers to praise, from faith to hope, from patience to obedience, and from loving God to loving one's neighbor."[32] It also involves certain "outlooks," "theories" and "explanations."[33] The latter, however, are "somewhat piecemeal" in nature, and "quite different in intent" from corresponding elements in natural science and other disciplines. Rather than "resolve a dispassionate query" a religious explanation "is a direct use of pathos." By means of it one "seeks a justification for one's life;" one seeks to know oneself and everything else in relation to one's God.[34]

On the question of religion's foundational judgments Wittgenstein and his followers are much briefer. In the context of a discussion of faith in personal survival Wittgenstein makes comments which recall some of the general ones noted earlier. Sometimes, he says, the issue between a believer and a non-believer "won't be a question at all of more or less knowledge, so that [they] can come together"—i.e., reach agreement according to shared procedures. "Sometimes it will be a question of experience," so that the believer might ultimately say to the non-believer, " 'Wait another 10 years' " (LRB, 63). Some people, says Wittgenstein, would find the believer's remark acceptable, while others would find it totally unacceptable. And "there would really be great differences" between the two sides—differences about what is ultimately to count as reasonable in human thought, judgment and expectation (LRB, 64). Moreover such differences—which Wittgenstein apparently feels crop up frequently in connection with religion—cannot be resolved by appeal to any wider criteria. Here, that is to say, efforts at justification must come to an end.

Phillips and Holmer, if anything, are even less sympathetic toward efforts at supporting religious forms of thought. According to Phillips "criteria for distinguishing between the real and the unreal" vary from language-game to language-game; thus "there can be no *general* justification of religion."[35] Holmer warns against the idea that "there is a 'foundation'—an abstract and general 'foundation'—for theology and everything else."[36] For Christians there is nothing more basic than *"Consummatum est*. Something was settled and is therefore ready...sin and death are vanquished, God is in Christ, and Christ has been born, has lived, has died, and has been raised from the dead." These taken together form "the foundation" for Christian belief.[37]

We find in these remarks many interesting suggestions about the natural history of religious faith—suggestions which might be further pursued, and often are pursued by our authors. However, in light of the main interests of the present essay a number of critical questions are in order. Regarding foundational issues, it may be granted that there is no completely general mode of justification, nor a common foundation for all language-games. Still it may be asked whether our authors isolate what is, in Wittgenstein's sense, foundational. Holmer calls the elements of the *Consummatum est "the foundation."* But do not these and all other theological beliefs contain implicit suppositions or assumptions—in particular, that reality is not exhausted by the types of thing that are directly available to human comprehension, i.e., the physical and measurable? In this connection we might recall Holmer's earlier remark about the irrelevance of speculative schemes, including "conceptual atheism." Can he be quite right about this, given that conceptual atheism presumably involves a rejection of the foundational supposition just mentioned? Further, supposing that it is possible to develop an alternative conceptual scheme, would this not be a way for believers to resist the atheistic one? Indeed, would this scheme not support believers' basic assumptions about reality? The whole topic of the foundations of religious forms of life is in need of further development.

Concerning the character of faith itself it should be asked whether Wittgensteinian philosophers do justice to the theoretical strand among religious interests. Granted that experiences and concerns of a personal sort may be the primary roots of faith, are these not—at least in some believers—intertwined with an interest in grand-scale explanation? Do not some believers as believers seek a comprehensive, reasoned account of the world in relation to God, rather than being content with a sense of wonder and certain personal and piecemeal outlooks?[38] Could anything other than a priori stipulation—so foreign to Wittgensteinian methodology—exclude a concern of the present sort from the realm of religious phenomena? Finally, regarding religious dogmas themselves—e.g., Creation and Last Judgment—do these not function in the thinking of at least some believers in ways that approximate statements of "how things stand"? Do they not have some of the same kinds of "connections" and "consequences"? To become clearer about these points, especially the latter, we must further explore the grammar of theological statements. This inquiry too parallels a topic in *Emergence*.

C. *The Use of Theological Pictures*. No thinker who takes religious faith seriously holds that its doctrines can be treated as ordinary statements. On the side of faith itself they are regarded as formulations of unfathomable mystery, which nevertheless is communicated to humankind. A proper task for philosophy of religion, as reconstructed by Collins, is to elaborate "the human meaning of religious mystery."[39] For Wittgensteinians this means describing the use or uses of religious "pictures." Let us begin by considering their accounts of certain examples, then proceed to questions about pictures' assessment.

The language of "pictures" recalls the theory of the *Tractatus*. It is clear, however, that Wittgenstein means something very different here. Indeed, when he says of a theological statement that "it uses a picture" (LRB, 71), he seems to mean precisely that it functions in some way other than to say "how things stand." Certainly religious statements do not represent literally. If they did, says Wittgenstein, we should have to conclude in connection with the statement "God's eye sees everything" that it makes sense to inquire about God's eyebrows (LRB, 71). To the question what then is the function of religious pictures we are given a variety of answers. The examples which are most fully discussed in the Lectures are those of Ressurection and Last Judgment. Wittgenstein variously says of these pictures that they give "guidance" for the believer's life, that they "regulate" his life and that they serve to "admonish" him (LRB, 53, 54, 56). The experiences mentioned in the lecture on ethics also relate to certain pictures—or, as Wittgenstein calls them in that lecture, "similes" and "allegories." The experience of wonder at the world Wittgenstein associates with the picture of God creating; the feeling of absolute safety he relates to the image of being in the hands of God; and the experience of guilt he says finds expression in terms of God as disapproving judge (LE, 9-10). Regarding the use of these similes or pictures the following suggestions can be made.[40] The picture of God as Creator focuses the believer's awe and enjoins love and respect for the world; the simile involving God's hands induces a sense of trust; and the picture of God as Judge again admonishes the believer—and also serves to warn and to explain. (Concerning the latter it will be recalled that Wittgenstein says that fear can be "part of the substance" of a religious belief [LRB, 56], and that believers sometimes regard events in their lives as rewards or punishments [LRB, 54].) Finally, the image of God's all-seeing eye issues a promise and, once again, a warning.[41] It should be noted, however, that although Wittgenstein expresses some hesitancy about the case of Last Judgment (see LRB, 63), he in general finds no comparison between the grammars of religious pictures and statements of fact. As earlier mentioned, he says of the Creation picture, for example, that it "has to be used in an entirely different way" (LRB, 63).

D. Z. Phillips and other Wittgensteinians offer similar analyses. For Phillips, it will be recalled, seeing the world as God's world involves relating oneself in love to people and things. One who does this finds a significance in his life that cannot be destroyed even by death. This, says Phillips, is the point of religious pictures of "eternity" and "immortality": to reassure the believer that his life is "not rendered pointless by death."[42] Rush Rhees adds that the notion of immortality is connected with "an attitude of 'trust' in God."[43] Paul L. Holmer discerns a range of uses of theological statements. The language of faith "straightens [the believer's] dispositions, and shakes him loose from worldly and transitory loyalties;" it tells him to steel himself against temptation and to "refer everything...completely to God's love and care."[44] Once again, however, there is no mention of uses of language which say "how things stand."

Given the distinctive character of religious statements is it possible to assess their adequacy? Wittgenstein approaches this question when he says, "The whole weight may be in the picture" (LRB, 72). There appear to be two aspects to this point. One is that religious pictures are so deeply rooted in peoples' lives that one is not "able to substitute anything else" (LRB, 71). For example, even if the point of the statement "You shall live forever" is to reassure the believer, this is not likely to be achieved if one substitutes "Your life has permanent significance." And if someone says of a case like this, "He's only changing the words," Wittgenstein's reply is, "What more could he do?" (LRB, 72). The other aspect to the point about pictures' weight is that there is no comparing a religious picture with its "object." Recalling his childhood instruction Wittgenstein notes that with pictures of God there were not "the same consequences as with pictures of aunts. I wasn't shown [that which the picture pictured]" (LRB, 59, brackets in original text). And in the lecture on ethics he points out that if we "try to drop the simile" and "state the facts which stand behind it, we find that there are no such facts" (LE, 10). This of course suggests difficult questions about whether we can speak of the truth or falsity of religious pictures. The difficulty is not lost on Wittgenstein. At one point he says of a believer, "Perhaps now he sees he was wrong." Then, stopping short, he asks (but does not attempt to answer), "What sort of remark is this?" (LRB, 71).

Wittgenstein's followers develop the above themes. Holmer stresses the importance for religion of theologians' staying with the Biblical story. Their task, he says, is "not to change the story," but to express it with vividness and freshness.[45] In particular, theologians should avoid "substituting general views, supernaturalistic, scholastic, ontological, or secular." It is a mistake to suppose that schemes of these sorts—which involve only "idle set[s] of speculations"—could convey the religious meaning as well, let alone that they could convey it better.[46] Phillips discusses the "weight" of religious pictures, and also addresses the concern about truth. The idea of "corresponding to reality" must, he says, be discussed in light of the grammar or "mode of discourse" in question.[47] This affects the meaning of "truth" as applied to religious pictures. For an individual to say that "he thinks these beliefs are true" is for him to say that "he can live by them," or that "they constitute food for him."[48] On the other hand, for an individual to reject a religious belief is not for him to discover that it fails to correspond to a realm of fact; rather it is for him to say, "[I]t does not regulate my life; I do not adhere to it; I do not aspire to what it stands for."[49] Thus, for example, a believer may find he is nourished by a picture of immortality, while a non-believer does not allow images of the world as God's world to regulate his life. But in neither case does the question of truth involve any sort of "comparison."

Once again we find in Wittgenstein and his followers a number of interesting points. They are not the first to emphasize the pictorial character of religious language, but they offer a distinctive means of coming to philosophical terms with that character. However, their views also invite a number of critical comments. Granted that religious pictures function principally in such ways as focusing awe, reassuring and warning, may there not be, at least for some believers, uses—or dimensions of use—which belong to the fact-stating variety? Indeed, *must* there not be such dimensions of use if certain others which are important to many believers are to be possible? That is, if the picture of God as Judge is to *warn* (not merely to admonish), must it not be part of the picture's meaning that *Judgment will come*;[50] if the image of being in God's hands is to induce a sense of *trust* (not merely to relate to a feeling of safety), must it not be part of the image's meaning that *true needs will be provided for*; and so on? Statements of "how things stand"—however they are to be described in the present context—cannot here be ignored by conscientious Wittgensteinians.

Related to this point are questions about the assessment of theological statements. Is it not the case that, again at least for some believers, Phillips' account of religious truth is inadequate? Further, for these believers, can there not be an interest (even if not exercised *while* statements are functioning in their primary religious modes) in passing beyond sheer allegory and imagery to more highly conceptualized forms of expression? And, notwithstanding Holmer's comment about the idleness of general schemes, may there not here be a genuine effort at "comparison"—not, of course, an attempt to empirically verify theological statements; but nevertheless an attempt to find some measure of intellectual warrant? Here again it emerges, in light of the tradition's own professed aims, that the general thrust of Wittgensteinian philosophy of religion needs to be reconsidered.

III. Wittgenstein and Realistic Theism

An application of themes from James Collins' *The Emergence of Philosophy of Religion* introduces an order into Wittgensteinian reflections on religion. Our study suggests that this tradition offers significant contributions to the field, and has the potential to offer still more significant ones. However, we have also found, in light of Wittgenstein's aims and methods and the religious phenomena themselves, that on a number of key points the present philosophers need to reconsider or develop their views. Further, it can be seen that on each of these points the philosophy of realistic theism might have an impact on the Wittgensteinian account—might serve, in Collins' words, to widen the range of effective positions open. Let us review the points in question, together with realism's potential impact, then discuss the conditions which must be met if this philosophy is to influence Wittgensteinian thought.

Our first critical point related to the intrinsic meaningfulness of speculative theories of God. In spite of the claims of Wittgensteinians no adequate analysis of such a theory has yet been produced. Realists might provide a detailed example or examples of theistic schemes. They also would be in primary position to describe the grammars of these schemes, together with the forms of life—the speculative concerns—in which they find their roots and point.

The second line of discussion concerned the foundations of religious practices, which so far have been little explored by Wittgensteinians. While there is no single line of justification common to all language-games, realistic philosophers might show that the conclusions of theistic reflection would, if accepted, provide a justification for certain suppositions of faith (in particular, that reality is not limited to the material), and also provide a means by which opposed conceptual schemes might be rationally resisted.

A third difficulty related to the ignoring by Wittgensteinians of a theoretical strand among the roots of religious language—language, for example, about God as Creator or the world as being God's world. Realistic theism might serve as a model of this interest, showing how reflective questioning about the world can be elaborated in a measured way, and also how such questioning can be related to and intertwined with the more personal and affective concerns in a life of faith.

Our fourth critical point concerned the uses or dimensions of use of theological statements. Wittgensteinians have neglected a fact-stating dimension, which nevertheless seems required if certain other dimensions important to many believers are to be intelligible. A theology which incorporates theism would place this dimension in the light, as well as develop highly conceptualized formulations of certain religious doctrines—e.g., God as *Ipsum Esse Subsistens*. Realistic philosophy might contribute to a Wittgensteinian account by indicating how, despite the uniqueness of their ontological referent and the high degree of analogicity in their terms, theological statements can follow grammatical rules (especially regarding the possibilities of assessment) which place them in the fact-stating family.

None of this is to say that realistic theism is *necessary* for a life of faith. Religion's assumptions, for example, might be recommended by simple persuasion, or by suggestions that the hearer "wait 10 years;" and a saying of "how things stand" might in the present context remain a matter of undeveloped intention, with the forms of religious language employed by a believer or community tailored to other, more practical purposes. Nonetheless it seems clear that realistic philosophy can have great importance for at least some people's faith; and thus that Wittgensteinians, as they come to note this importance, should amend their descriptions of the religious phenomena accordingly. In this way, it may be remarked, there would be an impact not only on Wittgensteinian philosophy of religion, but also on the developing Wittgensteinian account of human nature. Philosophers in this tradition would come to acknowledge concerning theistic speculation, "This language-game too is played."

What now is necessary if realistic philosophy is to influence the present tradition? The most general response is that it must be prepared to engage Wittgenstein and his followers on their own ground. It must, that is to say, take seriously the task of exploring its foundational assumptions, its mode of concept-formation, and so on. It must try to show, contrary to the suspicions of the writers we have studied, how its metaphysical scheme is no mere arbitrary and gratuitous invention, or an oversimplification of the grammar of everyday language. Considerations of space permit only a brief mention of two suggestions along these lines. First, while if accepted its conclusions would support certain assumptions of the practices of faith, realistic philosophy itself has foundational suppositions which are not subject to *any* direct justification, within this language-game or any other. Examples would be that being is intelligible, and that reality's most pervasive features can to some degree be discerned and described. Secondly, while metaphysical terminology is of course highly general, it does not result from a mere further abstraction along the same line as that of, c. g., natural science; rather it requires a qualitatively different insight or movement of thought. Because of this a term like "being" or "cause" is, in Wittgenstein's terminology, a family resemblance term. Its development and use in the context of realistic metaphysics is one specific instance among many, an instance having various relations with the others without being an over-generalized version of any of them. If points like the present can be developed with cogency realistic philosophy should indeed affect the Wittgensteinian accounts. And, it is worth noting, in doing so it would be affecting this tradition in its historical actuality, rather than, as in connection with the classical moderns, calling for a revision of views propounded a century and a half or more ago.

Let us consider, in conclusion, how the thinking of realistic theists might itself be affected by the encounter with Wittgenstein. It is hardly to be expected that realistic philosophers should accept as the final word on their enterprise, "This language-game too is played"! They will want, as Collins puts it, to "reinterpret the note of comprehensiveness,"[51] which sounds through Wittgensteinian philosophy as much as any other. They will want to develop their own distinctive account in philosophy of religion, an account of God, the human person and the religious relationship which is based on realistic principles and contains theistic metaphysics as a centerpiece.[52] However, in light of our study it may be suggested that as they do so they will find that their own thinking has been clarified—in particular concerning the nature and foundations of their metaphysical scheme, and concerning the precise types of significance, and limits on the significance, which this scheme can have for religious faith. Realists will find, that is, that they have profited from their encounter with Wittgenstein, even as they have made contributions to his very different mode of philosophizing. This too, it will be recalled, responds to an *Emergence* theme.

Notes

[1] James Collins, *The Emergence of Philosophy of Religion* (New Haven: Yale University Press: 1967). See especially Chapters 9 and 10.

[2] *Ibid.*, p. 430. See also pp. 420-22, 431.

[3] *Ibid.*, pp. 350-51. The following are the titles given by Collins for the six common issues he identifies: 1) Religion Within the Scope of Philosophy; 2) Religionizing the Theory of God; 3) The Ruptured Alliance: Morality and Religion; 4) The Natural History of Religious Faith; 5) The Mystery of the Revealing and Saving God; 6) The Religious Concretion: Symbol, Cult, and Community.

[4] *Ibid.*, pp. x-xi.

[5] *Ibid.*, By "realistic theism" or "realistic philosophy" Collins means "a philosophy which is realistic in its metaphysical and epistemological bases, and theistic in its ultimate interpretation of human experience." *Ibid.*, p. 423. He has primarily in mind theism of the Scholastic and in particular the Thomistic sort. *Ibid.*, p. 437n. However, he also refers to Whitehead and process philosophy. *Ibid.*, p. 499n. The present study will be neutral as to the relative merits of different types of theism.

[6] See in particular Norman Malcolm, *Ludwig Wittgenstein A Memoir* (New York: Oxford University Press, 1967). Wittgenstein's mother was a Roman Catholic, and he was baptized in the Catholic church. However, he was, by his own account, not a religious believer. He told Malcolm that "in his youth he had been contemptuous" of religion, but that in later years he "saw the possibility" of it. *Ibid.*, p. 70.

[7] L. Wittgenstein, *Lectures and Conversations on Aesthetics, Psychology and Religious Belief*, ed. Cyril Barrett (Berkeley and Los Angeles: University of California Press, 1967). The Lectures on Religious Belief date from around 1938. Although Wittgenstein did not himself check his students' notes, they are commonly regarded as accurately representing his meaning.
In the text below remarks from the Lectures will be designated in parentheses, by LRB, followed by the page number. Other internal references to Wittgenstein's works will be as follows: 1) *Tractatus Logico-Philosophicus*, trans. D. F. Pears & B. F. McGuiness (London: Routledge & Kegan Paul, 1961). (T, followed by the proposition number.) 2) *Philosophical Investigations*, 3rd ed., trans. G. E. M. Anscombe (New York: The Macmillan Co., 1968). (PI, followed by the section number of Part I, or the page number of Part II.) 3) *Zettel*, ed. G. E. M. Anscombe and G. H. von Wright, trans. G. E. M. Anscombe (Berkeley and Los Angeles: University of California Press, 1967). (Z, followed by the section number.) 4) *On Certainty*, ed. G. E. M. Anscombe and G. H. von Wright, trans. Denis Paul and G. E. M. Anscombe (New York and Evanston: J. & J. Harper Editions, 1969). (C, followed by the section number.) 5) "Wittgenstein's Lecture on Ethics," *Philosophical Review* LXXIV (Jan., 1965). (LE, followed by the page number.)

[8] Collins, *The Emergence of Philosophy of Religion*, p. 420.

[9] *Ibid.*, p. 416.

[10] These correspond to the second, the fourth and the fifth from Collins' list. See note 3 above. Limitations of space have dictated a selection of topics. The three I explore form, I believe, a natural grouping; they are also the ones on which realistic theism might have the most immediate impact.

[11] See Collins, *The Emergence of Philosophy of Religion*, p. 422. It should be noted that Wittgenstein gave the Lectures on Religious Belief relatively early in his mature period, and thus that he might have produced improved analyses (as well as more comprehensive ones) if he had returned to the subject in later years. It should also be noted that while those I call "Wittgenstein's followers" express a number of similar views they do not form a monolithic group. Each has certain distinctive interests and points of emphasis.

[12] *Ibid.*, p. 362.

[13] Malcolm, *Ludwig Wittgenstein A Memoir*, p. 71.

[14] Rush Rhees, *Without Answers* (New York: Schocken Books, 1969), pp. 111, 118.

[15] D. Z. Phillips, *Faith and Philosophical Enquiry* (New York: Schocken Books, 1971), p. 44.

[16] Paul L. Holmer, *The Grammar of Faith* (San Francisco: Harper and Row, 1978), pp. 170-71, 165.

[17] Norman Malcolm, "Is it a Religious Belief that 'God Exists'?" in John Hick, ed., *Faith and the Philosophers* (New York: St. Martin's, 1964), p. 107.

[18] Phillips, *Faith and Philosophical Enquiry*, p. 45.

[19] *Ibid.*, pp. 60, 26. See Rhees, *Without Answers*, pp. 114, 116.

[20] Phillips, *Faith and Philosophical Enquiry*, p. 56.

[21] Holmer, *The Grammar of Faith*, p. 170.

[22] *Ibid.*, p. 161.

[23] Collins, *The Emergence of Philosophy of Religion*, p. 426.

[24] Malcolm, *Ludwig Wittgenstein A Memoir*, p. 72.

[25] W. Donald Hudson, *Wittgenstein and Religious Belief* (London: Macmillan, 1975), p. 11.

[26] See, e. g., Phillips, *Faith and Philosophical Enquiry*, pp. 17, 63, 70-72.

[27] *Ibid.*, pp. 87-88.

[28] *Ibid.*, p. 97.

[29] *Ibid.*, p. 33.

[30] Rhees, *Without Answers*, p. 126.

[31] *Ibid.*, p. 119.

[32] Holmer, *The Grammar of Faith*, p. 178.

[33] *Ibid.*, pp. 69, 177.

[34] *Ibid.*, p. 69.

[35] Phillips, *Faith and Philosophical Enquiry*, pp. 70, 72.

[36] Holmer, *The Grammar of Faith*, p. 93.

[37] *Ibid.*, p. 109.

[38] In one place Holmer uncharacteristically appears to acknowledge the present point. See *Ibid.*, p. 38.

[39] Collins, *The Emergence of Philosophy of Religion*, p. 395.

[40] These suggestions do not come directly from Wittgenstein, but are constructions from things he does say.

[41] Another use of theological statements, alluded to at *Philosophical Investigations*, 373, is a "grammatical" use—i. e., an indication of the sorts of things that it either does or does not make sense to say of God.

[42] D. Z. Phillips, *Death and Immortality* (London: Macmillan, 1970), p. 50.

[43] Rhees, *Without Answers*, p. 112.

[44] Holmer, *The Grammar of Faith*, pp. 175, 71, 19. See also p. 53.

[45] *Ibid.*, p. 36.

[46] *Ibid.*, p. 49.

[47] Phillips, *Faith and Philosophical Enquiry*, pp. 89, 63. Compare Rhees, *Without Answers*, p. 132, and Wittgenstein, *Zettel*, 55.

[48] Phillips, *Death and Immortality*, p. 71.

[49] Phillips, *Faith and Philosophical Enquiry*, p. 114.

[50] On this point see Patrick Sherry, *Religion, Truth and Language-Games* (London: Macmillan, 1977), p. 15.

[51] Collins, *The Emergence of Philosophy of Religion*, p. 432.

[52] *Ibid.*, p. 447.

17.

JACQUES MARITAIN ON THE FUTURE: IN SEARCH OF A CONCRETE HISTORICAL IDEAL

Vincent C. Punzo

The editor of a 1968 symposium on hope observed, "But Kant's third question: 'What may I hope?', which has received only sporadic attention by theologians until now, appears at last to be coming into its own."[1] The question can be said to have come into its own in recent years not only in theology, but in the intellectual community at large, as can be seen with the beginning of a journal such as *Alternative Futures*, with the growing interest in utopian and dystopian literature, and with the interests of social scientists, philosophers, and theologians in questions concerning the impact of technology on the future of the human community. This essay will concentrate on the contribution which the socio-political writings of Jacques Maritain have to make as a response to Kant's third question. Although these writings pre-date the most recent coming to prominence of the question, there is a concern with the future running through them that marks them as a significant resource for contemporary discussion of this question.

Both his conception of the significance of historical development to the understanding of one's present situation and his commitment to bring the Gospel message to bear on the social order give the future an important place in Maritain's political thought.

> The present is but a limit, a line of demarcation between the past and the future. So we can understand the present only in terms of the past or in terms of the future. That is why I think it would be advisable for Christians to dedicate in their own way a bit of meditation to the future.[2]

Meditation on the future is helpful to understanding the present because the true significance of an idea or of a movement can best be understood when considered in terms of the future toward which it is moving, "when it is big with the future."[3] As temporal, the present is a movement toward a future. Hence, if this present is to be understood, it should be reflected upon from a perspective that seeks to uncover the underlying dynamic principle of its movement and the future toward which it appears to be moving. Beyond this interest in understanding the present, there is the following question that leads Maritain to concern himself with the future: "How could men who believe in the Gospel as far as eternal life is concerned not believe in it for life here below—how could they resign themselves to men's earthly hope in the Gospel being disappointed?"[4]

The key ingredients in the attempt to avoid the disappointment of "men's earthly hope," are presented in the following statement in which Maritain spells out what must be done philosophically by "those Christians who are turned toward the future and who hope...for...a new Christianly inspired civilization."[5]

> The Christians of whom I am speaking have to establish and develop a sound philosophy of modern history, as well as to separate from the genuine growth of time, from the genuine progress of human consciousness and civilization, the deadly errors which have preyed upon them, and the tares which are also growing among the wheat and which foster the wickedness of the time. In order to conceive our own concrete historical image of what is to be hoped for in our age, we have to determine and take into account, as an existential frame of reference, the basic typical features which characterize the structure of our age, in other words the *historical climate* or the *historical constellation* by which the existence and the activity of the human community is conditioned today.[6]

The specific point of focus for this exposition will be on Maritain's development of the concrete historical ideal "of what is to be hoped for in our age." The exposition will be divided into three major sections. The first will consider what is meant by a concrete historical ideal and the methodological factors involved in the attempt to "develop a sound philosophy of modern history" as the rational foundation for the development of the ideal. A second section will concentrate on the critical evaluation of the modern age that is directed to separating "from...the genuine progress of human consciousness and civilization, the deadly errors which have preyed upon them." A final section will center in the content of the ideal and the resources that need to be brought into play in working toward its realization.

I shall not deal with Maritain's distinction between the new Christendom toward which the concrete ideal for the modern age is directed and the Christendom of the Holy Roman Empire which he rejects as being neither appropriate nor morally desirable in the modern age, however appropriate it may have been to its own time and situation.[7] Rather, I shall limit the exposition to that aspect of his treatment which he has in mind, when he says that although he appeals to Christians because he himself is a Christian, his analysis and critique of the modern age are grounded in reason and are thus open to Christian and non-Christian alike.[8] He addresses the analysis and critique to Christians because he is concerned to call them specifically to their social responsibility and to help them meet this responsibility in a reflective manner. He also thinks that they have their own unique resources to bring to bear on the problems and fatalities of the modern age. The last section of this paper will point to such resources, but will not go into a detailed and full account of them.

I

Unlike a utopia which tries to achieve a vision of absolute social and political perfection apart from reference to the exigencies and possibilities of any given historical period, a concrete historical ideal is developed out of a consideration of the specific possibilities for human good found in the tendencies of an historical period. Such an ideal is a "dynamic image" rather than a detailed blueprint of the future. It is meant to provide a sense of the direction that must be given the forces of an historical period and a sense of the powers that must be employed if the age is to move toward a more humane future. Although there is a thrust toward realization in an ideal, its significance does not lie exclusively in whether or not the future toward which it is pointing is ever fully achieved. Such an ideal "is to be realized as a movement and a line of force."[9] Whether realized or not in the future, it helps guide human life in the present by opening that present to possibilities for human good which would have been absent, had no attempt been made to challenge this present from the perspective of the future toward which it ought to be directed. An ideal can thus be realized as a movement and a line of force in so far as human beings use that ideal as a principle whereby they will do what they can in the present to regulate their lives in a manner appropriate to the possibilities envisioned by the ideal.[10] So understand, it is "realizable not as something made, but as something on the way to being made."[11]

The development of a sound philosophy of modern history that is needed for the development of an ideal appropriate to the modern age must avoid two traps concerning the relationship between history and eternity. It must avoid, on the one hand, the abandonment of the eternal, and, on the other hand, a freezing of the eternal into a given historical period which would entail a denial of the process character of history. The Christian's task is to think of "the passing changing world in the light of eternity."[12] Maritain refers to those who fall into the first trap as the "Sheep of Panurge."[13] They "rather suffer the world than think it; they are acted upon by the world and do not act upon it otherwise than as instruments of the very forces of the world; they glide like fluttering leaves or sodden tree trunks on the water down the stream of history."[14] They usually have their hearts in the right place as regards social and political issues, but they tend to botch things up when they try to develop an intellectual defense of what they are about or when they undertake to realize what their hearts tell them they ought to do. In their concern to be up-to-date, such people fail to use the resources of the human mind to grasp the unchanging principles of being that would enable them to gain a critical perspective on the present and to act within it as real agents rather than as instruments of prevailing fads.[15] Those who fall into the trap of identifying eternity with a given period of history are referred to as the "Ruminators of the Holy Alliance."[16] This position is able to maintain a certain tension between itself and the fads of the moment. Unfortunately, it is tension based on a confusion of eternity with one's own attachment to a certain frozen period in the past. The present historical period is rejected without any attempt to understand it.[17] An embalmed past is used as a refuge from confronting the task of alleviating human misery and injustice in one's own day.[18] The position is connected with a failure to realize that the work of human reason is not restricted to a passive recognition of an order created by God. Reason as practical has also a contribution to offer to the making of the world. "The whole order of human life is not ready-made in nature and in things; it is an Order of Freedom; it has not just to be discovered and accepted: it has also to be made."[19] Reason's role is to continue, and to collaborate with, God's action by contributing to a fashioning of the contingent and to renewing the world of time in conformity with the demands of eternity.[20] The Ruminators of the Holy Alliance fail to use reason in such a constructive way because "a certain narrowness of heart prevents them from 'knowing the work of men' and doing justice to the work of God in time and history."[21] In the last analysis, Maritain finds that both the Sheep and the Ruminators share a fundamental and essential weakness. Each, because of its own peculiar zeal, fails to make a concern with truth its highest priority. It is not truth, but prudence that is the main concern of the Ruminators, "to bar the way to threatening dangers, to lock the doors, to build dikes." The Sheep are moved primarily by a "Deference to public opinion: to do as everyone does, at least as all those who are not fossils."[22]

The mediation between eternal principles and changing historical times and climates that Maritain seeks is to be developed through a process of analogical predication in which the principles grasped by the mind are seen to be in themselves eternal and unvarying, but are applied to the changing historical situations in different ways so that those situations may be brought to conform to the demands of the principles in ways appropriate to the distinctiveness of the different situations. Such analogical predication requires that one move beyond a conception of the processes and phases of history that is purely empirical and toward a rational philosophical conception, one that tries to capture the underlying dynamism of such processes and phases.[23]

Maritain's attempt to develop such a rational philosophical conception of the modern age is predicated on the view that the movement of any historical period involves both advance and dissipation and that "both exist at the same time, *to one degree or another.*"[24] He holds that Christians who engage in a wholesale rejection of the modern age are being as foolish as the rationalist historians who identified the Middle Ages with darkness and error.[25] Similar to every other age or civilization, the modern world "contains a positive element of ontological tension and vitality... But this positive element, good in itself, is accompanied by a privation."[26] Hence, the attempt to find a concrete historical ideal appropriate to the modern age consists in trying to find and nurture its "positive element of ontological tension and vitality." So understood, the ideal is not imposed on an age as an alien force totally extrinsic to it. It is rather the discovery of those dimensions of the age that hold promise for a better future, with the discovery functioning as a call to action to do what one can to build a future on such dimensions.

Maritain seeks to distinguish the positive elements from the errors and evils of the age through an exploration of "the concrete logic of the events" of the age.[27] Such an exploration seeks to understand the historical climate of the age by uncovering at its basis "the dialectic of the concrete, conceived as an historical development due to the internal logic of a principle, or of an idea, in action in the human concrete."[28] Viewing the movement of history as "the development of ideas or logical loads incarnate in time," Maritain seeks to understand the modern age by discovering in its movement the underlying intellectual outlook on life that gives unity and coherence to the age as constituting its spirit, its principle of movement.[29] A study of the philosophers of the period is of utmost importance to this approach because they are often like mirrors reflecting the deepest currents obscurely at work in the human spirit during different historical epochs, thereby bringing these currents to consciousness and making them available for critical analysis.[30]

The following statement of a tri-dimensional approach to the study of a philosophical position is an excellent summary of the way in which Maritain analyzes the ideas of an age as a clue to the underlying dynamism of that age.

> Three things must be distinguished in the consideration of any philosophy: first, the sentimental values which lure the reason or the simply human aspirations to which its adherents actually, even though unwittingly, respond; secondly, what the philosophy itself states; thirdly, what it *does* and the results to which it leads.[31]

Maritain's socio-political writings do not offer a simple, straightforward exposition of the positions taken by philosophers. They concentrate rather on the first and third approaches as instruments to help in the understanding of an age. The first approach seeks to clarify the age's underlying value orientation by distinguishing within the complexity of such an orientation between those elements that constitute legitimate human aspirations and those that constitute these aspirations gone astray. The third approach is at the very heart of his "dialectic of the concrete." It seeks to determine the existential meaning and significance of the "logical loads" incarnate in a period by noting the repercussions of such logical loads or principles as these are worked out in the actual movement of events.

II

As Maritain moves to his critique of the modern age with respect to its socio-political legacy, he is concerned to avoid the errors made by those in the sixteenth and seventeenth centuries who undertook to criticize modern science on behalf of Christian principles. Because they failed to make necessary discriminations, these critics confused the legitimate growth of modern science with the philosophical errors that accompanied this growth.[32] Maritain's more discriminating critique of the socio-political legacy of the modern age leads him to uncover much in this age which is worth preserving and nurturing. Speaking of this age, he says, "But this world has been great and has done great works."[33] Any account of these great works must keep in mind Maritain's point that any historical period involves both advance and dissipation. It is possible to list on paper these great works in isolation from the underlying errors and shortcomings of the age. However, as found in the actual movement of the age, these works are themselves infected with such errors and weaknesses, and are thus perverted. The development of a concrete historical ideal is directed to uncovering both these great works and the source of their perversion, and indicating what is to be done if these works are to be freed from such perversion so that human beings may enjoy them in their proper reality.

The advance that seems to underlie all the other achievements of the modern period is that whereby the temporal or secular order has come of age in the sense of asserting a value and reality of its own that is not reducible to being a mere instrument for a supernatural order.[34] Within the context of such coming of age, human beings have come to consciousness of themselves as beings whose task it is to transform the temporal world within which they live. They have been in the process of transforming their world from earliest times, and will continue to do so in their day-to-day labors. The modern advance consists in their coming to a direct and explicit consciousness of themselves as "activator[s] of the world," whereas in the past they changed the world through their labors unconsciously, as it were, "like moss or lichen in the process of invading a piece of land little by little."[35] Such consciousness can be said "somewhat allegorically" to have begun to take shape with Descartes' declaration that human beings must master and possess nature, but it was left to Marx to render this consciousness fully explicit.[36]

As it has attempted to carry out the demands of this consciousness, the modern age has made itself the great age of ways and means. It has made significant progress in the development of instrumentalities for living. Maritain refers to such progress as "material" progress, taking the word "in its widest philosophical extent, for the equipment of culture has progressed not only in the order of the scientific and industrial means of exploiting nature, but also in the order of intellectual, artistic, and spiritual means and techniques."[37]

There have also been advances in the moral areas of life. Practices such as slavery and torture now appear to lead to spontaneous feelings of revulsion among more people than they did in the past and are officially disapproved, at least on a verbal level.[38] A more significant advance during the modern age was the growing realization in the eighteenth century of the importance of rights, as distinct from the ancient and medieval emphasis on obligations and duties. Without denying the suffering and disorder that was tied in with such growing moral awareness and the French Revolution's proclamation of the ideals of liberty, equality, and fraternity, Maritain is not willing to surrender the emphasis on rights or to stifle the search for the realization of these ideals. "One would need to have the soul of a slave to wish for the destruction of this very sense of freedom and justice."[39] Finally, underlying such socio-political tendencies of the modern age is not only the coming of age of the temporal but also a "*prise de conscience* of self." Human beings have come to a more explicit consciousness of the interiority of their lives as revealed in science, art, poetry, and in the very expressions and articulations of their own passions and vices.[40] The coming to consciousness of the working person and of the working community that developed in the nineteenth century is to be included in this *prise de conscience*. Without denying the economic significance of development, Maritain holds that its moral significance is greater. It represents a step toward liberty and dignity for those persons and that community closest to the material foundations of life who have been exploited and humiliated throughout history.[41]

Granted such advances, the modern age appears to be a paradise that fulfills all that humanity could hope for. It is at this point, as we try to evaluate the modern age, that Maritain's notion that any age involves both advance and dissipation is helpful.

> One of the fundamental axioms of a sane philosophy of history, I have often noted, is that the history of the world progresses *at the same time* in the line of evil and in the line of good. In certain periods—our own, for example—one sees the effects of this simultaneous double progress erupting in a kind of explosion. This does not make it easy to describe these moments in man's history. It then becomes necessary to propose several contradictory descriptions, all of which will be true.[42]

The modern age is also the age of concentration camps, of totalitarianisms of the right and left, of two world wars, and of the atomic bomb. "Everything we trusted seems to have failed. Science and progress are turned to our own destruction. Our very being is threatened by mental and moral atomization. Our very language has been perverted: our words have become ambiguous and seem only able to convey deception. We live in Kafka's world."[43] Maritain is not satisfied with simply proposing "several contradictory descriptions." He tries to uncover the underlying factor or factors of the age that help us to understand in a unified and coherent manner why the age is open to such descriptions. He does not accept the fact that human beings cannot achieve perfection in this world as a justification for passively accepting the evils and broken promises of this age.

> To wish paradise on earth is stark naïveté. But it is surely better than not to wish any paradise at all. To aspire to paradise is man's grandeur; and how should I aspire to paradise except by beginning to realize paradise here below?[44]

Arguing that the advances detailed above must be preserved and used as a foundation for a better future, he sets out to uncover the underlying factor or factors peculiar to this age that have kept modern humanity from fulfilling the promise for human good that such advances offer.

The age has failed to live up to its promise because it is infected by "the dialectic of anthropocentric humanism," which constitutes its underlying philosophical orientation.[45] Maritain's critique is directed not toward the humanism of this position, understood as holding that there is an inherent value and dignity to human life in the temporal order and as resisting the reduction of this life and order to being mere instruments for an eternal order. Rather it is the anthropocentric character of this humanism which he rejects, viz., that aspect whereby human and temporal goods were to be sought "in a separation from God," rather than as open to God and to the eternal.[46] Maritain contends that "the concrete logic" of the movement of events in the modern age reveals the dialectic, or self-defeating internal logic, at work in such a humanism of separation. There may be no internally self-defeating logic revealed as anthropocentric humanism is conceived in the mind. However, as lived in the modern age, it reveals its self-defeating character in that its anthropocentric emphasis on separation from God and the eternal is destructive ultimately of its humanistic emphasis on the dignity and value of human life.[47]

Maritain's conception of the fundamental institutional and spiritual legacy of this humanism is succinctly summarized in the following: "It is only too clear that the march of humanity under the sway of money and mechanics marks a progressive materializing of the intellect and of the world."[48] The first steps in this march were taken at the very beginning of the modern age, during the sixteenth and seventeenth centuries. This period is marked by the growth of modern science on the intellectual level of life, and on the appetitive level by the growth of "a great aspiration of the heart of man for the blessings of worldly goods, which is the source of capitalism, mercantilism and industrialism in the economic order."[49] Maritain sees these two movements as mutually reinforcing in that each in its on way sought possession and control of the material order. A humanity whose heart is set on the accumulation of material wealth is eager to support an intellectual enterprise that offers the possibility of controlling and domesticating the material universe, thereby turning it into an instrument to be used on behalf of such an accumulation.[50]

Maritain finds a basis for understanding these developments in the deterioration of the Middle Ages from being an age of magnanimity and humility to an age of humiliation. Human beings began to feel themselves oppressed and crushed by the structures of the age which viewed itself as God's fortress on earth. They thus sought to overcome this sense of oppression and to rehabilitate themselves by separating themselves not only from its structures and authorities, but also from the God in whose name they ruled.[51] It is this separation from God and the eternal that is at the heart of Maritain's critique of the modern age. Acknowledging that science "is a good in itself," he directs his criticism of its role in modern life to the fact that the conditions of its birth, which involved a pushing aside as irrelevant to human activity and human intellection any reference to God or the eternal, have engendered a reductionistic view of the nature and role of the intellect in human life.[52] Specifically, his criticism is directed against a "scientific imperialism," which reduces the intellect to nothing more than an instrument for the domestication of matter in so far as the intellect is denied any way of knowing other than the physico-mathematical way of modern science. Such a reduction constitutes a materialization of the intellect and sets the stage for the modern age to repeat in its own way the confusion or identification of knowledge with power found in the magic cultures of primitive times.[53]

It was during the bourgeois period of the eighteenth and nineteenth centuries that the confusion of knowledge with power born of a scientific imperialism began to make itself felt in the political and economic spheres. Depending solely on the intellect's ability to dominate and control nature, humanity set out to achieve human happiness and freedom through the simple expedient of reigning over external nature through technology.[54] "Modern man placed his hope in mechanism, in techniques, and in mechanical or industrial civilization...; he expected freedom from the development of external techniques themselves, not from any ascetic effort toward the internal possession of self."[55] Intrinsic to such hope is a movement toward the enslavement of human beings to "the empire of technique," in that humanity is required to submit its life and intelligence to the very techniques in which this hope resides.[56] Instead of functioning as a compliant tool for human liberation, technique has tended to insinuate itself in every area of human life in such a way that "everything which is amenable to any technique whatever in human life tends to resolve itself into a closed world, separate, independent. Things like politics and economics in particular will become contrivances removed from the specific regulation of the human good; they will cease to be, as the ancients wished, subordinated intrinsically and of themselves, to ethics."[57] If it is only through technological control over nature that human beings are to achieve happiness and freedom, it follows that there is no point in complicating the search for these values with ethical or religious considerations.[58]

The tendency of modern pedagogy to become so wrapped up in developing ways and means of education that it loses any sense of what ought to be its proper end exemplifies the way in which the empire of technique tends to assume control over key areas of life. Moreover, even when modern educators are able to tear themselves away from their concern with ways and means and to undertake a consideration of the ends of education, they again fall victim to the domination of techniques. An age which sees technology as the supreme wisdom and ruling principle of human life treats the minds of students as though their sole end were to be able to measure and to manage matter. What does not fall under the domain of the technological enterprise is either ignored or treated as myth, and thus as not a factor to be included as an end in the education of the human reason.[59] Such a technologizing of human life is not limited to science and to the class room. It has led to a "kind of political and economic physicalism [that] has really poisoned modern culture."[60]

Acknowledging that the social sciences have uncovered significant data relating to the workings of the political and economic orders, Maritain nonetheless is critical of them to the extent that they have been infected by such a physicalism which tends to treat the political and economic orders as machines similar to the Cartesian conception of the human body as a machine governed by purely chemical and mechanical laws.[61] Such a physicalism transforms the political order into a "technocracy," i.e., an order in which there is no wisdom beyond technology and in which the intellect is restricted to dealing with quantifiable phenomena.[62] Once political rationality is thus equated with a "technical rationalization," politics becomes a matter of sheer efficiency, "the art of conquering and keeping power by any means whatsoever."[63] Such a society is ultimately incompatible with a truly democratic order because human beings are being treated as mere objects either to be dominated through the use of force or to be manipulated by catering to their desires for pleasure.[64]

A technical rationalization also infects the three major socio-economic systems of the modern age, viz., capitalism, communism, and socialism. Although Maritain accepts the morality of a private property system, he criticizes the capitalistic system in its historic reality as being a "vicious economy" which slowly kills the social body by making the cult of worldly wealth the soul of civilization.[65] Such a civilization is ruled by the "fecundity of money." Instead of money being the food which fuels the living productive process enabling it to secure the material equipment and replenishment necessary to it, it is money that becomes the living organism with the productive process which includes human labor becoming the food for money.[66] Such a system is incompatible with the person of both rich and poor, enslaving both to the task of endlessly seeking the increase of material possessions. At its best, when not engaged in brutally exploiting the poor as mere instruments of production, the system engages in a more manipulative exploitation by promising a life of freedom and happiness based exclusively on the development of technology's capacity to cater to their every wish and desire. In short, capitalism lives off the promise of the modern age that "an appropriate technique should permit us...to satisfy our desires without any interior reform of ourselves."[67] The futurologists Herman Kahn and Anthony Wiener provide an excellent insight into the nature of this promise when they tell us that by the year 2000 technological developments will provide "physically non-harmful methods of over-indulging."[68] Maritain views the fulfillment of such a promise as a step not toward freedom but toward enslavement, disarming and weakening human beings by making them available to every demand of the material universe. It is a fulfillment that reduces the person to a "consumer crowned by science."[69] What passes for emancipation in such a life is a debilitating dispersal of human existence, a "waste and disposal of the human substance in the endless multiplication of needs and sadness."[70]

The problem with both communism and socialism as remedies to the evil of a capitalist culture is that neither reaches to the spiritual roots of this evil. For all their respective critiques and disagreements with capitalism, each in its own way shares in capitalism's underlying technocratic orientation toward human freedom and happiness. Communism is seen as accentuating rather than rejecting the fundamental orientation of capitalism in so far as its own highest ideal continues to be the enjoyment of earthly goods in a way that brings to fruition the materialization of human intelligence and life.[71] It also has liabilities of its own, such as its excessive reliance on state coercion and force as the fundamental means to be used to achieve what it considers to be a more just distribution of goods and services, as well as its reduction of the individual to the status of a mere cog in the productive process.[72]

Maritain is much more sympathetic to the socialist tradition. He praises it for having taken the initiative in putting capitalist civilization on trial and for calling that civiliation to a sense of justice and of the dignity of human labor.[73] Acknowledging that one "can only criticize it effectively while remaining on many points in its debt," he finds socialism guilty of taking a technocratic orientation toward remedying the evils of capitalism.[74] By 1942, he saw signs that those working in the socialist tradition were becoming aware of its excessive reliance on economic technique and of its tendency to submit everything to State authority as remedies to a capitalistic culture.

The State is to be the Administrator of human happiness. However much socialism wishes to avoid totalitarianism, there is in such a reliance a thrust toward a technocratic brand of totalitarianism.[75] At the basis of the tradition's technocratic bent is its inability to do justice to the immanent dimensions of personal existence. There seems to be a suspicion of the immanence of personal existence in socialism's attempt to defend the dignity of human labor by denying the value of contemplation.[76]

Such a weakness is not peculiar to the socialist tradition. Indeed, from Maritain's perspective, the materialization of human intelligence and life that characterizes the modern age and that prevents it from properly realizing and living up to the values which it itself has discovered is grounded ultimately in the failure of this age to do justice to the richness and value of personal existence. The equation of human intelligence with physico-mathematical knowing and its subsequent reduction to a mere instrument of technological advance, the search for freedom exclusively in such advance, the search for societal unity either in coercive force alone or in the manipulative expansion of human needs and desires, are all symptoms ultimately of the failure of the modern age to rely on those resources in personal existence that are self-perfective rather than self-destructive. Hence, Maritain holds, "To my mind it is through a sound philosophy of the person that the genuine, vital principle of a New Democracy, and at the same time, a new Christian civilization, can be rediscovered; and this involves an extensive work of purification of the ideas that the world has received from the eighteenth and nineteenth centuries."[77]

III

It is important to emphasize at the very beginning of this section that Maritain's concrete historical ideal is not offered as a precise tactical plan for bringing about a certain type of future. The ideal is meant rather to give point and guidance to the search for such a plan by providing a reflective perspective as to the nature and scope of the problems confronting a society and by indicating both the direction in which the society ought to move as it tries to resolve these problems and the resources that need to be brought into play to effect this move. As one would expect from the preceding section, Maritain holds that the realization of the ideal calls for radical changes in modern society.

> Modern civilization is a worn-out garment. One cannot sew new patches on it. It requires a total and, I may say, substantial recasting, a transvaluation of cultural principles.[78]

Such a transvaluation is not to be equated with a violent insurrection. Although Maritain accepts a just war position, he opposes the belief that substantial changes in history can occur only through war and violence. Comparing such changes to the birth of a child, he argues that there are times when "violence" in the form of a caesarean section may be necessary. However, normally birth occurs with the sufficient maturation of the fetus. Similarly, revolutions normally occur in history as a result of hidden maturation within the womb of a civilization that issues in the birth of a new order.[79] Finally, although the needed transvaluation must include a change in institutional arrangements, it calls for more than "mere technical adjustment or material improvement."[80] It must be first and foremost a moral and spiritual revolution in the sense that the maturation must take place in the hearts and souls of persons.[81] Specifically, the revolution must call persons to realize the possibilities intrinsic in them for a way of knowing that is not reducible to physico-mathematical knowledge, to a freedom that does not subordinate human life to purely technological determinations, and to a social order that is grounded neither in force alone nor in the manipulative expansion of needs and desires.[82]

Essential to any remedy for the ills of the modern world is the liberation of the human intellect from the imperialism of science.[83] Maritain emphasizes that his critique of the role of science in modern culture is from an "epistemo-sociological" perspective which means that it is directed toward the impact which the development of the scientific enterprise has had on the modern mind and not toward what science is in itself or toward the demands placed on the mind when it undertakes a scientific approach to reality.[84] Because of the imperialism of science, modern humanity has failed to recognize the range and richness of its own cognitive resources. It has thus opened itself to being victimized by its own technological advances by depriving itself of a cognitive resource whereby it would be able to evaluate such advances from a person-centered perspective. The stage for such a reductionistic imperialism was set in the sixteenth and seventeenth centuries when humanity cast aside reference to God and the eternal as irrelevant to its concern to understand the human situation in nature. Such a development constituted a break not only with the specifically Christian roots of Western culture, but also with its more general intellectual roots which were nurtured by a focus on the transcendent. "I call 'transcendent' all forms of thought, however diverse they may otherwise be, which find as principle of the world a spirit superior to man, which find in man a spirit whose destiny goes beyond time, and which find at the center of moral life a natural or supernatural piety."[85] With the breaking of the bond with the transcendent, humanity seemed to lose hold of "the natural working of the metaphysical intelligence, the natural pursuit of and feeling for the absolute."[86]

The breaking of this bond deprived the human intellect of the call which Christian faith makes to the intellect to reach toward a life and truth beyond time. "For faith, which believes, and does not see, dwells...in the intellect, the law of which is to see. From this it follows that it is essential for faith not to be quiet, to suffer a tension, an anxiety, a movement, which beatific vision alone shall end. *Credo ut intelligam.* Essentially, faith is an élan toward vision."[87] Faith as a virtue of the intellect is a source of creative tension in so far as it pushes the intellect to seek that which is believed, to be dissatisfied until it gains a vision of Subsistent Truth.[88] Faith thus functions as a liberating principle of the human intellect against any imperialism that would claim to exhaust its richness and variety in the fulfillment of a purely instrumental task such as the prediction and control of the material universe. It prods the intellect to be true to its own élan which is not simply to be an instrument to control matter, but to "see" in the sense of entering into the object known and sharing intentionally in its being and life.

Maritain's epistemology is directed to doing justice to "the structural differentiations and...diversity of dimensions" in the life of the mind and to its élan toward being and truth that underlies such differences.[89] At the center of this élan is the capacity of the mind for metaphysical wisdom which Maritain describes as "the reflexive knowledge of the relation of thought to being (critique), the knowledge of being as being (ontology in the strict sense), the knowledge of pure spirits and the knowledge of God according as these knowledges are accessible to reason alone (pneumatology and natural theology)."[90] Engaged in such a reflexive undertaking, the mind shows itself capable of dealing with being or reality precisely in its character as being and not simply as that which is to be controlled or as a process to be ordered according to certain mathematical relations. Moreover, once the mind is set to the task of reflexively grasping its own immanence in relation to the world and of trying to comprehend being as being, it finds itself dealing with reality as reaching beyond time and materiality to the eternal dimensions of spirit and the life of God. Such wisdom "was born when the intelligence of the philosopher lifted its head above time."[91]

Maritain's concern to claim a central role for metaphysical wisdom in modern culture is not directed to forcing science "to live in the livery of philosophy," but to distinguish between science and wisdom so as ultimately to integrate both in human life, restricting each to the problematic aspects of life and reality appropriate to its resources and approach.[92] Science is not a source for valid normative principles for the regulation of life, whereas wisdom is, because the task of such regulation concerns the immanent and not simply the transient order of life. The reflexive character of wisdom provides a cognitive resource that enables human beings to break the rule of the empire of technique in so far as it enables them to evaluate the achievements of technology from the perspective of their lives as persons. This perspective is central to Maritain's concrete historical ideal, which seeks to replace the empire of technique with a person-centered or personalist social order, which takes as its fundamental normative principle not the demands of technique but the nature and requirements of the personal dimension of human existence.[93] The equation of freedom with power that underlies the empire of technique is destructive of such an order because it fails to recognize that freedom in the lives of persons is a complex affair, involving both a freedom of choice and a freedom of autonomy.[94]

By freedom of choice, Maritain understands freedom as absence of necessity, either external or internal to the human organism. It can be said to be a gift of nature in that it arises directly out of the nature of the will. Because the human will is by nature attracted only to that which is good absolutely, human beings are not necessarily determined to action by the non-absolute, partial and fragmentary goods of their experience. They are thus free to choose among these goods.[95] The simple identification of freedom with the growth of technological power fits in nicely with this conception of freedom in that such growth of power increases the range of choices open to human beings. Maritain opposes such an identification because it fails to do justice to the existence of human beings as persons, i.e. as beings capable of using the resources of intellect and will to hold their own lives in their hands, to exist as self-possessed agents.[96] Freedom of choice is a necessary but not sufficient condition for the realization and fulfillment of this personal dimension. Hence, in so far as human beings are capable of existing as persons, their freedom must include the freedom of autonomy in addition to the freedom of choice. Unlike the latter freedom, freedom of autonomy is not given simply by the natural abilities of intellect and will. Rather, it is an achievement to be won by human beings through effort and struggle not only against external forces, but also against the organism's internal forces of inclinations and desires. It is the freedom whereby a human being becomes properly a person by attaining a life of self-possession and self-mastery in the face of both internal and external forces.[97]

The failure to recognize this second dimension of freedom leads to the confusion of freedom with technological power which provides the basis for a technocratic morality that glorifies power and that caters to those drives and inclinations that lead to the dispersal and fragmentation of human existence. The emphasis on freedom of autonomy is meant to call attention to the need to develop an ascetic morality. Such a morality does not deny that technological power and possessions have a proper role to play in human life. Rather it is directed toward assuring that neither technological power, nor possessions, nor the organism's own tendencies and inclinations become the governing principles of human life. It seeks to submit these factors to reflexive wisdom's grasp of what must be done if human beings are to achieve that freedom of autonomy, that "inner spiritual freedom" which is the metaphysical root of personality as a self-possessed wholeness of life and agency.[98]

The demands of an ascetic morality underlie Maritain's characterization of capitalism as a vicious economy and his rejection of communism and socialism as adequate remedies. Such a morality calls for a transvaluation of the roles played by poverty and material abundance in a capitalist culture. Within such a culture, those who possess a superabundance of material goods are understood to be the key sources of the well-being of the whole society.

The hope for the poor lies in the superabundance of the rich from whose material superabundance will be generated the economic wherewithal to improve the lives of the poor. Poverty is, at best, passive in all this; at worst, a disease to be cured by the overflowing material prosperity of the rich. Maritain's transvaluation of capitalism's poverty of misery and penury requires that a liberating poverty understood as a detachment from material things replace the capitalist cult of material wealth and possessions as the basis of social life. Such a detachment is not predicated on a manichean rejection of the material as evil, but on the belief that material possessions are not to be the ruling or dominating interests of life, whether that life be the life of an individual or of a society. The poverty of detachment is meant to dethrone wealth and possessions from their lofty status as the motivating power of society and to replace them with an economy of sufficiency nurtured by a bond of fraternity.[99] A social order united by such a bond is one in which persons do not simply "act for" another, but "exist with" another. The wealthy person who benevolently shares a portion of his or her superabundance with the less fortunate is said to "act for" them. The sharing involved is restricted to a sharing of things. "'To exist with" another is to move beyond such sharing to a sharing of self in love, "in the sense of becoming one with him, of bearing his burdens, of living a common moral life with him, of feeling with him and suffering with him."[100]

An economic order based on such a sharing is an order that rejects the bourgeois axiom that one gets nothing for nothing and replaces it with the Thomistic principle of *usus communis*. This principle holds that persons have a right to the fulfillment of their primary material and spiritual needs grounded in their very character as persons and not in their ability to pay for such fulfillments. A community grounded in fraternal love involves a free passing on of the heritage from the past to care for the fundamental material and spiritual needs of its members. The realization of such a community demands the building of a social order in which the ability and responsibility for the passing on of such a heritage rests primarily not in the State, but in the different communities, beginning with the family, that constitute society's economic structure.[101] Central to such a social order is the replacement of the capitalist wage system of production with a system of communal ownership and management. This replacement asserts that the worker has a right to the work for which he or she is qualified and does not work at the whim of management. Maritain's quarrel with capitalism is not that it is based on the human right to property, but that it does not extend this right to wage earners. Hence, the primary point behind the call for communal ownership and worker management is not simply to get a larger share of the economic pie for the worker, but to insure that workers enjoy the protections and supports which a right to property provides for persons.[102] Such an arrangement is also valuable as a means of keeping the control of an enterprise and the ownership of the means of production from passing to the State. It provides for worker incentive that comes not from a dependence on some statist parliamentary body, nor from coercion, nor from some mystical loss of the individual in his or her work, but rather from an interest generated from shared proprietorship and operative responsibility.[103] Finally, it avoids the danger inherent in attempts to overcome the class tensions generated by a capitalist system while still retaining the capitalist structure. Whatever may be one's desires, such attempts lead inevitably to a fascist totalitarianism in which political power is used to preserve not the liberty, nor even the possessions of the owning class, but their privilege to rule and to control workers.[104]

Just as the Christian emphasis on the eternal dimension of human existence served as a principle to liberate the human mind from its materialization as a mere instrument for technological domination, so also does it function as a liberating principle of human life from its materialization in a social order whose soul is defined by such domination by material possessions and the fecundity of money. Christian faith calls persons to a recognition that the fullness of their being and the meaning of their existence are not fully captured by such factors. They are called to a life that reaches toward an eternal union in truth and love with God, the Wholeness of Life. Possessions and power will play a significant role in life on earth for such persons. However, their significance will no longer be that of functioning as the soul and center of life. Rather, they will become instruments to serve and to be incorporated in a life of freedom of autonomy whose soul is the lives of persons as centers of love and truth.[105] For all his criticism of capitalism, Maritain acknowledges that there is a certain boldness about it that stimulates the active and inventive capabilities of human beings.[106] He holds that there need be no surrendering of a spirit of adventure and boldness in a social order characterized by a freedom of autonomy and the poverty of detachment, granted the eternal dimension of personal existence, granted its character as "a microcosm in which the great universe in its entirety can be encompassed through knowledge and through love."[107] The transvaluation involved in such a social order will mean the redirection of human boldness and inventiveness from technological advance for its own sake and from the rule of money to the rule of wisdom. "The vocation of man is great enough, his needs and desires sufficiently capable of growth, that we may rest assured that such a measure [the subjecting of the things of the world to the measure of the person] would not imply a renunciation of greatness."[108] To build a social order that at one and the same time meets the material needs of human beings and does justice to them as immanent centers of truth and love is a task befitting human genius and creativity.

The building of such a social order will not occur in a day. "Time is necessary to make reason able to control the formidable material means which industrial and technological revolution has put in our frail hands. Time is necessary to stir up, from the depths of human bewilderment, the moral and spiritual revolution."[109] Time may be said to be the soil for the needed revolutionary transformation. It is hope that is the seed planted in time out of which that revolution is to grow. Writing during the second World War, Maritain described hope as "force and a spiritual weapon, as necessary a dynamic agent of effective transformation and victory as material weapons and munitions."[110] This conception of hope is at work throughout his sociopolitical writings and is not a passing point appropriate only to the wartime situation. A life of hope mediates between the destructive and progressive factors at work in the modern age. On the one hand, it stands in opposition to the dominant institutional relations and reigning cultural forces of the age. On the other hand, it both builds on, and nurtures, those values and aspirations of the period that have been perverted and frustrated by such institutions and forces.

The future called for by the concrete historical ideal will not be achieved automatically, as it were, by the dynamic intrinsic to the age's ruling institutions and culture. If the needed transvaluation is to occur, those who accept this ideal must ardently guard and nourish in their souls and in their actions "the germ and the ideal of the new civilization which we—each according to his measure—are called to prepare in time and for time, for the terrestrial history of this poor earth."[111] To guard and nurture this ideal is to live in opposition to the reigning powers in so far as its realization is seen to be impossible from the perspective of these powers, although philosophical reflection can show on the basis of its analysis of the possibilities and requirements of human nature that this realization is morally demanded and not impossible in itself.[112] The transformation of what is institutionally impossible into the possible begins in a life of hope which is not simply a passive waiting for a future, but "a dynamic agent of effective transformation" whose guiding principle is not the dominant institutional arrangements but the morally demanded future.[113]

Although contrary to the dominant institutional and cultural forces of the age, the concrete historical ideal is not contrary to the fundamental aspirations of humanity. Maritain maintains that a key contribution to be made by philosophers and others dedicated to the work of the mind is to probe beneath these dominant forces and to uncover and to give voice to those fundamental human aspirations of the age that are being ill-served and perverted by these forces and by the anthropocentric humanism that is at the heart of such forces. The point is to bring modern humanity to an awareness of itself so that it will come to see that it is not the life of hope called for by the concrete historical ideal, but the life dominated by material possessions and technological power that is foreign and hostile to its true liberation and its deepest aspirations.[114]

Notes

[1] Walter H. Capps, "The Hope Tendency," *Cross Currents* XVII (Summer, 1968), 2.

[2] Jacques Maritain, *Man and the State* (Chicago: The University of Chicago Press, 1951), 179. Hereafter to be cited as *MS*.

[3] Jacques Maritain, *Three Reformers: Luther, Descartes, Rousseau* (New York: Charles Scribner's Sons, 1940), 3.

[4] Jacques Maritain, "Blessed are the Persecuted," *The Range of Reason* (New York: Charles Scribner's Sons, 1942), 221. Hereafter the book will be cited as *RR*. See also Jacques Maritain, *Integral Humanism: Temporal and Spiritual Problems of a New Christendom*, trans. by Joseph W. Evans. (Notre Dame, Indiana: University of Notre Dame Press, 1973), 6. Hereafter to be cited as *IH*.

[5] *MS*, 159.

[6] *MS*, 160.

[7] On the distinction between these two types of Christendom, see IH, 143-207. See also the distinction among three levels of Christian activity in Jacques Maritain, "Catholic Action and Political Action," *Scholasticism and Politics*, translation edited by Mortimer J. Adler, (Garden City, New York: Image Books, 1960), 185-211. Hereafter this book will be cited as *SP*.

[8] *IH*, 268.

[9] *IH*, 259, 127-129. See also Jacques Maritain, *Freedom in the Modern World*, trans. by Richard O'Sullivan, K.C. (New York: Charles Scribner's Sons, 1936), 112-113. Hereafter will be cited as *FMW*.

[10] See *IH*, 211-212, 259.

[11] *See IH, 128.*

[12] Jacques Maritain, *Religion and Culture: Essays in Order*, trans. by J. F. Scanlan, with an intro. by Christopher Dawson (London: Sheed and Ward, 1931), 54. Hereafter to be cited as *RC*.

[13] Jacques Maritain, *The Peasant of the Garonne: An Old Layman Questions Himself about the Present Time*, trans. by Michael Cuddihy and Elizabeth Hughes (London: Geoffrey Chapman, 1968), 25. Hereafter to be cited as *PG*.

[14] *RC*, 56.

[15] *RC*, 56. See also *PG*, 26, and *IH*, 207-208

[16] *PG*, 26. *IH*, 207-208.

[17] *RC*, 56-57.

[18] *IH*, 55.

[19] *FMW*, 80.

[20] *FMW*, 79-80.

[21] *RC*, 56-57.

[22] *PG*, 26.

[23] *FMW*, 103-104, 110-111.

[24] Jacques Maritain, *On the Philosophy of History*, ed. by Joseph W. Evans (New York: Charles Scribner's Sons, 1957), 47. See also *PG*, 4.

[25] *FMW*, 84. *On the Philosophy of History*, 52.

[26] *RC*, 13, also 23.

[27] Jacques Maritain, "Integral Humanism and the Crisis of Modern Times," *SP*, 11.

[28] Jacques Maritain, "Science and Philosophy," *SP*, 57.

[29] Jacques Maritain, "Philosophical Co-operation and Intellectual Justice," *RR*, 45.

[30] Jacques Maritain, "La philosophie dans la cité," *La philosophie dans la cité* (Paris: Alsatia, 1960), 10-11.

[31] Jacques Maritain, *The Person and the Common Good*, trans. by John J. Fitzgerald (Notre Dame, Indiana: University of Notre Dame Press, 1966), 90. Hereafter to be cited as *PCG*.

[32] "Catholic Action and Political Action," *SP*, 196. See also *IH*, 209.

[33] Jacques Maritain, *Christianity and Democracy*, trans. by Doris C. Anson (New York: Charles Scribner's Sons, 1945), 21-22. Hereafter cited as *CD*.

[34] *IH*, 176-177.

[35] *PG*, 200-201, 211, ftn. 77.

[36] *PG*, 199-200.

[37] *RC*, 15. See also *CD*, 22. See also Jacques Maritain, *Education at the Crossroads* (New Haven: Yale University Press, 1943), 3. Hereafter cited as *ECR*.

[38] *RC*, 15.

[39] *CD*, 21-22, 42-43. See also *MS*, 94. *On the Philosophy of History*, 48-49.

[40] *IH*, 26. *RC*, 16.

[41] Jacques Maritain, *Les droits de l'homme et la loi naturelle* (New York: Editions de la Maison Francaise, Inc., 1942), 115-116.

[42] *PG*, 4.

[43] Jacques Maritain, "A Faith to Live By," *RR*, 201-202.

[44] Jacques Maritain, "Action and Contemplation," *SP*, 182.

[45] *IH*, 80, also 8, 30-31.

[46] Jacques Maritain, "Christian Humanism," *RR*, 194. See also Jacques Maritain, *The Twilight of Civilization* trans. by Lionel Landry (New York: Sheed and Ward, 1944), 4-5. Hereafter to be cited as *TWC*.

[47] *TWC*, 4-6. See also "Integral Humanism and the Crisis of our Times," *SP*, 11. "Science and Philosophy," *SP*, 57.

[48] Jacques Maritain, *The Degrees of Knowledge*, trans. from the fourth French edition under the supervision of Gerald B. Phelan (New York: Charles Scribner's Sons, 1959), 15. Hereafter to be cited as *DK*.

[49] *FMW*, 117. See also Jacques Maritain, *The Dream of Descartes*, trans. by Mabelle L. Andison (New York: Philosophical Library, 1944), 102. Hereafter to be cited as *DD*.

[50] Jacques Maritain, *Science and Wisdom*, trans. by Bernard Wall (New York: Charles Scribner's Sons, 1940), 30. Hereafter to be cited as *SW*.

[51] Jacques Maritain, "A New Approach to God," *RR*, 92-93. See also "Christian Humanism," *RR*, 194. *IH*, 12-15.

[52] See *RC*, 19. *FMW*, 94-95. *IH*, 31-32. *SW*, 32.

[53] Jacques Maritain, "On Human Knowledge," *RR*, 11, 15-16. See also *DD*, 178, 164.

[54] *IH*, 32. *FMW*, 95.

[55] "Christian Humanism," *RR*, 187.

[56] *PG*, 154. Also *IH*, 32.

[57] *DD*, 181.

[58] The "technopolitan man" of Harvey Cox's secular city is a fine example of such an outlook. "He devotes himself to tackling specific problems and is interested in what will work to get something done. He has little interest in what have been termed 'borderline questions' or metaphysical considerations. Because religion has concerned itself so largely precisely with these things, he does not ask 'religious' questions." Harvey Cox, *The Secular City: Secularization and Urbanization in a Theological Perspective* (New York: The Macmillan Company, 1965), 62, 63.

[59] *ECR*, 3-4, 14, 114-115. An excellent contemporary account of the reductionistic conception of human knowledge at work in a technocratic society is found in Peter Drucker, *The Age of Discontinuity: Guidelines to our Changing Society* (New York: Harper Colophon Books, 1978), 349-371.

[60] *RC*, 26.

[61] *SW*, 169. *RC*, 26.

[62] *ECR*, 114-115.

[63] *MS*, 56. See also *PG*, 92.

[64] *ECR*, 114-115.

[65] *FMW*, 128-129. *IH*, 114-115.

[66] *RC*, 62. See also *FMW*, 61-62.

[67] *DD*, 182-183. *IH*, 114-115. *FMW*, 129-131.

[68] Herman Kahn and Anthony Wiener, *In the Year 2000—A Framework for Speculation on the Next Thirty-Three Years* (London: Macmillan Co., 1967), 52.

[69] *DD*, 182-183.

[70] *RC*, 20-21.

[71] *FMW*, 132-133.

[72] *FMW*, 211, 213-214.

[73] *IH*, 88.

[74] *IH*, 88.

[75] *Les droits de l'homme et la loi naturelle*, 121-122.

[76] *IH*, 87, ftn. 32.

[77] Jacques Maritain, "Foreword," *SP*, 7.

[78] *IH*, 207.

[79] *FMW*, 164-165.

[80] Jacques Maritain, "To Exist with the People," *RR*, 127. *IH*, 94.

[81] *FMW*, 135. See also *IH*, 89.

[82] See *IH*, 207.

[83] Jacques Maritain, *On the Use of Philosophy: Three Essays* (Princeton, New Jersey: Princeton University Press, 1961), 49-50.

[84] *DK*, 189.

[85] *IH*, 4-5.

[86] Jacques Maritain, "Bergson's Morality and Religion," *Ransoming the Time*, trans. by Harry Lorin Binsse (New York: Charles Scribner's Sons. 1941), 98.

[87] Jacques Maritain, "The Ways of Faith," *RR*, 209-210.

[88] "The Ways of Faith," 211.

[89] *DK*, 315-316. *SW*, 33.

[90] *DK*, 218.

[91] Jacques Maritain, "The Metaphysics of Bergson," *Ransoming the Time*, 62-63.

[92] *SW*, 26-27.

[93] *PG*, 50-51. *IH*, 192-195.

[94] Jacques Maritain, "The Thomist Idea of Freedom," *SP*, 117-118.

[95] "The Thomist Idea of Freedom," *SP*, 120-128.

[96] *ECR*, 7-9, 34. *PCG*, 1, 39-41, 47.

[97] *ECR*, 10-11. "The Thomist Idea of Freedom," *SP*, 117-118, 120. *FMW*, 30.

[98] *ECR*, 34, 47. *FMW*, 96. *DD*, 182-183. *PCG*, 43-46.

[99] *IH*, 7, 114-115, 191. The rather recent work of the economist E. F. Schumacher is very much in keeping with Maritain's critique of the modern age. His opposition to the notion that the best foundation for peace is to be found in universal prosperity is in accord with Maritain's call for a poverty of detachment. Moreover, he also opposes the development of a scientific imperialism and calls for a return to wisdom. E. F. Schumacher, *Small is Beautiful: Economics as if People Mattered* (New York: Harper and Row, 1975). On the opposition to universal prosperity as the soundest foundation for peace, see 23-39. On the opposition to a scientific imperialism and the necessity to return to wisdom, see 79-101. The whole of this book is useful to anyone interested in building on, and up-dating, Maritain's critique of the modern age. See also E. F. Schumacher, *A Guide for the Perplexed* (New York: Harper and Row, 1977), 9, where Schumacher quotes Maritain's critique of the reductionistic character of Descartes' conception of human knowledge.

[100] "To Exist with the People," *RR*, 121.

[101] *IH*, 192.

[102] *IH*, 186-187. See also *Les droits de l'homme et la loi naturelle*, 117-120. Schumacher provides a contemporary example of an enterprise that practices worker ownership and worker democracy, i.e., the Scott Bader Commonwealth. He also provides figures which show that the business has not suffered financially because it has accepted the principles of worker ownership and democracy. *Small is Beautiful*, 272-292. See also Jeremy Rifkin, *Own Your Own Job: Economic Democracy for Working Americans* (New York: Bantam Books, 1977). In addition to arguing for worker democracy, this book also provides three examples of enterprises that are organized in keeping with the principles of worker democracy and that are also financially successful. The bimonthly journal *Working Papers for a New Society* is an excellent continuing source of information and discussion on the problems and prospects for worker democracy in the contemporary world.

[103] *IH*, 186-187. See also *FMW*, 61-62.

[104] *Les droits de l'homme et la loi naturelle*, 123-124.

[105] "The Ways of Faith," *RR*, 215-216. See also "A Faith to Live By," *RR*, 202. See also *ECR*, 8-9.

[106] *FMW*, 130-131.

[107] *ECR*, 7-8. *IH*, 191.

[108] *IH*, 191.

[109] "A Faith to Live By," *RR*, 203-204.

[110] *CD*, 13-14.

[111] *IH*, 265.

[112] Jacques Maritain, "The Possibilities for Co-operation in a Divided World," *RR*, 174-175. Also *MS*, 200.

[113] See *CD*, 13-14. See also *IH*, 265.

[114] "The Possibilities for Co-operation in a Divided World," *RR*, 173-174. *IH*, 274-275. "Integral Humanism and the Crisis of Modern Times," *SP*, 19. "Action and Contemplation," *SP*, 182.

18.

HISTORY, FUTUROLOGY AND THE FUTURE OF PHILOSOPHY

Vernon J. Bourke

Every now and then someone comes up with the claim that philosophy is dead or dying. At one point in his amazing career Ludwig Wittgenstein seemed to be telling us that philosophy is a sort of disease that can be cured by showing, from an analysis of philosophical questions, that such pseudo-queries are meaningless nonsense.[1] More recently and under the influence of Wittgenstein's contention that philosophers need psychoanalysis, Morris Lazerowitz has argued that philosophy "is a linguistically contrived illusion" which should be abandoned.[2]

Commenting on Lazerowitz, Dennis Rohatyn admits that he himself has been thinking for years "that philosophy is a pile of garbage" but he now realizes that Lazerowitz's "hatred of philosophy" exceeds his own antipathy toward his subject.[3] Elsewhere Rohatyn challenges two basic claims long associated with philosophy: (1) the dogma that philosophy is a branch of knowledge; and (2) the notion that the essence of philosophy lies in reasoned argument. It is his conviction that: "To understand philosophy means to realize that philosophers have been engaged in a constant, self-defeating, and heretofore unsatisfactory struggle for vindication of their own occupation as a reliable form of knowledge-yielding inquiry."[4] Moreover, Rohatyn argues that there is "no philosopher... who does not feel this way... to some extent."[5] This is too sweeping a conclusion but it must be admitted that many people are now asking whether philosophers have any proper function in mankind's future.[6]

Just last year Chaim Perelman published his lectures on the history of ethics (*Introduction historique à la philosophie morale*, 1980). He taught at Brussels for a long time and, year after year apparently, he started with the Greeks, touched lightly on Augustine and Aquinas, and then analyzed the moral philosophies of the modern period. From the twentieth century he selected Lévy-Bruhl, Durkheim, Bergson and Dupréel. Of course it is understandable that for a French-speaking class one will refer mostly to writers in that language—but no mention of any figures in recent German, British or American ethics? It is not that Perelman is unacquainted with non-French philosophers; he has been active for decades in international philosophical circles. Seemingly he did not feel that his classes needed to know anything about recent ethics written in German or English. (It is well known, of course, that Jacques Maritain shared this negative view, particularly of British ethics.) And in all honesty, if one looks over the thousands of names in the membership lists of American philosophical associations, the question sometimes arises: what have all these teachers contributed to the life of philosophy?

Not only have some philosophers become disillusioned with the value of their work, administrators and educational theorists have started to replace philosophy as a core discipline. Where the nineteenth-century educated person recognized philosophy as the "guide of life," (as the founders of Phi Beta Kappa believed) today's educational leaders are not so convinced. Now people are asking why the highest degree in most academic fields should be the doctorate in "philosophy." Colleges and universities under religious auspices, particularly Catholic ones, have traditionally stressed the importance of philosophy. But in recent decades this emphasis has decayed. Gradually the idea that philosophers are not really needed in higher education has gained acceptance. Perhaps this is but part of a growing antitheoretical trend among academics. The 1980 Phi Beta Kappa Oration laments the "Uncertainty of Science" and regards this as a general academic malaise.[7] Reviewing a book on the same phenomenon in the field of mathematics (Morris Kline, *Mathematics: The Loss of Certainty*, 1980), Ernest Nagel notes how the claim to absolute certainty in geometry and number theory has been replaced by "probabilistic conceptions of knowledge." There has been, as Nagel suggests, "a steady decline in the authority of self-evidence as a criterion of truth." Yet Nagel thinks that it is excessive to contend that "there are no truths in the axioms or theorems" of mathematics.[8]

For these and other reasons it is not inappropriate to give a little thought to the future of philosophy.

Philosophy and Its History

While one motive for the study of the history of philosophy lies in the satisfaction of knowing more about past thought, a more practical stimulus is the desire to improve the quality of future philosophical thinking. That a philosopher who ignores the history of his subject is condemned to repeat the false starts and errors of his predecessors has been noted by many writers. Most of the great philosophers have used the work of earlier thinkers to some extent. Nearly all Aristotle's treatises open with some discussion of what his predecessors thought, yet Aristotle was not much interested in history for its own sake. A good many philosophers do what Descartes did in such a striking way: first show that all previous work in the field is open to question, and then use this "useless" background to erect one's own system of philosophy.

THE FUTURE OF PHILOSOPHY

James Collins has explored this forward-looking, "prospective," character of the work of the historian of philosophy.[9] This he sees as one aspect of the "problem of creativity" confronting every serious philosopher. While any present-day thinker may well wonder how he can go beyond the visions of the great philosophers of the past, he should see "his program as a hostage to futurity, as a beckoning ideal not yet realized in terms of his own creative effort." Thus has Collins argued that one of the four traits essential to the understanding of the history of modern philosophy is that it "incorporates a futural reference."[10]

Closely related to this theme is the notion of a perennial philosophy. Following the appearance of the papal encyclical *Aeterni Patris* a century ago, it became quite common for Catholic philosophers to expound the thought of St. Thomas Aquinas as the culmination of a basic and true philosophy, running through every century of its history. Thus Yves Simon once wrote in regard to metaphysics:

> With qualifications due to the peculiar difficulty of the subject and to several historical accidents, it can be said that for centuries the science of metaphysics has been available to men, just as calculus has been available to them since the time of Newton and Leibniz. But quite a few can manage calculus, and almost none metaphysics.[11]

Of course Simon meant that the metaphysics of Thomas Aquinas is this knowledge that has been available perennially. He had the grace to add that indefinite progress is possible in the future of metaphysics, and so Simon did not claim, as many have, that Thomas' thought is a closed system with no capacity for future development.

Indeed there are two ways of looking at philosophy as perennial.[12] In the strong sense perennial philosophy is taken to be a body of knowledge lasting through the ages, and containing at least implicitly the true answers to all the great problems of philosophy. One of the difficulties inherent in this strong sense is the fact that interpreters of St. Thomas differ radically on his essential teachings. Such differences are observable among his first followers in the fourteenth century. Similar divergences are evident in the "second scholasticisms" of Cajetan, Sylvester of Ferrara, John of St. Thomas, and Francisco Suarez. They are still more evident today. Some twentieth-century "Thomists" reject what they call the excessive "objectivity" of traditional expositions of Aquinas' theory of knowledge, and they substitute the subjectivity of a phenomenological analysis of introspective consciousness.[13] In the moral area we have seen lengthy disputes among Thomists as to the primacy of the common or the private good. Now, if Thomists cannot agree on the basic tenets of their philosophy, how can they hope to convince others that Thomism is the philosophy for all times?

A second difficulty in the strong meaning of perennial philosophy is the fact that non-Thomists of various persuasions have taken over the term. Aldous Huxley understood it to mean some sort of evolutionary scientism.[14] Karl Jaspers took perennial philosophy to be pluralistic; it runs through many different historical patterns which are in continual process of counter-action and development.[15] The Futurist writer, Willis Harman, views perennial philosophy as an amalgam of the Bhagavad Gita, the Cabbala, Freemasonry, and Aldous Huxley.[16] Such diversity of viewpoints beclouds the whole notion of a philosophy that is perennial in the strong sense.

However there is a more limited and modest meaning for *philosophia perennis*. Not only may it signify a continuing and hopeful search for answers to ultimate questions, it also implies the discovery of some answers that are meaningful in all ages and places. The terminology may make such basic solutions appear diverse but the understanding should be fundamentally the same. I am convinced, for instance, that there is something unassailable in the Thomistic theory of potency and act. If others see it in terms of polarity, or Yin and Yang, that matters little. The point is that (apart from the sphere of divine activity which humans cannot explain) all events and all existents require a passive and an active principle for their occurrence and explanation. This is probably the kind of thing that Yves Simon had in mind, when he said that there already exists a standard metaphysics.

All the foregoing is related to the problem of pluralism in philosophy—and to the difficulty of finding an acceptable definition of philosophy. Just recently, when the owner of a baseball club fired his manager, the dismissal was attributed to a difference of baseball philosophies. Philosophy does not always enjoy univocity of meaning. Some years ago, James Feibleman defined it as, ''the most general science... the general principles under which all facts could be explained, in this sense, indistinguishable from science.''[17] Many philosophers would reject this; and the definition might irritate some scientists. International congresses of philosophers are the scenes of the complete inability of one school of thinkers to understand their colleagues from another school. One gets the impression, for instance, that Continental phenomenologists are not looking for the same thing that British analysts seek. It has always been a problem for organizing committees of such meetings to know a philosopher when he lays claim to that title. In my experience with such congresses, there was only one occasion on which a man was told that he was not a philosopher. This was in 1953 at Brussels when a Swiss thinker, Maurice Schaerer, submitted a paper entitled, ''Essai d'une philosophie basée sur les données récentes des sciences de la nature.'' It was rejected: apparently because at one point he reduced all reality to zero. But even on this occasion the organizing committee did not venture to define philosophy. Now, if there is no standard univocal meaning for philosophy, it is hardly the case that there is one basic philosophy that has lasted from the time of the ancient Greeks. A striking comment on this confusion of meanings was written by Joseph Owens in his explanation of metaphysics:

> If someone should define ichthyology as the philosophy of law, who would take time out to tell him that he was getting his fishes mixed up with court decisions? Yet one writer can state that metaphysics is a doctrinal study treating of suprasensible being. Another can say that metaphysics is not a doctrinal study and has nothing to do with objective being whatsoever but is an historical cataloguing of human presuppositions. One can say that metaphysics is the most profound of the sciences and the most desirable of human intellectual pursuits. Another can say that it is literally nonsense.[18]

Plural meanings for philosophy do indeed complicate any study of its history. But for the purposes of this article we will think of philosophy in terms of its etymology, as the love of wisdom. And wisdom will be given the traditional sense of the knowledge of the highest causes of the real and good, plus a developed habit of willing and doing what is good. In other words, the wise person would use all his powers to the fullest and best extent—and the philosopher would strive to achieve such wisdom. Perhaps the best way to appreciate this meaning of philosophy, then, is to study how some of its most highly regarded practitioners have worked at it, in its long history.

Futurology and Philosophy

Now there is a rapidly growing field of investigation which aspires to become the science of future developments. It has already spawned a swarm of journals and hundreds of articles and books looking to the future. There are national and world organizations devoted to this study. Several universities now have courses in, or centers for, studies of the future. The University of Houston (Clear Lake City) has begun to offer a master's degree in futurism.[19] The movement is world-wide but not much more than twenty-five years old. As early as 1964 a symposium entitled, *Comment vivre demain?* was published in Switzerland. Several of Bertrand de Jouvenel's writings deal with the future; he is sometimes called the father of futurology.[20] In the summer of 1980 more than 5000 persons attended the first global meeting of the World Futurists, in Toronto. A number of courses and seminars were scheduled: Teaching Futures; Futurics: Perceiving Things to Come; Values and the Future; and so on. The Canadian Futures Society announced an award to that well-known philosopher of the future, Marshall McLuhan. But at the time of the conference, as a result of a serious illness, Marshall was unable to appear. His son, Eric, accepted the award.[21] So much for futurist foresight and the contingency of particulars.

Most efforts of futurists are directed toward predicting economic, financial, industrial, political and social developments. The *Club de Rome* (founded by Aurelio Peccei) was a pioneer group in this field. Today, according to the estimate of James Traub, more than two hundred research centers are grinding out studies of predicted future events. Many have lucrative government and industrial contracts for their services.[22] Techniques of forecasting involve probability theory, computer technology, the use of graphs, and other statistical methods.[23] It is difficult to see how such techniques can be applied to the study of the future of philosophy, for quantification and measurement are not germane to philosophical investigation.

However there are futurists interested in philosophy and other humanistic studies. An example is found in some of the work of Willis Harman who is widely respected by other futurists. His exposition of perennial philosophy is clearly indebted to the views of Aldous Huxley:

> In its Western form, the ethic deriving from the perennial philosophy comprises an intermittently visible stream and has had a profound effect on Western civilization. Thales, Solon, Pythagoras and Plato journeyed to Egypt to be initiated into the ancient Mysteries. Much of the perennial philosophy is woven into the structure of Christianity. In its Hermetic, Cabbalistic, Sufistic, Rosicrucian, and Freemasonry forms it greatly influenced the history of the Middle East, Europe, and the United States.[24]

Obviously Harman's genius does not lie in the knowledge of historical facts, for it is quite unlikely that any of the Greeks that he names visited Egypt. And it is rather clear that what he means by perennial philosophy is far distant from the usual sense of the term. Yet Harman is much more than a statistical technologist. He stresses throughout his work an interest in the "transcendental" in human consciousness and quotes Huxley to the effect that there is a "metaphysic that recognizes a divine Reality substantial to the world of things and lives and minds."[25]

A similar interest in value theory is found in Thomas Kuhn's treatment of paradigms. Broadly considered, paradigm means to Kuhn, "the entire constellation of beliefs, values, techniques, and so on shared by the members of a given community." And Kuhn maintains that "probably the most deeply held values concern predictions."[26] But his approach to the philosophy of values and the future is much more sociological than Harman's. Of course popular writers, such as Alvin Toffler, are not shy about forecasting in practically all areas of human concern. The author of *Future Shock* and *The Futurists* has recently projected a coming era in which most people will work at home, utilizing electronic communication devices instead of travelling daily to office or factory. Thus may the values of family life be revived.[27]

Perhaps the most common-sense explanation of how men may know future events is found in Thomas Aquinas' *Summa of Theology*.[28] He first distinguishes between knowing future happenings directly in themselves *(in seipsis)* and knowing such events in their causes *(in suis causis)*. To know a futurible in itself is directly to see it as presently occurring. This sort of vision of the future, here and now, is the prerogative of God alone. Of course Thomas grants the possibility that God, through grace, may enlighten the minds of prophets so that they may see more of the future than others do. But this is not man's ordinary way of knowing. On the other hand, Thomas recognizes that men may foresee some future events by considering their presently knowable causes. If an earthquake or tornado devastates a city, any rational person may foresee that there will probably be many consequent cases of looting. This is foresight of futuribles *"ut in pluribus"*; that is, it is probable that certain consequences will follow observable phenomena, *in most cases*. Such results are foretold *per quandam coniecturam*, by guesswork based on prior experience. (Modern probability theory merely puts such conjecture on a definite mathematical foundation.) But in regard to another type of future events which are the *necessary* consequences of present causes, Thomas thinks that experts may foresee with certainty the occurrence of such futuribles. This sort of vision Thomas exemplifies in the work of astronomers predicting eclipses. As long as nature continues to run its present course, astronomical predictions are quite reliable. Unfortunately most events of human consequence lie in the area of contingent probability and not in the field of reliable certainty.

One futurist technique that may have some application to forecasting future developments in philosophy is "Trend Impact Analysis." This term has been popularized by the Future Group of Hartford, Connecticut.[29] Something like this technique has been applied to philosophy by Bertrand de Jouvenel in his efforts to project the occurrence of new ideas.[30] It is also interesting to note how Frederick Copleston, S.J., in several recent studies has turned to the question of recurring trends in the history of philosophy.[31] Possibly certain discernible patterns in the past life of philosophy may point toward what is to come in this field. To this possibility we turn in the following section.

Philosophy's Future

There are two different questions concerning the future of philosophy. One is: does it have any future? And the other is: what kind of future may confront philosophy? As to the first, while we have seen that some pessimistic thinkers say that philosophy is practically dead, it is not probable that this subject will disappear from the human scene. It may decrease in popularity or emphasis in educational institutions, partly as a result of the takeover of many philosophical problems by the partitioning of disciplines such as physics, psychology, mathematical logic, social studies, and economics. All these were originally part of the work of philosophers. It matters little what name is put on man's efforts to satisfy intellectual curiosity in the search for ultimate solutions. A change of name is not equivalent to death. Yet it would be well to remember that the term, philosophy, is a modest name: for it does not imply that the "lover of wisdom" necessarily possesses the object of his admiration.

The second question is more significant. What will be the distinctive features of the philosophy of the next few decades? In the attempt to answer this we will look at some of the discernible trends in the history of philosophy. To facilitate the examination of such patterns, we will use four key philosophical questions: 1) What is the ultimate character of reality? 2) How is human knowing to be explained? 3) What are the distinctive functions of man? 4) How may man live a good life?

A metaphysical question. Recorded philosophy began with efforts to identify the stuff(s) out of which all things came. Some said water or fire; others said little pieces of stuff that could not be cut any smaller; still others said there were several kinds of original materials. Soon these early Greek thinkers went beyond physical stuffs to more ultimate sources, such as "mind," or indeterminate potentiality, or non-material archetypes. Certain thinkers taught that everything in the universe was made from nothing by an all-powerful divine Maker. Through the twenty-five centuries from which we have records various versions and combinations of these theories about basic reality appear in history.

Sometimes the ultimate sources, or causes, of all things are reduced to one (monism); at other times they are many (pluralism). The origin of all has been seen as divine, or as blind chance, or as no origin at all. Sometimes the whole of reality is thought to have neither beginning nor end; in other cases the real is considered to have started at a certain point and possibly to have a termination in time. In some cases all reality is reduced to bodily stuff; at other instances to non-bodily origins. In the twenties we used to laugh at Bertrand Russell analyzing all that was mental into matter, and all that was material into mental data. Some philosophers have seemed to say that reality never changes at all: that change is but an illusion. Other critics of the metaphysics of permanence have held that change itself, the process, is what is most real. And there have been profound philosophers who have argued that the ultimately real is unknowable; while others have said it is knowable but they cannot quite describe it, as yet.

Now in these, and similar, metaphysical speculations is there a discernible pattern? It would appear not. There are periods in the history of philosophy where one over-all answer is most favored. In the Middle Ages, for instance, Christians, Jews, Moslems, and some pagans in the Stoic tradition, supported the general view that the ultimate source is a divine Creator. Many religious-minded thinkers today still hold this—but general philosophical literature in the twentieth century pays little attention to creationism, or to any other-worldly metaphysics. There have been sporadic attempts to transcend the presentations of sense experience and individual personal consciousness, but such transcendentalisms represent a minority position in present-day thought. Very distinctive of our era is the negative attitude, that one should not ask metaphysical questions.

The lack of orderly patterns in metaphysical thinking is evident not only in the whole history of philosophy but particularly in the varied types of twentieth-century thought. The dominant philosophies of our time are positivistic empiricism, dialectical materialism, linguistic analysis, and phenomenology. No one of these is accepted in academic circles as the standard philosophy. In the thirteenth century every writer knew that "the Philosopher" was Aristotle: today no one merits that title. So, the history of philosophy provides us with an abundance of attempted metaphysical positions but with no reliable suggestions or probabilities as to the future of speculation on the ultimate character of the real.

An epistemological question. In asking how human knowledge is to be explained, we are making the supposition that cognition is central to the work of philosophers. A few persons would deny that philosophy is concerned with the attempt to satisfy intellectual curiosity. But it is not easy to support the view that philosophizing consists in emoting, or desiring, or simply existing. Through the ages, as an academic discipline, philosophy has been presumed to be a kind of knowledge and to be teachable. Non-cognitive attempts at philosophy are eccentric.

Historically, answers to the question, "What does it mean to know?" have moved from the view that one knows when some "thing" is present to awareness (realism) to the contrary view that knowing is an activity of mind which constructs its own objects (idealism). Before the last three or four centuries there were no idealists. Even as great an introspectionist as Augustine never dreamed of claiming that his mind created realities. Epistemological idealism is an invention of modern philosophies.

Some realistic thinkers have explained knowing as simply the awareness of various aspects of individual bodies (sense empiricism). But most philosophers have looked for general meanings in reality, either the essential but universal natures of things sensed, or some sort of generalized constructs that constitute a world of thought objects. These objects may be either dependent on sense experience, or only remotely related to it. Not many have equated understanding with simple sense experience. Theories of understanding vary chiefly in *what* they take to be understood. Some stress the individual thing-object; others say that to understand is to grasp some rational character derived from, or projected onto, primary sense percepts.

Today the notion that thoughts are simply the re-presentations of physical entities is not widely accepted. There may be a few naive realists but they are not many. The trend in recent epistemology is toward thinking in terms of models, constructs of what is there, or what is going on, "as if" it were such and such. But the oddity in this is the fact that these *als ob* constructs are usually pictured from man's crudest sense experiences. Thus a highly sophisticated explanation in physics, cosmology or philosophy of science may utilize models that are constellations of balls or pictograph waves. This may represent an effort to get into the neutral stuff area between mind and matter.

The present trend in theories of knowledge is nominalistic. That is to say, the medieval view of realistic universals is not now popular. Balancing this is the tendency in the hard sciences to seek ultimate verification of constructural theories in realistic experiment. Pragmatism is not as important as it was fifty years ago—but it is still with us. It may be that the epistemology of the immediate future will become more rather than less realistic.

Still another historical variation in theories of scientific knowledge has been the ancient/medieval tendency to seek understanding of the *qualities* of things, as opposed to the modern/recent inclination to think in terms of the *quantities* of the objects of understanding. The remarkable progress of modern physics has been due in great part to the use of mathematics for the quantification of its objects. This is not always helpful. Many modern thinkers are under the impression that they improve their understanding of colors (for instance) by reducing their perceptions to something measured in millimicrons. This is to substitute quantity for quality. But the knowing of differences of kind is not reducible to quantitative measurement. The future may see a return to the realization that qualities are at least as important in epistemology as quantities.

A psychological question. Here we are using psychology to designate the study of man's psyche, the seat of his distinctive life activities. We have noted already that cognition is one of these functions and of primary philosophical interest. However in addition to rational understanding, are there other specially human functions?

To many it would seem that willing is another distinctive human activity. Recent decades have seen attempts to improve the process of decision-making, by using probability theory. Game theory has been tried by some ethicists. A good deal of this effort to introduce calculating techniques into the regulation of man's desires is the result of a confusion of prudence with moral science. It is quite a different thing to reason well about one's own moral problems (prudence) and to develop a rational explanation of various types of moral actions in terms of universal good or evil (ethics). Opponents of rule ethics fail to see this distinction. The truth remains, of course, that volitional activity is at the heart of human rationality and is central to all human action. Solutions of human problems by computers seem but poor substitutes for reasoned willing, yet it is likely mathematical technology will continue to be used in decision-making. This is another case of substitution: for however well a machine operates—it does not will.

In addition to cognition and appetition, a third aspect of human activity is man's emotional life. Feelings are closely related to desires and aversions but the affective side of human consciousness is not identical with movements of will. Traditional treatments of the emotions, as passions of the soul, were much indebted to Stoic psychology, in which four basic emotions (love, hate, fear and anger) were discussed. Through the ages philosophers analyzed these four feelings and their variations. With the nineteenth-century development of various schools of psychology and psychoanalysis, new terminologies came into use. However, it is generally recognized that the study of emotive experience as distinctive of mankind has not yet reached its full development. That more will be done in affective analysis in the future is highly probable.

In the social arena we find another dimension of human functioning. There has been in the last hundred years a perhaps understandable trend toward seeing the human person as a cog in the vast machine of human society. Indeed Aristotle is the source of the description of man as a *zoon politikon*—a societal being. But it is easily possible to stretch this conception to the point where individuality is lost in the human person.

One version of this sort of thing is present in all totalitarian philosophies of human nature. Both Fascism and Marxism see the meaning of human existence in terms of participation in societal organization. Even some radical types of democracy insist that man must achieve his peak in functioning *as a citizen*. The domination of such claims is evident in the arguments of people who defend abortion: they do not think that a child is human until it has begun to socialize, that is, to function as part of a group. Of course no scientific proof supports this contention that in the first eighteen months or more of its life a child is not a human person. The view depends on an arbitrary definition of personality. Until recent decades philosophers have considered any individual member of the human species to be a person, whether actually functioning in group activities, or not. There are other contemporary evidences of the spread of this totalitarian error.

This trend to reduce the ontological status of the human person to mere membership in a group can hardly continue. Even the most noted attempts at fascistic or communistic societies soon develop into personality cults. One leader becomes the personification, as an individual "hero," of the spirit of the group. Many humans, some the greatest geniuses, have been solitary workers. One might expect in the future a swing back to the long established meaning of person: a complete existing individual substance capable of reasoning and willing.

An ethical question. Our last query is concerned with how a human person may live a good life. Over the centuries a great many ethical prescriptions have been offered. Some philosophers have thought that one should use man's highest powers to the fullest extent possible, thereby perfecting one's personality. In contrast, other ethicists have assumed that the good man must act primarily for the welfare of others. Parallel to, but not identical with, the foregoing, is the contrast between deontological and consequence ethics. One view is that a person should do his "duty" whatever the consequences; the contrary view is that the results of one's moral actions are of primary moral value. Strangely, this problem of the relative importance in ethics of intention and consequences has come, in the last decade, to heated dispute among Catholic moral experts.[32]

One might hope that the future would enable ethicists to take more balanced positions. There is no reason why ethics should ignore the importance of prior intent, or the value of significant consequences.

Another polarity in ethics lies in the contrast between intrinsicism and extrinsicism. Throughout the history of philosophy there have been those who have thought that good conduct depends primarily on conformity to a set of commands issued by some superior authority. Where this conviction means that one must conform to external commands, whatever the consequences or the inner intention of the agent, this is an example of ethical extrinsicism. On its surface, at least, the Old Testament story of Abraham's decision to kill his son in deference to a divine command is a bald instance of this extrinsic position. On the other hand an intrinsic explanation of moral obligation need not exclude the relevance of external commands; all that the intrinsicist must hold is that a moral act is good or bad in terms of the nature of the agent and the real circumstances of his action. Thus Thomas Aquinas (who firmly believed in the importance of divine commands) argues that fornication is immoral because it is rationally unfitting to human agents under certain conditions.[33]

Here again the future may bring better understanding. There is no necessary incompatibility between an ethics founded on divine commands and a naturally grounded explanation of rights and duties. Just as primary and secondary causality are not mutually exclusive, so are moral intrinsicism and extrinsicism mutually supportive. However we are still in a cultural climate in which other-worldly explanations (even in ethics) are not widely popular. The trend among the general public toward the re-establishment of religious values is not matched by a similar conviction in the minds of ethicists.

A Final Word

After examining some trends in past ways of dealing with these four questions, one must acknowledge that there are few ongoing patterns in the material surveyed. Philosophical fashions come and go and why they occur is not evident. Trends seem to occur at random. Most of the preceding attempts to foresee the future of philosophy are but pious expectations, indicative of the prejudices of the writer rather than the projections of objective evidences.

It is one thing to admit the impact of prior philosophers on their heirs; quite a different matter to decide whether subsequent thinkers will agree or disagree with items in their past history. Perhaps it is just as well that the thinking of philosophers should not be rigidly determined by tendencies in the thought of their predecessors. Robert Oppenheimer may have been right when he wrote: "But for good or ill, tomorrow is novelty... What makes tomorrow is that it cannot be foretold today: it is not implied by today."[34]

Notes

[1] This seems to be the general drift of the *Tractatus Logico-Philosophicus*.

[2] *The Language of Philosophy. Freud and Wittgenstein*. Dordrecht/Boston: D. Reidel, 1977, p. 163: "The thesis developed in these pages is that academic, reasoned philosophy, exemplified by the central doctrines of Aristotle, Anselm, Descartes, Hume, G. E. Moore, is an illusion... a linguistically contrived illusion."

[3] Rohatyn, "Review of Lazerowitz' *The Language of Philosophy*," *The Modern Schoolman* LVI, 2 (Jan. 1979) 171-178.

[4] Rohatyn, *Two Dogmas of Philosophy and Other Essays in the Philosophy of Philosophy*. Cranbury, NJ: Fairleigh Dickinson University Press, 1979, pp. 16 and 66. See R. J. Henle's review of this book in *TMS* LVI, 1 (Nov. 1978) pp. 98-99.

[5] See Rohatyn's review cited above in note 3, at p. 173.

[6] Cf. Jean-Francois Revel, "L'élitisme de masse," in *L'Express Magazine* (20 oct. 1979) p. 32; and his book, *Pourquoi des philosophes?* Paris: Collection Pluriel, 1971.

[7] Lewis Thomas, "On the Uncertainty of Science," *The Key Reporter: Phi Beta Kappa* XLVI, 1 (autumn 1980) pp. 1-3; reprinted from *Harvard Magazine* (1980).

[8] See Nagel's comments on the Kline book, in *The New York Review* (6 Nov. 1980) under the title, "Crises in Mathematics."

[9] Collins, "Inquiry-Model on Philosophical Advancement," *TMS* LII, 1 (Nov. 1974) pp. 8 ff.

[10] Collins, *Interpreting Modern Philosophy*. Princeton University Press, 1972, p. 190.

[11] Simon, *Philosophy of Democratic Government*. Chicago: University of Chicago Press, 1961, p. 262. My colleague, Vincent Punzo, drew my attention to this passage.

[12] For a fuller discussion see J. Collins, "The Problem of a Philosophia Perennis," *Thought* XXVIII (Winter 1953-4) pp. 571-597.

[13] For such a critique of epistemological objectivity see the Aquinas Lecture of Bernard Lonergan, *The Subject*. Milwaukee: Marquette University Press, 1968. Several schools of interpretation are surveyed in Helen James John, *The Thomist Spectrum*. New York: Fordham University Press, 1967.

[14] Huxley, *The Perennial Philosophy*. New York: Harper & Bros., 1945.

[15] Jaspers, *The Perennial Scope of Philosophy*. Trans. Ralph Manheim. New York: Philosophical Library, 1949.

[16] Harman, *An Incomplete Guide to the Future*. San Francisco: SF Book Co., 1976, pp. 100-101.

[17] *Dictionary of Philosophy*, ed. D. Runes. New York: Philosophical Library, 1942, p. 235.

[18] Owens, *An Elementary Christian Metaphysics*. Milwaukee: Bruce, 1963, p. 12.

[19] See the journal, *Futurist* XIV, 2 (April 1980) p. 26; and for a popular survey of the literature: James Traub, "Futurology. The Rise of the Predicting Profession," *Saturday Review* (Dec. 1979) pp. 24-30.

[20] B. de Jouvenel, *L'Art de la conjecture*. Paris: Editions du Rocher, 1956; translated as *The Art of Conjecture*, New York: Basic Books, 1967; see also "Back to Basics: the Concrete Economy" *Futurist* XIV, 3 (June 1980) pp. 11-15; and of course Jouvenel's autobiography, *Un voyageur dans le siècle, 1903-1945*. Paris: Laffont, 1979.

[21] Recorded in *Futurist* XIV, 5 (Oct. 1980) p. 6.

[22] Traub, *art. cit.* p. 24.

[23] See Louis H. Bean, *The Art of Forecasting*. New York: Random House, 1969; and Wm. G. Sullivan and W. W. Claycombe, *Fundamentals of Forecasting*. Reston, VA: Reston Publishing Co., 1977.

[24] Harman, *An Incomplete Guide*, pp. 101-102.

[25] *Ibid.*

[26] Kuhn, *The Structure of Scientific Revolutions*. 2nd ed. Chicago: University of Chicago Press, 1962/1970, pp. 175 and 184-5.

[27] For international interest in Toffler's *The Third Wave* (1980) see *L'Express* (7 juin 1980) pp. 74-78.

[28] *S.T.* I, 57, 3, considers how angels (i.e. created intellects without the dependence that human intellects have on sense experience) may discern the future. *S.T.* I, 86, 4, asks the same question about men. In both places St. Thomas offers much the same explanation. Cf. *Summa contra Gentiles*, Bk III, 154, in my trans. (Notre Dame University Press, 1975) Part II, p. 243.

[29] Cf. Traub, *art. cit.*, pp. 26-28.

[30] Part V of de Jouvenel's *Art of Conjecture* is entitled "The Forecasting of Ideas." On the study of *"penchants"* and *"modes"* in recent French intellectual circles, see Revel, *art. cit.*, p. 32.

[31] This was written before the delivery of Father Copleston's Wade Lecture (1981) at St. Louis University, on the question: "Are There Recurrent Problems in the History of Philosophy?" [The text of this lecture is published for the first time in the present volume.—Ed.] Consult also J. Collins, "Developing Patterns in Philosophy," in Walter Ong (ed.), *Knowledge and the Future of Man*. New York: Holt, Rinehart and Winston, 1968, pp. 215-244.

[32] The article arose in connection with discussions of the principle of double effect, on which see the many articles by Peter Knauer, S.J. For some of the literature, Richard A. McCormick S.J., *Ambiguity in Moral Choice*. Milwaukee: Marquette University Press, 1973, pp. 107-111.

[33] *Summa contra Gentiles* III, c. 122.

[34] Robert Oppenheimer et al., *Comment vivre demain?* Neuchâtel: La Baconnière, 1964, p. 13.

A BIBLIOGRAPHY OF PROFESSOR JAMES COLLINS' PUBLICATIONS

(Compiled by Lee C. Rice and Joseph W. Koterski)

I. BOOKS

1. *The Thomistic Philosophy of the Angels.* Washington: Catholic University of America Press, 1947.

2. *The Existentialists, a Critical Study.* Chicago: Regnery, 1952.

3. *The Mind of Kierkegaard.* Chicago: Regnery, 1953.

4. *A History of Modern European Philosophy.* Milwaukee: Bruce, 1954.

5. *God in Modern Philosophy.* Chicago: Regnery, 1959.

6. *Readings in Ancient and Medieval Philosophy* (editor). Westminster, Md.: Newman, 1960.

7. *Philosophical Readings in Cardinal Newman* (editor). Chicago: Regnery, 1961.

8. *The Lure of Wisdom.* Milwaukee: Marquette University Press, 1962.

9. *Three Paths in Philosophy.* Chicago: Regnery, 1962.

10. *Communism: Why It Is and How It Works.* With Thomas P. Neill. New York: Sheed and Ward, 1964.

11. *The Emergence of Philosophy of Religion.* New Haven: Yale University Press, 1967.

12. *The British Empiricists: Locke, Berkeley, Hume.* Milwaukee: Bruce, 1967.

13. *The Continental Rationalists: Descartes, Spinoza, Leibniz.* Milwaukee: Bruce, 1967.

14. *Crossroads in Philosophy: Existentialism, Naturalism, Theistic Realism.* Chicago: Regnery, 1969. (Reprint of *Three Paths in*

Philosophy, with an added chapter, another revised, notes and bibliography updated.)

15. *Descartes' Philosophy of Nature.* Monograph in *American Philosophical Quarterly* series, no. 5. London: Basil Blackwell, 1971.

16. *Interpreting Modern Philosophy.* Princeton, N.J.: Princeton University Press, 1972.

II. ARTICLES

17. "Aristotle's Philosophy of Art and the Beautiful," *New Scholasticism* 16 (July, 1942), 257-284.

18. "Edith Stein and the Advance of Phenomenology," *Thought* 17 (Dec., 1942), 685-708.

19. "Przywara's 'Analogia Entis'," *Thought* 17 (March, 1942), 119-135.

20. "Gabriel Marcel and the Mystery of Being," *Thought* 18 (Dec., 1943), 665-693.

21. "Kant's 'Opus Postumum'," *New Scholasticism* 17 (July, 1943), 251-258.

22. "Kierkegaard's Critique of Hegel," *Thought* 18 (March, 1943), 74-100.

23. "Olgiati's Conception of Modern Philosophy," *Thought* 18 (Sept., 1943), 478-504.

24. "The Role of Monistic Idealism in Croce's Esthetic," *New Scholasticism* 17 (Jan., 1943), 32-58.

25. "Catholic Estimates of Scheler's Catholic Period," *Thought* 19 (Dec., 1944), 671-704.

26. "For Self-Examination of Neoscholastics," *Modern Schoolman* 21 (May, 1944), 225-234.

27. "The German Neoscholastic Approach to Heidegger," *Modern Schoolman* 21 (March, 1944), 143-152.

28. "An Approach to Karl Jaspers," *Thought* 20 (Dec., 1945), 657-691.

29. "Progress and Problems in the Reassessment of Boethius," *Modern Schoolman* 23 (Nov., 1945), 1-23.

30. "The Neo-Scholastic Critique of Nicolai Hartmann," *Philosophy and Phenomenological Research* 6 (Sept., 1945), 109-132.
31. "Philosophy of Existence and Positive Religion," *Modern Schoolman* 23 (Jan., 1946), 82-100.
32. "A Congress on Existentialism," *Modern Schoolman* 25 (Nov., 1947), 34-38.
33. "Bertrand Russell's 'A History of Western Philosophy': Book Two, Catholic Philosophy," *Franciscan Studies* 7 (June, 1947), 193-218.
34. "Louis Lavelle on Human Participation," *Philosophy Review* 56 (March, 1947), 156-183.
35. "Philosophical Discussion in the United States: 1945," *Modern Schoolman* 24 (Jan., 1947), 61-84.
36. "Philosophical Themes in G. M. Hopkins," *Thought* 22 (March, 1947), 67-106.
37. "Religious Thoughts of a Scientist," *Modern Schoolman* 24 (May, 1947), 235-238.
38. "The Absolute and the Relative as a Problem in Modern Philosophy," *Proceedings of the American Catholic Philosophical Association* 22 (1947), 80-94.
39. "Mr. Lewis and the *A Priori*," *Journal of Philosophy* 45 (Oct., 1948), 561-571.
40. "The Existentialism of Jean-Paul Sartre," *Thought* 23 (March, 1948), 59-100.
41. "The Meaning of Existence," *New Scholasticism* 22 (Oct., 1948), 371-416.
42. "The Mind of Kierkegaard, I: The Problem and Personal Outlook," *Modern Schoolman* 26 (Nov., 1948), 1-22.
43. "The Mind of Kierkegaard, II: The Sphere of Existence and the Romantic Outlook," *Modern Schoolman* 26 (Jan., 1949), 121-147.
44. "The Mind of Kierkegaard, III: The Attack upon Hegelianism," *Modern Schoolman* 26 (March, 1949), 219-250.
45. "The Mind of Kierkegaard, IV: Becoming a Christian in Christendom," *Modern Schoolman* 26 (May, 1949), 293-322.
46. "Contemporary Theories of Man," *Thomist* 12 (Jan., 1949), 17-47.
47. "History in the Service of Metaphysics," *Review of Metaphysics* 2 (June, 1949), 105-125.

48. "Karl Jaspers' Philosophical Logic" *New Scholasticism* 23 (Oct., 1949), 414-420.

49. "The Ethical View and Its Limits," *New Scholasticism* 23 (Jan., 1949), 3-37.

50. "The Nature of the Human Individual," *New Scholasticism* 23 (April, 1949), 147-185.

51. "A Quarter-Century of American Philosophy," *New Scholasticism* 25 (Jan., 1951), 46-80.

52. "Kierkegaard and Christian Philosophy," *Thomist* 1 (Oct., 1951), 441-465.

53. "Kierkegaard's Divine Unrest," *Journal of Arts and Letters* 3 (Spring, 1951), 68-82.

54. "Review of Philosophy: Philosophers of 1949-1950," *Thought* 26 (Spring, 1951), 146-159.

55. "Scheler's Transition from Catholicism to Pantheism," *Philosophical Studies,* ed. J. K. Ryan (Westminster, Md.: Newman, 1952), 179-207.

56. "Review of Philosophy: Philosophers of 1951-1952," *Thought* 27 (Spring, 1952), 101-124.

57. "Marxism and Secular Humanism," *Social Order* 3 (May-June, 1953), 207-232.

58. "Review of Philosophy: Philosophical Trends of 1952,"*Thought* 28 (Summer, 1953), 287-308.

59. "God as a Function in Modern Systems of Philosophy," *Proceedings of the American Catholic Philosophical Association* 28 (1954), 1-16. Reprinted in *Classical and Contemporary Metaphysics,* ed. R. T. DeGeorge (New York: Holt, Rinehart and Winston, 1962), 294-304.

60. "Review of Philosophy: Philosophy in 1953," *Thought* 29 (June, 1954), 271-296.

61. "The Defender of Human Intelligence," *Commonweal* 60 (June 11, 1954), 246-249.

62. "The Problem of a Philosophia Perennis," *Thought* 28 (Winter, 1953-1954), 571-597.

63. "Review of Philosophy: The Year in Philosophy, 1954," *Thought* 30 (March, 1955), 84-104.

64. "Philosophic Problems, 1955," *Thought* 31 (March, 1956), 114-140.

65. "Jaspers on Science and Philosophy," in *The Philosophy of Karl Jaspers,* ed. P. A. Schilpp (New York: Tudor, 1957), 75-88.
66. "Art and the Philosopher," *University of Houston Forum* 1 (Summer, 1957), 26-30.
67. "Faith and Reflection in Kierkegaard," *Journal of Religion* 37 (Jan., 1957), 10-19.
68. "God and Contemporary Philosophy," *Commonweal* 85 (Feb. 10, 1957), 528-534. Reprinted in *God, Jesus, Spirit,* ed. D. Callahan (New York: Herder & Herder, 1969), 75-88.
69. "Toward a Philosophically Ordered Thomism," *New Scholasticism* 32 (July, 1958), 301-326.
70. "The Nature of Theological Discourse" (with Jason Xenakis, V. C. Aldrich, and P. Wheelwright), *The Christian Scholar* 41 (1958), 601-613.
71. "Darwin's Impact on Philosophy," *Thought* 34 (June, 1959), 185-248.
72. "Philosophy in the Nineteenth and Early Twentieth Centuries," *Philosophy in the Mid-Century* (1959), 175-186.
73. "Newman and Philosophy," Introduction to *Philosophical Readings in Cardinal Newman,* ed. J. Collins (1959; see no. 7 above), 1-33.
74. "The Genesis of Dewey's Naturalism," in *John Dewey: His Thought and Influence,* ed. J. Blewett (New York: Fordham University Press, 1960), 1-32.
75. "Philosophy in Catholic Life," *Religion in Life* 29 (Spring, 1960), 179-188.
76. "Leo XIII and the Philosophical Approach to Modernity," in *Leo XIII and the Modern World,* ed. E. T. Gargan (New York: Sheed and Ward, 1961), 181-209.
77. "Analytic Theism and Demonstrative Inference," *International Philosophy Quarterly* 1 (May, 1961), 235-263.
78. "The Bond of Natural Being," *Review of Metaphysics* 15 (June, 1962), 539-572.
79. "Philosophy and Religion," in *The Great Ideas Today, 1962,* ed. R. M. Hutchins and M. J. Adler (Chicago: Encyclopedia, 1962), 315-371.
80. "The Work of Rudolf Allers," *New Scholasticism* 38 (July, 1964), 281-309.

81. "Christian Philosophers and the Modern Turn," *Proceedings of the American Catholic Philosophical Association* 39 (1965), 14-37.
82. "Weiss's Exploration of Religion," *Review of Metaphysics* 19 (Dec., 1965), 301-328.
83. "John Henry Newman," in *The Encyclopedia of Philosophy,* ed. Paul Edwards (New York: Macmillan, 1967), 480-485.
84. "A Kantian Critique of the God-Is-Dead Theme," *Monist* 51 (Oct., 1967), 536-558.
85. "Developing Patterns in Philosophy," in *Knowledge and the Future of Man,* ed. W. J. Ong (New York: Holt, Rinehart & Winston, 1968), 215-244.
86. "Josiah Royce: Analyst of Religion as Community," in *American Philosophy and the Future,* ed. M. Novak (New York: Scribner's, 1968), 193-218.
87. "Karl Jaspers: A Tribute," *America* 133 (Mar. 22, 1969), 328-330.
88. "Interpretation: The Interweave of Problems," *New Literary History* 4 (Winter, 1973), 389-403.
89. "Innovation and Consequence: Interpreting Modern Philosophy," *Studi Internazionali di Filosofia* 5 (Autumn, 1973), 43-52.
90. "Inquiry-Model on Philosophical Advancement," *Modern Schoolman* 52 (Nov., 1974), 3-25.
91. "Kant's 'Logic' as a Critical Aid," *Review of Metaphysics* 30 (Mar., 1977), 440-461.
92. "Functions of Kant's Philosophy of Religion," *Monist* 60 (April, 1977), 157-180.
93. "Interpreting Spinoza: A Paradigm for Historical Work," *Speculum Spinozanum 1677-1977,* ed. S. Hessing (London: Routledge and Kegan Paul, 1977), 119-132.
94. "A Telos Approach to Leibniz," *Review of Metaphysics* 33 (Dec. 1979), 347-369.
95. "Spirituality and Scholarly Intent," *Communio* 6 (Winter, 1979), 386-391.
96. "Kierkegaard's Imagery of the Self," in *Kierkegaard's Truth: the Disclosure of the Self,* ed. J. H. Smith (New Haven: Yale University Press, 1981), 51-84.

III. COMPREHENSIVE REVIEWS OF THE LITERATURE

[For the last thirty years extended review articles have appeared annually, at first in *Thought* (see entries 54, 56, 58, 60, 63, 64) and since 1957 in *Cross Currents* under the title "Annual Review of Philosophy." Items 97 to 121 are listed here by volume, issue, year and page numbers of *Cross Currents*.]

97.	7.1	Winter	1957	68-93
98.	8.1	Winter	1958	67-90
99.	9.2	Spring	1959	160-191
100.	10.2	Spring	1960	147-180
101.	11.2	Spring	1961	145-176
102.	12.3	Summer	1962	345-377
103.	13.2	Spring	1963	187-216
104.	14.3	Summer	1964	361-388
105.	14.4	Autumn	1964	451-474
106.	15.2	Spring	1965	213-236
107.	16.2	Spring	1966	167-196
108.	17.2	Spring	1967	197-226
109.	18.2	Spring	1968	175-202
110.	19.2	Spring	1969	198-228
111.	20.2	Spring	1970	173-200
112.	21.2	Spring	1971	186-210
113.	22.2	Spring	1972	183-201
114.	23.1	Spring	1973	49-72
115.	23.4	Winter	1974	437-460
116.	25.1	Spring	1975	67-92
117.	26.1	Spring	1976	79-106
118.	27.1	Spring	1977	57-82
119.	28.2	Summer	1978	167-188
120.	29.1	Spring	1979	39-62
121.	30.1	Spring	1980	38-60

CONSPECTUS

James D. Collins

It is a great pleasure and honor for me to receive these papers. I want to express my gratitude to my colleagues and other friends who contributed the essays, and to others who helped in preparing this Festschrift. They have shown an intellectual generosity and fidelity to the discipline of history of philosophy that I deeply appreciate.

In reading the typescript, I have noticed some methodological points that hold good generally for historical work in philosophy and not solely for the particular issue under investigation. I would like to call attention to three of these topics having a broad significance for historical procedures. All references are to the present volume.

1. Several contributors make prominent use of the term *theme*. Frederick Copleston finds that one cannot make much headway on the recurrence of philosophical problems until the latter are reconceived as themes. This is a way of formalizing a move that we often must make in order to establish comparisons among any two philosophers, let alone among different eras. A comparison between Descartes and Spinoza on the meaning of will can be thwarted, for instance, if the will is considered solely within the very determinate network of problems where either philosopher sets forth his particular solution. It often pays to step back a bit from the immediate set of problems and to regard will as one of those very general themes which the philosophical community of the time expected Descartes and Spinoza to address. The meaning for will at which these two thinkers arrive is colored in part by their awareness of this thematic expectation among their own contemporaries and, indeed, of a long tradition on the subject.

Another aspect of the issue stands forth in W. Norris Clarke's account of action theory in St. Thomas. Here, thematization does not signify primarily a comparison between several philosophers or eras but rather an explication internal to one philosopher. What he regards as the chief objectives of his inquiry get formally explicated, but the resolution of difficulties may require him to employ some general propositions without treating them at great length for their own sake. To thematize these relatively implicit meanings in a philosopher belongs among the historian's offices. But often the choice of this rather than that topic for thematic analysis is determined by lively developments in the historian's own time. The emphasis today upon action theory makes a study of St. Thomas on action all the more interesting, as long as the exegesis remains faithful to the text.

This latter condition is not always observed, as Albert William Levi brings out. Whitehead was an inveterate thematizer, but not in the historical sense except indirectly. The same can be said of Dewey, who established many of his positions through polemical references to earlier philosophers and schools. In such cases, I would distinguish between thematizing done in the service of better historical understanding and that done mainly to advance one's own doctrines. Both sorts of thematizing are legitimate, as long as the thematizer clearly indicates the purpose of his treatment of the sources. Since I do not rigidly segregate historical work from present theorizing, I think it advisable to attend closely to both kinds of thematizing. Historians should take into account the whole range of interpretations and uses of the sources, lest a valuable implication of some sort be overlooked. And it does no harm to remind today's theorizers of the discrepancy between their invocation of a source thinker and the latter's actual intent.

Finally, Vernon J. Bourke asks whether historical patterns in philosophy determine its future course and supply a firm basis for our musings thereon. This is a question about philosophical thematics, which I take in either a weaker or a stronger sense. In the weaker sense, a historically grounded thematics does have some predictive value. It identifies those themes that have had a relatively long history, under many different cultural conditions, and hence that are likely to be discussed by a coming generation of philosophers. But this likelihood must be carefully qualified. A monothematic development does not constitute a philosophy by itself, since even a highly specialized philosophical field involves several themes combined in various ways. And the history of multithematic patterns shows a wide diversity both in meanings assigned to each ingredient theme and in their systematic interrelations.

The freedom of philosophizing does not exist apart from thematic variations, but consists precisely in the shaping of new themes and the reshaping of older ones. Hence there is no good reason for taking philosophical thematics in the stronger sense of a deterministic settlement of what the future turn of speculation must be. As Bourke remarks, it is just as well for us not to be saddled by such a determinism.

2. *Access.* There is an instructive difference between the specialized epistemologist and the working historian on the question of knowing the philosophical sources. The former is apt to formulate this question in the mode of possibility: whether we are able to obtain any reliable understanding of the philosophical past. But the historian tends to work in the mode of actuality: whether we can improve upon the existing welter of different and often conflicting interpretations. I do not regard these approaches as unrelated, since sometimes a person feels driven by the fact of conflicting historical interpretations to ask whether any knowledge of past philosophies

is open to us. This question is valid enough, but part of the evidence for responding to it comes from reflecting on the actual practice of historians of philosophy. Their aim is to take methodological initiatives that will improve a process of historical understanding which is already under way but which always requires fresh readings and correctives.

Indeed, I venture to suggest that people attracted to historical work are concerned less about the inaccessibility of the sources than about their overfamiliarity. Can any research of ours make a significant difference in how some major text is interpreted, or has everything of consequence been said already about the text? Leonard J. Eslick asks this about Plato's famous Divided Line and the Allegory of the Cave. His response is that Plato's thought is inexhaustible and contains depths yet unplumbed. The same can be said about other great philosophers. Their writings have unnoticed aspects that come to light only when the investigator asks a different question, makes a new comparison of texts, or draws upon his knowledge of other disciplines operating upon the source thinker's mind.

The great philosophical writings are neither wholly opaque nor instantly manifest to the reader. Through language, they give some access but never surrender their meaning effortlessly and completely. The sources offer an access that is limited yet constantly expandable. I regard this characterization as the minimal working premise upon which all thoughtful work in history of philosophy depends. It is the middle way that avoids both discouragement and delusion about the prospect for study.

3. *Religion and philosophy of being.* The contributors of papers on Boethius and Aquinas, Duns Scotus and Suarez, Hobbes and Kierkegaard, bear witness to the mutual influence of religious faith and philosophical teaching. After analyzing the penultimate chapter of my *The Emergence of Philosophy of Religion*, John E. Smith asks whether the interplay of religion and philosophy can be more fruitful within the context of Hume and Kant or within that of Hegel. As I try to show in the last chapter of that book, each context carries its own values and requires unceasing comparison with the other. An historically informed realistic theism does not ally itself with one approach, to the exclusion of the other. Rather, it tries to keep these philosophers of religion in communication, acknowledges the contributions of each, and permits each to underscore the drawbacks of the others. A realistic theist must be *at least* as well aware as Hume about the rooting of religious beliefs and activities in our passional human nature, as alert as Kant to the limits of our efforts to know God and act honestly before him, and as perceptive of philosophically significant meanings in revelational religions as is Hegel.

Smith's paper has a twofold contemporary bearing as well. First, it cites existentialism and process philosophy as the only points of entrance today for a metaphysically oriented study of the relation between philosophy and religion. But an important reason for working in history of philosophy is to uncover and freshly restate other methods and doctrines that can be used in contemporary philosophical treatments of God and religion. We need not be landlocked into the latest forms of metaphysics and philosophy of religion, since historical research makes other resources available for present philosophizing on religion.

Second, Smith suggests that little can be expected on the religion-and-philosophy issue from linguistic and analytic philosophy. But there has been a good deal of analytic work done on the distinctive features of religious discourse and on the reality disclosures of religious talk and experience, in their European, American, and Eastern forms. On the specific point of whether any worthwhile contributions come from Wittgenstein and his adherents, John W. Carlson's paper sets forth some positive evidence why their religious views deserve closer study and a dialogue.

The question of how best to relate a philosophy of being to recent methodologies is also raised by James L. Marsh. He asks whether it is more appropriate to ground and expand the theory of interpretation by means of the method and conception of being in Thomistic realism or that in phenomenological hermeneutics. I have always found it rewarding to study the hermeneutical theories of Heidegger, Gadamer, and Ricoeur. Perhaps due to his penetration of Kant, Ricoeur is cautious about expanding hermeneutics into a general theory of being. I find most congenial his limited reflection upon humanly interpreted existence and upon the reading of a text as a glimpse into our actions, desires, and orientation toward the sacred. Through his self-limitation, Ricoeur is also able to appreciate the work done by analytic, linguistic, and literary approaches to hermeneutics.

In the light of these many perspectives in hermeneutics, it is appropriate to use them all in sharpening our reading of St. Thomas himself. A primary historical task today is to make, not so much a transcendental turn of Thomism as a re-examination of the integral text of St. Thomas, in the light of questions suggested by modern hermeneutical philosophers. The views of St. Thomas on God's pervasive active presence, the modalities of human expressive action, word and text, intention and context, have to be better understood and brought closer together.

One further consideration is that the interpreting process is a thoroughly human operation. It can be analyzed in its own structures and acts, as well as judged for effectiveness by its use in improving our understanding of actual texts and their relationships. The hermeneutical theory in my *Interpreting Modern Philosophy* remains close to the fieldwork. My intent is to develop an interpretive pattern specifically responsive to the writings and historical procedures involved in classical modern philosophy. As far as I know, the working justification of a proposed interpretation concerning a classical modern philosopher does not consist primarily in a relation of applying or concretizing a general philosophical hermeneutics, however valuable may be the latter's suggestions. In respect to historical sources, any general theory about hermeneutical methods and conceptions of being must itself be evaluated by its contributions to, or deformations of, a study of the major writings in question.

My final word of thanks is reserved for Linus J. Thro, the general editor, and the editorial committee consisting of Richard J. Blackwell and Marianne M. Childress. They have devoted their time and judgment to this project in a way that well represents the spirit of Saint Louis University's Department of Philosophy, to which it is my honor to belong.

NOTES ON THE CONTRIBUTORS

RICHARD J. BLACKWELL is a professor of philosophy at St. Louis University. His research and writing have concentrated on the history of philosophy and the philosophy of science, including especially *Discovery in the Physical Sciences*. He is presently compiling a book-length bibliography of contemporary philosophy of science.

VERNON J. BOURKE, who came to the St. Louis University philosophy department in 1931 and retired in 1975, is at present research professor of philosophy in the Center for Thomistic Studies at the University of St. Thomas, Houston. During these fifty years of teaching and scholarship he has specialized in ethics and the history of medieval philosophy and has published a number of books in both fields. His most recent publication (with Terry L. Miethe) is *Thomistic Bibliography, 1940-1978* (Greenwood Press, 1980).

JOHN W. CARLSON is an associate professor of philosophy and director of the honors program at St. Louis University. His doctorate is from Notre Dame, where his dissertation was on Wittgenstein. His interests in traditional systematic philosophy and in philosophy of language have converged in a number of published studies in the philosophy of religion and in ethics.

W. NORRIS CLARKE, S.J., is a professor of philosophy at Fordham University and editor of the *International Philosophical Quarterly*. He has been president of the Metaphysical Society and of the American Catholic Philosophical Association. His most recent book is *The Philosophical Approach to God: A Neothomist Perspective* (1980). He has published numerous philosophical essays, especially in metaphysics.

FREDERICK C. COPLESTON, S.J., is at present the Austin Fagothey professor of philosophy at Santa Clara. He was formerly professor of history of philosophy at Heythrop College (1939-1970) and of metaphysics in the Gregorian University, Rome. He was instrumental in the affiliation of Heythrop with the University of London, on whose faculty he held a professorship in history of philosophy. He was the 1979-1980 Gifford lecturer at Aberdeen, and over the years was the recipient of numerous professional honors and awards. He is the internationally acclaimed author of many books and published papers.

CHARLES A. CORR is a professor of philosophy at Southern Illinois University at Edwardsville. Besides publishing a dozen articles in history of philosophy, notably on Kant and Wolff, he is editor of two volumes (forthcoming) for the *Gesammelte Werke* of Wolff. In the last several years, he has collaborated in a number of books devoted to the problems of death and dying, as contributor or as co-author or as co-editor. His doctoral work was completed at St. Louis University in 1966 under Dr. Collins.

DANIEL O. DAHLSTROM, whose doctoral dissertation on Hegel's science of logic under Dr. Collins led to his Ph. D. from St. Louis University in 1978, is at present assistant professor of philosophy at the Catholic University of America. For the past two years he has been secretary of the American Catholic Philosophical Association.

CORNELIUS F. DELANEY is a professor of philosophy and chairman of the department (since 1972) at the University of Notre Dame. His first book was *Mind and Nature* (1969). Besides publishing numerous articles on American philosophy, he is co-author of a book on the thought of Wilfred Sellars, editor of a collection of essays in philosophy of religion and co-editor of another in the general problems of philosophy.

JOHN P. DOYLE, a professor of philosophy at St. Louis University, is interested in the whole of Greek and medieval philosophy, but specializes in the impact of thirteenth and fourteenth century thought upon the metaphysics and theory of knowledge among the influential renaissance scholastics. He has produced a variety of articles in this field and is now engaged in a long-term research project on the significance of extrinsic denomination in Suarezian thought.

JOHN W. ELROD is a professor of philosophy and chairman of the department at Iowa State University. He is author of a number of articles on Kierkegaard and of two books: *Being and Existence in Kierkegaard's Pseudonymous Works* (1975) and *Kierkegaard and Christendom* (1981). He is also on the international advisory board for *Kierkegaard's Writings*.

LEONARD J. ESLICK has his degrees from the Universities of Chicago, Tulane and Virginia. He taught at Drake and in the Great Books Program at St. John's College before coming in 1948 to St. Louis University, where as professor of philosophy he has particularly concerned himself with the metaphysics of Plato and with Bergson and Whiteheadian thought. Among his many published articles are a number on Plato related to the one in the present volume.

JOSEPH W. KOTERSKI has had extensive bibliographical experience as graduate assistant to Dr. Collins, under whose direction he is completing his dissertation at St. Louis University. He has published several articles and has recently collaborated with Dr. Francis Lescoe in a project of translating Polish philosophers into English.

ALBERT WILLIAM LEVI, the David May Distinguished University Professor since 1952 at Washington University, has been on several occasions a Fulbright professor at the Universities of Vienna and Graz. He was educated at Dartmouth and the University of Chicago and subsequently taught at both institutions. Among his best known books are *Philosophy and the Modern World* (1959) and *Philosophy as Social Expression* (1974).

JAMES L. MARSH received his doctorate from Northwestern university in 1971 and has taught philosophy at St. Louis University since 1970, especially in the areas of existentialism, phenomenology, Hegel and Marx. He has published considerably in these areas and has recently completed a book in phenomenology, *Post-Cartesian Meditations*. He is a Danforth associate, won the A. C. P. A. Matchette award (1976) and was visiting professor a year ago at Fordham University.

THOMAS P. McTIGHE, long a professor of philosophy at Georgetown University and for a considerable period chairman of the department there, received his doctorate in 1955 at St. Louis University, writing his dissertation on method in Galileo under the direction of Dr. Collins. He has collaborated in the work of various professional associations and has published a number of studies on Boethius, Nicholas of Cusa and Galileo.

J. PATRICK MURRAY is an assistant professor of philosophy at Creighton University. A re-working of his dissertation (on Marx — under Dr. Collins) is nearing publication in book form; in preparing this Dr. Murray has profited from repeated grants for study in Germany from the German Academic Exchange Service. His publications include essays on Habermas and the Frankfurt School.

RICHARD H. POPKIN has been a professor of philosophy at Washington University since 1973, having come there from the University of California at San Diego, where he had taught for ten years, was chairman for five, and began editing the *Journal of History of Philosophy*. Before that he had been at Claremont and at Iowa State University. A principal focus of his research interests has been the history of skepticism through the sixteenth to eighteenth centuries. Among his many publications is his well known book in this area.

VINCENT C. PUNZO is a professor of philosophy at St. Louis University, where twenty years ago he was a graduate assistant to Dr. Collins and wrote a dissertation under his direction on Royce. His research and writing have been devoted mainly to topics in ethics and political philosophy and to figures in American philosophy. Among his publications in ethics is his book, *Reflective Naturalism*. He is at present preparing a book on Royce.

LEE C. RICE, following his doctoral studies at St. Louis University, has taught in the department of philosophy at Marquette University, where he is associate professor and has been chairman since 1977. He has published a number of articles on Spinoza and is completing a book on his thought and influence.

JOHN E. SMITH, well known philosopher of religion, is Clark Professor of Philosophy at Yale University. He is president of the American Philosophical Association (Eastern Division) and has been the recipient of many professional awards, including a doctorate from the University of Notre Dame. Among his publications are *The Spirit of American Philosophy* (1963), *Experience and God* (1968), *Religion and Empiricism* (1967) and *The Analogy of Experience* (1973).

LINUS J. THRO, S. J., began teaching philosophy at Regis College, Denver (1938-1941) and after a University of Toronto doctorate came to St. Louis University in 1949, where he is still teaching philosophy, but since 1981 as emeritus professor. His areas of special interest have been ancient and medieval philosophy, epistemology and ethics. He has been chairman of the department and has held other administrative posts.

ALLAN B. WOLTER, O. F. M., since 1963 has been a professor of medieval philosophy at Catholic University, where forty years ago he was a classmate of James Collins. He was for years editor of *Franciscan Studies* and Franciscan Institute publications. From the time of his first book, *The Transcendentals and Their Function in the Metaphysics of Duns Scotus* (1946) he has ranked among the foremost students of the works and thought of Scotus. Besides many translations of medieval authors he has published essays in a variety of journals and collections. In the Spring and Summer the last several years he has been a visiting research professor at the University of California at Los Angeles.